John Tregaskis

Souvenir of the Re-Union of the Blue and the Gray

on the battlefield of Gettysburg, July 1, 2, 3 and 4, 1888. How to get there, and what is to be done during the year

John Tregaskis

Souvenir of the Re-Union of the Blue and the Gray
on the battlefield of Gettysburg, July 1, 2, 3 and 4, 1888. How to get there, and what is to be done during the year

ISBN/EAN: 9783337284473

Printed in Europe, USA, Canada, Australia, Japan

Cover: Foto ©ninafisch / pixelio.de

More available books at **www.hansebooks.com**

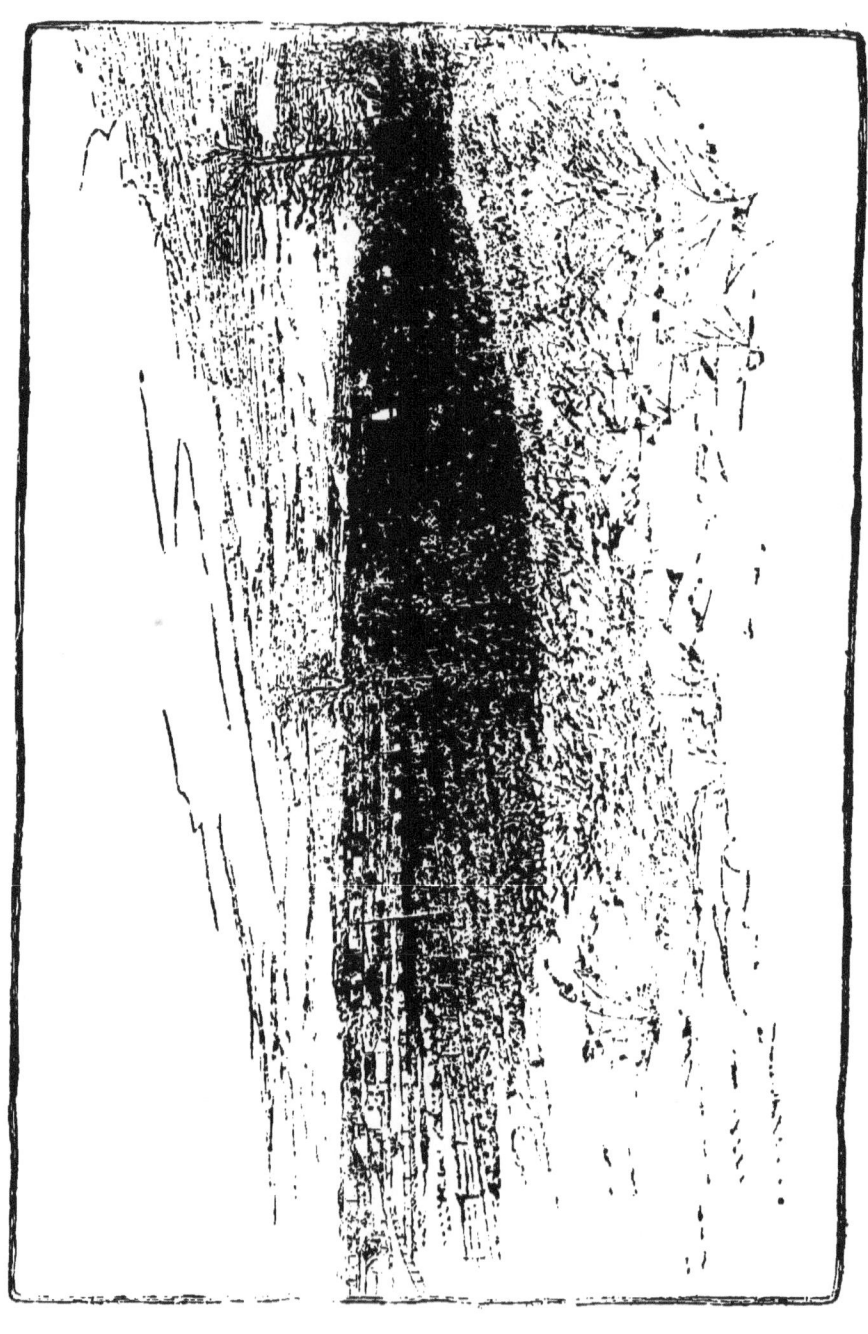

AUTHORIZED AND COPYRIGHT EDITION.

SOUVENIR

OF THE

RE-UNION

OF

THE BLUE AND THE GRAY,

ON THE

BATTLEFIELD OF GETTYSBURG,

July 1, 2, 3 and 4, 1888.

HOW TO GET THERE,

AND

WHAT IS TO BE DONE DURING THE YEAR.

NEW YORK.
THE AMERICAN GRAPHIC CO.
1888.

Entered according to act of Congress, in the year 1888, as the
OFFICIAL PROGRAMME,
and Copyrighted by
JOHN TREGASKIS,
In the Office of the Librarian of Congress, at Washington.

TABLE OF CONTENTS.

	Chapter.
Frontispiece—" First Glimpse of the Battlefield."	
Introduction	I.
Poem—" '63 and '88 "	II.
How to Reach Gettysburg and What it Will Cost	III.
Twenty-fifth Anniversary of the Battle of Gettysburg; Illustration—Memorial Church	IV.
Annual Meeting of the Army of the Potomac	V.
What the Society of the Army of Northern Virginia Will Do	VI.
Monuments to be Dedicated during 1888—Lists of Exercises and 18 Illustrations	VII.
Meade and his Commanders; 21 Portraits	VIII.
Organization of the Army of the Potomac, with Commanding Officers at Gettysburg	IX.
Lee and his Commanders; 5 Portraits. How Well They Fought	X.
Organization of the Army of Northern Virginia, and Commanding Officers at Gettysburg	XI.
Detail of Losses in each Army at the Battle	XII.
Description of the Battlefield, with Table of Elevations, and Map showing the Location of the Monuments to be Dedicated during 1888	XIII.
Tables of Distances to Points of Interest on the Battlefield	XIV.
Proceedings of the Last Meeting of the Army of the Potomac	XV.
Proceedings of the Last Meeting of the Army of Northern Virginia	XVI.
Officers of each Society and Committees having the Re-Union in charge	XVII.
Provision made for all who attend the Re-Union	XVIII.
Hotels and Boarding-Houses in and around Gettysburg	XIX.
The Blue and the Gray—Re-Union of Philadelphia Brigade and Pickett's Division, 1887; 2 Illustrations	XX.
Poem—"The Hand-Clasp at the Wall;" Illustrated	XXI.
Proposed Monument to General Armistead; Illustrated "The Historic Clump of Trees"	XXII.
The National Cemetery at Gettysburg	XXIII.
National Cemeteries of the United States and Interments therein to April 30, 1888	XXIV.
Organizations Mustered into the United States Service during the Rebellion	XXV.
Total Number of Troops Furnished by each State and Territory	XXVI.
Average of Infantry Losses by Brigades at Gettysburg	XXVII.
Total Casualties during the War	XXVIII.
Chronological List of Battles and Skirmishes during the War	XXIX.
Veteran Associations—Names and Addresses of Secretaries	XXX.
A Wounded Prisoner's Experience in Gettysburg	XXXI.
The Forces Engaged at Gettysburg	XXXII.
Absolution Under Fire; Illustrated. Baby's Shoe	XXXIII.

TREGASKIS & CO.

Publishers of the Official Programme.

WILL ISSUE AFTER THE RE-UNION

AN ACCOUNT OF ALL THE

Proceedings of this Anniversary,

INCLUDING THE DEDICATION OF MONUMENTS.

The work will include a Short History of Every Organization that took part on the field; a Biographical Sketch of Every Commander who was present in the Battle; of Every Army Corps, Brigade, Regiment, Battery, Staff and Company that can be obtained. Portraits of all will be given with the sketches.

ANY VETERAN WHO PARTICIPATES IN THIS RE-UNION CAN HAVE HIS OWN PORTRAIT AND BIOGRAPHICAL SKETCH IN-
CLUDED BY PAYING THE COST OF THE PICTURE
AND SUBSCRIBING FOR THE BOOK.

Write for Circular containing Further Particulars.

TREGASKIS & CO., 767 Broadway, Room 8, New York.

*Secretaries of Veteran Associations are requested to send Local News-
papers containing notices of their affairs.*

I.

INTRODUCTION.

GETTYSBURG.

Twenty-five years ago the valley in which is situated the borough of Gettysburg was resonant with the roar of artillery, the rattle of musketry, and the angry voices of over one hundred and fifty thousand combatants. For three long and sultry days the tide of battle swept through and around the little town, drenching with blood the only spot north of Mason and Dixon's line on which a general engagement between the Union and Confederate forces took place. Thousands joined the great majority during the battle, and many thousands more from injuries received on those eventful days.

The Battle of Gettysburg was the turning point in the great Civil War, which, beginning at Sumter, ended at Appomattox. All the force and antagonism of the conflict was concentrated here, and such an idea as this Re-Union gathering would have been laughed to scorn at that time by every combatant.

But the survivors of those contesting armies now meet on the battlefield, not again as foes; not as representatives of any party or issue; but as American citizens, who, having tested each other's courage, endurance, and love of principle, unite in demonstrating that the war is over: that as honorable foes, having accepted the arbitrament of the sword, they now meet to grasp each other's hands as friends and brothers, rejoicing in a result which enables them to claim joint interest in one great, growing and prosperous country; and that as a united people they are capable of the greatest things, in peace, in war, or in any position that the Ruler of the Universe may call upon them to occupy.

The programme of this great, this unique gathering of the Veterans of the Army of the Potomac and the Army of Northern Virginia, together with many facts concerning the Battle of Gettysburg, the Armies who fought there, the men who held command there, and the services at the dedication of the several monuments, will be found within these pages.

JOHN TREGASKIS.

A WORD FOR OURSELVES AND OUR ADVERTISERS.

A series of delays in the issuance, acceptance and promulgation of the official formalities, indispensable to a Re-Union of such dimensions and importance, postponed the date of this publication from May 1 to June 1, and again to June 15. One compensating incident was the fact that its publishers were thus enabled to better estimate and provide for the wide popular demand for their Memorial Magazine. Orders for it came in through G. A. R. Posts in every State of the Union in such quantities as to justify an initial edition of thirty thousand copies, instead of ten thousand, as at first proposed. They were also enabled to make more adequate provisions for the demand sure to come from the general travelling and reading public. THE RE-UNION SOUVENIR PROGRAMME AND REPORT will be sold on all trains leading to and from the scene of the celebration, on the grounds, and may be had from newsdealers everywhere, or during the remainder of the year from the office of the publishers, No. 769 Broadway, New York City (removed from Room 31, Cooper Institute).

The vast amount of research, arrangement and correspondence involved in this work have prevented its publishers from expending much time in bringing it to the attention of advertisers. Our advertising patronage is accordingly all the more select, and the more worthy of the confidence of readers. It comprises only those whose patriotic sympathies and national instincts led them readily to identify themselves and their businesses with the most unique soldier jubilee in history.

OUR RAILROAD ADVERTISERS.—To the railroad enterprises represented in these pages we especially invite attention. While almost every railroad in the land had a direct interest in an event so inviting to tourists, and so directly calculated to promote fraternal feeling and inter-communication between all sections, we bespeak for those which are here catalogued the good will and patronage of our reader.

THE GETTYSBURG AND HARRISBURG RAILROAD passes through the heart of the South Mountains, and as picturesque scenery as can be found in America. The gap is narrow and funnel-shaped, causing a constant current of air along the line of the road that tempers the heat of the day and makes the nights delightfully cool and pleasant. One of the attractions of the Re-Union will be to sojourn along the line of the Gettysburg and Harrisburg, visiting the battlefield each day, and returning to the road side village selected, by the 10:20 train each night.

THE PENNSYLVANIA RAILROAD, one of the most enterprising and far reaching in the extent of its territory, scarcely requires us to call attention to its facilities for accommodating the travelling public. It is intitled to the patronage of all who desire to visit the battlefield, and we hope every veteran, his family, and his friends, will buy the tickets by this line —the first to concede the reduced rate, and the first to look after the soldiers' interest while paying due regard to its own.

A GREAT INDUSTRY AND ITS FOUNDER.— The attention of manufacturers among our readers the country over will be concentrated upon the full page cut representing the world-famed Reliance Works of Messrs. Edward P. Allis & Co., located in Milwaukee, Wisconsin. This establishment derives additional general interest from the fact that it is the product of a single contemporaneous lifetime, and is the largest of its kind in this country under individual, as distinguished from corporate, ownership. It sends grist and saw mills, engines and other machinery to England, Japan, Australia, and to South America, as well as to the remotest points of the North American Continent. One of its latest contracts was to furnish Chicago with new pumping engines for $360,000. The senior proprietor, a man of rare simplicity of manners and fineness, combined with force of character, is known in this metropolis and in the capitals of Europe as a discriminating and munificent patron of art. In the Northwest he is a power alike in thought, in politics, and in practical affairs. He never has any unadjustable differences with the vast community of those whom he employs.

BATTLEFIELD MONUMENTS.—One of the most enterprising and successful firms engaged in erecting monument stones on the field at Gettysburg is Messrs. Frederick & Field of Quincy, Mass. This is the only establishment possessing their own quarry ; and from this, situated on Culp's Hill, they supply material not only for all their own work, but to other parties in the same line of business. Another feature of this house is that it does all its own work in every branch of the trade. It is ready and able to put up monumental work in every section of the country.

FINE ART BRONZE WORK.—Notably among the increasing number of bronze founderys in this country is that of Hon. Maunce J. Power of New York, known as the Natural Fine Art Foundery. Its reputation, always of the best, is steadily increasing, and its success in business is only another evidence of what business capacity and strict integrity can accomplish.

THE WASHINGTON LIFE is an insurance company which we can personally recommend with peculiar heartiness and sincerity. Aside from its universally recognized soundness and conservatism, and the attractiveness of its improved and unique system of Combination Insurance, it is commended to our approbation and regard by fourteen years' experience as a policy holder of the uniform spirit of friendliness and hospitality which animates all its officers and departments. From the day when introduced to the Washington Life, to the present, we have noted what seemed to be a family resemblance in the geniality of its officers and efficient corps of agents, among whom are many well known business men distributed throughout the country. Those who deal with this company will find themselves, as we have done, unexpectedly in a circle of friends. " Devotion to the interest of its policy holders" is justly the motto of the Washington Life, and we have no doubt but that the spirit of that motto inspired the system of Combination Insurance mentioned by the Company on another page and fully described in its catalogues and circulars which may be had on application by mail.

THIS EDITION IS 10,000 COPIES.

20,000 more will be printed and in circulation on July 1.

ADVERTISEMENTS FOR WHICH WILL BE ACCEPTED UP TO JUNE 26.

EXTRA EDITIONS WILL BE PRINTED AS CALLED FOR.

During the entire year THE SOUVENIR will be for sale in quantities from 1 to 1,000 by

TREGASKIS & CO., 767 BROADWAY (Room 8),

New York City.

JOHN TREGASKIS.   GEO. W. COONEY.

II.

'63 AND '88.

Cover with a mantle of roses
  The graves of our dead.
  Who were the heroes who bled.
  Whether they followed or led,
    Nothing discloses.

Weed-grown the ramparts, and still
  Are the desolate trenches.
The fort on the crest of the hill,
The cannon that mangle and kill,
The frosts of the winter now chill,
    The early rain drenches.

What though we thought they were wrong!
  Were they worse than all others?
From the same mountains and plains,
With the same losses and gains,
With the same blood in their veins,
    They were our brothers.

Slumber the sword in its sheath;
Unto the carnage of death
  Let no man draw it.
How earth is likest to hell
Nobody better can tell
  Than we who saw it.
Limb torn asunder from limb,
Blood till our eyesight grew dim,
Filling the cup to the brim
    As devils bore it.

Peace comes again to the land—
Friendship we must not withstand—
Offers once more her hand
  Now and forever.
Keep us, O God, in Thy sight,
Guard us and guide us aright;
Never may factionist blight
    Or traitors dissever.
                      FRANKLIN

III.

HOW TO REACH GETTYSBURG AND WHAT IT WILL COST.

The energetic efforts of General Daniel Butterfield, Chairman of the Committee on Transportation of the Army of the Potomac, resulted in a very great reduction in the rates of fare on all the railroads. The New England Passenger Association, however, with the money-loving proclivity of the wooden nutmeg Yankee, repudiated their agreement after it was made, so that the Boys in Blue from that section will have to pay higher rates of travel than their comrades in more liberal parts of the country. The Pennsylvania Railroad is the best line to travel by. All veterans should purchase their tickets from agents of that road at Harrisburg, and thence through the picturesque route of the Gettysburg and Harrisburg Railroad to the Battlefield.

Lower rates can be obtained in any locality by clubbing together and purchasing tickets. The actual rates from the principal points for Single Round Trip Tickets will be as follows from the points named:

	Parties Single of 25 or more			Single Rate		Single Rate		Single Rate
	Rate.	More.	Wilkesbarre	$5 00	Greenville, O.	$14 50	Mansfield, O.	$12 25
Danville	$10 85	$8 70	Erie	11 25	Richmond, Ind.	15 25	Crestline, O.	12 25
Augusta, Ga.	19 85	15 35	Altoona	5 45	Cambridge City, Ind	15 75	Bucyrus, O	12 65
Montgomery	25 30	20 35	Pittsburg	8 95	Indianapolis, Ind.	16 00	Upper Sandusky, O.	13 15
Mobile, Ala.	28 85	23 05	Baltimore, Md	2 15	Union City, Ind.	14 75	Forest, O	13 45
New Orleans	30 85	26 15	Washington, D. C.	3 35	Hartford, Ind.	15 75	Lima, O	14 35
Atlanta	20 85	16 85	Washington, Pa.	10 00	Marion, Ind.	16 00	Van Wert, O.	15 00
Boston, Mass., $18.97 Rail road, $12.55 Steamer.			Wheeling, W. Va.	10 00	New Castle, Ind.	15 75	Fort Wayne, Ind.	15 00
			Steubenville, O.	10 00	Anderson, Ind.	15 75	Columbia City, Ind.	15 25
	Single		Cadiz, O	10 85	Elwood, Ind.	16 10	Warsaw, Ind.	15 75
	Rate.		Urichville Junc., O.	10 60	Kokomo, Ind	16 75	Plymouth, Ind.	16 40
New York, N. Y.	$6 55		NewComerstown, O.	10 60	Logansport, Ind.	16 75	Valparaiso, Ind.	17 50
Jersey City	6 55		Coshocton, O.	11 05	Chicago, Ill.	17 50	New Castle, Pa.	10 50
Brooklyn	6 75		Newark, O.	12 15	Columbus, Ind.	16 20	Sharon, Pa.	10 75
Newark, N. J.	6 35		Columbus, O.	12 75	Madison, Ind.	16 80	Greenville, Pa.	10 75
Elizabeth, N. J.	6 20		London, O.	13 50	Seymour, Ind.	16 05	Tiffin, O.	13 00
Trenton, N. J.	4 85		Xenia, O.	14 00	Louisville, Ky.	17 50	Toledo, O.	13 50
St Louis, Mo.	21 50		Cincinnati, O.	14 00	Beaver Falls, Pa.	9 90	Wellesville, O.	10 00
Peoria, Ill.	21 00		Springfield, O.	14 00	Salem, O	10 75	Bellaire, O.	10 00
Detroit, Mich.	15 50		Dayton, O.	14 00	Alliance, O.	10 75	Ravenna, O.	10 80
Corry, Pa	10 65		Milford Centre, O.	13 60	Canton, O.	11 50	Cleveland, O.	11 00
Philadelphia	4 05		Urbana, O	14 60	Massillon, O.	11 50	NewPhiladelphia, O	11 00
Lancaster	2 55		Piqua, O.	14 00	Orrville, O	11 90		
Williamsport	4 30		Bradford Junc., O.	14 25	Wooster, O.	12 25		

Tickets will be of the iron-clad form and must be stamped at Gettysburg to insure return passage.

The good faith of the veterans has been pledged to use every effort to prevent any misuse of tickets or abuse of the concessions granted by those not going to the Re-Union, and it is expected that veterans will notify railroad agents of any such misuse or abuse within their knowledge.

Where large parties go the rates are fixed at one mile each way, so that if 500 can arrange to charter a train the price of tickets will reach the low sum of $4.40 each from New York City, $4.45 from Elmira, $4.20 from Newark and 3.10 from Wilmington, Del.

After the Re-Union is over the folowing are the regular single ticket excursion rates to Gettysburg and return from the places named :

Altoona, Pa $7 30	Cape May, N. J $8 20	MonongahelaC'y,Pa$13 20	Reading, Pa $7 45
Atlantic City, N. J... 7 70	Chester, Pa 6 75	Newark, N. J 9 50	Renovo, Pa 7 85
Avondale, Pa 5 10	Connellsville, Pa 11 70	Newark, N. Y 11 85	Schuylkill Haven, Pa 8 70
Bellefonte, Pa 7 20	Cresson, Pa 7 90	New Brunswick, N.J. 8 60	Shamokin, Pa 4 90
Belona, N. Y 10 90	Curwensville, Pa 8 60	New York, N. Y 9 80	Shenandoah, Pa 9 55
Beverly, N. J 7 00	Deal Beach, N. J 10 20	Norristown, Pa 6 20	Sodus Point, N. Y ... 12 55
Bordentown, N. J.... 7 3	Elbero , N. J 10 20	Ocean Beach, N. J .. 10 05	Trenton, N. J 7 45
Braddock, Pa 11 55	Elizabeth, N. J 9 30	Ocean Grove, N. J ... 10 20	Tyrone, Pa 6 70
Bridgeton, N. J 7 70	Elmira, N. Y 8 85	Penn Yan, N. Y 10 65	Waterford, Pa 14 00
Bristol, Pa 7 15	Erie, Pa 15 65	Philadelphia, Pa 6 20	Watkins, N. Y 9 75
Brooklyn, N. Y 10 00	Germantown, Pa 6 45	Phillipsburg, Pa 7 65	West End, N. J 10 20
Bryn Mawr, Pa 5 80	Jersey City, N. J 9 80	Pittsburg, Pa 11 05	Westmoreland, Pa .. 6 40
Buffalo, N. Y 15 45	Lancaster, Pa 3 45	Pottsville, Pa 8 98	Wilkesbarre, Pa 6 70
Burlington, N. J 7 15	Long Branch, N. J .. 10 20	Princeton, N. J 7 10	Williamsport, Pa 5 75
Canandaigua, N. Y .. 11 60	Monmouth Junc.,N.J. 8 20	Rahway, N. J 9 05	Wilmington, Del 7 30
Canton, Pa 7 35			

In addition to the above, special excursions are arranged with tickets good for the round trip and for one day's accommodation (breakfast, dinner, supper, and lodging) at Eagle Hotel. It is good for passage three days from and including date of sale. but is not good to stop off. The rates for these are :

Altoona, Pa $7 45	Lewisburg, Pa $5 40	Northumberland, Pa $5 20	Shamokin, Pa $5 70
Brooklyn, N. Y ... 9 20	Manayunk, N. J 6 05	Philadelphia, Pa 6 50	Shenandoah, Pa 9 80
Columbia, Pa 4 10	Nanticoke, Pa 6 85	Pottstown, Pa 7 70	Sunbury, Pa 5 15
Germautown, Pa... 6 80	Newark, N. J 8 80	Pottsville, Pa 9 35	Tyrone, Pa 7 05
Huntingdon, Pa... 6 45	New York, N. Y 9 00	Reading, Pa 8 25	Wilkesbarre, Pa 7 05
Lancaster, Pa 4 60	Norristown, Pa 7 00	Schuylkill Haven, Pa 9 25	Williamsport, Pa ... 6 30

The rates of boarding generally in Gettysburg are $1 per day in private houses. The hotels charge : Springs Hotel, $2.50 and $3 per day, and from $10 to $16 per week : Eagle Hotel, $1.50 and $2 per day. The other hotels charge from $1 to $2 per day.

Time Table of Gettysburg and Harrisburg Railroad that will be in effect from June 25 to July 7, 1888:

TRAINS TO GETTYSBURG.					TRAINS FROM GETTYSBURG.				
Leave.	P. M.	P. M.	A. M.	A. M.	Leave.	A. M.	P. M.	P. M.	P. M
Pittsburgh (P. R. R)....	7:15	9:00	—	8:00	Gettysburg............	9:00	1:00	5:00	*10:20
Altoona "	....10:55	1:00	7:00	11:50	Arrive.				
New York "	.... 8:00	12:15	—	9:00	Mount Holly Springs...10:03		2:00	6:08	11:20
		A. M.			Carlisle.................	10:25	2:15	6:20	11:40
Philadelphia "	....11:25	4:30	7:40	11:50	Harrisburg............	10:10	3:00	7:25	12:20
	A. M.			P. M.		P. M.			A. M.
Lancaster "	.... 1:25	6:25	9:35	2:00	Chambersburg	1:45	5:11	7:45	0:23
Williamsport "	.... 1:25	—	8:15	12:20	Hagerstown	2:40	6:00	—	7:05
Sunbury "	.... 2:50	—	9:40	1:43	Sunbury..............	12:52	5:30	—	5:10
	P. M.								
Hagerstown (C. V. R. R.).10:30		—	8:20	12:01	Williamsport.........	2:15	7:00	—	6:50
Chambersburg "	..10:45	7:00	9:15	12:58	Lancaster..............	12:58	4:45	9:35	2:20
	A. M.								
Harrisburg "	. 4:45	7:45	11:45	3:30	Philadelphia..........	3:15	6:50	—	4:25
			P. M.						
Carlisle (G. & H. R. R.)..	5:20	8:35	12:35	4:10	New York.............	6:20	9:35	—	7:10
Mount Holly "	.. 5.35	8:50	12:50	4:25	Altoona...............	3:30	7:50	—	4:05
Arrive.									
Gettysburg "	.. 6:50	10:00	1:50	5:33	Pittsburgh............	8:20	11:55	—	7:45

* Special trains that will be run only from June 25 to July 7 inclusive.

VISITING THE BATTLEFIELD.

A short rapid transit railroad extends from the Gettysburg and Harrisburg Depot to Little Round Top Park, a walk of only three minutes to the summit, where General Weed was killed, and from which point General Meade viewed the progress of the battle.

The hack rates at all times, except during such a thronged season as the Re-Union, is likely to be, are as follows: Three dollars for one or two persons; a horse and buggy for one, or a two seated carriage with one horse, and a driver that acts as guide for two persons, or a carriage with two horses and guide, for $5. The carriage seats five persons besides the guide. For all parties above five, the charge is $1 per head. These charges entitle the passengers to a ride over the battlefield of the second and third days' fight, and includes Culp's Hill, Cemetery Hill, National Cemetery, Emmittsburg Road to the Peach Orchard, the Wheat Field, Devil's Den, Round Top, and in Battlefield Avenue to the Angle where Hancock repulsed Pickett's charge, Ziegler's Grove, and back to Gettysburg. It requires from four to five hours to make the drive, and the time depends on how long the passengers wish to spend at the different points of interest. The distance is about eleven miles.

At the time of the Re-Union the town will be filled with hacks from all around the country, the owners of which hope to make all the money they can. They cannot be regulated, charge what they please, and Gettysburg gets the blame for it. There will be hacks from places fifty and sixty miles away. Most of them will deal fair, but some will take advantage of any one.

IV.

THE TWENTY-FIFTH ANNIVERSARY OF THE BATTLE OF GETTYSBURG

The celebration of the Twenty-fifth Anniversary of the Battle of Gettysburg promises to be one of the most striking events in history.

In spite of the foolish efforts of a few cranks at Washington, who profit by the privilege given them by the rules of the House to interpose capricious objection, and thus defeat the measure to provide the means to shelter the thousands of expected veterans, preparations are steadily going on, and the Blue and the Gray will fraternize on the field of battle, furnishing the world with a lesson that every nation should take to heart.

The celebration of the anniversary is counted from the first moment a dedicating party reaches the field until the last visit for such purpose is paid; or, during 1888, from June 12 to October 10. This period of time will include the Re-Union of the Two Armies, and the programme in chronological order is as follows (details of exercises are given in Chapter VII. of this book):

BEFORE THE RE-UNION

JUNE 12, 13 and 14.—Visit of Shaler's Brigade and dedication of the Monuments of the 65th and 122d New York, and 23d and 82d Pennsylvania Volunteers. June 21—Dedication of the 96th Pennsylvania Volunteers' Monument. June 30—The States of New Jersey and Wisconsin will dedicate all the Monuments to their troops engaged in the battle. The 76th New York Volunteers will also dedicate its Monument on that day. On that same Saturday the Department Encampment of the G. A. R. of Pennsylvania will convene for its summer session on East Cemetery Hill.

THE RE-UNION.

SUNDAY, JULY 1.—The 147th New York Volunteers will open the campaign by dedicating their Monument at 10 A. M., the 39th New York Volunteers following suit at 1 P. M. At th same hour the Society of the First Corps will meet in Reynolds' Grove for memorial services and to dedicate a Corps Monument. During the afternoon the following New York regiments will dedicate their Memorials—83d Infantry (9th Militia), 41st, 45th, 54th, 68th, 97th, 119th, 134th, and 121st Pennsylvania. In the afternoon there will be a concert at the G. A. R. Encampment.

MONDAY, JULY 2, will be the great day of this fraternal jubilee. The following Monuments will be dedicated—Greene's Brigade, 78th, 102d, 60th, 137th, and 149th New York, on Culp's Hill, commencing at 10 A. M. In the afternoon the Excelsior Brigade, 70th, 71st, 72d, 73d, and 74th New York Regiments; a special Monument by the 73d (2d Fire Zouaves), and 86th, 64th, 62d, 145th, and 152d New York Infantry, 9th New York Cavalry, Battery D, 15th, and 4th Battery, New York Artillery; 98th 68th, 110th, 105th Pennsylvania Infantry.

During the afternoon the Confederate Veterans will come in detachments, and will be welcomed as soon as they arrive. When all are on the ground, or when General Cooke shall notify General Sickles, the "Assembly" will be sounded, and the formal Re-Union will take place. Circumstances alone will dictate the place, and accident the method, but the programme for the speech-making is as follows: General Daniel E. Sickles will call the assemblage to order, Major George W. Cooney, as Secretary, recording the ceremony. After his introductory remarks, General Sickles will present Governor and Lieutenant-General John B. Gordan of Georgia, who will introduce to the Southern Veterans Governor and Major-General James A. Beaver of Pennsylvania. Governor Beaver, in the name of that Commonwealth and the Veterans of the Union Army, will welcome them as fellow citizens, friends and brothers, to the hospitalities of the Keystone State. General Sickles will then present, or some gentleman will be assigned by him to the pleasant duty of presenting, to the Union Army Veterans, Captain and Professor McCabe of Petersburg, Va., who will respond to the address of welcome. Then, if President Grover Cleveland is present, he will address the gathering as the Chief Magistrate of one people, with one glorious destiny before it. Speeches by Governors of States present may possibly follow, and then the camp fires will be started and kept up all night. Business meetings of the Corps Societies and Army of the Potomac will precede the Re-Union ceremonies.

TUESDAY, JULY 3.—Meetings of the several societies will take place during the morning, notably that of the 6th United States Regular Cavalry, and the Encampment of the Sons of Veterans of Pennsylvania will commence. During the day the following Monuments will be dedicated: 3d Battery, 13th Battery, and Battery B. New York Artillery; 5th New York Cavalry, 42d, 67th, and 146th New York Infantry, the Stone to General Hancock, and the 99th Pennsylvania Infantry. The corner stone of the Memorial Church will be laid in the morning, and the public exercises of the Society of the Potomac in the afternoon will be followed by a banquet in the evening.

WEDNESDAY, JULY 4, will be spent in fraternizing by the Blue and the Gray all over the field.

AFTER THE RE-UNION.

Many of the Monuments on the field, or now being erected, will be dedicated later in the season; those who have reported dates are as follows: August 8, General Warren's bronze Statue, by Duryee's Zouaves, 94th New York Infantry. August 9, 88th Pennsylvania Infantry. August 29, 4th New York Cavalry. September 4, 108th, 123d New York Infantry, and 1st Light Battery. September 17, 107th New York Infantry. September 20, all Michigan Monuments. September 26, 10th New York Cavalry. Last week in September, 80th, and 44th New York Infantry, all Maryland, Maine, and Vermont Monuments, and 2d New Hampshire Monuments. October, 84th, and 110th Pennsylvania.

NATIONAL MEMORIAL CHURCH.

Several years ago a plan was conceived and matured of erecting a Memorial Church on the Battlefield of Gettysburg, whose stones shall be inscribed, and donated as memorials of the dead of both armies, and thank offerings of the living. The church is to be named National

Memorial Church of the Prince of Peace. Nothing can well appeal more movingly to the hearts of churchmen than the plan here set before them. That Church, upon whose loving unity the terrible events of the Civil War made no mark, is surely the one above all others to embrace the memorials of both sides in rearing a lasting Temple to the Prince of Peace. Hundreds of memorial stones have already been contributed, and the corner stone will be laid on the morning of July 3, when probably the largest gathering of veterans of both sides that will ever take place will be witnessed.

The architect, Mr. Dempwolf of York, Pa., says that $20,000 will be the entire cost of the beautiful edifice, and the special memorials to be donated may be windows, bells, furniture and decorations, stones and tablets, suitably inscribed and to be placed in the large monumental tower. Also, tiles with names burned therein. Designs and full particulars will be furnished upon application to any one who wishes a stone or tablet to the memory of friend, comrade or relative. The Church is to be located on the corner of Baltimore and High streets, and the ceremonies will be under the direction of Bishop Howe of the Diocese of Central Pennsylvania; addresses will be made during the services by representatives of both the Blue and the Gray.

GRAND ARMY ENCAMPMENT —The Semi-Annual Encampment, Department of Pennsylvania, Grand Army of the Republic, will be held on East Cemetery Hill from June 30 to July 6, inclusive. The meetings will be held under a large canvas, owned by the Department. This being the summer encampment there is no settled programme. Tents are erected on Cemetery Hill for the use of comrades and Posts. Straw is put in them, and the comrades provide, or bring with them, everything else. Concerts are given in camp morning and evening by a band. Dress parade takes place every evening, and two or three camp fires will be lighted during the week. The idea of the encampment is to have a grand Re-Union and week of pleasure; and everything done, tends to that end; so the comrades are given the fullest latitude. None but comrades of the G. A. R. are provided with quarters in this section of the ground, under the rules and regulations of the Department. The officers of the Department are: Frank J. Magee, D. C.; W. R. Jones, S. V. C.; George R. Hart, J. V. C.; H. G. Williams, A. Q. M. G.; Thomas J. Stewart, A. A. G.; John V. Miller, Insp.; Thomas E. Merchant, J. A.; W. W. Greenland, C. M. O.; S. F. Chapin, M. D., and Rev. John W. Sayers, Chap.

SIXTH UNITED STATES CAVALRY.—The survivors of the Sixth United States Cavalry are ordered to report for duty on the Battlefield of Fairfield, near Gettysburg, Pa., on Tuesday, July 3, 1888, at 2 o'clock P. M., sharp, to take part in the Fifth Re-Union of that glorious old regiment, and the anniversary of one of the greatest battles that ever took place between troopers. George C. Platt, President; H. G. Mueller, Secretary.

CUSHING'S BATTERY. A, 4th United States Artillery, will take part in the Re-Union, firing the several salutes during the celebration.

BATTERY B, 1st Pennsylvania Light Artillery, will meet at the Tablet on East Cemetery Hill, at 4 P. M., July 2, for a good and hearty meeting, and to perfect the arrangements for the dedication of its Monument in 1889.

SONS OF VETERANS of Pennsylvania will hold a Division Encampment at Gettysburg, commencing on July 3, and closing on the 5th.

V.

ANNUAL MEETING OF THE ARMY OF THE POTOMAC.

Aside from the Re-Union of the Two Armies and Anniversary of the Battle, the members of the Society of the Army of the Potomac will hold their Annual Meeting at Gettysburg.

The members of the Society and of the several Corps Societies will assemble during Saturday. June 30, and Sunday, July 1. The main body from the vicinity of New York City will leave the depot at Jersey City on special trains at 11 A. M. and 11 P. M., June 30. Tickets for these trains can be obtained for $5 each, holders of which must return either on Tuesday evening or Thursday morning. Tickets are not good on other trains. The following is the programme:

MONDAY, JULY 2.—The various corps societies will hold their meetings at such places as can be secured on that day. The meeting of the Fifth Corps will be presided over by General Fitz John Porter; Sixth Corps by General Charles A. Whittier, Ninth Corps, General Gilbert H. McKibben; Twelfth Corps, Lieutenant-Colonel William Fox; Nineteenth Corps, General W. H. Emory; Cavalry Society, General Samuel E. Chamberlain. The hour set for each is 10:30 A. M. The general business meeting of the Army of the Potomac will be held in the Rink at 1 P. M. General John C. Robinson will preside. The business will conclude at an early hour to allow of the reception of the various parties of Confederate veterans as the trains roll in. In the evening the Society will join in the welcome and Re-Union exercises.

TUESDAY, JULY 3.—The public exercises before the Society and its guests will begin at 3:30 P. M. The Orator of the day will be George William Curtis; the poet, George Parsons Lathrop. In the evening the annual banquet of the Society will be held. On this occasion the Blue and the Gray will fraternize at the festive board, expressing their feelings of mutual esteem and pledging each other's united efforts for the country's advancement under the old flag in the future. Any one desiring to participate in the banquet can obtain tickets at the Springs Hotel at $5 each; spectators' tickets, $1 each.

WEDNESDAY, JULY 4—Independence Day.—A general jubilee will take place on the Battle-field, in the town, and at every hotel and home in Gettysburg.

VI.

WHAT THE ARMY OF NORTHERN VIRGINIA WILL DO.

The various detachments of Confederate Veterans will be welcomed at the depots during the day on Monday, July 2, and escorted to the quarters selected for or by them, by details from the Union veterans who have volunteered for that agreeable service.

In the evening, when General Tallafiero shall have notified General Sickles that the main body of his party are in town, the "Assembly" will be sounded, and under leadership of the Headquarter Band all will march to the point selected for the formal Re-Union of the Blue and the Gray.

The Court House will be placed at the disposal of the society for any meetings they may choose to hold. All business matters connected with the Re-Union or their personal movements will be discussed at the meetings they expect to hold every morning in that hall at 7:30 o'clock. Committee meetings will be held in the special hotel car reserved for the leading officers of the Confederate Army, which will be stationed on the special side track recently erected.

The full affiliation and fraternization will take place all along the lines of the battlefield on the Anniversary of Independence day. No special festivities have been arranged for by the contingent in Gray.

As an evidence of the general desire of the Boys in Gray to participate we publish one letter of many received by the Committee of Arrangements:

VETERANS OF THE ARMY OF NORTHERN VIRGINIA,
BRIGADE ASSOCIATION, LOUISIANA DIVISION,
NEW ORLEANS, June 4, 1888.

General Daniel E. Sickles.

MY DEAR SIR: Will you kindly give me information in regard to the celebration of the anniversary of the Battle of Gettysburg to be held on July 1, 2 and 3 of this year. A delegation from this Association may attend, composed of soldiers who participated and who desire to be present. * * * We speak for ourselves as the survivors of Louisiana's Contingent serving under General Robert E. Lee. Very respectfully your obedient servant,

FRED. A. OBER,

Formerly of the 5th Louisiana Infantry, Hays' Louisiana Brigade.

✠ Fine Monuments ✠

From New and Artistic Designs in Granite and Real Bronze.

ESPECIAL ATTENTION PAID TO
SOLDIERS' MONUMENTS AND GETTYSBURG MEMORIALS.

Quarries and Works, Quincy, Mass.

- A. L. MYERS - Agent, -
78 SOUTH AVENUE, ROCHESTER, N. Y.

THE FOLLOWING SOLDIERS' MONUMENTS ARE AMONG THOSE ERECTED BY US

Port Jervis, N. Y.,	Leominster, Mass.,	West Roxbury, Mass.,
Norristown, N. J.,	Monmouth Battle Monument,	Springfield, O.,
Lawrence, Mass.	Manchester, N. H.,	Findley, O., Etc.

GETTYSBURG MEMORIALS ERECTED AND NOW IN PROCESS OF CONSTRUCTION:

20th N. Y. S. M. (80th N. Y. Vol. Inf.)	1st N. J. Cavalry,	12th N. J. Vol. Inf.,
Battery K, 1st Ohio Light Artillery,	6th Ohio Cavalry,	Clark's Battery,
6th N. J. Vol. Inf.	5th N. J. Vol. Inf.,	1st N. J. Artillery.
8th N. J. Vol. Inf.,	7th N. J. Vol. Inf.,	39th N. Y. Inf.,
43d N. Y. Inf.,	67th N. Y. Infy.,	86th N. Y. Infy,
49th N. Y. Inf.	68th N. Y. Inf.	97th N. Y. Inf.,
57th N. Y. Inf.,	70th N. Y. Inf.,	104th N. Y. Inf.
6th N. Y. Inf.,	80th N. Y. Inf.,	121st N. Y. Inf.,
125th N. Y. Inf.,	137th N. Y. Inf.,	Battery D, 1st N. Y. Artillery,
126th N. Y. Inf.,	146th N. Y. Inf.,	5th N. Y. Independent Battery,
134th N. Y. Inf.,	147th N. Y. Inf.,	9th N. Y. Cavalry,
136th N. Y. Inf.	Battery B, 1st N. Y. Artillery,	83d Penn. Inf.

PRIVATE MEMORIALS OF ALL DESCRIPTIONS, COSTING FROM $50 TO $100,000. ERECTED COMPLETE IN ANY PART OF THE COUNTRY.

VII.

MONUMENTS TO BE DEDICATED DURING THE YEAR 1888.

WITH SKETCHES OF THE ORGANIZATIONS AND LISTS OF EXERCISES.

In order that the various dedicatory exercises may be more easily referred to, we have divided this programme into three sections: 1—Before the Re-Union. 2—During the Re-Union. 3—After the Re-Union.

That some idea of the number of Monuments erected, or to be erected, on the Battlefield may be given those interested, the following statement has been compiled from official sources; and will show the number of organizations from each State engaged on the Union side at Gettysburg; the amount appropriated by the State to each organization to mark its position on the field; the amount appropriated by the State to the Gettysburg Battlefield Memorial Association, for purchase of lands, &c., and the total amount appropriated by each State, including, in some instances, special appropriations for Monuments to distinguished officers who fell on the field:

States represented by Troops in the Union Army at Gettysburg.	Number of Organizations.	Amount to each Organization.	Amount to Gettysburg Battlefield Mem. Association.	Total Amount Appropriated.
New York........................	92	$1,500	$20,000	$216,000
Pennsylvania....................	85	1,500	16,000	150,000
Massachusetts...................	25	540	5,000	18,500
Maine............................	14	900	3,000	15,600
New Jersey......................	15	1,000	3,000	18,000
Ohio.............................	19	1,500	11,500	40,000
Michigan........................	12	1,350	5,000	21,000
Vermont.........................	9	722	2,500	9,000
Connecticut.....................	8	....	2,500	2,500
Indiana..........................	6	500	....	3,000
New Hampshire.................	4	600	1,100	3,500
Rhode Island....................	3	666	1,000	3,000
Delaware........................	2	1,000	500	2,500
Minnesota.......................	1	1,000	1,000	2,000
Wisconsin.......................	6	1,500	1,500	10,500
Maryland........................	5	900	1,000	6,000

Of the intended Monuments nearly ninety were in position and dedicated before the close of 1887. Those to be dedicated during this year, the twenty-fifth anniversary of the battle, will be mentioned in the following sections:

I.—BEFORE THE RE-UNION.

SHALER'S BRIGADE.—The first gathering of Veterans on the Battlefield during the year will be that of the survivors of Shaler's Brigade on Tuesday, Wednesday and Thursday, June 12, 13 and 14. This was the First Brigade, Third Division, Sixth Army Corps—comprising the 65th, 67th and 122d New York, and the 23d and 82d Pennsylvania Volunteers. It is expected that the Regimental Associations, excepting the 67th New York, will reach Gettysburg on the morning of Tuesday, the 12th, and remain during the three days. The programme as arranged is:

June 12, Tuesday.—9 A. M., arrival of the 122d New York Volunteers. 1. P. M., arrival of the 65th New York Volunteers, 23d and 82d Pennsylvania Volunteers, who will be escorted upon their arrival to their respective headquarters by the G. A. R. Band of Gettysburg. 7:30 P. M , assemble at Brigade headquarters to attend the Camp Fire at Court House; General Alexander Shaler will deliver an address, followed by music, songs, recitations, Army reminiscences, &c. William J. Wray, 23d Pennsylvania, Master of Ceremonies.

June 13, Wednesday.—9 A. M., assemble at Brigade headquarters to march to the Dedication Grounds at Culp's Hill. The Monument Dedication Ceremonies will begin with an address by General John Cochrane of New York City, one of the former Brigade Commanders, followed by the dedication of Monuments in the order named—23d Pennsylvania, 82d Pennsylvania, 65th New York and 122d New York. Should General Cochrane not recover his health in time for the ceremonies General Martin T. McMahon, United States Marshal for the Southern District of New York, will probably deliver the address. Each of the dedicatory ceremonies is expected not to exceed thirty minutes'. 2 P. M., assemble at Brigade headquarters for visit to the Battlefield of the second and third days' actions, passing along the lines at Cemetery Hill, Peach Orchard, Devil's Den, the Round Tops, Culp's Hill and National Cemetery. 9 P. M., reassemble at Brigade headquarters to attend the complimentary ball and reception, given in honor of the event, by the 23d Pennsylvania Volunteers' Survivors' Association, at the Rink Building. Colonel John F. Glenn of Philadelphia, Grand Conductor. Music by McKnightstown Cornet Band.

June 14, Thursday.—9 A. M., assemble at Brigade headquarters to visit the Reynolds Monument and field of the first day's action. Noon—Departure for home.

The officers of the Brigade Association are: President—General Alexander Shaler, Ridgefield, N. J.; Vice-Presidents—Colonel John F. Glenn, 23d Pennsylvania Volunteers, Philadelphia, Pa.; Colonel Silas Titus, 122d New York Volunteers, Syracuse, N. Y.; Colonel John M. Wetherill, 82d Pennsylvania Volunteers, Pottsville, Pa.; Lieutenant-Colonel Henry G. Healy, 65th New York Volunteers, Washington, D. C.; Colonel William P. Roome, Headquarters Staff, New York City. Secretary and Treasurer—William J. Wray, 23d Pennsylvania Volunteers, 3923 Reno street, Philadelphia, Pa. Brigade Committee—General Alexander Shaler, Headquarters, Ridgefield, N. J.; Colonel Samuel Truesdell, 65th New York Volunteers, New York City; Captain Robert H. Moses, 122d New York Volunteers, New York City ; Colonel John M. Wetherill, 82d Pennsylvania Volunteers, Pottsville, Pa.; William J. Wray, 23d Pennsylvania Volunteers, Philadelphia, Pa.

It was deemed best that the Re-Union should occur in June, it being the beginning of the vacation season, and the Regimental Tablets would be erected in time for inspection by the great crowd of people who will visit the historic field of Gettysburg in July. Following are the Regimental Programmes:

23D PENNSYLVANIA INFANTRY (Birney Zouaves) will unveil their Birney Zouave Statue June 13, the order of dedicatory exercises being: Prayer, by Rev. James G. Shinn, Atlantic City, N. J., late Chaplain 23d Pennsylvania Volunteers; Address, by Colonel John F. Glenn, Philadelphia, late Colonel 23d Pennsylvania Volunteers; Music, McKnightstown Cornet Band; Presentation of Statue to the Battlefield Association, by William J. Wray, Philadelphia, late F Company 23d Pennsylvania Volunteers; Unveiling of Statue—Music; Acceptance of Statue by the Battlefield Association's Secretary; Singing, "My Country, 'tis of Thee"; Doxology, by Chaplain Shinn. During the stay of the Brigade in Gettysburg the 23d will give a ball and reception at the Rink Building. The regimental headquarters will be at the Eagle Hotel.

82D PENNSYLVANIA INFANTRY.—This command will dedicate a Tablet on Wednesday morning, June 13. The programme of exercises is: Address, by the President, Colonel J. M. Wetherill; Prayer, by the Chaplain; Music—Band; Oration, Captain George W. Waterhouse; Singing, "My Country, 'tis of Thee"; Doxology. The Committee on the Tablet are: Colonel John M. Wetherill, Captain Charles Williams, Captain Albert Ivers, William H. Aiment and W. H. Redheffer. The excursion party of this regiment have arranged for their train to leave Broad Street Station, Philadelphia, on Tuesday, June 12, 1888, at 7:20 o'clock A. M. Headquarters have been established at the Keystone Hotel.

65TH NEW YORK INFANTRY (Chasseurs), was raised in New York City, and mustered in during October, 1861, and fought at Fair Oaks, Malvern Hill, Antietam, Fredericksburg, Marye's Heights, Salem Heights, Gettysburg, Wilderness, Spottsylvania, Cold Harbor, Petersburg, Opequan and Cedar Creek. Regimental headquarters will be at the McClellan House in the square. The Monument will be dedicated on June 13.

122D NEW YORK INFANTRY, raised at Syracuse, and mustered in during August, 1862. It smelt powder at Marye's Heights, Gettysburg, Rappahannock Station, Wilderness, Spottsylvania, Cold Harbor, Petersburg, Fort Stevens, Opequan, Fisher's Hill, Cedar Creek. The order of exercises at the Monument is: Calling to order, by the President of the Survivors' Association, A. H. Hubbs; Presentation of Monument, by Major Davis Cossett, Chairman of Monument Committee; Unveiling of Monument; Music, by Band; Acceptance of Monument, by President A. H. Hubbs; Oration, by Major J. B. Davis. Regimental headquarters will be at the Globe Hotel.

NOTE.—The regiments met as arranged, and the programme was thoroughly and successfully carried out.

THE STATE OF WISCONSIN will dedicate on June 30 seven Monuments to the memory of the dead from that State who participated with their several commands in the engagement. Each regiment will have its own appropriate exercises, and then the general exercises on behalf of the State will be held in the grove where General Reynolds fell on July 1, 1863. The Society of the First Corps has tendered the State the use of the rostrum it has erected for exercises on the following Sunday, and the offer has been accepted. The platform, built by Peter Culp, a scout employed by General Reynolds on the morning of the first day's fight, is thirty two feet square. State Senator L. E. Pond was the prime mover in obtaining the appropriations which enable the State to place her seven stately and unique Memorials in granite and marble. The Senator was Captain of Company E of the 7th Regiment at Gettysburg, and fell shot in the breast early in the engagement—so early, in fact, that it is said he was the first man wounded in the battle. The company faltered for a moment. He cried out: "Press on, boys; never mind me," and they pressed on. He was subsequently wounded twice at Petersburg, and was compelled to withdraw from the service December 30, 1864. Captain Pond was appointed President of the Wisconsin Gettysburg Monumental Association, and to his efforts the prompt execution of the will of the Legislature is due. The Wisconsin delegation will reach Gettysburg early on the morning of the day of dedication. The programme for the general gathering is arranged as follows: The procession will wend its way from the town, and at ten o'clock, under the direction of L. E. Pond, President of the State Commission, and Chairman of the Committee on Excursion, and H. B. Harshaw,

Secretary, will gather around the First Corps platform in Reynold's Grove. Comrade and Captain Levi E. Pond will then transfer the Monuments to the Governor of Wisconsin, General Jeremiah M. Rusk, who will formally accept them in the name of the State. The Oration, by United States Senator John C. Spooner will follow. At its conclusion the Memorial Stones will be presented to and accepted by the Battlefield Memorial Association. Short addresses will be made by General Lucius Fairchild, General R. R. Dawes of Ohio, Colonel W. W. Dudley of Indiana, and other prominent officers. Other exercises will follow at each of the regimental stations. The following were appointed as the Commission to erect the Monuments by Governor Rusk: 2d Regiment, General Lucius Fairchild, Madison; Captain Henry B. Harshaw, Oshkosh; Henry Sanford, Manitowoc. 3d Regiment, Colonel G. W. Stevenson, Wiota; Colonel Warham Parks, Oconomowoc; Herman Buchner, Lancaster. 5th Regiment, General T. S. Allen, Oshkosh; Captain Henry Curran, Stevens Point; Frank E. Pease, Menominee. 6th Regiment, General E. M. Rogers, Viroqua; Captain J. H. Marston, Appleton; Lieutenant H. J. Huntington, Green Bay. 7th Regiment, General H. Richardson, Chippewa Falls; Captain L. E. Pond, Westfield; Captain M. C. Hobart, Fall River; 26th Regiment, General F. C. Winkler, Major George P. Træmur, Captain William Steinmeyer, Milwaukee. Company G, Berdan's 1st Regiment, United States Sharpshooters, Sergeant J. S. Webster, Madison; J. K. Hawes, Baraboo; C. W. Baker, Soldiers' Grove. Lieutenant H. J. Huntington was made Secretary of the Commission. It is expected that at the regimental exercises Colonel H. B. Harshaw, 2d Regiment, will speak; also Colonel G. W. Stevenson, 3d Regiment; General T. S. Allen, 5th Regiment; Judge H. J. Huntington and General R. R. Dawes, 6th Regiment; Alexander Hughes of Bismarck, D. T.; General H. Richardson, 7th Regiment; General F. C. Winckler of the 26th Regiment, and Captain F. E. Marble of Company I, 1st Regiment of Sharpshooters. The excursion party from Wisconsin will number 200, including all the State officials.

NEW JERSEY always was a patriotic State, and this year she steps to the front again, inviting every soldier who fought at Gettysburg, now residing in the State, to take a trip to the scene of that great conflict at her expense. The dedication of all the Monuments to New Jersey troops who participated in the battle will take place on June 30. Trains will leave Pennsylvania Railroad depot at Jersey City on the morning of Friday, June 29, at 9 o'clock, stopping at the principal stations between Jersey City and Trenton, and at Philadelphia, and running through to Gettysburg without change. Subsistence and quarters in tents will be furnished at Gettysburg, by the Quartermaster-General. The New Jersey trains returning will leave Gettysburg, Saturday evening, June 30, but soldiers will be at liberty to return on any regular train within the limit of time expressed on their tickets. The Commission, composed of Robert S. Green, Governor; William S. Stryker, Adjutant-General; Edward J. Anderson, Comptroller; James N. Duffy, Newark; Gottfried Krueger, Newark; William H.

Corbin, Elizabeth, thoroughly satisfied that it would be impossible to carry out the programme incident to such a dedication as is proposed, on either July 2 or 3, the anniversary of the battle, fixed upon a date prior to the anniversary for the dedication of the State Monuments, and have named a day that will be specially appropriated to the soldiers of New Jersey. The encampment will be pitched on the historic wheat field, and after a brief sojourn in the tents on the morning of June 30, the procession will form at 9 A. M., and move to the site of the Brigade Monument on the north slope of Little Round Top, where the dedicatory exercises will be held. The Oration will be delivered by the Governor, Hon. Robert S. Green; Colonel James N. Duffy, Chairman of the Monument Commission, will also make an address. The procession will then move to the site of the Monuments erected to the 5th,

6th, 7th, 8th (Hooker's Old Guard), 11th and 12th Regiments of Infantry and Battery A of the Artillery; brief remarks by a surviving officer of each of the commands will be included in the exercises. The formal programme was not completed in time for this publication.

96TH PENNSYLVANIA INFANTRY will dedicate their Monument on June 21. The President of the Veteran Association is Samuel R. Russell, and the Secretary, John A. Schweer. This command was composed of sturdy miners from Schuylkill, Dauphin, Berks, Luzerne and Montgomery Counties. It was mustered in at Pottsville in 1861. Rev. Dr. Powers of Pottsville, will open the exercises with prayer; Colonel Henry Royer is the Orator of the occasion, and the music will be furnished by the Grand Army Band and Choir of St. James Church, Gettysburg.

76TH NEW YORK INFANTRY will reach Gettysburg on the morning of June 30. At 10 A. M. sharp the party will assemble around the base of the Monument. The old Drum Corps, or as many as they can get there, will then beat the "Assembly," and after prayer, singing by a Glee Club, and addresses by Benjamin F. Taylor and A. P. Smith, the Monument will be transferred to the Battlefield Memorial Association. Between 200 and 300 persons will be in the party, which will leave Cortland, N. Y., on the 29th of June under the following officers: President, Benjamin F. Taylor, Cortland; Vice-Presidents—Dr. William J. Burr, Newark Valley; Charles H. Smith, Washington, D. C.; Ira C. Potter, Utica; Secretary, A. P. Smith, Cortland; Treasurer, William H. Myers, Cortland. Executive Committee—Major Aaron

Sager, David C. Beers, Norman G. Harmon, all of Cortland. This regiment mustered in at Albany in January, 1862, and was recruited from Albany, Otsego and Cortland Counties. Its record is: Rappahannock Station, Warrenton, Gainesville, Bull Run (1862), South Mountain, Antietam, Upperville, Fredericksburg, Chancellorsville, Gettysburg and Mine Run.

DURING THE RE-UNION.

THE SOCIETY OF THE FIRST CORPS will meet on the spot where General Reynolds fell and will commence the celebration of the Twenty-fifth Anniversary of the Battle of Gettysburg on July 1 by interesting exercises in commemoration of their renowned chieftain. It was intended to have commenced these exercises at 1 P. M., but that being in the heat of the day and too early for those who leave New York and Philadelphia by the first trains the exercises will be deferred a little as an act of courtesy to intended participants. The arrangements have been left entirely in the hands of the Historian of the Corps, Mr. J. H. Stine of Washington, and he reports the following as the programme—except one Confederate speaker, that may not be filled: Presiding Officer, Major E. P. Halstead; Address of Welcome, Governor James A. Beaver of Pennsylvania; Response, General Abner Doubleday; Addresses by War Governor A. G. Curtin of Pennsylvania, Austin Blair of Michigan, Frederick Holbrooke of Vermont, S. J. Kirkwood of Iowa, J. Gregory Smith of Vermont, Frederick Smythe of New Hampshire and William Sprague of Rhode Island. Addresses by General John C. Robinson, General James Longstreet, General Lucius Fairchild, General J. H. Stine, Historian First Corps, General James A. Hall, General Joseph Dickinson and General J. P. Rea, Commander-in-Chief of the Grand Army of the Republic. Music will enliven the proceedings at intervals. The officers of the Society of the First Corps are: E. P. Halstead, President, Washington, D. C.; Charles E. Coon, Vice-President, New York City; Charles E. Phelps, Vice-President, Baltimore, Md.; Patrick De Lacy, Vice-President, Scranton, Pa.; John A. Reynolds, Vice-President, Rochester, N. Y.; Abram Merritt, Corresponding Secretary, Nyack, N. Y. (deceased); James M. Andrews, Jr., Recording Secretary, Saratoga, N. Y.; Walter J. Gibson, Treasurer, Buffalo, N. Y.; J. H. Stine, Historian, 323 C Street, S. E., Washington, D. C.

54TH NEW YORK INFANTRY will plant their old battle flag in the position occupied by them on July 1, and the Color Sergeant who rescued it on that day will again bear it—Sergeant Will C. Smith. Seventy-five persons will constitute the party that will leave this city to dedicate the Monument on Sunday, the first day of the Re-Union. The Committee of Arrangements are Captain William Townsend, Chairman; Sergeant Will C. Smith, Secretary; Sergeant P. Bellburg, Treasurer. The veterans of the 54th will leave New York on June 30, and among them will be the Theodore Koerner Liedertafel, which was organized September 17, 1863, when the regiment was stationed on Folly Island, S. C. The living members of the Liedertafel who will go to Gettysburg to dedicate the Monument are: Jacob Meinzer, President; Ludwig Meister, Vice-President; F. Prengkowitz, Corresponding Secretary; C. Wangenstein, Treasurer; William Braumann, Musical Director; Fritz Angersbach, Adam Becker, Charles Berger, John Doscher, August Durholz, Theodore Frost, Henry Heutschel, Martin Hofer, Christian Hettenbach, Charles Hohle, Wilhelm Holzschuh, Adam Iselhardt, Adolph Konig, Freidrich Lofller, Martin Mink, Richard Nicolai, Peter Oschman, Fritz Schafer, George Schwim, George Stock, George Wack and Fritz Weimer. At the dedicatory services the programme will be: Prayer; Singing, "Nachtlied der Krieger," by Wreide, Koerner Liedertafel; Addresses by Colonel Bankson T. Morgan, Colonel George F. Hopper, Captain W. Townsend, Captain Ed. Wertheimer and Samuel Minnes; Original Poem, "The Muffled Drum," Colonel Samuel S. Wood, Jr.; Singing, "Wachtfeur," by Kern, Koerner Liedertafel; Benediction. The 54th was raised in New York City, and was mustered in during October,

1861; it bears the following record: Cross Keys, Freeman's Ford, Bull Run (1862), Chancellorsville, Waterloo Bridge, Cedar Mountain, Gettysburg, Rappahannock Station, Sulphur Springs.

39TH NEW YORK INFANTRY (Garibaldi Guards) intend to dedicate their Monument on Sunday, July 1, some fifty of the survivors of the old command participating in the exercises. The programme will include instrumental and vocal music and an oration by Captain Frank M. Clark of New York City. The regiment, recruited in New York City, was mustered in May, 1861, and fought at Bull Run, Cross Keys, Gettysburg, North Anna, Bristow Station, Po River, Mine Run, Spottsylvania, Wilderness, Tolopotomy, Cold Harbor, Petersburg and Deep Bottom. The officers of the Veterans' Association are A. E. Seifert, President; John H. Erben, Vice-President; Charles Hoffmann, Treasurer; Richard Marschall, Secretary.

97TH NEW YORK INFANTRY (Conkling Rifles) will dedicate their Monument on July 1, the "Social Union" of its veterans taking charge of the exercises. The Company, over 200 strong, will leave Utica on June 30. Had the lamented ex-Senator Conkling lived, after whom the regiment was named, he would have been the Orator of the Day. Now, Mr. H. E. Turner of Lowville will take his place. The officers of the "Social Union" are C. D. Fenton, President; Dr. George S. Little, Vice-President; Arch B. Snow, Secretary; John Peattie, Isaac Hull, C. D. Collins, Executive Committee. The regiment was recruited in Oneida, Herkimer, Lewis, Fulton and Hamilton Counties, and its battle roll included Cedar Mountain, Bull Run (1862),

Chantilly, South Mountain, Antietam, Fredericksburg, Gettysburg, Mine Run, Wilderness, Spottsylvania, North Anna, Tolopotomy, Bethesda Church. The order of exercises at the dedication will be prayer, Rev. J. V. Ferguson, late Chaplain of the regiment; Introductory remarks by Dr. George S. Little, M. D., of Brooklyn, late Surgeon of the Regiment, and now President of the Regimental Veterans; Reminiscences of the Battle, by Brevet-Major Isaac Hall of Leyden, N. Y.; Poem, Captain John E. Norcross, late United States Volunteers, Brooklyn, N. Y.; Address, H. E. Turner, Esq., Lowville, N. Y.; Benediction, by the Chaplain. Members of the Monument Committee: George S. Little, ex-officio; Major Isaac Hall, Chairman; Captains A. B. Snow, Secretary; G. M. Palmer, C. D. Fenton, Frank Favill, Sergeant W. B. Chambers, Captains J. V. Furgeson, C. D. Collins, Lieutenant John T. Comstock, John Peattie and R. B. Maxfield, Esq.

134TH NEW YORK INFANTRY will take a party 400 strong from Schenectady to dedicate their Monument on July 1. The Mayor and Common Council of that city and the Board of County Supervisors will accompany the Veterans, the 36th Separate Company of the National Guard acting as escort. The addresses at the dedication will be made by Hon. H. Low Barhyat and Hon. A. A. Yates. Charles Griffin is President of the Regimental Organization, A. G. McMullin of the Local Association, and Henry V. Bradt is Secretary of both. The regiment was recruited in Schoharie and Schenectady Counties, mustered in during September, 1862, and started for the front on the 25th of that month. Its battle record is Chancellorsville, Gettysburg, Mission Ridge, Knoxville, Atlanta, Resaca, Dallas, Pine Knob, Lost Mountain, Pine Tree Creek, Savannah and Goldsboro. The following history of the colors of this regiment is furnished by a comrade: The colors of the 134th were presented at New York City by Governor Horatio Seymour, in behalf of the State of New York, and were carried by the regiment through all its skirmishes, battles and marches. At Gettysburg they were carried by Sergeants Carroll and Seaman. Sergeant Seaman received a severe wound from a minnie ball in the right arm, and was unable to bring the regimental colors from the field. At this critical moment Carroll seized both colors, and started for the Cemetery Heights, where the Corps had retired and were taking position, but had not proceeded far before he received three severe wounds, which laid him prostrate. The Confederates were close behind and bent upon obtaining the colors, but they were foiled. A gallant officer seized the National colors and bore them off, and Sergeant Carroll tore the State color from its staff, and wound it round his body underneath his clothing, where he kept it for four days, during which time he was a prisoner, and at the expiration of which he returned them to the regiment. For this act of gallantry Sergeant Carroll received the thanks of the commanding General, and also the thanks of the entire regiment. Both Color Sergeants being now disabled, new ones were appointed in the persons of Sergeants Bradt and Rosa. The last named was killed at the Battle of Peach Tree Creek, Ga., and his place filled by Sergeant Mickle. At the Siege of Savannah, Ga., Sergeant Bradt was severely wounded, and Sergeant Dey was appointed to the vacancy. By these Sergeants they were carried through the campaign of the Carolinas and in the grand review at Washington, at which latter place they were cheered along the whole line of march. They were brought to Albany and deposited in the Hall of Military Records, where they remain as lasting mementos of the bravery and patriotism of the sons of Schenectady and Schoharie.

147TH NEW YORK INFANTRY proposes to dedicate its Monument at the Railroad Cut, on July 1 at 10 o'clock in the morning. This was the hour in which they were most busily engaged in 1863, twenty-five years before. The dedication service will consist of the reading of a "History of the Regiment During the Battle," by Surgeon A. S. Coe, and an Oration, by General J. Volney Pierce of Walnut, Kan., formerly a Captain in the 147th. About seventy-five persons will participate in the services, among whom will be General J. Volney Pierce, Surgeon A. S. Coe, Major N. A. Wright, Captain James McKinley, Captain A. R. Penfield, Walnut, Kan.; Amos Allport, Oswego; John S. Coe, Scriba; Lieutenant P. J. Brown (Capitol), Albany; Captain E. D. Parker, Auburn; Lieutenant W. R. Potts, Williamstown; Lieutenant J. F. Box, Burns Parkhurst, Elisha Burr, Pulaski; H. H. Cole, Laeona; Dr. Crockett, Sandy Creek; Colonel George Hugmuir, Captain William Gillett, Syracuse, and H. H. Lyman, Oswego, N. Y.

GREENE'S BRIGADE, Geary's Division, Slocum's Corps (2d Division 12th Corps) will have their Re-Union on Culp's Hill, the extreme right of the line, at 11 A. M. on July 2, immediately after the dedication of the regimental Monuments. Major-General Henry W. Slocum and Brigadier-General George S. Greene will speak, and poems, addresses and singing will be interspersed in the exercises.

60TH NEW YORK INFANTRY was organized in October, 1861, in St. Lawrence County, and fought at Chancellorsville, Gettysburg, Lookout Mountain, Mission Ridge, Pea Vine Creek, Ringgold, Atlanta, Resaca, Mount Hope Church and Peach Tree Creek.

78TH NEW YORK INFANTRY, recruited in Erie, Monroe, Steuben, Niagara and Oneida Counties, was organized in New York City in the fall of 1861, and served in the following battles: Harper's Ferry, Chantilly, South Mountain, Antietam, Winchester, Chancellorsville, Gettysburg, Wauhatchie, Lookout Mountain, Mission Ridge, Pea Vine Creek, Ringgold, Mill Creek Gap (Dalton), Resaca, Cassville, New Hope Church (Dallas), Pine Mountain, Culp's Farm. This regiment was consolidated with the 102d New York Infantry, Veteran Volunteers, in July, 1864, and the two regiments will join in the dedication of one Monument on July 2, at 10 A. M.

102D NEW YORK INFANTRY, recruited in Brooklyn and New York City during the summer and fall of 1861, was mustered into service in April, 1862, and fought at Harper's Ferry, Cedar Mountain, Chantilly, South Mountain, Antietam, Winchester, Chancellorsville, Gettysburg, Wauhatchie, Lookout Mountain, Mission Ridge, Pea Vine Creek, Ringgold, Mill Creek Gap (Dalton), Resaca, Cassville, New Hope Church (Dallas), Pine Mountain, Culp's

Farm, Peach Tree Creek, Atlanta, Savannah, Bentonsville and Gordonsville. At Gettysburg Captain Lewis R. Stegman took command when Colonel James C. Lane was wounded. The loss of the regiment during the engagement was 32 out of a total of 135. The joint Monument of this and the 78th Regiment will be dedicated at ten o'clock on the morning of July 2. The services will take place on Culp's Hill as follows: Delivery of Monument, by builder and designers; Reception of Monument, by Committee of Regiments; Unveiling; Anthem, "America;" Poem, Colonel Juan Lewis; Reading of the Official Reports of the two Regiments as written immediately after the battle; Oration, Major-General Henry W. Slocum; Anthem, "Star Spangled Banner;" Delivery of Monument to the Gettysburg Battlefield Memorial Association; Response.

137TH NEW YORK INFANTRY mustered into service in September, 1862. Fought at Gettysburg and Lost Mountain.

BATTERY D, 1ST NEW YORK LIGHT ARTILLERY, will dedicate its Monument on July 2. The Orator of the Day will be Captain Thomas W. Osborn of New York City, and the Poet, Mr. G. S. Conger of Gouverneur, St. Lawrence County, N. Y. This battery was commanded by Captain T. W. Osborn; when promoted Major, Captain George Winslow succeeded him. Captain Winslow, who has answered the last "roll call," was wounded in the Wilderness, and Lieutenant L. J. Richardson, now Superintendent of the Cortland Water Works, took command, and though subsequently succeeded by Captain A. Matterson, on the promotion of the latter Lieutenant Richardson was again the Battery Commander and held the position until the war was over.

62D NEW YORK INFANTRY (Anderson Zouaves). Organized in the City of New York in 1861, they first felt the enemy at Yorktown, and were subsequently engaged at Williamsburg, Fair Oaks, Malvern Hill, Antietam, Salem Heights, Fredericksburg, Marye's Heights, Opequan, Cedar Creek, Gettysburg, Rappahannock Station, Fisher's Hill, Petersburg, Wilderness, Spottsylvania, Cold Harbor and Fort Stevens. The survivors expect to dedicate their Monument on July 2. The Committeemen are: Colonel T. B. Hamilton, Chairman; H. W. Lawrence, Secretary; Louis Hoer, Treasurer; Captain Edward Brown, George R. Patterson, Lyman Upson, Major William Baker and James R. Evans. It is proposed that the trip to Gettysburg shall take somewhat of a military character—the ex-members placing themselves as near as possible under command of their old line officers, Colonel T. B. Hamilton having supreme control to leave New York on Sunday Night, July 1, and arriving at Gettysburg, if possible, to camp on the ground they occupied twenty-five years ago. The dedication of the Monument to take place on the afternoon of the 2d, when the order of exercises will be as follows: Reveille, by Trumpeter; Roll Call (on the battlefield), by Acting-Adjutant; Prayer, by Chaplain, Rev. Charles Travis; Unveiling of Monument, by Colonel T. B. Hamilton; Poem, by H. W. Lawrence; Oration, by Hon. Edward Browne; Short Speeches, by Comrades of the Regiment; Benediction, by Chaplain; Tattoo, by Trumpeter; Taps, by Trumpeter; "Farewell" (Lost Chord), by Trumpeter. We expect the following survivors of the regiment will participate in the excursion: Colonel T. B. Hamilton, Major William Baker, Captain William Ackerman, Captain George Moser, Captain Jacob Duryee Lieutenant Thomas Judge, Lieutenant W. Stewart, George R. Patterson, William Jones Louis Heuer, W. H. Foster, Charles Morse, James R. Evans, P. Sheilds, H. W. Lawrence, Edward Browne, William Brady, W. Montgomery, F. Miner, James E. Gill, R. P. Wheeler, Daniel Skidmore, T. J. Wilson, Lyman Upson, George Howe, James Huested, William Vandevoort, Andrew Monroe, James McDowell, John Perine, N. Bancroft, Daniel Ames, Edward Willis, T. G. Hall, Edward Tracy, W. Harnden, Joseph Wright, William Barnett, W. A. Sharpe, P. McCune, William Dinan, James Boyle, James E. Moore, J. H. Brown, William Gunn, Daniel Mulligan, August Schaffer, Martin Bergen, Chris Daley, Charles Sheffield, Martin Schenck, Peter Sherer, James A. White, George W. Faulkner, L. Gaffney, George Kelly, William Lewis, Christopher Miller, Daniel Mullen, Robert Davis, Edward Daley and Thomas Brady.

64TH NEW YORK INFANTRY will dedicate their Monument on July 2. The Veteran Association held a meeting in January last to raise a fund to pay the expenses of all the survivors of the regiment, who might otherwise be unable to go, in order that every living member of the old command should once more visit the scene of the ever memorable conflict. The officers of the Association are: Surgeon George W. Barr, Chairman; Rodney R. Crowley, Secretary. Committee of Arrangements, O. H. Willard, R. R. Crowley, George W. Barr, W. W. Henry, W. A. Day, Colonel William Glenny, F. C. Jones. This regiment was mustered in at Elmira in December, 1861, from Alleghany, Cattaraugus, Chatauqua, Tioga and Tompkins Counties, and was engaged at Yorktown, Fair Oaks, Gaines' Mill, Savage Station, Peach Orchard, White Oak Swamp, Glendale, Malvern Hill, Antietam, Fredericksburg, Chancellorsville, Gettysburg, Brandy Station, Mine Run, Wilderness, Po River, Spottsylvania, North Anna, Tolopotomy, Cold Harbor, Petersburg, Strawberry Plain, Deep Bottom and Reams.

5TH NEW YORK CAVALRY will dedicate their Monument on July 3. General Hammond, Lieutenant-Colonel James A. Penfield, Major S. B. Ryder, Colonel A. H. White and Captain C. M. Pease, who located the site last year, will all take part in the exercises. The regiment was recruited in New York, Kings, Alleghany, Tioga, Wyoming, Essex and Greene Counties. Mustered into service on Staten Island on October 1, 1861, it participated in the battles at Bull Run, Yorktown, Hanover C. H., Mechanicsville, Gaines' Mill, Peach Orchard, Savage Station, White Oak Swamp, Glendale, Malvern Hill, Bull Run (1862), Antietam, Fredericksburg, Chancellorsville and Gettysburg. Among the survivors who will participate in the services on the Battlefield will be: General John Hammond, Crown Point, N. Y.; Colonel A H. White, Detroit, Mich.; Lieutenant-Colonel James A. Penfield, Boston, Mass; Lieutenant-Colonel E. J. Barker, Sergeant H. Underhill, Crown Point, N. Y.; Lieutenant A. S. Thompson, Rawson, N. Y.; Captain Dickinson, Portsville, N. Y.; Lieutenant E. D. Toller, Attica, N. Y.; Captain W. D. Lucas, Des Moines, Iowa; Major S. L. Abbott, Lexington, Mississippi; Major A. H. Krone, Candor, N. Y.; Lieutenant Mat Straight, Franklinville, N. Y.; Captain E. B. Geere, Owego, N. Y.; Lieutenant D. B. Merriman, Eau Claire, Wis.; Captain S. B. Ryder, Elizabeth, N. J.; Captain George Morton, New York City; Sergeant J. Gorham, Stillwater, N. Y.; Captain E. B. Haywood, Davenport, Iowa; Captain J. G. Viall, Washington, D. C.; Dr. Isaac Mead, Amenia, N. Y.; Sergeant D. F. Wolcott, Bradford, Pa.; Lieutenant W. H. Whitcomb, Catskill, N. Y.; Rev. J. H. Bond, Benson, Vt.; Sergeant Andrew Bridgman, Mount Vernon, N. Y.; Sergeant C. T. S. Pierce, Vergennes, Vt.; Surgeon O. W. Armstrong, New York City; Sergeant G. W. Toms, Stamford, Ct.; Captain C. M. Pease, Crown Point, N. Y. On the rear of the Monument, an illustration of which is given, is the following inscription: " July 3, 1863, this regiment, under command of Major John Hammond, here supported Battery E. 4th U. S. Horse Artillery, Lieutenant S. S. Elder losing six men. This regiment, June 30, 1863, met and repulsed a portion of Lee's Cavalry, under the personal command of General J. E. B. Stuarts, in the streets of Hanover, Pa. (the first battle on free soil), in a hand to hand fight, capturing Lieutenant Colonel Paine and seventy-five men, with a loss of twenty-six officers and men killed and wounded July 2, 1863, this regiment attacked General Stuarts' Cavalry at Hunterstown, Pa., and at night moved to Round Top, where we opened on General Longstreet's right."

146TH NEW YORK INFANTRY was organized in Rome under the direction of the Senatorial Committee of the Nineteenth District. It was mustered into service October 10, 1862. Originally known as the "5th Oneida," afterward as the "Halleck Infantry," its familiar title was "Garrard Tigers," by which the officers and men were wont to speak of themselves, as a compliment to the stern discipline and soldierly enthusiasm of Colonel Kenner Garrard, a graduate of West Point, who had accepted the command of the 146th at the suggestion of

General Halleck. The regiment was assigned to the Third Brigade of General Sykes' Division of the Fifth Corps, then under the command of General Meade. During the battle of Gettysburg the 140th was in the brigade commanded by Brigadier-General Weed; and in a charge supported the Third Corps, which had met with a temporary reverse. Here also it was that the 146th, with the 140th New York and 91st and 155th Pennsylvania Regiments, at a severe loss of officers and men, charged up and obtained possession of the "Little Round Top," the key to the position, and held it during the entire engagement. Among the killed were Brigadier-General Weed, who commanded the brigade; Colonel Patrick O'Rourke of the 140th; and Captain Hazlett, commanding the famous "Battery D," 5th United States Artillery, which the 146th supported. In consequence of the death of General Weed and Colonel O'Rourke the command devolved upon Colonel Garrard, and for his gallant conduct on that occasion he was commissioned Brigadier-General. Colonel David F. Jenkins then took command of the regiment. In 1863 the 146th adopted the Zouave uniform, which rendered it as beautiful on parade as it was gallant in action. It numbered in all from first to last 1,568 men, receiving additions from the old 5th New York Duryea Zouaves, the Seventeenth New York D'Espeneuil Zouaves and the 44th New York "Ellsworth Avengers," receiving at each time a body of splendid soldiers. The regiment was thrice complimented in general orders for distinguished gallantry; first at Laurel Hill, Va., when as two lines of battle in front broke, it stood firm and repelled the attack, losing severely; second, at Cold Harbor, when Mahone's Division burst on its lines, the Brigade to which the 146th belonged checked their career, thus saving the position; third, at Hatcher's Run, where it held its ground at great odds until its ammunition was entirely gone, when it was withdrawn a short distance, its cartridge boxes replenished, and the line again advanced. Its battle record includes twenty-three engagements, among them Fredericksburg, Chancellorsville, Gettysburg, Rappahannock Station, Mine Run, Wilderness, Spottsylvania, Tolopotomy, Petersburg, North Anna, Chapel House, Bethesda Church, Weldon Road and Hatcher's Run. The regiment will dedicate its Monument on July 3 on the Little Round Top. Brief addresses only will be made at the dedication. The Monument will be of sarcophagus pattern, and one of its inscriptions will be "From this point General Meade directed the battle of July 3."

MAJOR-GENERAL W. S. HANCOCK was wounded during Pickett's charge on July 3, 1863. On the twenty-fifth anniversary of that incident and during the afternoon a stone appropriately marked and which has been placed on the position will be visited by the admirers of the gallant commander of the Fighting Second Corps. No services are contemplated.

67th NEW YORK INFANTRY (1st Long Island Volunteers), also called the "Brooklyn Phalanx" and "Beecher's Regiment," participated in twenty-three battles of the Army of the Potomac from Fair Oaks in 1862 to Appomattox in 1865. It was mustered into service in June, 1861, and there are now about 147 survivors of the regiment, all of whom it is proposed to take to Gettysburg to be present at the dedication of the Monument on July 3. The Orator on that occasion will be the Rev. Thomas K. Beecher of Elmira, N. Y. The following are the Monument Committee: General Nelson Cross, Chairman; Sergeant William Reid, Secretary; Private James N. Mills, Treasurer; Major Thomas M. K. Mills, Sergeant Joseph C. Sealy, Brevet-Colonel George W. Stillwell, Brevet-Colonel Henry B. Beecher, First Lieutenant Charles Crowell, Quartermaster A. H. Doty, Adjutant George B. Lincoln, Jr., Private Burleigh L. Crans, Captain William H. Partridge, Washington, D. C., and Sergeant James Mackin, Wellsville, N. Y. It was first proposed to join with the other regiments of Shaler's Brigade in the exercises of June 12, 13 and 14, but that resolution was unanimously rescinded at a special meeting held February 14, 1888, in order to allow the surviving Veterans to meet the survivors of the Confederate Army on the twenty-fifth anniversary of the Battle. It will also be the first Re-Union of the regiment, and the "Roll Call on the Battlefield" will be an interesting feature of the ceremonies. A large delegation from Plymouth Church will accompany the Survivors' Association to the Battlefield. In addition to the committee named the following survivors will be present at the dedication: John S. Bliss, Sergeants Edward Fahey, Miles O'Reilley, John Morris, W. W. Dodge, Henry Metcalf,

Corporals Robert Ramsey and G. D. Cunliff, J. H. Kershaw, Emery Brown, John H. Bogart, B. L. Crans, William H. Pink, Lewis Walker, R. F. Johnson and G. A. Haley. The flags of the 1st Long Island Volunteers have the following battles inscribed on them; Yorktown, Williamsburg, Seven Pines, Glendale, Turkey Bend, Malvern Hill, Chantilly, Antietam, South Mountain, Williamsport, Fredericksburg, Salem Heights, Gettysburg, Rappahannock Station, Locust Grove, Mine Run, Wilderness, Spottsylvania, Cold Harbor, Petersburg.

3D NEW YORK INDEPENDENT BATTERY was organized and mustered in the United States Service May 21, 1861, as Company D, 2d Regiment, N. Y. S. M. Subsequently permanently detached from the regiment, it was, June 17, 1861, re-mustered as the 3d New York Independent Battery Volunteers—Captain T. P. Mott, First Lieutenant P. J. Downey, Second Lieutenant J. V. Bryant, Orderly Sergeant J. Warren and fifty non-commissioned officers and privates. Under the successive commands of Captains Mott, Stewart and Harn, it participated in the engagements of Lewinsville, Ball's Cross Roads, Lee's Mills, Williamsburgh, Chickahominy, Gaines' Mill, Golding's Farm, White Oak Swamp, Malvern Hill, Krampton's Gap, Antietam, Williamsport Road, Fredericksburg, December 11 and 13, 1862, May 5, 1863, Marye's Heights, Salem Heights, Gettysburg, Fairfield Pass, Funkstown, Rappahannock, Mine Run, Wilderness, Spottsylvania C. H., North Anna, Cold Harbor, Petersburg Siege and Sailors' Creek. After four years' active service in the Sixth Corps, it was mustered out June 24, 1865—Captain W. A. Harn, 1st Lieutenants A. McLain and G. W. Kellogg, Second Lieutenants G. P. Fitz Gerald and L. Rheims, and sixty-seven non-commissioned officers and privates, with the reputation "second to none in the Army of the Potomac." Sergeant William A. Moore sent out a call for the formation of a Veteran Association, to which the following named members of the Battery responded: Lieutenants J. V. Bryant, H. M. Fitz Gerald, G. W. Kellogg, Leon Rheims. Non-commissioned Officers and Privates—Warren, Meister, O'Hanlon, Dwyer, Frost, Glenn, Malloy, O'Reilly, Merritt, Burghstreem, Regan, O'Brien, Nuley, Shueman, Moran, Hansen, Ryan, Audesuer, Draflin, Stiles, Craw, Buskuhl, Thornton, Baublger, Van Nostrand, Flattich, Werner, Odell, Van Seinburgh, Miller and Sullivan; and on June 16, 1887, a permanent Veteran Association was established by the election of W. A. Moore President, R. O. Frost Vice-President, H. M. Fitz Gerald Treasurer, J. Warren Secretary. By arrangement of an ex-committee, consisting of W. A. Moore, H. M. Fitz Gerald and H. L. Stiles, at 10 A. M., July 3, 1888, about twenty-five members of the 3d N. Y. I. Battery Veteran Association propose to meet on the spot their Battery occupied "in Battery" ready to repel "Pickett's charge" in the battle of July 3, 1863, to unveil and dedicate their Battery Monument. Major-General William S. Rosecrans will deliver the Oration. No further ceremonies are contemplated otherwise than to fraternize in good fellowship with the surviving members of the Army of Northern Virginia, notwithstanding they did their best that same day twenty-five years ago to drive us off the field—if not the earth.

149TH NEW YORK INFANTRY was recruited and mustered into service at Syracuse, Onondaga County early in 1862. Its battle record is Chancellorsville, Gettysburg, Wauhatchie, Lost Mountain, Kenesaw, Ringgold, Malvern, Pine Tree Creek, Mission Ridge, Resaca, Dalton, Pumpkin Vine Creek, Dallas, Atlanta, Savannah, Raleigh, Pine Knob and Fort McAllister. It will dedicate its Monument on July 2. General Henry A. Barnum, the former Colonel of the regiment will be the Orator of the day. The regiment will also join in the exercises of Greene's Brigade on Culp's Hill. The Committee of Arrangements are : Captain George K. Collins, Chairman ; Lieutenant-Colonel Henry N. Burhans, Lieutenant-Colonel Abel G. Cook, Captain Orsen Coville, Captain Thomas Merriam and Lieutenant John Gebhardt, Jr.

4TH NEW YORK INDEPENDENT BATTERY will dedicate its Monument on July 2. The survivors will march from the Square to the scene of their participation in the conflict, with their old commanding officer, Captain J. E. Smith, at their head. A photograph of the group around the stone will be taken, and then the Memorial will be turned over to the Battlefield Association, the Orator telling the story of the gallant charge made by the "Orange Blossoms" and their charge in front of the battery at the Devil's Den. Quite a number of the "Blossoms," 124th New York Volunteers, will be present at the exercises, and the survivors will include, besides the Captain, James R. Hill, Secretary, New York; Lieutenant W. T. McLean, Los Angeles, Cal.; General James S. Fraser, Lieutenant James E. Nairn, Captain Dexter S. Bingham, Lieutenant John B. Johnston, Lieutenant Richard Hamlin, Sergeants Robert S. Beaver, Fred S. Walkins, New York City; D. H. Smith, Wahpeton, Dak.; Joseph A. Charlton, Spotswood, N. J.; John Shaw, Hugh Cullum, —— Spencer, —— Byrnes, —— Lambert, —— Hope, —— McCullough, —— Burnam and —— Quatlander. The battle record of the 4th Battery is: Yorktown, Williamsburg, Fair Oaks, Savage Station, Glendale, Malvern Hill, Fredericksburg, Chancellorsville, Gettysburg. The survivors meet at 781 Eighth avenue, New York.

9TH NEW YORK CAVALRY VETERAN ASSOCIATION will hold their Re-Union on the battlefield July 1, 2 and 3, taking a party of about 300, including wives and families. The Monument will be dedicated on July 2 at eleven o'clock A. M., the Orator of the day being Lieutenant Colonel W. G. Bentley of Chicago. The officers of the Association are : Major W. B. Martin, President; Captain Edward Goodrich, Vice-President; A. C. Robertson, Secretary, and Thomas Beaumont, Treasurer. Organized in November, 1861, the 9th was recruited from Chautauqua, Cattaraugus, Wyoming, Rensselaer, Washington, St. Lawrence and Clinton Counties. Mustered in at Albany, it passed through the following engagements before it was mustered out : Cedar Mountain, Brandy Station, Aldie, Upperville, Gainesville, Bull Run (1862), Chantilly, Antietam, Gettysburg, Kelley's Ford, Rappahannock Station, Sulphur Springs, Opequan, Wilderness, Cold Harbor, Mechanicsville, Deep Bottom, Winchester, Fisher's Hill, Cedar Creek, Petersburg and Richmond. This regiment repulsed the first charge made by the enemy at Gettysburg, and lost the first man killed, and captured the first

prisoner in that memorable battle. Now, after a quarter of a century, they hope to meet and clasp hands with each other and with those who were their enemies on the historic battlefield.

SICKLES' EXCELSIOR BRIGADE (United States Volunteers), composed of the 70th, 71st 72d, 73d and 74th regiments of New York Infantry, will dedicate an imposing Brigade Monument, one of the most striking on the field, on a commanding location near the Peach Orchard on the 2d day of July. The Rev. C. H. A. Buckley of Howard University, Washington, D. C., will conduct the religious exercises, Rev. J. H. Twichell of Hartford, Ct., being the Orator of the day. The Monument will be a pentagonal Doric Temple, the dome supported by five polished Labrador granite pillars, with spar in blue and green, surmounted by a bronze eagle. On each of its sides will be the record in stone and bronze of one of the regiments of the Brigade, so that the one programme of exercises will include the five regiments in the Brigade The officers of the Brigade Association are: President, Major-General Sickles; Vice-Presidents—First Excelsior, Colonel Daniel Mahom; Second Excelsior, Colonel Rafferty, deceased; Third Excelsior, General N. Taylor; Forth Excelsior, General Henry E. Tremaine; Fifth Excelsior, General Charles K. Graham ; Secretary and Treasurer, Colonel John N. Coyne ; Chaplains, Professor C. H. A. Buckley and Rev. Charles Twichell, now an eminent divine of Hartford, Ct. The Monument Committee are : First Regiment, Major W. J. Kay ; Second, Colonel H. L. Potter; Third, Sergeant N. W. Leighton ; Fourth, Private William Sweeney; Fifth, Major Willard Bullard. The regiments forming the Brigade were known as Excelsior Regiments, were all recruited in New York City and vicinity, and as a Brigade took part in the following battles: Yorktown, Williamsburg, Fair Oaks, Glendale, Malvern Hill, Brandy Station, Bull Run (1862), Chantilly, Fredericksburg, Chancellorsville, Gettysburg, Kelley's Ford, Mine Run, Wilderness, Spottsylvania, North Anna, Tolopotomy, Cold Harbor, Petersburg, Strawberry Plains, Deep Bottom, Poplar Springs Church and Boydton Road. The 1st Regiment went into action at Gettysburg with a total of 326 and lost 117; 2d Regiment 230, loss 91; 3d Regiment 305, loss 111; 4th Regiment 507, loss 162; 5th Regiment 275, loss 89. The programme at the dedication will be: General Sickles, the presiding officer, will unveil the Monument; Dr. Buckley, formerly Chaplain of the 1st Regiment, will deliver the prayer; the Oration, by Dr. Twichell, will be followed by a poem, "Excelsior," by Dr. Buckley. Appropriate musical selections will intervene. Colonel John N. Coyne, the Secretary of the Brigade Association, will wear the medal of honor bestowed on him by Congress. The following representatives of each regiment will be at the ceremonies: 1st Regiment—Daniel E. Sickles, Daniel Mahem, John N. Coyne, William S. May, Charles L. Young, J. F. Denniston, M. J. Foote, A. Duflor, R. McKinstry. 2d Regiment—Henry L. Potter, W. A. Donaldson, J. Foller, H. Holmes, W. H. Elwood, J. J. Webb, B. Franklin, W. S. Requa. 3d Regiment—Nelson Taylor, John Leonard, N. W. Leighton. C. C. Abell, S. H. Bailey, H. Hemphill, L. W. Norton, P. Anderson. 4th Regiment—H. E. Tremain, W. Sweeney, J. G. Noonan, C. Wilson, M. Feeney, J. A. Kent, M. McCulloch, F. Moran, P. Smith. 5th Regiment—C. K. Graham, L. Purdy, W. Bullard, W. Lounsbury, W. B. Miller, D. M. Watt, J. R. Ferret, W. Conway, J. D. Stewart.

73D NEW YORK INFANTRY (2d Fire Zouaves and 4th Excelsior) will leave New York City by special train on June 30, and remain on the battlefield until the evening of July 3, making their headquarters at the Eagle Hotel. A strong delegation from Mansfield Post, G. A. R., and the Veteran Associations of the Regiments will accompany the Fire Zouaves. Of the survivors of the regiment the following expect to take part in the Gettysburg celebration: Officers of the Association—President, William Sweeney; Vice-President, Michael Feeny; Corresponding Secretary, John Ross; Financial Secretary, Alexander A. McClave; Treasurer, John J. Ware; Sergeant-at-Arms, Henry A. Kraus; Trustees—Henry E. Tremaine, John G. Noonan, John T. Lawrence, Thomas Fair, John Coffee; Members—Patrick Boyle, John Benson, William Bary, John Brady, John Bayne, John Brooks, William Buckle, Daniel Crowley, James Conlan, Francis Collum, Peter J. Comber, Edward Corbery, John H Doherty, John Downey, Christ. Dacey, H. Eckhart, James Forrest, Michael Gleason, William Gleason, Lyman S. Green, Daniel Glacker, George Gibbins, Francis Gratlan, James P. Gill, Thomas Graves, William H. Haley, Daniel Hurley, Patrick Hanlon, Daniel Judge, Joseph N. Kent, Michael J. Keenan, Peter Kimmer, William T. Lackey, Elias Loyde, Owen Lewis, J. H. Lesson, Christ. Lynch, C. K. Mellon, James J. Murphy, Richard Malone, Matthew McCollough, John F. Mackey, T. McKeon, William McMenomey, Frank Moran, F. J. McDonald, William Nelson, James Owens, William E. Perkins, Michael T. Sullivan, Martin Short (Captain of Brooklyn police), Frederick Shaln, Michael C. Shay, James Sheridan, Thomas Shaunon. George Thoner, Adolph Shepperd, John J. Smith, Elisha Thomas, M. H. Whistler, William Weise, John Walsh. The Second New York Fire Zouaves, recruited chiefly from the Fire Department of the city of New York, was organized May 3, 1861, went into Camp Decker, Staten Island, and departed for the field on August 23, 1861. Its first duty was building fortifications and doing picket duty on the Eastern shore of Maryland, and its first engagement near Stafford Court House, Va., in April, 1862. It was the first regiment to enter Yorktown, and under Little Mac took part in the battles of Williamsburg, Seven Pines, Fair Oaks, Oak Grove, Savage Station, Glendale and Malvern Hill. Under General Pope it fought at Bristow Station, Second Bull Run and Chantilly, met Burnside at Fredericksburg, and Hooker at Chancellorsville. At Gettysburg it held Barksdale's Mississippians in check until reinforcements arrived after the Confederate attack on General Graham's forces. Its record is, in fact, from that great day, that of the Army of the Potomac, and is a bright one. It was mustered into the service as United States Volunteers and left for the seat of war as an independent organization, not being recognized by the State of New York. It formed part of General Sickles' Brigade, and when the State finally concluded to accept the Brigade, on November 27, 1861, the officers received their commissions, and the regiment was thereafter known as the 73d New York Volunteers. The command left New York 800 strong, received during its term of service 500 recruits and the 163d New York Regiment, which was consolidated with it in January, 1863. It was mustered out at Hart's Island, N. Y., June 29, 1865, about 200 strong after a term of service of 4 years, 1 month and 27 days.

86TH NEW YORK INFANTRY, recruited from Chemung, Steuben, and Onondaga Counties, was mustered in at Elmira in November, 1861, and passed through fire at Bull Run (1862), Fredericksburg, Chancellorsville, Gettysburg, Mine Run, Wilderness, Spottsylvania, North Anna, Tolopotomy, Cold Harbor, Petersburg, Deep Bottom and Boydton Road. It will dedicate its Monument on Monday, July 2, at 3 P. M. Regimental line will be formed in front of the Eagle Hotel at 2 P. M., and after marching to the site the exercises will consist of: Invocation, by the Rev. and Captain H. B. Seeley; Unveiling and Presentation of the Monument, by a Representative of the New York State Commission; Acceptance of Monument, by Colonel B. L. Higgins, President of the 86th Regiment Veteran Association; Transfer of Monument to the Gettysburg Battlefield Memorial Association; Acceptance, by a representative of the Gettysburg Battlefield Memorial Association; Oration, by Charles H. McMaster, Esq. The Regimental Re-Union will follow the exercises on the field. The officers of the Association are: President, Benjamin L. Higgins, Syracuse; Secretary, A. M. Dunham, Knoxville, Pa.; Treasurer, C. H. Wombough, Hornellsville, N. Y. Monument Committee, Colonel B. L. Higgins, Major S. H. Leavitt, Adjutant Charles W. Gillet.

15TH NEW YORK LIGHT BATTERY was organized in the City of New York in December, 1861, and its battle record notes its efficient service at Chancellorsville, Gettysburg, Rappahannock Station, Mine Run, Spottsylvania, North Anna, Tolopotomy, Bethesda Church and Petersburg. At Gettysburg it was engaged in the Peach Orchard on July 2 and on Cemetery Ridge on July 3. The Monument will be dedicated in the Peach Orchard July 2 next. The programme will be: Prayer; Patriotic Airs, Mrs. Florence Rice-Knox and Miss Rilla E. Bronson; Address, Captain E. M. Knox, only surviving officer of the Battery; Music.

BATTERY B, NEW YORK ARTILLERY, will dedicate its Monument at 1 P. M. on July 3, the Oration to be made by the Rev. W. M. Beauchamp. The Committee in charge of the dedication are: A. S. Sheldon, Chairman; Sanford Weeks, Treasurer, and John M. Scoville, Secretary. They expect to take at least fifty persons in their party. Battery B was organized in Baldwinsville, Onondaga County, in August, 1861. Its first commander, Captain Rufus D. Pettit, resigned May 31, 1863, and was succeeded by Captain A. S. Sheldon, who was wounded at Gettysburg on July 3, and again at Bethesda Church, June 2, 1864. When mustered out on account of his wounds, the command of the battery fell to Captain R. E. Rogers, who held it until the close of the war.

68TH PENNSYLVANIA INFANTRY (Scott's Legion) will dedicate their Monument on July 2. During the battle, on the highest crest of the exposed ridge at the Peach Orchard angle, stood the 68th Pennsylvania Volunteers. This celebrated regiment, surnamed the Scott Legion, was recruited in Philadelphia and vicinity, in the summer of 1862. Many of the officers and men were veterans of the Mexican War. In the exposed position occupied by this regiment they were obliged to receive the full force of the enemy's artillery fire, which went sweeping through their ranks, cutting down rows of men long before the infantry at this point had become engaged. When General Graham was wounded and captured at this point,

Colonel Tippin of the 68th, succeeded to the command of the Brigade. Both the Lieutenant-Colonel and Major were wounded, and of the fourteen company officers, ten were killed or wounded. Among the killed were Captain McLean and Lieutenants Black, Reynolds and Ealer. The programme arranged by the regiment is as follows: July 2—Assemble at Headquarters, house of John E. Pitzer, Chambersburg street, at 9 A. M.; assemble at house of John J. Sherfy, Peach Orchard Farm, at 2:30 P. M.; Formation of line and march to Monument at 3 P. M., sharp; Introductory Remarks and Announcement of the Committees' Work, by Comrade Alfred Craighead, Secretary of Association; Unveiling of Monument, by Color Sergeant of 68th P. V. V., Comrade James McLarnon; Prayer, by the Chaplain of the regiment, Rev. William Fulton; Oration, by Speaker of House of Representatives of Pennsylvania, Hon. Henry K. Boyer; History and Exploits of the Regiment and its Officers, and Presentation of Monument to the Gettysburg Battlefield Memorial Association, by Captain Thomas H. Leabourn of General John F. Reynold's Post, No. 71, G. A. R.; Reception of Monument by Battlefield Memorial Association; Survivors of Regiment and Monument photographed, by Comrade Marcellus Rhoades of the 68th Regiment; July 3—Assemble at Headquarters at 9 A. M.; Grand Picnic over the Battlefield, visiting important and historic points of interest. Evening—Grand Re-Union of 68th Regiment at 9 P. M. The following are the officers of the Veterans' Association of the Regiment: President, Major Michael Fulmer, Philadelphia; First Vice-President, William H. Jones, Pottstown, Montgomery County, Pa.; Second Vice-President, Christian Ottinger, Philadelphia; Secretary and Treasurer, Alfred Craighead, Philadelphia. Monument Committee: Chairman, George C. Jackson; Secretary, Alfred Craighead; George H. Sowers, James McLarnon and Charles F. Runner.

98TH PENNSYLVANIA INFANTRY, at 6 P. M. on July 2, will hold the dedicatory exercises at their Monument, Comrade J. Fred Loeble of Co. E, delivering the Oration. The officers of the Association are: J. Fred Loeble, President; A. B. Boemish, Secretary. Monument Committee: Jacob A. Schmid, John F. Ballier, John M. Schniffe and G. W. Kishner.

145TH NEW YORK INFANTRY will dedicate their Monument on Monday, July 2. General George H. Sharpe will be the chief Orator of the occasion, and addresses will be made by a Confederate officer and Joseph Hayes. The following survivors of the regiment will go to Gettysburg to participate in the exercises: Philip S. Clark, Frank Hubbs, John Mallay, William H. Bennett, George W. Kierstead, James Conway, Brooklyn; Martin Long, Henry Seabelt, H. C. Daniell, William E. Rabell, William Haines, New York City; Philip De Waters, William De Waters, David Newberry, Henry Stillwell, Stephen Stillwell, John W. Gibbs, Staten Island; Philip Darby, Highlands, N. J.; James Firth, West Bergen, N. J. John Norton, St. Johnland, Long Island; and Thomas B. Birtchell, Mineola, Long Island. About twenty relatives of deceased members of the regiment, and several persons from Tottenville and Pleasant Plains, Staten Island and Brooklyn will accompany them.

110TH PENNSYLVANIA INFANTRY will, on July 2, listen to an Oration by Captain J. C. M. Hamilton of Company C of the Regiment, dedicating their Memorial Stone, and will then place it in the hands of the Battlefield Memorial Association. The regiment was recruited in Blair, Huntingdon, Bedford, Centre, Clearfield Counties and in Philadelphia, was mustered into service in 1861, and was in the most important battles fought by the Army of the Potomac.

83D NEW YORK INFANTRY (9th New York State Militia.) This was one of the first of the gallant bands who volunteered "for the war" when called out in April, 1861, and did not return after their militia service was over. The regiment participated in all the important battles of the Army of the Potomac, under Generals McDowell, McClellan, Pope, Burnside, Hooker, Meade and Grant. The 9th Regiment, National Guard, its successor in the militia, will accompany the Veteran Association of the 83d to Gettysburg, as escort to the Society of the Army of the Potomac, and as the representative organization of the Empire State. The Monument will be dedicated on Sunday, July 1, at 4 P. M. About one hundred survivors of the regiment, one hundred guests, and five hundred of the 9th N. G. S. N. Y., with band, will constitute the party which will leave this city on the morning of that day to attend the

eremonies. The following is the order of exercises. Prayer, by the Rev. Alfred C. Roe, Chaplain of the Veteran 9th Regiment, N. G. S. N. Y., and formerly of the 83d N. Y. Volunteers in the field; Unveiling of the Monument; Music, by the 9th Regiment, N. G. S. N. Y. Band; Reception of Monument by the Veteran Association from Chairman of Monument Committee; Delivery of Monument to the New York State Commission, and acceptance by the Gettysburg Memorial Association; Poem, by Rowland B. Mahany; Music, by the Band. Oration, by Hon. Orlando B. Potter; Music; Benediction. The roster of battles in which the 9th Regiment was engaged is: Harper's Ferry, Cedar Mountain, Rappahannock, Thoroughfare Gap, second Bull Run, Spottsylvania, Chantilly, South Mountain, Antietam, Fredricksburg, Fitzhugh Crossing, North Anna River, Chancellorsville, Gettysburg, Mine Run, Wilderness, Laurell Hill and Cold Harbor. The loss of the regiment during the war in killed, wounded and died of wounds, was 684. It is expected that Governor D. B. Hill, his Military Staff, and many State officials, will accompany the 9th Regiment, and that his Excellency, the Governor, will deliver an address during the services.

40TH NEW YORK INFANTRY was organized in New York City, June, 1861. Its battle record is: Yorktown, Williamsburgh, Fair Oaks, Glendale, Malvern Hill, Bull Run (1862), Chantilly, Fredericksburg, Chancellorsville, Gettysburg, Mine Run, Wilderness, Po River, Spottsylvania, North Anna, Tolopotomy, Cold Harbor, Petersburg, Strawberry Plains, Deep Bottom, Boydton Road. It will dedicate its Monument July 2.

119TH NEW YORK INFANTRY will dedicate its monument on July 1. The command was raised in New York City, mustered in September, 1862, and fought at Chancellorsville, Gettysburg, Wauhatchie, Mission Ridge, Knoxville, Resaca, Dallas, Pine Hill, Culp's Farm, Kenesaw, Pine Tree Creek and Atlanta. General John T. Lockman of 88 Nassau street, New York, has provided at his own expense a palace car for the survivors of this command, in which they will live and enjoy themselves on the side track at Gettysburg.

41ST NEW YORK INFANTRY will unveil their Monument on the afternoon of July 2. The command was recruited in New York City, and participated in the battles of Cross Keys, Rappahannock Station, Cedar Mountain, Freeman's Ford, Warrenton, Waterloo Bridge, Bull Run and Gettysburg.

105TH PENNSYLVANIA INFANTRY, the only veteran association that has a female secretary, will assemble on Monday, July 2, 1888, at the Sherfy House, at 3 P. M., and march to the site of the Monument, where the following will be the order of exercises: Prayer, Chaplain D. G. Steadman; Music, Brookville Male Quartet; Presentation of Monument, Committee ; Music, Brookville Male Quartet; Oration, Rev. H. T. McClelland ; Music, Brookville Male Quartet ; Short Addresses by Colonel L. G. Duff, Colonel James Miller, Colonel O. C. Redic, Captain A. C. Thompson, Captain G. A. Craig and others ; Music ; Benediction, Rev. W. J. Wilson. J. M. Shaaf, President 105th Regiment Association; Kate M. Scott, Secretary.

13TH NEW YORK INDEPENDENT BATTERY, organized in the City of New York in October, 1861, was engaged at Cross Keys, Waterloo, Bull Run (1862), Chancellorsville, Gettysburg, Mission Ridge, Chattanooga, Atlanta and Cedar Creek. The Battery Veteran Association will dedicate their Monument on July 3 ; a brief history of the command during its four years service will be told, and then the structure will be formally consigned to the Battle-field Memorial Association. The arrangements are in the hands of the following committee, who may be the only survivors of the 13th Battery on the field during that day : John P. McGurrin, President; Edward Baldwin, Secretary ; James Eskdale, William Boe, John White, Christian Klein, Diedrich Funk.

45TH NEW YORK INFANTRY, mustered into the United States service in New York City during October, 1861, took part in the actions at Cross Keys, Waterloo Bridge, Sulphur Springs, second Bull Run and Gettysburg. Its Monument will be dedicated July 1.

62D PENNSYLVANIA INFANTRY organized in Harrisburg in 1861, was raised in Alleghany, Classon, Jefferson and Blair Counties, and will dedicate its Monument on July 2, the following being the programme : Regimental Society called to order by Captain William Kennedy, President; Prayer, Chaplain; Dirge, Band; Reading the Record, by B. Coll, Secretary; Address, Lieutenant William J. Patterson ; "Star Spangled Banner," Band; Oration, General J. B. Sweitzer ; Music, Band; Benediction. The following is the Committee of Arrangements : General J. B. Sweitzer, Captain William Kennedy, Captain Dietrich Gruntz, Lieutenant W. J. Patterson, Sergeant B. Cole.

52D NEW YORK INFANTRY will dedicate their monument on July 2. It was raised in New York City, and its battle record is: Peach Orchard, Savage Station, White Oak Swamp, Malvern Hill, Antietam, Fredericksburg, Chancellorsville, Gettysburg, Brick Station, Mine Run, Wilderness, Po River, Spottsylvania, North Anna, Tolopotomy, Cold Harbor, Petersburg, Strawberry Plains, Deep Bottom and Reams.

68TH NEW YORK INFANTRY was mustered into service in New York City during August, 1861, and its battle record includes: Cross Keys, White Sulphur Springs, Waterloo Bridge, Freeman's Ford, Groveton, Bull Run (1862), and Gettysburg. The survivors of this command will dedicate their Monument on July 1.

IRISH BRIGADE.—This command was composed of the 63d, 69th and 88th New York Infantry. Recruited in New York City in the fall of 1861, it constituted General Francis Thomas Meagher's Brigade, which won a record second to none in the Army of the Potomac. The losses of the regiments had so heavily reduced them that towards the close of the great struggle they were consolidated and now they will dedicate one handsome Monument to commemorate the dead of the three organizations. The battle record of the Brigade is : Yorktown, Fair Oaks, Gaine's Mill, Savage Station, Peach Orchard White Oak Swamp, Malvern Hill, Antietam, Fredericksburg, Chancellorsville, Gettysburg, Brandy Station, Mine Run, Wilderness, Po River, Spottsylvania, North Anna, Tolopotomy, Cold Harbor, Petersburg, Strawberry Plains, Deep Bottom and Reams. The Monument will be unveiled on July 2,

the services including a solemn requiem mass in an improvised chapel. Rev. Fathers Quillette and Corby, Chaplains in the Brigade conducting the religious exercises. The Orator of the occasion has not been selected, but General Robert Nugent and Denis F. Burke will be among the speakers. Mrs. Rice-Knox and her sisters will sing during the exercises.

III.—AFTER THE RE-UNION.

5TH NEW YORK INFANTRY (Duryee's Zouaves), will dedicate a bronze Statue to Major-General Gouverneur K. Warren, their old commander, on the Little Round Top, near the spot occupied by the Signal Corps during the battle. The party, which will be very numerous, will leave New York on the morning of August 8 next, and in the afternoon the monument will be dedicated. The Rev. C. F. Hull of New Jersey, formerly a private in Company A of the Zouaves has been selected as the Orator for the occasion.

94TH NEW YORK INFANTRY, the last regiment of the Army of the Potomac that was mustered out of service, was mustered in at Sackett's Harbor, March 1862. Its battle record is: Cedar Mountain, Bull Run (1862), Chantilly, Chancellorsville, South Mountain, Antietam, Gainesville, Fredericksburg, Gettysburg, Mine Run, Tolopotomy, Bethesda Church, Petersburg and Weldon Road. The survivors of the regiment will visit Gettysburg on August 8, and dedicate their Monument.

88TH PENNSYLVANIA INFANTRY will dedicate their monument on August 9, the 27th anniversary of the acceptance of the regiment by the War Department in 1861. The stone will mark the spot from which the 88th charged on Iverson's Brigade on July 1, 1863, and captured almost all of the 23d North Carolina. The Committee on Monument are: General Louis Wagner, General G. W. Gile, General R. B. Beath, Captain S. G. Boone and J. D. Vautier.

4TH NEW YORK CAVALRY was raised in New York City, and was mustered in August 29, 1861. The regiment was never absent a day from the scene of active operations. At the second Battle of Bull Run, co-operating with the 1st Michigan, it made the only cavalry charge of the battle. It was engaged in every battle and skirmish in which the Cavalry Corps of the Army took part. The regiment participated in the following battles and skirmishes: Anandale, Rappahannock Station, Franklin, Strousburg, Harrisonburg, Cross Keys, Port Republic, Slaughter Mountain, Rapidan River, White Sulphur Springs, Manassas (Bull Run), Berryville, Kelly's Ford, Chancellorsville, Beverly Ford, Aldie, Middleburg, Upperville, Gettysburg, Brandy Station, Morton's Ford, Bealton Station, Oak Hill (Brentsville), Robertson's Tavern, Mine Run, Barnett's Ford, Piney Grove Church, Trevillian's Station, Deep Bottom, White Post, Cedarville, Kearneysville, Shepherdstown and Smithfield. On September 16, 1863, after chasing the enemy from Brandy Station across the Rapidan, and while a portion of the regiment was on picket duty at Racoon Ford, twenty-four of its men were captured, after being surrounded, and one officer and two men had been killed. For this disaster, arising from carelessness, the regiment was prohibited by General Pleasonton, from carrying its regimental colors. A full statement of the circumstances sent to the Secretary of War, resulted in having the colors restored on the 6th of January, 1864, on the ground of meritorious service. At Front Royal the regiment (numbering at this time one hundred and fifty men) charged on a regiment of Wickham's Brigade, which was driving our skirmishers, capturing in the charge the veteran battle flag of the 3d Virginia Cavalry, besides many prisoners. In this charge Captain Mann, while gallantly leading his squadron, was killed, having been shot through the heart. This entire affair was characterized by the Division General as "Superb."

44TH NEW YORK INFANTRY, with whom it is probable the 12th New York Infantry will unite, have prepared the design here shown for their Monument, at the position held by them on Little Round Top. The design will probably include a memorial of Colonel Rice, who succeeded to the command of the Brigade by the death of General Strong Vincent, who as Colonel of the 83d Pennsylvania, received his death wound at Little Round Top in the second day's fight. The old commander of the Brigade, General Daniel Butterfield, then Chief of Staff of the Army of the Potomac, received from Washington Vincent's promotion before his death. The design of the Monument is the work of Mr. Charles Zeilman of Albany, a

member of the regiment, and for years stamp clerk in the Albany Post-office. The 44th Regiment was organized in 1861 as an answer from New York to the assassination of Colonel Ellsworth in Alexandria. The original plan provided for one man from each ward and town in the State, the qualifications being that he should have a good character, be unmarried, not more than thirty years old, and should pay $20 for the purchase of a Zouave uniform, and started from Albany for the seat of war on October 1, 1861, numbering 1,061 men, under command of Colonel S. W. Stryker. At Washington they were armed with Springfield rifles and sent to General Butterfield's Brigade, in the Fifth Corps. This regiment and the 83d Pennsylvania were know during their service as "Butterfield's Twins" and "Butterfield's Pets." They particiated with the Army of the Potomac in the advance on Centreville, Seige of Yorktown, Battle of Hanover Court House, Gaine's Mill, Malvern Hill, second Bull Run, Antietam, Shepperdstown Ford, Fredericksburg, Chancellorsville, Aldie, Gettysburg, Jones' Crossing, Williamsport, Rappahannock Station, Mine Run, Wilderness, Spottsylvania Court House, North Anna, Bethseda Church, Petersburg and Weldon Railroad. The organization left the field September 24, 1864, and was mustered out October 11, 1864.

108TH NEW YORK INFANTRY expects to dedicate its Monument late in August or during the first week in September. This regiment was mustered in at Rochester, Monroe County, in August, 1861. Its record is Antietam, Fredericksburg, Chancellorsville, Gettysburg, Brandy Station, Wilderness, Spottsylvania, North Anna, Tolopotomy, Cold Harbor, Petersburg, Strawberry Plains, Deep Bottom, Reams', and Boydton Road.

123D NEW YORK INFANTRY expects to dedicate its Monument on the afternoon of Tuesday, September 4, 1888. The Chairman of the Committee on Monument is Seth C. Cary of Maplewood, Mass., the Adjutant of the regiment. The 123d was mustered at Salem, Washington County, in September, 1862, and was engaged at Chancellorsville, Gettysburg, Resaca, Cassville, Dallas, Pine Mountain, Lost Mountain, Culp's Farm, Chatahoochie River, Pine Tree Creek, Atlanta, Monteith Swamp, Savannah, Columbia, Averysboro and Raleigh.

1ST NEW YORK LIGHT BATTERY (Reynolds), will dedicate a Monument during the first week in September, it having been impossible to finish the structure in time for the Silver Re-union. About forty or fifty persons will accompany the few survivors to the Battlefield. The first commander of this battery was Captain John A. Reynolds who rose to the rank of Colonel; his successor, Captain Gilbert H. Reynolds was wounded in the side, and lost an eye at Gettysburg. Captain G. H. Reynolds was also taken prisoner; he resigned in 1864. Captain George Breck, who then took command of the battery, brought it home from the war, and was mustered out as Brevet-Major. The battle record of this command is the record of the Army of the Potomac.

107TH NEW YORK REGIMENT ASSOCIATION will dedicate their Monument near Spangler's Spring, and hold their Twenty-second annual Re-Union on Sept. 17, 1888, and the participants will probably number upwards of 200 persons. The programme is not fully complete, but among the speakers of the occasion will be Colonel N. M. Crane of the 107th and General Henry W. Slocum of Brooklyn. Lieutenant-Colonel William F. Fox will read the poem. The Association was organized December 20, 1867, and have held a Re-Union each year since, the able Secretary, A. G. Fitch, holding that position year after year from the date of his election, December 20, 1872. The officers of the Association besides him are: General N. M. Crane, President; Captain John M. Losie, Lieutenant E. Weller, Sergeant F. Pooley, Vice-Presidents; Rev. B. P. Tracy, Chaplain; Major C. P. Fox, Corresponding Secretary; Private Theodore G. Smith, Treasurer. The Monument and Excursion Committee are, in addition to the officers named: Lieutenant John Clawson, Major E. P. Graves, Lieutenant Paul Collson, Q. M. Sergeant Bray D. Hall, Sergeant Gilbert Wright, Private Theodore G. Smith. The battle record of the regiment, which was mustered in at Elmira in August, 1862, is Antietam, Chancellorsville, Gettysburg, Resaca, New Hope Church, Culps' Farm, Peach Tree Creek, Kenesaw Mountain and Averysboro.

THE STATE OF MICHIGAN has contracted for nine Monuments, all of which will be dedicated on September 20 next in presence of a large audience of officials, veterans and citizens of that State. The commands are Michigan Cavalry Brigade, 1st, 3d, 4th, 5th, 7th, 16th, 24th Infantry and 9th Battery. The Michigan Board of Commissioners of Gettysburg Battlefield Monuments are: Colonel George G. Briggs, Grand Rapids, Chairman; Lieutenant Peter Lennon, Lennon; and Lieutenant George W. Crawford, Big Rapids.

10TH NEW YORK CAVALRY, recruited in Chemung, Chenango, Courtland, Erie, Fulton, Steuben and Onondaga Counties, was mustered into the service at Elmira during December, 1861, and was engaged with the enemy at Leesburg, Brandy Station, Middleburg, Gettysburg, Shephardstown, Sulphur Springs, Auburn, Mine Run, Todd's Tavern, Richmond, Hawes' Shop, Cold Harbor, Trevillian Station, South Mountain, Chancellorsville, Malvern Hill, Charles City Road, Ream's, Vaughan Road, Boydton Road and Bellyfield. This Monument is to be located on Brinkerhoff Ridge, near the Hanover Road, about two miles east of

Gettysburg, the position held by the regiment on the afternoon of July 2. The design of the Monument was suggested by Lieutenant H. E. Hayes, and has some appropriate and distinctive features. The dedication ceremonies will take place on the 26th and 27th of September, and will be of an interesting character. The 10th New York Cavalry was quartered in Gettysburg during January and February, 1862, while waiting for their equipments, and was the only regiment stationed there before the great battle. The first Union soldier buried in the Gettysburg Cemetery was Private John Congdon of this regiment.

MARYLAND MONUMENTS. Maryland had three regiments of infantry, one of cavalry and one battery of artillery engaged at Gettysburg. The record of the Maryland troops at Gettysburg will compare favorably with those of any State represented at that, the decisive battle of the late war. It is a notable fact that wherever Maryland troops fought, whether in the Blue or Gray, their action was characterized by bravery and gallantry. In the last struggle for the Little Round Top, on the evening of the 2d of July, it was "Lockwood's Maryland Brigade" that bore the brunt of the gallant assault of the Confederates, and who, in the language of General Meade's report, with the aid of other troops present, "succeeded in checking and finally repulsing the assault of the enemy, who retired in confusion and disorder and ceased any further efforts." It was Colonel Maulsby's Maryland Regiment which held the most advanced position of the Army of the Potomac on the night of July 2. It was the 3d Maryland Regiment who opened the fight on the extreme right on the morning of July 3. And, later in the same day, the 1st Maryland P. H. B. checked the Confederate attack on Culp's Hill and practically ended their serious efforts in that direction. Rigby's Maryland Battery of three-inch rifles did their full share of service in each day's fight, and in repelling Pickett's supreme effort on the afternoon of the 3d no guns in that terrible line of nearly one hundred belching pieces of artillery of the Army of the Potomac did more effective service than those of Rigby. The 1st Maryland Cavalry received special mention for its services in the Cavalry fight on July 3. On March 3, 1888, the State Legislature appropriated $6,000 to erect a Monument to each of her commands who took part in the conflict. Under this act the following Monument Commission was appointed: Colonel Theodore F. Lang, Chairman, Baltimore; Hon. William D. Burchinal, Chestertown; Hon. Milton G. Urner, Frederick; Hon. Charles D. Gaither, Baltimore; Captain Frank Nolen, Secretary, Baltimore; George R. Graham, M. D., Corresponding Secretary, Baltimore. These gentlemen, with three survivors of each regiment and of the battery, will visit the field at noon on Thursday, June 14, and locate the sites to make the respective positions of the commands in the battle. Probably five hundred persons will visit the field on that day, and the Monuments erected on the positions chosen will be dedicated late in September or early in October.

VERMONT will erect five Monuments on the Battlefield, to be dedicated in October next. The most prominent of these, the State's Monument, will stand where the 2d Vermont Brigade struck Pickett's right flank, and on this will be inscribed the record of the 5,500 Vermont troops on the field. The Monument is to be a copy of the famous Nelson Monument in Trafalgar Square, London. The Monument proper will stand fifty feet high. The base, twenty feet square and nearly two feet high, is a massive block of granite, the die of Barre granite, and the fluted column, twenty-nine feet long, of Dummerston granite, with a carved cap. The Gettysburg Monument Commissioners from Vermont are: Governor E. J. Ormsbee, Brandon, Chairman; Colonel Albert Clarke, Rutland, Secretary; Colonel James H. Wallridge, North Bennington; General Thomas O. Beaver, Woodstock; Private French F. Carrick, St. Johnsbury; Captain Cornelius H. Forbes, Brandon; Captain Thomas B. Kennedy, St. Albans; Colonel G. Grenville Benedict, Burlington; Captain Noble F. Dunshee, Bristol; Colonel Redfield Proctor, Proctor; Colonel Wheelock G. Veazey, Rutland; General William Wells, Burlington; Sergeant Cassins Peck, Brookfield; Colonel M. R. Stoughton, Shelby Iron Works, Alabama; Corporal Curtis Abbot, 27 Tremont Row, Boston, Mass.; General Edward H. Ripley, Mendon; Colonel Fred E. Smith, Montpelier, and Colonel F. Stewart Stranahan, St. Albans.

42D NEW YORK INFANTRY (Tammany Regiment) will send a committee to Gettysburg on July 3 to select the position its Monument is to occupy. The Committeemen are: Eugene Sullivan, President; John McGuire, Vice-President; Frank Reynolds, Secretary; Thomas H Mallon, Treasurer, and Daniel O'Connell. Mustered into service in New York City in June, 1861, the 42 fought at Bull Run, Yorktown, West Point, Glendale, Malvern Hill, Antietam, Fredericksburg and Gettysburg.

114TH PENNSYLVANIA INFANTRY will dedicate their Monument in September.

84TH PENNSYLVANIA INFANTRY will dedicate their monument early in October next. The Committee in charge of the arrangements are: Captain Thomas E. Merchant, Chairman; General George Zinn, Adjutant Edmund Mather, Sergeant A. J. Hertzler, and Henry E. Bunker.

80TH NEW YORK INFANTRY, the 20th Regiment New York State Militia, will dedicate their Monument on the ridge south of Willoughby Run, about 300 feet east of the Hagerstown Pike, during the latter part of September next, the arrangements being in charge of the following committee: General Theodore B. Gates, Colonel John McEntee and Surgeon Robert Loughran. The regiment was mustered into the United States service at Kingston in October, 1861, and fought at Beverly Ford, Warrenton Springs, Gainesville, Groveton, Bull Run (1862), Chantilly, South Mountain, Antietam, Fredericksburg, Gettysburg, Petersburg and Appomattox.

53D PENNSYLVANIA (Veteran Volunteers), will hold their Re-Union at Gettysburg, Pa., on Monday, September 17, 1888. At the same time the Monument of the regiment, in the wheat field, will be unveiled. Every survivor of the regiment, with such of their friends as see fit to come, are expected, as well as all of those who had friends or relatives in the regiment. The Monumental Committee are: George C. Anderson, President; William Mentzer, Secretary; G. C. M. Eicholtz, P. N. Schriger, John Shields and Eli Chambers.

THE STATE OF MAINE has contracted for all her Monuments, but they are not to be completed until October 1, soon after which date a "Maine Day" will be selected on which all the Monuments will be dedicated. The contractors, as a special favor, will complete those of the 3d and 17th Regiments in time for the Re-Union. The following veterans will represent the State on the occasion of the reception to the survivors of the Confederate Army: Colonels Charles H. Smith, Fort Clark, Texas; Moss B. Lakeham, Malden, Mass.; Elijah Walker, Rockland, Clark S. Edwards, Bethel, B. F. Harris, Augusta, General Selden Connor, Augusta, Maine; Colonels John Bardsley, Washington, Ark.; Charles W. Tilden, Hallowell, Charles B. Merrill, Rutland, Francis E. Heath, Waterville, Maine; Generals Joshua Chamberlain, New York City; Charles Hamlin, Bangor, Maine; James A. Hall, Columbus, Ohio; Colonel G. T. Stevens, Oakland, Maine; Captain Edward B. Dew, New York City, and G. F. Stevens, Secretary Executive Committee Maine-Gettysburg Commission.

Secretaries of Veteran Associations will please forward at once to Tregaskis & Co., 767 Broadway, Room 8, New York City, dates and programmes of the dedication ceremonies at their Monument for insertion in subsequent editions of this Programme.

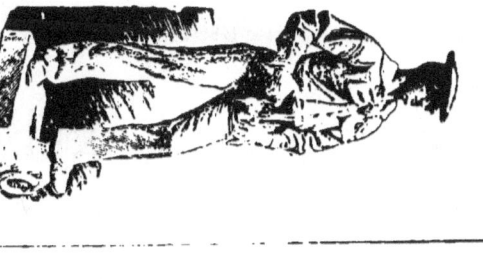

Copyright by
The Henry-Bonnard
Bronze Company

HENRY J. NEWTON, Pres. and Treas. ARTHUR MERWITT, Secretary.
EUGENE F. AUCAIGNE, Gen'l Sup't.

The Henry-Bonnard Bronze Company,

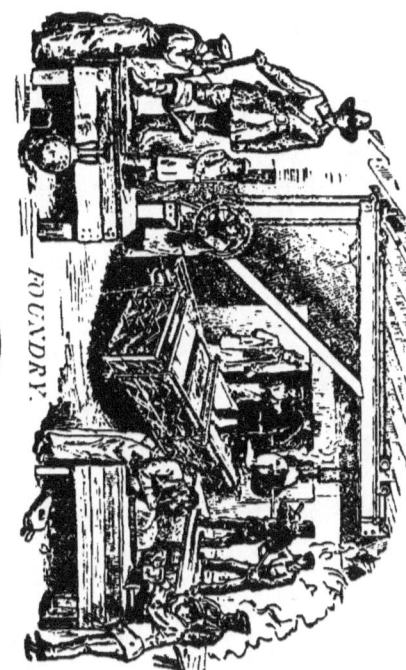

FOUNDRY.

Artistic
AND
Architectural
Bronze Work.

Office and Works,
430–436
West 16th St.,
New York.

The Coat-of-Arms for the New York Monuments on the Gettysburg Battlefield were all cast in this Foundry; also, the Equestrian Statue of Gen. Meade in Fairmount Park, Philadelphia; also, Hampton Battery Monument at Pittsburg, Pa., and the Soldiers' and Sailors' Monument at Binghamton, N. Y.

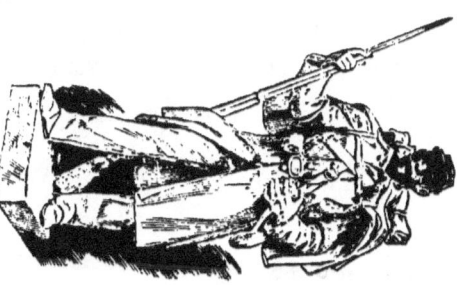

Copyright by
The Henry-Bonnard
Bronze Company

Established 1853.

F. BOOSS & BRO.

IMPORTERS AND MANUFACTURERS OF

FINE AT WHOLESALE FURS

Sealskin Garments a Specialty.

FUR TRIMMINGS IN ALL VARIETY.

449 BROADWAY - AND - 26 MERCER STREET,
(FOUR DOORS BELOW GRAND STREET,)
New York.

TREGASKIS & CO.

ARE READY TO SUPPLY COPIES OF THIS

Souvenir Programme

AT ANY TIME AND IN ANY QUANTITIES.

Address all orders to

TREGASKIS & CO., 767 Broadway, Room 8, New York.

PRICE 25 CENTS.   FREE BY MAIL FOR 30 CENTS.

VIII.

MEADE AND HIS COMMANDERS

A SERIES OF BRIEF BIOGRAPHIES.

(WITH PORTRAITS.)

MEADE, GEORGE GORDON, Major-General, was born at Cadiz, Spain, December 31, 1815, his father having been at that time United States Navy Agent at that port. He was graduated at West Point in 1835 and assigned to the Third Artillery, served in Florida and at Watertown Arsenal, Mass. He resigned in October, 1839. He was engaged in a survey of the Mississippi Delta and the boundary between the United States and Texas and of the northeastern boundary of Maine. In May, 1842, he was appointed Lieutenant in the Corps of Topographical Engineers. In September, 1845, he joined the staff of General Zachary Taylor at Corpus Christi, Tex., took part, May 8 and 9, 1846, in the battles of Palo Alto and Resaca de la Palma, and later, under General Worth, led the assault on Independence Hill at Monterey, for which he was brevetted. He was then engaged in various surveys and in building lighthouses. In May, 1856, he became captain, and served on the geodetic survey of the Northwestern lakes till 1861. He was appointed Brigadier-General of Volunteers August 31, 1861, and commanded the Second Brigade of Pennsylvania Reserves in the Army of the Potomac, engaged at Mechanicsville, Gaines' Mills and New Market Cross Roads, where he was severely wounded, but soon rejoined his command and took part in the second battle of Bull Run. At South Mountain he flanked the enemy from the right, showing such intrepidity that when General Hooker was wounded General McClellan on the field placed him in command of the First Corps. His division at Fredericksburg confronted the troops of Stonewall Jackson. It alone of all the Army drove all before it, broke through the Confederate lines, encountering their reserves, but for lack of timely support was finally forced to fall back. General Meade was promoted Major-General and given command of the Fifth Corps, leading it at Chancellorsville, and on the first day was successfully pressing the Confederates on the left when he was recalled. He took command of the Army of the Potomac June 27, 1863, while it was on the march to check the invasion of Pennsylvania by General Lee. Continuing the movement on the 29th by two forced marches, he gained positions which would enable him to deploy his forces along the line between Westminster and Waynesborough, and when Lee began to concentrate east of South Mountain, Meade occupied the slope along Pipe Creek, advancing his left wing to the neighborhood of Gettysburg, the force there and at Emmettsburg being intended to delay the march of the Confederates till the Union Army could be concentrated on the selected line fifteen miles in the rear. The great battle which ensued on the first three days of July is fully described in another part of this book. Meade was commissioned Brigadier-General in the regular army July 3, 1863. He continued in command of the Army of the Potomac for two years till General Grant had been made Commander of all the Armies of the United States and assumed direction of all the operations in person. He was promoted Major-General August 18, 1864, and after the war commanded successively the Departments of the East and of the South and the Military Division of the Atlantic, which latter position he held at the time of his death in Philadelphia, November 2, 1872, which resulted from pneumonia aggravated by complications incident to the gunshot wound he had received at New Market Cross Roads.

AMES, ADELBERT, Major-General, born in Maine in 1835, graduated at West Point in 1861 and assigned to the Fifth Artillery. He was wounded at Bull Run, and was present at the siege of Yorktown and the battles of Gaines' Mills, Malvern Hill, Fredericksburg, Chancellorsville, Antietam and Gettysburg, besides many minor engagements in Virginia. He commanded a Brigade and at times a Division in the Army of the Potomac and in the operations before Petersburg in 1864. He was brevetted Major-General of Volunteers for his conduct at the capture of Fort Fisher, March 13, 1865, and Major-General United States Army for "gallant and meritorious conduct in the field." On July 28, 1866, he was promoted to the full rank of Lieutenant-Colonel, Twenty-fourth Infantry. On July 15, 1868, he was appointed provisional Governor of Mississippi, and on March 17, 1869, his command was extended to include the Fourth Military District. In 1870 he was elected United States Senator, and in 1873 he was chosen Governor of Mississippi by a popular vote. His administration was so repugnant to the white population that bitter hostilities were engendered between them

1. MAJOR-GENERAL GEORGE G. MEADE 2. MAJOR-GENERAL ALPHEUS S. WILLIAMS.
3. MAJOR-GENERAL W. S. HANCOCK. 4. MAJOR-GENERAL ABNER DOUBLEDAY.
5. MAJOR-GENERAL H. W. SLOCUM 6. MAJOR-GENERAL O. O. HOWARD.
7. MAJOR-GENERAL JOHN F. REYNOLDS.

and the Republicans, mostly blacks, leading to serious riots in Vicksburg, with violence and murder through the State. The next election gave the Democrats control of the Legislature, and articles of impeachment were prepared against Governor Ames, who, knowing that conviction was certain before the partisan tribunal, tendered his resignation on condition that the impeachment be withdrawn. This was agreed to by the Democrats. Governor Ames laid down his office and removed to Minnesota.

AYRES, ROMEYN BECK, Major-General, born in New York, December 20, 1826, graduated at West Point in 1847, served through the war with Mexico as a Lieutenant in the Third Artillery, and subsequently on garrison and frontier duty. In May, 1861, he was promoted to be Captain in the Third Artillery, and he was present at all the early engagements of the war. After serving as Chief of Artillery in General W. T. Smith's Division and of the Sixth Army Corps, he accompanied the Army of the Potomac in the Peninsular Campaign of 1862 and the Maryland Campaign, ending with the Battle of Antietam, as well as in the battles of Fredericksburg, Chancellorsville and intervening actions. As Brigadier-General of Volunteers from November 29, 1862, he commanded a Division of the Fifth Corps at Gettysburg, and was then ordered to New York City to suppress the draft riots. In 1864 he led his command in the movement against Richmond, beginning with the Battles of the Wilderness (May, 1864). He was wounded at Petersburg, and was present at the final engagements ending with the surrender of Lee's Army at Appomattox, April 9, 1865. Since the war he has served on various important commissions and boards. He was promoted in regular course to the Colonelcy of the Second Artillery July 13, 1879.

BARLOW, FRANCIS CHANNING, Major-General, born in Brooklyn, N. Y., October 19, 1834. He was graduated at Harvard in 1855, studied law in the office of William Curtis Noyes, New York, and began practice in that city. In 1861 he enlisted in the 12th Regiment, New York State National Guard, and went to the front on the first call for troops. He re-entered the service as Lieutenant-Colonel of the 61st New York Volunteers, was promoted Colonel during the siege of Yorktown, and distinguished himself at the battle of Fair Oaks or Seven Pines. At Antietam, where his command captured two sets of Confederate colors and 300 prisoners, he was severely wounded, and carried apparently dead from the field. At Chancellorsville (May 2, 1863,) he commanded a Brigade in the 11th Corps, which harrassed "Stonewall" Jackson in his flank movement on the National right. At the battle of Gettysburg he was severely wounded and taken prisoner during the first day's fight. At Spottsylvania Court House, May 12, 1864, the 2d Corps was ordered to storm the Confederate works at dawn. General Barlow commanded the First Division, in the advance line.

The works were carried with a rush, and 3,000 prisoners captured, with two Generals, D. M. Johnson and G. H. Steuart. General Barlow participated in the final campaign under General Grant, was present at the assault on Petersburg, and at Lee's surrender. He was elected Secretary of State of the State of New York in 1865, and served until 1868, when President Grant appointed him United States Marshal of the New York Southern District. He resigned in October, 1869. In November, 1871, he was elected Attorney-General of the State, served through 1872-3. Since that date he has practiced law in New York City.

BARNES, JAMES, Major-General, born in Massachusetts in 1809, was graduated at West Point in 1829, fifth in a class which embraced Robert E. Lee, Joseph E. Johnson, Ormsby McK. Mitchell and others who rose to distinction. He went into the Artillery, became First Lieutenant in June, 1836, resigned the next month, and engaged in railroad building in New York, Massachusetts, Missouri and other States. He was Colonel of the 18th Massachusetts from July, 1861, to December, 1862, participating in most of the battles of the Army of the Potomac during that time. Promoted to Brigadier-General, he was engaged at Fredericksburg, Chancellorsville, Aldie and Upperville. At Gettysburg he commanded a Division, and was severely wounded. He was brevetted Major-General of Volunteers March 15, 1865. With health permanently impaired he was never able subsequently to engage in business. He died in Springfield, Mass., February 12, 1869.

BARTLETT, JOSEPH J., Major-General, was born about 1820. He was appointed Brigadier-General of Volunteers October 4, 1862, brevetted Major-General August 1, 1864, and was mustered out January 15, 1866. From 1867 till 1879 he was United States Minister to Sweden and Norway. He is now employed in the Pension Office at Washington, D. C.

BAXTER, HENRY, Major-General, was born in Sidney Plains, Delaware County, N. Y., September 8, 1821. He received an academic education, and in 1849 went to California overland in a company of thirty men, with ox teams, and was chosen as their Captain. He volunteered as a private early in 1861, and was active in raising a company of the 7th Michigan Infantry, and was elected Captain. He was made Lieutenant-Colonel May 22, 1862, and while in command of his regiment, at Fredericksburg, volunteered to cross the river and dislodge a company of Confederate sharpshooters. Colonel Baxter was shot through the lung in the attempt to cross, but the movement was successful, and he was promoted to Brigadier-General on March 12, 1863. He participated in most of the actions of the Army of the Potomac. In the Battle of the Wilderness two horses were killed under him. For conspicious gallantry he was brevetted Major-

General April 1, 1865. From 1866 till 1869 General Baxter was United States Minister to Honduras. He died in Jonesville, Mich., December 30, 1873.

BENHAM, HENRY W., Major-General, born in Connecticut in 1817, was graduated at the head of his class at West Point in 1837, assigned to the Engineers Corps, and engaged upon river and harbor work. In the Mexican War he won a Captain's brevet at Buena Vista, February 23, 1847. He was in charge of several important public works at Boston, Buffalo and Washington from 1848 to 1853, when he took charge of the Coast Survey Office. At the opening of the work was made Engineer of the Department of Ohio, was brevetted Colonel July 13, 1861, for gallantry at Carricksford, Va., was made Brigadier-General in August, 1861, and was engaged at New Creek, Carnifex Ferry and other sections in Virginia in that year. In 1862 he was present at the Capture of Fort Pulaski and James Island. He was highly efficient in throwing pontoon bridges across James River, the Potomac and the Rappahannock. He was brevetted Brigadier and Major-General in the regular army, and made Major-General of Volunteers for services during the war. In 1868 he became Colonel of Engineers, and subsequently had charge of Government work on the New York and New England coast. He was retired in 1882, and died in New York, June 1, 1884.

BIRNEY, DAVID BELL, Major-General, born at Huntsville, Ala., May 29, 1825, practiced law in Philadelphia from 1848 till 1861, when he entered the Union Army as Colonel of the 23d Pennsylvania Regiment, which he raised. He was promoted Brigadier and Major-General, and won distinction at Yorktown, Williamsburg, the second Battle of Bull Run, Fredericksburg, Chancellorsville and Gettysburg. He led the 3d Corps at Gettysburg after General Sickles was wounded, and on July 23d was given command of the 10th Corps. He died in Philadelphia October 18, 1864, from disease contracted in the service.

BREWSTER, WILLIAM R., Brigadier-General, was a Colonel in the Excelsior Brigade, organized by Daniel E. Sickles in 1861, and after the promotion of that officer was made a Brigadier-General of Volunteers. At the time of his death, December 13, 1869, he held a place in the United States Internal Revenue Department at Brooklyn, N. Y.

BROOKE, JOHN R., Major-General, was born in Pennsylvania. He enlisted in the 4th Pennsylvania Infantry in April, 1861, became Captain, and on November 7 was made Colonel of the 53d Pennsylvania Infantry. He was promoted Brigadier-General of Volunteers May 12, 1864, and brevetted Major-General of Volunteers August 1, 1864. In the regular service he was appointed Lieutenant-Colonel of the 37th United States Infantry July

28, 1866, and was transferred to the 3d Infantry, March 15, 1869. He was promoted Colonel 13th Infantry March 20, 1879, and retransferred to the 3d Infantry June 14, 1879. In the regular army he received brevets as Colonel and Brigadier-General for gallantry in several battles.

BUFORD, JOHN, Major-General, was born in Kentucky in 1825, graduated at West Point in 1848, assigned to the 1st Dragoons, and served in various sections of the Western States and Territories until the Rebellion began. He was made a Major in the Inspector-General's Corps, November 12, 1861. He was detailed to the Staff of General Pope in the Army of Virginia on June 26, 1862, and on July 27 made a Brigadier-General, assigned to the command of a Brigade of Cavalry under General Hooker. He was engaged at Madison Court-House, August 9; the passage of the Rapidan in pursuit of Jackson's force, August 12; Kelly's Ford, Thoroughfare Gap, August 28, and Manassas, August 29 and 30, where he was wounded. He served as Chief of Cavalry of the Army of the Potomac in the Maryland Campaign, being engaged at South Mountain, September 14, 1862; at Antietam, September 17, where he succeeded General Stoneman on General McClellan's Staff, and in the march to Falmouth. He was subsequently conspicuous in almost every Cavalry engagement, being at Fredericksburg, in Stoneman's raid toward Richmond in the beginning of May, 1863, and at Beverly Ford, June 9, 1863. He commanded the Cavalry Division of the Army of the Potomac in the Pennsylvania Campaign, and was engaged at Aldie, Middleburg and Upperville. At Gettysburg he began the attack on the Confederates before the arrival of Reynolds on July 1, and the next day rendered important services both at Wolff's Hill and Round Top. He participated in the pursuit of the Confederates to Warrenton, and in the subsequent operations in Virginia. A short time previous to his death he was assigned to the command of the Cavalry in the Army of the Cumberland, and had left the Army of the Potomac for that purpose. His last sickness was the result of toil and exposure. His commission as Major-General reached him in Washington on the day of his death, December 16, 1863.

BURBANK, SIDNEY, Brigadier-General, born in Massachusetts in 1807, was graduated at West Point in 1829, served in the Infantry on the frontier and at the Military Academy as instructor, was promoted Captain in 1839, fought the Seminoles in Florida, and was in charge of recruiting at Newport. During the Civil War he was Colonel of the 2d Infantry, and later led a Brigade in the Army of the Potomac. He was in the battles of Chancellorsville and Gettysburg, and received the brevet of Brigadier-General. After the war he commanded the 2d Infantry, and was retired in 1870 credited with forty years' service.

BUTTERFIELD, DANIEL, Major-General, was born in Utica, N. Y., October 31, 1831. His father, John Butterfield, was one of the best known citizens of Central New York, one of the founders of the American Express Company, builder of the first telegraph line between New York and Buffalo, and President of the Overland Mail Company. Daniel Butterfield was graduated at Union College in 1849, and became a merchant in New York City. He was Colonel of the 12th New York Militia when the war begun, went with it to Washington July, 1861, led the advance into Virginia over the Long Bridge, joined General Patterson on the upper Potomac, and commanded a Brigade. He was appointed Brigadier-General September 7, 1861, and assigned to Fitz-John Porter's Corps, with which he participated in the Campaign of the Peninsula, taking a conspicuous part in the actions at Hanover Court House, Mechanicsville, Gaines' Mills, where he wa wounded, and in battles fought during McClellan's change of base from White House to Harrison's Landing, when he commanded a force on the south side of the James River to cover the movement. He took part in the great battles under Pope and McClellan in August and September, 1862, and in October took command of Morrell's Division. He became Major-General of Volunteers November 29, 1862; was made Colonel of the 5th Regular Infantry July 1, 1863; commanded the Fifth Corps in the Battle of Fredericksburg; was Chief of Staff, Army of the Potomac, at Chancellorsville and at Gettysburg, where he was wounded. He was sent to re-enforce Rosecrans in October, 1863, and was Hooker's Chief of Staff at Lookout Mountain, Mission Ridge, Ringgold and Pea Vine Creek, Ga. He commanded a Division of the Twentieth Corps in the battles of Buzzard's Roost, Resaca, Dallas, New Hope Church, Kenesaw and Lost Mountain, Ga., and was brevetted Brigadier and Major-General U. S. Army for gallant and meritorious conduct. After the war he was Commandant of the forces in New York Harbor and General Superintendent of the recruiting service till 1869, when he resigned from the Army and was appointed Assistant Treasurer of the United States in charge of the Sub-Treasury at New York. Since his resignation from that position he has been connected with the management of the American Express Company, the Iron Steamboat Company, and a number of other enterprises of great importance. General Butterfield was the author of a book of great practical value in the organization and instruction of troops, "Camp and Outpost Duty," pubished in 1862, which became a most popular manual in the hands of both officers and men, and proved highly useful to the Federal cause in transforming peaceful and Union-loving citizens into that mighty military force which was destined after the long, and sometimes disheartening, struggle to win victory and ensure the perpetuity of our National unity.

CALDWELL, JOHN CURTIS, Major-General, born in Lowell, Vt., April 17, 1833, and graduated at Amherst in 1855. At the beginning of the Civil War he became Colonel of the 11th Maine Volunteers. He was made Brigadier-General of Volunteers April 28, 1862, and brevetted Major-General August 19, 1865. General Caldwell was in every action of the Army of the Potomac, from its organization till General Grant took command, and during the last year of the war he was president of an advisory board of the War Department. He was a member of the Maine Senate, Adjutant-General of the State in 1867, and in 1869 was United States Consul at Valparaiso, Chili. From 1873 till 1882 he was Minister at Uruguay and Paraguay, and in 1885, having removed to Kansas, was President of the Board of Pardons of that State.

CARR, JOSEPH B., Major-General, was born in Albany, N. Y., August 16, 1828, and educated in the public schools. He embarked in business in Troy, N. Y., and became a Colonel in the State Militia. In April, 1861, he was appointed Lieutenant-Colonel, and in May, Colonel of the 2d New York Volunteers, the first volunteer regiment to leave the State and the first to encamp on the soil of Virginia. He participated in the Battle of Big Bethel, and in May, 1862, fought through McClellan's Peninsula Campaign, being attached to General Hooker's command. Colonel Carr was acting Brigadier-General in the engagements of the Orchards, Glendale and Malvern Hill, and was promoted Brigadier-General September 7, 1862, for gallantry at Malvern Hill. He fought with credit at Bristow's Station, Chantilly and Fredericksburg. In January, 1863, he commanded an expedition that severed the rebel communications at Rappahannock Bridge. At Chancellorsville, May 3, 1863, he commanded the Division after the fall of General Berry. At Gettysburg, where his horse was killed under him, he was injured, but held his troops in order, though two-thirds of them were killed or wounded. Commanding the Third Division of the Fourth Corps he participated in the actions at Brandy Station, Locust Grove and Mine Run. He afterwards commanded divisions in the First Corps, had charge of the defence of James River, and on June 1, 1865, was brevetted Major-General. He took a prominent part in the politics of New York, being elected by the Republicans Secretary of State in 1879 and re-elected in 1881 and 1883. In 1885 he was his party's candidate for Lieutenant-Governor.

CARROLL, SAMUEL SPRIGG, Major-General, born in Washington, D. C., September 21, 1832; graduated at West Point in 1856, assigned to the 10th Infantry, and became a Captain November 1, 1861. He was appointed Colonel of the 8th Ohio Volunteers December 15, 1861, and served in Western Virginia till May 23, 1862. He commanded a Brigade of General Shield's Division, taking part in the pursuit of the rebels up the Shenandoah in June, 1862, and in the Battle of Cedar Mountain. On August 14 he was wounded in a skirmish on the Rapidan. He took part in the Maryland Campaign, and on the Rappahannock from December, 1862, till June, 1863, being engaged in the battles of Fredericksburg and Chancellorsville, and receiving the brevet of Major for bravery. In the Battle of Gettysburg he earned the brevet of Lieutenant-Colonel, and in the Wilderness fight that of Colonel. Near Spottsylvania he was twice wounded and disabled for further service in the field. He was brevetted Brigadier-General, U. S. A., for gallantry at Spottsylvania, and Major-General for services during the Rebellion. On January 22, 1867, he became a Lieutenant-Colonel in the Regular Army. In 1868 he was Acting Inspector-General of the Division of the Atlantic, and on June 9, 1869, retired as Major-General for disability from wounds received in battle.

CLARKE, HENRY FRANCIS, Major-General, born in Brownsville, Pa., November 9, 1820, graduated at West Point in 1843, entered the Artillery, was distinguished at Chapultepec where he won the brevet of Captain, was Professor of Mathematics at West Point, became Captain on January 12, 1857, and was in the Expedition to Utah, as Chief Commissary, remaining till 1860. He ordered the relief of Fort Pickens, April 1, 1861, and became McDowell's Chief Commissary July 2, 1861, served in the Manassas Campaign, and was Chief Commissary of Subsistence in the Army of the Potomac from August, 1861, to January, 1864, being present at the Seige of Yorktown, and the battles of South Mountain, Antietam, Fredericksburg, Chancellorsville and Gettysburg, and was brevetted Brigadier and Major-General. He was Chief of the Commissariat of the Division of the Missouri in 1868-75, and of the Division of the Atlantic from 1879 till he was retired November 9, 1884, with the rank of Colonel.

CRAWFORD, SAMUEL WYLIE, Major-General, was born in Pennsylvania November 8, 1829. He was graduated at the University of Pennsylvania in 1846, studied medicine, and in 1851 became an Assistant Surgeon in the United States Army. He served in the Southwest until 1860, when he was stationed at Fort Sumter, being one of the garrison when that fort was fired upon by the rebels from Charleston at the beginning of the war and having command of a battery during the bombardment. In August, 1861, he was appointed Major in the 13th Infantry, and in 1862 Brigadier-General of Volunteers. General Crawford served with distinction in the Shenandoah Campaign, being present at the battles of Winchester and Cedar Mountain, loosing one-half of his Brigade in the last named action. At Antietam he succeeded General Mansfield in command of his Division and was severely wounded. Early in 1863 he was placed in command of the Pennsylvania Reserves, then stationed about Washington, and with these troops, forming the Third Division of the Fifth Army Corps, he was engaged at Gettysburg, serving with great bravery. Subsequently he participated in all the operations of the Army of the Potomac until the close of the war. He was brevetted successively from Colonel in 1863 up to Major-General in 1865 for conspicuous gallantry. After the war he became Colonel of the 16th Infantry and later of the 2d Infantry. In February, 1873, owing to disability resulting from wounds, he was retired with the rank of Brigadier-General.

CROSS, EDWARD EPHRAIM, Brigadier-General, born at Lancaster, N. H., was educated at the Lancaster Academy and began life as a printer. In 1854 he became an editor of the Cincinnati *Times*, and four years later he made a trip across the plains to Arizona in connection with a mining company in which he was interested, taking the first steam engine and printing press that ever crossed the Rocky Mountains. He became a Lieutenant-Colonel in the Mexican Army, and when the news of the attack on Fort Sumter reached him had command of a large garrison at El Fuere. He resigned, and, returning to New Hampshire, organized the 5th Regiment of Volunteers, which under his command distinguished itself as "The Fighting Fifth" in many engagements. He was mortally wounded at Gettysburg, July 2, 1863, where he commanded the First Brigade of the First Division of the Second Corps.

CUSTER, GEORGE ARMSTRONG, Major-General, born in New Rumly, Harrison County, Ohio, December 5, 1839. He was graduated at West Point in June, 1861, was assigned to the 5th Cavalry, and participated, on the day of his arrival at the front, in the first Battle of Bull Run. In June, 1862, he was appointed an aide to General McClellan with the rank of Captain. He at once asked leave to attack a picket post he had discovered, surprised the enemy, drove them back and captured the first colors that were taken by the Army of the Potomac. For gallantry at Aldie and Brandy Station he was appointed Brigadier-General of Volunteers June 29, 1863, and given command of the Michigan Brigade. At Gettysburg his Brigade, together with those of Gregg and McIntosh, defeated General Stuart's efforts to turn the Federal left flank. For this action he was breveted Major in the United States Army. He took part in General Sheridan's Cavalry raid toward Richmond in May, 1864, and was brevetted Lieutenant-Colonel for meritorious services in the Battle of Yellow Tavern, May 11. In General Sheridan's second raid on Richmond the Michigan Brigade made a most gallant fight at Trevillion Station. On September 19, 1864, he was made Brevet-Colonel, United States Army, for gallantry at Winchester, and Brevet-Major-General of Volunteers. On September 30 he assumed command of the 3d Division of Cavalry, with which he fought the brilliant Battle of Woodstock on October 9. At Cedar Creek he confronted the enemy from the first attack in the morning until the battle ended in a brilliant success,

The 3d Division recaptured, before the day was over, guns and colors that had been taken from the army earlier in the fight, together with many Confederate flags and cannon. In the spring of 1865 Custer's Division alone fought the Battle of Waynesboro, March 2. The enemy's works were carried and they lost eleven guns, 200 wagons, 1,600 prisoners, and seventeen battle flags. For gallant and meritorious services at the battles of Five Forks and Dinwiddie Court House, General Custer was brevetted Brigadier-General, United States Army, March 13, 1865. General Custer never lost a gun or a color and was never defeated. General Custer received the first flag of truce from the Army of Northern Virginia, and was present at Lee's surrender. He was brevetted Major-General for services in the campaign of 1865, and appointed Major-General of Volunteers. After the war closed General Custer asked permission to accept from President Juarez the place of Chief of the Mexican Cavalry in the struggle against Maximilian. President Johnson refused him the leave of absence, and Custer accepted the Lieutenant-Colonelcy of the 7th Cavalry and served on the plains until 1871. On November 27 he fought the decisive battle of the Washita, in Indian Territory, completely defeating the Cheyennes. On May 15, 1876, General Custer commanded his regiment in a campaign against the confederated Sioux tribes. The Indians were encamped on the Little Big Horn River, in a region almost unknown. Their eleven tribes numbered nearly 9,000. The Government expedition consisted of 1,100 men. The attack was made June 25 by a portion of the regiment numbering fewer than 200 Cavalry, while General Custer with 277 troopers charged on the village from another direction. They were met by overwheming numbers, and General Custer with his entire command was slain.

CUTLER, LYSANDER, Major-General, was born in Maine in 1806. He offered his services to the Government, and was given command of the 6th Wisconsin Regiment, which he soon made one of the best in the Union Army. He was later in command of the "Iron Brigade" of the Army of the Potomac, to which his regiment was attached, and won promotion to Brigadier and Major-General. He was twice wounded, and died at Milwaukee July 30, 1866.

DAY, HANNIBAL, Brigadier-General, born in Vermont about 1802. He was graduated at West Point in 1823. He served in the Florida Seminole War, was commissioned Captain July 7, 1838, Major February 23, 1852, Lieutenant-Colonel February 25, 1861, and Colonel January 7, 1862. He commanded a Brigade of the Fifth Corps in the Pennsylvania Campaign in 1863, taking part in the Battle of Gettysburg. He was retired from active duty "on his own application after forty consecutive years of service."

August 1, 1863, and employed on military commissions and courts martial from July 25, 1864. On March 13, 1865, he was brevetted Brigadier-General for long service.

DE TROBRIAND, PHILIPPE REGIS, Major-General, born near Tours, France, June 4, 1816. He studied in various French military schools till 1830, when he entered the University of Orleans and was graduated as "bachelier of lettres" in 1834, and at Goitiers, with license to practice as a lawyer, in 1838. He came to the United States in 1841, edited and published the *Revue de Nouveau Mode* in New York in 1849-50, and was joint editor of the *Courier des Etats-Unis* in 1854-61. He joined the Army as Colonel of the 55th New York Regiment, August 28, 1861; was engaged at Yorktown and Williamsburg, commanded a Brigade of the Third Army Corps in 1862-63, and was at Fredericksburg, Chancellorsville and Gettysburg. He was made Brigadier-General of Volunteers in January, 1864, and placed in command of the defences of New York City. As commander of a Brigade in the Second Army Corps he was at Deep Bottom, Petersburg, Hatcher's Run and Five Forks, and he led a Division in the operations that ended in Lee's surrender. He was brevetted Major-General of Volunteers on April 9, 1865; entered the Regular Army as Colonel of the 31st Infantry on July 28, 1866, was brevetted Brigadier-General, United States Army, March 2, 1867, and commanded the District of Dakota. He was transferred to the 13th Infantry on March 15, 1869, and was retired at his own request, on account of age, on March 20, 1879, since which date he has resided in New Orleans, La.

DEVIN, THOMAS C., Major-General, born in New York City in 1822. He received a common school education, followed the trade of a painter, and became Lieutenant-Colonel of the 1st New York Militia Regiment. Just after the Battle of Bull Run he told Mr. Thurlow Weed that he wished authority to raise a Cavalry company for immediate service. Mr. Weed telegraphed to Governor Morgan, obtained the desired commission, and in two days the company had been recruited and was on its way to Washington. Three months later he was given a command as Colonel of the 6th New York Volunteers, attached to the Cavalry Corps of the Army of the Potomac, and he participated in all the battles fought by that Corps from Antietam to Lee's surrender. At Five Forks he commanded his Brigade, and carried the Confederate earthworks. He was brevetted Brigadier-General of Volunteers August 15, 1864, for bravery at Front Royal, where he was wounded, and Major-General March 13, 1865, for his service during the war. He entered the Regular Army as Lieutenant-Colonel of the 8th Cavalry July 28, 1866, commanding the District of Montana. On March 2, 1867, he was brevetted Colonel, United States Army, for gallantry at

Fisher's Hill, and Brigadier-General for services at Sailor's Creek. He subsequently commanded the District of Arizona, and on June 25, 1877, became Colonel of the 3d Cavalry. He died in New York City April 4, 1878. General Grant, in a conversation with Thurlow Weed, called General Devin, next to General Sheridan, the best Cavalry officer in the Army.

DOUBLEDAY, ABNER, Major-General, born at Ballston Spa, N. Y., June 26, 1819; was graduated at West Point in 1842, served in the Artillery through the Mexican War, was promoted to First Lieutenant in 1847 and Captain, March 3, 1855. He was in the garrison of Fort Sumter, and aimed the first gun fired in its defence, April 12, 1861. He was made Brigadier-General, February 2, 1862, and assigned to command all the defences of Washington; was engaged at the second Battle of Bull Run, where he succeeded to the command of Hatch's Division. At Antietam his Division, on the extreme right, opened the fight and lost heavily, but captured six battle-flags. He was promoted Major-General of Volunteers, October 29, 1862; was at Fredericksburg and Chancellorsville, and succeeded General Reynolds in command of the First Corps. On July 1, 1863, he was sent to Gettysburg to support Buford's Cavalry, and on the fall of General Reynolds took command of the field till the arrival of General Howard, some hours later. In the repulse of Pickett's charge on the 3d, his Division was prominent. In July, 1864, he had command of the Southeastern defences of Washington, when Early's raiders threatened the Federal Capital. He was brevetted Colonel, Brigadier and Major-General for meritorious services, became Colonel of the 35th Infantry in 1867, and was retired in 1873.

EUSTIS, HENRY LAWRENCE, Brigadier-General, was born at Fort Independence, Boston, Mass., February 1, 1819, graduated at Harvard in 1838, and at West Point at the head of his class in 1842, being assigned to the Engineer Corps. He assisted in the construction of Fort Warren and Lovell's Island Seawall, in Boston harbor, in 1843-5, and engineering operations in Newport harbor. In 1847 he was made the Principal Assistant Professor of Engineering at West Point. He resigned in 1849, becoming Professor of Engineering at Harvard, organizing the Scientific Department there, and held the position until his death, January 11, 1885. In the Civil War he was Colonel of the 10th Massachusetts Volunteers, serving at Williamsport, Fredericksburg, Marye Heights, Salem, Gettysburg, Rappahannock Station, Mine Run, Wilderness, Spottsylvania, Cold Harbor and many minor actions. He was brevetted Brigadier-General on September 12, 1863, and resigned on June 27, 1864, owing to impaired health.

FARNSWORTH, ELAN J., Brigadier-General, born in Green Oak, Livingston County, Mich., in 1837, educated in the public schools, and spent a year at the University of Michigan. Leaving college in 1858, he served in the Quartermaster's Department of the Army during the Utah Expedition of that year. In 1861 he became Assistant-Quartermaster of the 8th Illinois Cavalry, was soon promoted Captain, and took part in all the battles of the Peninsula, and in those of Pope's Campaign. He was appointed aid to General Pleasonton in May, 1863, promoted to Brigadier-General June 29, and was killed July 3, while leading a charge during the Battle of Gettysburg.

GARRARD, KENNER, Major-General, was born in Cincinnati, Ohio, in 1830; graduated at West Point in 1851, entered the Dragoons, became a Captain, March 3, 1855; was engaged in frontier service in Texas, and captured by the Confederates on April 12, 1861. After being exchanged, he was commissioned, September 27, 1862, Colonel of the 146th Regiment of New York Volunteers, and engaged in the principal battles of the Rappahannock and Pennsylvania Campaigns. On July 23, 1863, he was promoted Brigadier-General; took part at Rappahannock Station and in the Mine Run operations, and in 1864 commanded a Cavalry Division of the Army of the Cumberland, and participated in the operations around Chattanooga and the invasion of Georgia, being constantly engaged in detached expeditions. He was brevetted Colonel in the United States Army for services in the expedition to Covington, Ga. From December, 1864, till the end of hostilities he commanded the Second Division of the Sixteenth Army Corps. He distinguished himself at the Battle of Nashville, earning the brevets of Major-General of Volunteers and Brigadier-General in the Regular Army, participated in the operations against Mobile, led the storming column that captured Blakeley, and was placed in command of the District of Mobile. He received the brevet of Major-General, United States Army, for services during the war. On November 9, 1866, he resigned his commission in the Regular Army, and died in Cincinnati, May 15, 1879.

GEARY, JOHN WHITE, Major-General, born in Westmoreland County, Pa., December 30, 1819. After a partial course in Jefferson College he was employed as a civil engineer in Kentucky, studied law and was admitted to the bar. At the opening of the war with Mexico, in 1846, he became Lieutenant-Colonel of the 2d Regiment of Pennsylvania Volunteer Infantry, and commanded his regiment at Chapultepec, where he was wounded, but resumed his command the same day at the attack which carried the Belengate. He was detailed by General Scott at the first command of the City of Mexico. He was appointed in 1849 to be the first Postmaster of San Francisco, with authority to establish the postal service throughout California. He was also the first American Alcalde of San Francisco, and a "Judge of the first instance." In 1850 he became the first Mayor of that city and took a leading part in the formation of the new Constitution of California. In 1852 he retired to his farm in Westmoreland County, Pa. In 1856 he was appointed Lieutenant-Governor of Kansas, which office he held one year. At the beginning of the war raised the 28th Pennsylvania Volunteers. He commanded in several engagements, and won distinction at Bolivar Heights, where he was wounded. He occupied Leesburg, Va., in March, 1862, and routed General Hill. On April 25, 1862, he was commissioned Brigadier-General. He was severely wounded in the arm at Cedar Mountain, August 9, 1862. At Chancellorsville and Gettysburg he led the Second Division of the Twelfth Corps, and he took part in the battles of Wauhatchie and Lookout Mountain, in both of which he was distinguished. He commanded the Second Division of the Twentieth Corps in Sherman's march to the sea, and was the first to enter Savannah, of which place he was appointed Military Governor. He was brevetted Major-General in 1865. He was selected Governor of Pennsylvania in 1866, and held this office until two weeks before his death, which took place at Harrisburg February 8, 1873.

GIBBON, JOHN, Major-General, born near Holmesburg, Pa., April 20, 1827. He was graduated at West Point in 1847, assigned to the Artillery, served through the Mexican War at the City of Mexico and afterwards on frontier and garrison duty. He was assistant Instructor of Artillery at West Point in 1854–'57 and Quartermaster there in 1856–'59. On November 2, 1859, he became Captain in the 4th Artillery. He was Chief of Artillery under General McDowell from October 29, 1861, till May 2, 1862, and at the latter date made Brigadier-General of Volunteers ; he commanded a Brigade through the Northern Virginia, Maryland, Rappahannock and Pennsylvania Campaigns in 1862–'63, receiving the brevets of Major in the Regular Army, September 17, 1862, for Antietam ; Lieutenant-Colonel December 13, 1862, for Fredericksburg ; and Colonel, July 4, 1863, for Gettysburg. He became a Major-General of Volunteers on June 7, 1864, and was engaged at the Wilderness, Spottsylvania and Cold Harbor. After January 15, 1865, he commanded the Twenty-fourth Army Corps, and was before Petersburg from June 15, 1864, till April 2, 1865, taking part in the assaults of the last two days and carrying two redoubts. He was brevetted Brigadier-General and Major-General United States Army, March 13, 1865, and was one of the Commissioners to carry into effect the stipulations for Lee's surrender. Since the war he has commanded various posts as Colonel of the 36th Infantry in 1866–'69 and of the 7th Infantry in 1869–'86. He had charge of the Yellowstone Expedition against Sitting Bull in 1876, and on August 9, 1877, commanded in the action with the Nez Perces Indians at Big Hole Pass, Montana, where he was wounded. On July 10, 1886, he was promoted to Brigadier-General.

GRAHAM, CHARLES KINNAIRD, Major-General, born in New York City June 3, 1824. He entered the United States Navy as midshipman in 1841, and served in the Gulf during the war with Mexico, at the close of which, in 1848, he resigned. About 1857 he was appointed Constructing Engineer of the Brooklyn Navy Yard, the dry dock and landing ways being built under his supervision. At the beginning of the war he volunteered with about 400 in his employ, entering the Excelsior Brigade, in which he became Colonel and was actively engaged in the Army of the Potomac, being, in November, 1862, commissioned Brigadier-General and fighting at the Battle of Gettysburg, where he was severely wounded. He was afterwards assigned to the command of a gunboat flotilla on the James River under General Butler, and was the first to carry the National Colors up that river. He subsequently took part in the attack on Fort Fisher, and remained on duty at different points until the close of the war, when he returned to the practice of engineering in New York City. He was brevetted Major-General, March 13, 1865. General Graham was Chief Engineer of the New York Dock Department from 1878 till 1883, when he became Naval Officer of the Port, and held that post until 1885. He is now the Engineer of the New York State Commission on Gettysburg Monuments.

GRANT, LEWIS A., Major-General, born in Vermont about 1820. He was commissioned Major of the 5th Vermont Infantry August 15, 1861; Lieutenant-Colonel September 25, 1861, and Colonel September 16, 1862. He commanded the Twentieth Brigade of the Second Division of the Sixth Corps at the Battle of Chancellorsville, and was commissioned Brigadier-General of Volunteers April 27, 1864. He was brevetted Major-General of Volunteers October 14, 1864, and mustered out of service August 24, 1865.

GREENE, GEORGE SEARS, Major-General, born in Rhode Island May 6, 1801, graduated at West Point in 1823, second in his class. He served in various garrisons and as Instructor at West Point until 1836, when he resigned and became a civil engineer, building many railroads in several of the Eastern and Middle States, and for several years had charge of the New York City Water Works. He re-entered the army in 1862 as Colonel of the 60th New York Regiment, and became Brigadier-General of Volunteers April 28, 1862. He commanded his Brigade at Cedar Mountain, and was in command of the Second Division of the Twelfth Army Corps in the Battle of Antietam. He also led his Brigade at the Battle of Chancellorsville. At Gettysburg, on the night of July 2, 1863, with a part of his Brigade, he held the right wing of the Army of the Potomac at Culp's Hill against more than a Division of Confederate troops, thereby averting a threatened disaster. In a night engagement at Wauhatchie, near Chattanooga, October 28, 1863, he was dangerously wounded in the jaw. With Sherman's Army in North Carolina he participated in the engagements preceding Johnston's surrender, and was brevetted Major-General March 13, 1865. In 1867 he became Chief Engineer and Commissioner of the New York Croton Aqueduct Department till 1871, when he was made Chief Engineer of Public Works in Washington, D. C., but resigned in 1872. Since that date he has been engaged as consulting engineer on various works.

GREGG, DAVID MCMURTIE, Major-General, born in Huntingdon, Pa., April 10, 1833, graduated at West Point in 1855, assigned to the Dragoons, served for several years in New Mexico and California and became Captain in the 6th Cavalry in May, 1861. In January, 1862, he was appointed Colonel of the 8th Pennsylvania Cavalry, and was engaged at the Battle of Fair Oaks, the seven days' fight and otherwise during the Virginia Peninsula Campaign in 1862. He became Brigadier-General of Volunteers on November 29, commanded a Division of Cavalry in the Army of the Potomac from December, 1862, till June, 1863, and was engaged at Beverly Ford, Aldie, Gettysburg, Rapidan Station and New Hope Church. He commanded the 2d Cavalry Division, April 6, 1864, to February 3, 1865, in the Richmond Campaign, and the Cavalry of the Army of the Potomac from August 1, 1864, when he was brevetted Major-General, till his resignation, February 3, 1865. He was appointed United States Consul at Prague, Bohemia, in 1874, and in 1886 became Commander of the Pennsylvania Order of the Loyal Legion.

GREGG, JOHN IRVIN, Major-General, born in Bellefonte, Pa., July 19, 1826. He volunteered for the Mexican War as a private in December, 1846, was appointed a Lieutenant of the 11th Regular Infantry in February, 1847, and Captain on September 5, 1847. At the close of that war he engaged in the iron business in Centre County, Pa. He was appointed Captain in the 6th United States Cavalry in May, 1861, Colonel 16th Pennsylvania Cavalry in October, 1862, and commanded a Cavalry Brigade in the Army of the Potomac from April, 1863, till April, 1865. He participated in numerous battles, including Deep Bottom, where he was severely wounded. For gallant and meritorious services he was brevetted Major-General of Volunteers, and Brigadier-General United States Army at the close of the war. He became Colonel of the 8th Cavalry July 28, 1868, and was with his regiment on the Pacific coast till he was retired for disability incurred in line of duty April 2, 1879.

HANCOCK, WINFIELD SCOTT, Major-General, born at Montgomery Square, Pa., February 14, 1824, was graduated at West Point July 1, 1844, and assigned to duty in the 6th Infantry at Fort Tonson, Indian Territory. In the summer of 1847 he joined the Army of General Scott in its advance upon the Mexican Capital, participated in the chief battles of the campaign and was brevetted First Lieutenant. From 1848 till 1859 he served with the regiment at various frontier posts in line and staff duty. From 1859 till 1861 Captain Hancock was Chief Quartermaster of the Southern District of California. At the beginning of the Civil War in 1861 he asked to be transferred to more active service at the seat of the war. In a letter to a friend at this time he said: "My politics are of a practical kind—the integrity of the country, the supremacy of the Federal Government, an honorable peace or none at all." He was commissioned a Brigadier-General of Volunteers September 23, 1861, and aided in organizing the Army of the Potomac. During the Peninsula Campaign under General McClellan he was especially conspicuous at the battles of Williamsburg and Frazer's Farm. He took an active part in the subsequent campaign in Maryland, at the battles of South Mountain and Antietam, being assigned to command the First Division of the Second Army Corps on the battlefield at Antietam September 17, 1862. He was made a Major-General of Volunteers, November 29, 1862, and commanded a Division in the attempt to storm Marye's Heights at the Battle of Fredericksburg, December 13, 1862. In this assault General Hancock led his men through such a fire as has rarely been encountered in warfare. He commanded 5,006 men, and left 2,013 of them on the field. In the three days' fight at Chancellorsville, in May, 1863, Hancock's Division took a prominent part. In the decisive action at Gettysburg of July 3 Hancock commanded the left centre, the main point assailed by the Confederates, and was shot from his horse. Though dangerously wounded he remained on the field till the enemy was repulsed, when he sent this message to General Meade: "We have gained a great victory. The enemy is now flying in all directions in my front." Out of fewer than 10,000 men, the Second Army Corps lost at Gettysburg about 4,000 killed or wounded. It captured 4,500 prisoners and about thirty colors. On April 21, 1866, Congress passed a resolution thanking General Hancock for his services in the Campaign of 1863. Disabled by his wound, he was not again employed on active duties till the spring of 1864, when he resumed command of the Second Army Corps, and bore a prominent part in the battles of the Wilderness and Spottsylvania, where the fighting was almost continuous from the 5th to the 26th of May. In the engagement at Spottsylvania Court House General Hancock, on the night of the 11th, moved to a position within 1,200 yards of General Lee's right centre, where he formed a sharp salient since known as "The Bloody Angle," and early on the morning of the 12th he gave the order to advance. His heavy column overran the Confederate pickets without firing a shot, burst through the abatis, and after a short hand-to-hand conflict inside the entrenchments captured nearly 4,000 prisoners, twenty pieces of artillery, with horses, caissons and material complete, several thousand stand of small arms and upward of thirty colors. The fighting at this point was as fierce as any during the war, the battle raging furiously and incessantly along the whole line throughout the day and late into the night. General Lee made five separate assaults to retake the works, but without success. In the subsequent operations of the army, at the crossing of the North Anna, the second Battle of Cold Harbor and the assault on the lines in front of Petersburg, General Hancock was active and indefatigable. He was appointed a Brigadier-General in the Regular Army, August 12, 1864, "for gallant and distinguished services in the battles of the Wilderness, Spottsylvania and Cold Harbor, and in all operations of the Army in Virginia under Lieutenant-General Grant." On August 21 the Second Corps was brought to Petersburg by a long night march, and on the 25th occurred the only notable disaster in Hancock's career. While he was entrenched at Ream's Station his lines were carried by the enemy and many of his men captured. In this hour of defeat the intrepid commander, covered with dust, begrimed with powder and smoke, laying his hand upon a staff officer's shoulder, said: "Colonel, I do not care to die, but I pray to God I may never leave this field." In February, 1865, he was assigned to the command of the Middle Military Division and ordered to Winchester, Va., to relieve General Sheridan from the command of the Army of the Shenandoah. After the assassination of President Lincoln General Hancock's headquarters were transferred to Washington, and he was placed in command of the defences of the Capital. On July 26, 1866, he was appointed a Major-General in the Regular Army. He subsequently commanded the Department of the Missouri, the Fifth District, comprising Texas and Louisiana, the Department of Dakota and the Division of the Atlantic. General Hancock's name was favorably mentioned in 1868 and 1872 as a candidate for Presidential honors, and he was nominated by the Democratic party in the Cincinnati Convention, June 24, 1880, receiving on the first ballot 171 votes in a convention containing 738 members, and on the second ballot he had 320 votes, Senator Bayard of Delaware 153 1-2, the remainder of the votes scattering among twelve candidates. On the second ballot General Hancock received 320 votes, Senator Thomas F. Bayard 111 and Speaker Samuel J. Randall of the House of Representatives 128 1-2. The third ballot gave General Hancock 705 votes, and the nomination was made unanimous. The election in November resulted in the following popular vote: James A. Garfield, Republican, 4,454,416; Winfield S. Hancock, Democrat, 4,444,952; James B. Weaver, Greenback, 308,578; Neal Dow, Prohibition, 10,305. General Hancock continued in the discharge of official duty. His last notable appearance in public was at General Grant's funeral, all the arrangements for which were carried out under his supervision. The esteem in which he was held as a citizen and a soldier was, perhaps, never greater than at the time of his death, which occurred at Governor's Island, New York Harbor, February 9, 1886.

HARROW, WILLIAM, Brigadier-General, was born about 1820. He was engaged as Colonel of the 14th Indiana Infantry, at the Battle of Antietam, where more than half of his regiment were killed or wounded. He was commissioned as Brigadier-General of Volunteers on November 29, 1862, and resigned on April 20, 1865.

HAYS, ALEXANDER, Brigadier-General, born at Venango County, Pa., July 8, 1819, was killed in the Battle of the Wilderness May 5, 1864. He was graduated at West Point in 1844. As a Lieutenant of the 8th Infantry in the Mexican War he won special distinction in the engagement near Atlixco. In April, 1848, he resigned and engaged in manufacturing iron in 1848–'50, was an engineer on railroad construction in 1850–4, and from 1854 till 1861 was a civil engineer in Pittsburg. When the war began in 1861 Hays reentered the service as Colonel of the 63d Pennsylvania Regiment. At the close of the seven day's contest around Richmond he was brevetted Lieutenant-Colonel. He took part in the Maryland Campaign, and was appointed Brigadier-General of Volunteers September 29, 1862. He was wounded at Chancellorsville while at the head of his Brigade. He commanded the Third Division of his Corps at the Battle of Gettysburg, and, after Hancock was wounded, was temporarily in command, gaining the brevet of Colonel in the United States Army. When the Army of the Potomac was reorganized, Hays was placed in command of the Second Brigade of Birney's Division of the Second Corps, and gallantly met his death during the terrible struggle toward the junction of the plank and brook roads, which was the feature of the first day's fighting in the Wilderness.

HAYS, WILLIAM, Brigadier-General, born in Richmond, Va., in 1819, was graduated at West Point in 1840, served in the Artillery, received several brevets for gallant and meritorious conduct in the Mexican War and was promoted to the rank of Major. He commanded a Brigade of Horse Artillery in 1861–2 in the Army of the Potomac, participating in the battles of Antietam and Fredericksburg, and was appointed Brigadier-General of Volunteers in November, 1862. He was wounded and taken prisoner at Chancellorsville May 6, 1863, rejoined the army at Gettysburg, and in November was appointed Provost Marshal of the Southern District of New York. In February, 1865, he returned to the front at Petersburg, and served with the Second Corps and in command of the Reserve Artillery until the close of the war, when he was brevetted Brigadier-General in the Regular Army for gallant conduct. He served at various posts, commanded at Fort Independence, Boston Harbor, from April 29, 1873, till his death, February 7, 1875.

1. MAJOR-GENERAL JOSEPH HOOKER.
2. MAJOR-GENERAL G. K. WARREN.
3. MAJOR-GENERAL JOHN SEDGWICK
4. MAJOR-GENERAL ALFRED PLEASONTON
5. MAJOR-GENERAL D. B. BIRNEY.
6. MAJOR-GENERAL D. E. SICKLES.
7. MAJOR-GENERAL JOHN NEWTON
8. MAJOR-GENERAL GEORGE SYKES.
9. MAJOR-GENERAL CARL SCHURZ.

HOWARD, OLIVER OTIS, Major-General, was born in Leeds, Me., November 8, 1830, graduated at Bowdoin in 1850, and at West Point in 1854, became First Lieutenant and Instructor in Mathematics in 1854, and resigned in 1861 to take command of the 3d Maine Regiment. He commanded a Brigade at the Battle of Bull Run, and for gallantry in that engagement was made Brigadier-General of Volunteers September 3, 1861. He participated in the Battle of Antietam, and commanded the Eleventh Corps during Hooker's operations at Chancellorsville in May, 1863; served at Gettysburg, Lookout Mountain and Missionary Ridge. He was with the Army of the Tennessee in the march through Georgia, was engaged at Dalton, Resaca, Adairsville, and Pickett's Mill, where he was again wounded, was at the surrender of Atlanta, and joined in pursuit of Hood's Confederates in Alabama from October 4 till December 13, 1864. In the march to the sea and through the Carolinas he commanded the right wing of General Sherman's army. He became Brigadier-General in the United States Army December 21, 1864; commanded the Army of the Tennessee, and engaged in all the important battles from January 4 till the surrender of General Joseph E. Johnston at Durham, N. C., April 26, 1865, and was brevetted Major-General for gallantry. He was Commissioner of the Freedmen's Bureau at Washington from March, 1865, till July, 1874. In 1877, while commanding the Department of the Columbia, he led the expedition against the Nez Perces Indians, and in 1878 led the campaign against the Bannacks and Piutes. In 1881-2 he was Superintendent of the United States Military Academy. In 1886 he was commissioned Major-General and assigned to the command of the Division of the Pacific.

HOWE, ALBION PARIS, Major-General, born in Standish, Me., March 13, 1818, graduated at West Point in 1841, entered the 4th Artillery, and from 1843 till 1846 was a teacher of mathematics at the Military Academy. He served with credit in the Mexican War, and was brevetted Captain for his conduct at Contreras and Chucubusco. He was General McClellan's Chief of Artillery in Western Virginia in 1861, and commanded a Brigade of Light Artillery in the Army of the Potomac during the campaign on the peninsula in 1862. He was appointed Brigadier-General of Volunteers July 11, 1862, and commanded a Brigade in Couch's Division, Fourth Army Corps. He was in the battles of Manassas, South Mountain, Antietam, Fredericksburg and Gettysburg, commanded the Artillery depot at Washington, D. C., in 1864-6, and was brevetted Major-General, United States Army, March 13, 1865, for meritorious service during the Rebellion. He was retired from the army in 1882, after serving for several years on the Pacific coast with the 4th Artillery, of which he was Major,

HUMPHREYS, ANDREW ATKINSON, Major-General, was born in Philadelphia, Pa., November 2, 1810, graduated at West Point in 1831, assigned to the 2d Artillery, and served at the Military Academy and in Florida. In September, 1836, he resigned and was employed as a civil engineer and by the United States Light House Board. On July 7, 1838, he was reappointed in the United States Army as First Lieutenant of Topographical Engineers, and served in charge of works for the improvement of various harbors and the Mississippi Delta, and in Washington in 1842–9 as assistant in charge of the Coast Survey Office. He was sent to Europe in 1851 to study systems for the improvement of the mouth of the Mississippi. He was made Major in August, 1861, was Chief of Topographical Engineers of the Army of the Potomac, and was made Brigadier-General of Volunteers on April 28, 1862. In September, 1862, he was given command of a Division of new troops in the Fifth Corps of the Army of the Potomac, with which he led in the Maryland Campaign. He was engaged in the Battle of Fredericksburg and Chancellorsville, receiving the brevet of Colonel. He served in the Battle of Gettysburg under General Daniel E. Sickels, and was promoted Major-General. On July 8, 1863, he became Chief of Staff to General Meade. In November, 1864, he was given command of the Second Corps, which was engaged under his direction at the siege of Petersburg, the actions at Hatcher's Run, and the consequent operations ending with Lee's surrender. General Humphreys received the brevet of Major-General in the United States Army. From December, 1865, till August, 1866, he was in charge of the Mississippi levees. He was then made Brigadier-General and given command of the Corps of Engineers, the highest scientific appointment in the United States Army, with charge of the Engineer Bureau in Washington. This office he held until June 30, 1879, when he was retired at his own request. He died in Washington December 27, 1883.

HUNT, HENRY JACKSON, Major-General, born in Detroit, Mich., September 14, 1819, was graduated at West Point in 1839, served in the Artillery on frontier and garrison duty till the outbreak of the Mexican War, during which he was brevetted Captain for gallantry at Contreras and Churubusco, and Major at Chapultepec, and was at Vera Cruz, Cerro Gordo, San Antonio, Molino del Rey, where he was twice wounded, and at the capture of the City of Mexico. He was then on frontier duty till the Civil War, with the exception of service in 1856–7 and 1858–60 on a Board to revise the system of Light Artillery tactics. He had become Major of the 5th Artillery May 14, 1861, and commanded the Artillery on the extreme left in the Battle of Bull Run. He was Chief of Artillery in the defence of Washington from July to September, 1861, and on September 28 became aide to General McClellan with the rank of Colonel, and organized the Artillery Reserve of the Army of the Potomac, commanding it in the Peninsula Campaign of 1862,

In September, 1862, he was made Brigadier-General of Volunteers, and became Chief of Artillery of the Army of the Potomac, holding the office till the close of the war, and taking an active part in all the battles that were fought by that army. He was brevetted Colonel July 3, 1863, for Gettysburg, Major-General of Volunteers July 6, 1864, for "faithful and highly meritorious services," Brigadier-General in the Regular Army for services in the campaign ending with Lee's surrender, and Major-General United States Army, March 13, 1865, for services during the war. He was President of the Permanent Artillery Board in 1866, and then commanded various forts, being promoted to Colonel of the 5th Artillery April 4, 1869. He was retired from active service September 14, 1883, and became Governor of the Soldier's Home, Washington, D. C.

INGALLS, RUFUS, Major-General, born in Demark, Me., August 20, 1820, graduated at West Point in 1843, served in the 1st Dragoons, was in the battles of Embudo and Taos, New Mexico, in 1847, and became Assistant Quartermaster January 12, 1848, with rank of Captain. He was appointed Lieutenant-Colonel and Aide-de-camp to General McClellan September 26, 1861, and was Chief Quartermaster in the Army of the Potomac from 1862 to 1865. He was promoted Brigadier-General May 23, 1863, and was present in the battles of South Mountain, Antietam, Fredericksburg, Chancellorsville, Gettysburg and the subsequent actions till the surrender of Lee. He was brevetted Brigadier-General in the Regular Army in 1864, and Major-General for meritorious services during the war, March 13, 1865, was stationed in New York as Chief Quartermaster from 1867 till 1876, and again in 1881, and on March 14, 1882, became Quartermaster-General of the Army. He was retired at his own request after forty years' service, July 1, 1883.

KANE, THOMAS LEIPER, Brigadier-General, born in Philadelphia, Pa., January 27, 1822; educated in Paris, studied law, and was admitted to the bar in Philadelphia in 1846. In April, 1861, he organized, in Northwestern Pennsylvania, a Regiment of hunters and loggers known as the "Bucktails," which became famous for valor and endurance. He was wounded at Dranesville, where he led the advance. On September 7, 1862 he was made a Brigadier-General for gallant services in the field. At the beginning of the Battle of Gettysburg he was absent on sick leave, yet he hastened to Washington for orders, took to General Meade the information that the National telegraphic cipher was known to the Confederates, joined his Brigade on the morning of the second day, and held an important position on the extreme right. He resigned on November 7, 1863, being disabled by wounds and exposure.

KILPATRICK, HUGH JUDSON, Major-General, was born near Deckerton, N. J., January 14, 1836; was graduated at West Point in 1861, appointed a Captain in Duryea's Zouaves, 5th New York Volunteers; was wounded at Big Bethel and disabled for several months. In August, 1861, he assisted in raising a Regiment of New York Cavalry, of which he was made Lieutenant-Colonel. In 1862 he was engaged in various skirmishes in Northern Virginia and the second Battle of Bull Run. He commanded a Brigade of Cavalry in the Rappahannock Campaign, being engaged in Stoneman's raid toward Richmond and at Beverly Ford. He was promoted Brigadier-General of Volunteers on June 13, 1863, and commanded a Cavalry Division in the Battle of Aldie, and was brevetted for bravery there. He took part in the Battle of Gettysburg, earning there the brevet of Lieutenant-Colonel in the United States Army, and in the subsequent pursuit of the Confederates was engaged in constant fighting at Smithburg, Hagerstown, Boonsboro and Falling Waters. In the operations in Central Virginia, during the autumn of 1863, he commanded a Cavalry Division, which he led with credit in many actions. In March, 1864, he commanded in a raid toward Richmond and through the Virginia Peninsula, in which he destroyed much property and had many severe fights. He took part, in 1864, in the raid into Georgia as Commander of a Cavalry Division of the Army of the Cumberland, rendering very important service to the Union cause, and being severely wounded at Resaca. In the March to the Sea and through the Carolinas he participated in many skirmishes and engagements with signal success. He was brevetted Colonel for bravery at Resaca, Brigadier-General for the capture of Fayetteville, N. C., and Major-General for services throughout the Carolina Campaign. He was promoted Major-General of Volunteers on June 18, 1865. He was conspicuous for inspiring confidence in the soldiers under his command, and gained a high reputation as a daring, brilliant and successful Cavalry leader. In 1865 he was appointed Minister to Chili by President Johnson, and was recalled in 1868. In 1880 he was an unsuccessful Republican candidate for Congress in New Jersey. In March, 1881, President Garfield appointed him again Minister to Chili, and he died at Valparaiso, December 4, 1881.

LOCKWOOD, HENRY HAYES, Brigadier-General, born in Kent County, Del., August 17, 1814, was graduated at West Point in 1836, assigned to the 2d Artillery, and after service in Florida resigned September 12, 1837, and engaged in farming in Delaware until 1841. He was then appointed Professor of Mathematics in the United States Navy and ordered to the frigate United States, on which he participated in the capture of Monterey, Cal., in October, 1842. After his return he was ordered to the Naval School at Annapolis as Professor of Natural and Experimental Philosophy. In 1851 he was transferred to the chair of Field Artillery and Infantry Tactics, serving also as Professor of Astronomy and Gunnery till 1866. During the Civil War he served as Colonel of the 1st Delaware Regiment, and was made Brigadier-General of Volunteers on August 8, 1861. He commanded an expedition to the eastern shore of Virginia, then had charge of Point Lookout and the defence of the lower Potomac, commanded a Brigade at Gettysburg, and from December, 1863, till 1864, was at the head of the Middle Department, with headquarters at Baltimore. He then participated in the Richmond campaign in May and June, 1864, and commanded provisional troops against General Jubal A. Early in July, 1864. From that date until August, 1865, he commanded a Brigade in Baltimore. He was mustered out of service on August 25, 1865, and returned to the Naval School in Annapolis. He was retired on August 4, 1876.

McGILVERY, FREEMAN, Colonel, born in Prospect, Me., in 1823, became a sailor and master of a vessel in the South American trade. He raised a Battery in Maine which first came into action at Cedar Mountain, August 9, 1862, where he helped to save the left flank of the Union Army. He was engaged at Sulphur Springs, the second Battle of Bull Run, Chantilly and Antietam. Having been promoted Major February 5, 1863 he was given command of the 1st Volunteer Artillery Reserve, Army of the Potomac. He became Lieutenant-Colonel June 23, 1863. By the rapid and destructive fire of his guns at Gettysburg he repelled their infantry charges on General Sickles' position and saved the Union line. He was promoted Colonel, and in June, 1864, commanded the Reserve Artillery before Petersburg. He was made Chief of Artillery of the Tenth Corps, and was shot in the hand at Deep Bottom. An amputation became necessary, and while undergoing it September 2, 1864, he died from the effects of chloroform.

MEREDITH, SOLOMON, Major-General, born in Guilford County, N. C., in 1810. He removed to Wayne County, Ind., in 1829, and gained an education by manual labor; was twice elected Sheriff and four times Member of the Legislature. In 1861 he was Colonel of the 19th Indiana Volunteers, which lost half its effective force at Gainesville, where he was wounded. He was promoted Brigadier-General in October, 1862, and led what was known as the "Iron Brigade," receiving special thanks in general orders for a gallant crossing of the Rappahannock in April, 1863. He took part in the Battle of Chancellorsville, and opened the Battle of Gettysburg, where he was very severely wounded. He was brevetted Major-General in 1865. In 1867-69 he was Surveyor-General of Montana, and then retired to his farm near Cambridge City, Indiana. He was six feet six inches in height, of commanding presence and an effective speaker. His three sons were all in the Union Army, and two lost their lives in the service.

MERRITT, WESLEY, Major-General, born in New York City, June 16, 1836, was graduated at West Point in 1860, assigned to the Dragoon service, became First Lieutenant May 13, 1861, and Captain April 5, 1862. He took part in Stoneman's raid toward Richmond April and May, 1863, was commissioned Brigadier-General of Volunteers in June and commanded the reserve Cavalry Brigade in the Pennsylvania Campaign. He was brevetted Major for gallant service at Gettysburg. His Brigade was engaged in the various actions in Central Virginia in 1863-64, and he received the brevets of Lieutenant-Colonel and Colonel in the Regular Army and Major-General of Volunteers for gallantry in the battles of Yellow Tavern, Hawe's Shop and Winchester, and on March 13, 1865, he was brevetted Brigadier and Major-General in the Regular Army for bravery at Five Forks, and commissioned Major-General of Volunteers April 1, 1865. After a long tour of frontier duty he was in 1882 placed in command at West Point, which post he held till June, 1887, when he was sent to command at Fort Leavenworth as Brigadier-General.

NEILL, THOMAS H., Brigadier-General, born in Pennsylvania in 1825, graduated at West Point and was assigned to the Infantry in July, 1847. He served mainly on frontier duty and at West Point until 1861, when he organized the 23d Pennsylvania Volunteers, and served as its Commander through the Peninsula Campaign in 1862. Appointed Brigadier-General in November, he commanded a Brigade of the Sixth Corps at the Battle of Fredericksburg, December, 1862; Marye Heights, May, 1863; Gettysburg, July, 1863, and was in command of a Division during the campaign of '64 around Richmond and Petersburg. He was engaged at Winchester, October 19, 1864, and at the close of the war was brevetted Major-General for gallantry. In 1870 he was transferred to the 6th Cavalry as Lieutenant-Colonel, and after a campaign in the Indian Country was in 1875 assigned to West Point as its Commandant. He was subsequently retired with the full rank of Colonel, and resides in Philadelphia.

NEWTON, JOHN, Major-General, born in Virginia in 1823, graduated at West Point, and was appointed Lieutenant of Engineers in July, 1842, and then became Assistant to the Board of Engineers up to the end of 1843. He was then transferred to West Point as Chief Instructor in his branch of the service, remaining there three years; subsequently, and up to the breaking out of the Civil War, in 1861, with the exception of his acting as Chief Engineer of the Utah Expedition in 1858, he was engaged in the construction of sea coast fortifications. In August, 1861, he was appointed Brigadier-General of Volunteers, and given the construction of the defences of Washington till 1862. With the Army of the Potomac he participated in its movements, commanding a Division at Fredericksburg in December, 1862;

was promoted Major-General in March, 1863. He commanded the Third Division, Sixth Corps, at Marye's Heights, and the First Corps at Gettysburg on July 2, 1863, which position he held until the reorganization of the army in March, 1864, when he was transferred to the West, leading a Division in the campaign around Atlanta. At the close of the war he resumed duty with the Engineer Corps, in which he had risen to the full rank of Lieutenant-Colonel. Since then he has performed several important Engineering duties, and is now Commissioner of Public Works for the City of New York.

OSBORN, THOMAS W., Major, was born in Scotch Plains, N. J., March 9, 1836, graduated at Madison University, N. Y., in 1860, studied law at Watertown, N. Y., was admitted to the bar in 1861, and at once entered the Union Army as Captain in the 1st New York Artillery, and served as Chief of Artillery of various Army Corps and of the Army of the Tennessee. He was three times wounded in battle. In the Battle of Gettysburg he was serving under General Howard in the Eleventh Corps. After the war he resided in Florida, serving in the State Constitutional Convention and State Senate, and in the United States Senate from June 30, 1868, till March 3, 1873.

PATRICK, MARSENA R., Brigadier General, born at Houndsfield, N. Y., March 15, 1811, was graduated at West Point in 1835, brevetted Major for meritorious conduct in the Mexican War, resigned in 1850, engaged in farming in Jefferson County, N. Y., and in 1859 was appointed President of the New York State Agricultural College. In 1861 he was made Inspector-General of New York Militia, and Brigadier-General of Volunteers in March, 1862, served with General McDowell in the Shenandoah Valley and Northern Virginia, and with the Army of the Potomac at South Mountain and Antietam. Later he was Provost Marshal-General of the Armies operating against General Lee. He resigned in June, 1865. Since 1880 he has been Governor of the Central Branch of the National Home for Disabled Soldiers in Ohio.

PAUL, GABRIEL R., Brigadier-General, born in Missouri, April, 1813; graduated from West Point and became Second Lieutenant of Infantry, July, 1834. He served with his company in the Florida War, was wounded in the Mexican War at Cerro Gordo and was made Brevet-Major for Chapultepec. In 1861 he was Major of the 8th Infantry stationed in New Mexico; in December of that year he was appointed Colonel of the 4th New Mexico Volunteers, and in September, 1862, was assigned to the Army of the Potomac as Brigadier-General of Volunteers. He participated in the Battles of Fredericksburg, Chancellorsville and Gettysburg, completely losing his sight in the latter engagement from a severe bullet wound. He was retired in 1865 as Colonel of the 14th Infantry, but in 1866 Congress granted him the full pay and allowances of a Brigadier-General. He subsequently served as Deputy-Governor of the Soldiers' Home at Washington, D. C., and as Manager of the Military Asylum at Harrodsburg, Ky.

PLEASONTON ALFRED, Major-General, born in the District of Columbia, in December, 1823, he graduated from the United States Military Academy, and was appointed to the 1st Dragoons in July, 1844. He took part in the Mexican War, and served subsequently on the frontier and in the Adjutant General's office. He marched his regiment from Utah to Washington in September and October, 1861, and as Major of the 2d Cavalry took part in the defence of the Capital until March, 1862. He next served the Army of the Potomac on the Peninsula of Virginia; was made Brigadier, and in September commanded the Cavalry Division following Lee's Army in the invasion of Maryland; engaged at Boonsboro, South Mountain, Antietam and subsequent pursuit. He constantly engaged the Confederate Cavalry at Fredericksburg and at Chancellorsville by his brilliant action. He stayed the further advance of Jackson's Corps, which threatened to sweep all before it. Promoted Major-General in June, 1863, he was in the many actions that preceded Gettysburg, where he also commanded in chief the Cavalry. Transferred in 1864 to Missouri, he drove Price's invading forces from the State. After the war he was United States Commissioner of Internal Revenue, and later President of Terre Haute and Cincinnati Railroad Company.

REYNOLDS, JOHN F., Major-General, born in Pennsylvania in 1820, graduated at West Point in 1841, assigned to artillery, served in the Mexican War, winning brevets of Captain and Major, and was employed in garrison and frontier duty till 1860, when he commanded at West Point. In August, 1861, he was made Brigadier-General. He commanded a Brigade of Pennsylvania Reserves in the Virginia Peninsula Campaign of 1862, in the actions at Mechanicsville, Gaines' Mill and at Glendale, where he was taken prisoner. He commanded a Division in the second Battle of Bull Run. In the Maryland Campaign of 1862 he was selected to command the Pennsylvania Militia for defence of the State, for which he received, through the Governor, the thanks of the State. He was promoted Major-General of Volunteers in November, 1862, commanded the First Corps of the Army of the Potomac, and took part in the Battle of Fredericksburg, December 13, 1862. At Chancellorsville his Corps was held in reserve and not allowed to join in the contest. After having made the disposition of his troops in person for the opening of the fight at Gettysburg, July 1, 1863, having urged his men with animating words, he saw the successful charge under way, when he was struck with a rifle shot that caused almost instant death.

RICE, JAMES CLAY, Brigadier-General, born at Worthington, Mass., December 27, 1829, graduated at Yale College; taught school; edited a paper and studied law at Natchez, Miss., 1855-56; settled in New York City in 1856; enlisted in a New York regiment as a private in 1861, was rapidly promoted for gallantry and intelligence in many battles in Virginia; became Colonel of the 44th New York Volunteers; commanded a Brigade at Gettysburg and was made Brigadier-General August 17, 1863. He died from wounds received at the Battle of Spottsylvania Court House, Va., May 11, 1864.

ROBINSON, JOHN C., Brigadier-General, born in Binghamton, N. Y., April 10, 1817, entered West Point in 1835, but left in 1838 to study law. In 1839 he was appointed Lieutenant in the 5th Infantry; served in the Mexican and Seminole Wars. In September, 1861, he was made Colonel of a Michigan regiment and in 1862 Brigadier-General of Volunteers. He commanded a Brigade with the Army of the Potomac in the Virginia Peninsula Campaign of 1862, at the second battle of Bull Run, Chantilly and Fredericksburg. At Gettysburg and in the Richmond Campaign he commanded a Division with great bravery, losing a leg on the third day of fighting in the latter campaign at Tod's Tavern. He was brevetted Brigadier and Major-General for gallantry. In 1866 he was made Colonel of the 43d Infantry, and in 1869 was retired with the rank of Major-General. He was elected Lieutenant-Governor of the State of New York in 1872, and has filled the position of Commander-in-Chief of the Grand Army of the Republic.

RUGER, THOMAS H., Major-General, born in New York in 1823, graduated at West Point in 1854, assigned to the Engineer Corps, resigned in 1855, practiced law at Janesville, Wis., was appointed Brigadier-General in November, 1862, commanded a Division in the Battle of Franklin, won the brevet of Major-General, commanded the Department of North Carolina until June, 1866, was Colonel of the 33d Infantry, transferred to the 18th Infantry in 1869, and became Brigadier-General in the Regular Army March 19, 1886. He was Superintendent at West Point from 1871 to 1876. In the Battle of Gettysburg he commanded the First Divison in the Twelfth Corps.

RUSSELL, DANIEL ALLEN, Major-General, born at Salem, N. Y., December 10, 1820, graduated at West Point in 1845, served in Infantry through the Mexican War, brevetted First Lieutenant for gallantry, on frontier duty till the opening of the Rebellion. Appointed Colonel of the 7th Massachusetts Volunteers in January, 1862, he led it through the Virginia Peninsula Campaign of that year, was brevetted for services at Antietam, appointed Brigadier November, 1862; he commanded a Brigade of the Sixth

Corps at Fredericksburg, Chancellorsville, Gettysburg and minor actions of that Corps. In the Richmond Campaign of 1864 he was given command of a Division in the 6th Corps, and had a share in all the fighting from the Wilderness to Petersburg, winning brevets for meritorious service from Colonel to Major-General. He was killed at the Battle of Opequan, September 19, 1864.

SCHIMMELFENNING, ALEXANDER, born in Germany in 1824, was an officer under Kossuth in the Hungarian Insurrection, after which he came to this country, published in 1854 "The War Between Russia and Turkey," became in 1861 Colonel of a Pennsylvania regiment, served under Sigel and Pope in Virginia, was appointed Brigadier-General November 29, 1862, and commanded a Brigade of the 11th Corps at Chancellorsville and Gettysburg. He died at Minersville, Pa., September 7, 1865.

SCHURZ, CARL, Major-General, born near Cologne, Prussia, March 2, 1829, educated at Bonn, was engaged on a liberal newspaper after the revolutionary outbreak in 1848, and in an attempt at revolution in Bonn in 1849; fought in the defence of Rastadt; went to Paris in 1851, taught and corresponded with liberal German newspapers; came to Philadelphia in 1852; settled at Madison, Wis., in 1855; was prominent in the Republican party and ran for Lieutenant-Governor in 1857; made his first speech in English in Illinois during the Senatorial contest between Lincoln and Douglas in 1858; lectured in New England in the winter of 1859-60, spoke in the election contest of 1860 for Lincoln; was appointed Minister to Spain March, 1861, and resigned in December. He was made Brigadier in April, 1862, and Major-General in March, 1863, commanded a Division in the second Battle of Bull Run and at Chancellorsville. He was temporarily in command of the Eleventh Corps at Gettysburg, took part in the Battle of Chattanooga; visited the Southern States as Special Commissioner by appointment of President Johnson in 1866, and the same year founded the *Post* newspaper at Detroit. He was subsequently Editor of the *Westliche Post* in St. Louis; was United States Senator from Missouri, 1869-75, won a high reputation for speeches on finance; antagonized General Grant's Administration; supported Horace Greeley for President in 1872; became a resident of New York in 1875; advocated the election of Hayes as President, and was by him made Secretary of the Interior, March 7, 1877. He has since 1881 resided in New York, being part of the time employed in literary and journalistic work.

SEDGWICK, JOHN, Major-General, born at Cornwall, Ct., September 13, 1813, graduated at West Point in 1837, assigned to Artillery, won brevets of Captain and Major for gallantry in the Mexican War, made Major of 2d Cavalry in 1855, and Colonel of the 4th Cavalry in August, 1861. In the Virginia Peninsula Campaign of 1862 he commanded a Division in Sumner's Corps; in the Battle of Fair Oaks, May 31, after a tedious march, he arrived in time to save the day for the Unionists; was wounded at Glendale; appointed Major-General he commanded a Division at Antietam, where he was severely wounded three times. Transferred to the command of the 6th Corps, February, 1863, he was ordered by Hooker to carry the Heights of Fredericksburg and join the main Army at Chancellorsville. He carried the works successfully, May 3, after a stubborn fight in which he lost nearly 5,000 men, but his column was checked at Salem Heights about four P. M. by the force which Lee sent against him after his repulse of Hooker. In the Pennsylvania Campaign of 1863 the 6th Corps encamped June 30 at Manchester, thirty-five miles from Gettysburg. This distance Sedgwick covered in thirty hours, reaching the field at two P. M., July 2, and at once joined in the fight, as he also did on the 3d and the pursuit of Lee, July 5. He was conspicuous in subsequent engagements, especially at the Wilderness and at Spottsylvania where, while placing his artillery in an advanced position early in the day, he was killed by a sharpshooter's bullet. He was greatly beloved by the whole Army. A monument wrought of cannon captured by the 6th Corps was erected to his memory at West Point in 1868.

SHALER, ALEX., Major-General, born in Haddam, Ct., March 9, 1827, joined the New York State Militia as a private in 1845, rose rapidly, and in 1867 was Major-General of the 1st Division National Guard. At the outbreak of the Rebellion he was Major in the New York 7th Regiment; in June, 1861, he was appointed Lieutenant-Colonel of the 65th New York Volunteers, became its Colonel July, 1862, serving with the Army of the Potomac in its many engagements. He commanded a Brigade, Sixth Corps, from March to November, 1863, and the Military Prison, Johnson's Island, Ohio, during the winter of 1863–64. Returning to the front he was taken prisoner May 6, 1864, and held three months in Charleston. After his exchange he served in the Southwest till the end of the war, and was brevetted Major-General for gallantry. He was subsequently President of the New York Fire Department and of the Board of Health.

SICKLES, DANIEL E., Major-General, born in New York, October 20, 1822, was educated at the University of New York, studied law, and was admitted to the bar in 1843. He was prominent in Democratic politics, and elected to the State Legislature in 1847. In 1853 he was appointed Corporation Attorney of New York City, and in the same year went with Minister Buchanan to England as Secretary of Legation. He was elected State Senator in 1855, and in 1856 a Member of Congress, and re-elected in 1858 and 1860. At the commencement of the civil war General D. E. Sickles did not relish the idea of taking a second place, so he raised the Excelsior Brigade, and started with it as its commander, during September, 1861, was appointed Brigadier-General. His Brigade was attached to General Hooker's Division of the 3d Corps, to the command of which he succeeded as Major-General of Volunteers in April, 1863, and was engaged with credit at Chancellorsville May 3-4. At Gettysburg he lost a leg early in the second day's fight. In 1866-67 he commanded the Military District of North and South Carolina, and was retired in April, 1869, with the rank of Major-General in the Regular Army. In the latter year he was appointed United States Minister to Spain, which position he resigned in 1874. He received the brevets of Brigadier and Major-General United States Army for gallantry.

SLOCUM, HENRY WARNER, Major-General, born at Pompey, N. Y., September 24, 1827, graduated at West Point in 1852; served in the Artillery till November, 1856, when he resigned and was a lawyer at Syracuse and a member of the Legislature in 1859. He was appointed Colonel 27th New York Volunteers and led it at Bull Run July 21, 1861, being severely wounded. He was promoted a Brigadier in Franklin's Division, Army of the Potomac, and in 1862 was at the siege of Yorktown and the action of West Point, and took command of the Division May 15. His command rendered important service at Gaines' Mill; it held the right of the main line at Glendale, June 30, and the same position at Malvern Hill July 1. Appointed Major-General, he took part in the second battle of Bull Run, of South Mountain and of Antietam. In October, 1862, he took command of the Twelfth Corps, which he led at Chancellorsville and at Gettysburg, where he had command of the right of the Army. He was sent with his Corps to the West and commanded at Vicksburg. In August, 1864, he succeeded General Hooker in command of the Twentieth Corps, which was the first to occupy Atlanta, Ga., September 2. During Sherman's "March to the Sea" and invasion of the Carolinas he commanded the left wing, participating in all the operations till the surrender of Johnston's army. He was subsequently a resident of Brooklyn, N. Y., engaged in various enterprises, and was a member of the Forty-first and Forty-second Congresses.

STANNARD, GEORGE J., Brigadier-General, born in Georgia, Vt., October 20, 1820, educated in common schools, became clerk and afterwards manager of a foundry at St. Albans; in 1860 he was Colonel of Vermont Militia; assisted to raise the 2d Vermont Volunteers, was made Lieutenant-Colonel, and went to the front in May, 1861; in May, 1862, was appointed Colonel 9th Vermont Volunteers, serving in Pope's Command, promoted Brigadier March 18, 1863. His Brigade was conspicuous at Gettysburg in the repulse of the final charge; wounded severely in the cannonade with which Longstreet strove to cover Lee's retreat. Engaged again at Cold Harbor he was again wounded. In the movement of the Eighteenth Corps on Petersburg, June 14, he led the advance with his Brigade, and was the third time wounded. On September 19, in the storming of Fort Harrison, which he captured and held, he lost his right arm. He retired from the Army in 1876, and was appointed Collector of Customs Third District of Vermont. In 1881 he became Doorkeeper of the House of Representatives, and held the position till his death at Washington, D. C., May 31, 1886.

VON STEINWEHR ADOLPH, WILLIAM FREDERICK, Baron, Brigadier-General, born at Blankenburg, Germany, September 25, 1822, educated in the Brunswick Military Academy, became a Lieutenant in 1841, resigned in 1847 and came to the United States, applied for a commission in the war against Mexico and went back to Germany. In 1854 he settled at Wallingford, Ct., as a farmer. He raised the 29th New York Volunteers in 1861, commanded it in the Battle of Bull Run, was made Brigadier in October, 1861, was Commander of the Second Division Eleventh Corps in the campaign on the Rapidan and Rappahannock, and took part in the battles of Chancellorsville and Gettysburg. He died at Buffalo, N. Y., February 25, 1877.

SYKES, GEORGE, Major-General, born at Dover, Del., October 9, 1822, graduated at West Point in 1842, served in the Infantry with credit in the Mexican War, was brevetted Captain for gallantry at Cerro Gordo, was on frontier duty till 1861, when he was appointed Major in the 14th Infantry, and at the Battle of Bull Run commanded a Brigade of Regulars. He commanded the division of regulars in Porter's Corps which so stubbornly held its position on the right in the Battle of Gaines' Mill. He continued to command this division in the second Battle of Bull Run, Antietam, Fredericksburg and Chancellorsville. When General Meade became Chief of the Army of the Potomac General Sykes succeeded him in the command of the Fifth Corps, which a week later was engaged at Gettysburg, and he retained this command till April, 1864. He was brevetted Colonel, Brigadier and Major-General for gallant service. He became Colonel of the 20th Infantry in January, 1868, and died February 8, 1880.

TORBERT ALFRED T. A., Major-General, born in Delaware in 1833, was graduated at West Point in 1855, served on the frontier, and became Captain 5th Infantry September 21, 1861. He commanded the 1st New Jersey Regiment in the Virginia Peninsula Campaign of 1862, being engaged in most of the battles. Was assigned a Brigade of the Sixth Corps, being present at the second battle of Bull Run, South Mountain (where he was wounded) and Antietam. He led his Brigade in the Gettysburg battles and in the subsequent operations of the Sixth Corps during the winter of 1863–64. In the Richmond Campaign of 1864 he commanded the Cavalry, remaining with General Grant during Sheridan's raid on the Confederate Capital, an of the 1st Division till August; engaged in frequent important actions, including the battles of Hawes' Shop and Cold Harbor. Made Chief of Cavalry of the Middle Military Division, he was in all the movements and actions of the Shenandoah Campaign, and frequently in command. He was in command of the Army of the Shenandoah from April to July, 1865. He won brevets for gallantry from Major to Major-General. Resigning his Captaincy of 5th Infantry October 31, 1866, he was appointed Consul-General at Havana in 1871 and Consul-General at Paris in 1874.

TYLER, ROBERT OGDEN, Major-General, born in Greene County, N. Y., December 22, 1831, graduated at West Point in 1853; served on the Pacific coast in Artillery, appointed Colonel 4th Connecticut Volunteers Heavy Artillery September, 1861; commanded siege batteries before Yorktown, in battles of Hanover Court House, Gaines' Mill and Malvern Hill, promoted Brigadier November 29, 1862, engaged at Battle of Fredericksburg December 13, commanding artillery of Sumner's grand Division; the Artillery Reserve of the Army of the Potomac at Chancellorsville, Gettysburg and subsequent operations till January, 1864. He commanded a Division Twenty-second Army Corps covering Washington, January, 1864, a Division of Heavy Artillery Second Corps in the Richmond campaign of 1864 from the Wilderness battles to Cold Harbor, where he was severely wounded and disabled for further duty in the field. He was employed after the war in Quartermasters' duties, becoming Deputy Quartermaster-General July, 1866. He was brevetted for gallantry from Major to Major-General. He died at Boston, December 1, 1874.

WADSWORTH, JAMES S., Major-General, born at Geneseo, N. Y., October 30, 1807, educated at Hamilton College and Harvard University, studied law at Yale and in the office of Daniel Webster, was admitted to the bar and devoted himself to the management of his large landed estate on the Genesee River. When railway communication with Washington was interrupted on the outbreak of hostility in 1861 he provisioned two vessels at New York, and went with them to Annapolis, where he superintended the delivery of the supplies to the Union troops. At the Battle of Bull Run he served with conspicuous efficiency and bravery as Volunteer Aide-de-Camp to General McDowell. He was commissioned a Brigadier-General, commanded in front of Washington, and was Military Governor of the Federal City. He was engaged in the Battle of Fredericksburg. At Gettysburg his Division was the first to engage the Confederates, July 1, 1863, and during that day it lost 2,400 out of its 4,000 men. On the second and third days he rendered conspicuous service, as he also did in the succeding operations of that Campaign. In Grant's Richmond Campaign of 1864

General Wadsworth commanded the 4th Division of the Fifth Corps, crossing the Rapidan May 5, and joinging in the action of that day with severe loss. Next morning his command engaged with the Second Corps, and the enemy were repulsed, but being reinforced at noon they took up the offensive, and Wadsworth, while heroically endeavoring to prevent his men from falling back when fiercely pressed by superior force, was struck in the head by a bullet, and without regaining consciousness he died on Sunday, May 8, 1864.

WARREN, GOUVERNEUR KEMBLE, Major-General, born at Cold Spring, N. Y., January 8, 1830, graduated at West Point in 1850, and assigned to Topographical Engineers. As Lieutenant-Colonel of the 5th New York Volunteer Zouaves he was engaged at Big Bethel, June 10, 1861, and became Colonel in August. In the Virginia Peninsula Campaign of 1862 he commanded a Brigade in Sykes' Division of Porter's Corps, was wounded at Gaines' Mill and brevetted Lieutenant-Colonel. His command was hotly engaged at Manassas, August 30, and at Antietam. He became a Brigadier September 26, 1862, and led a Brigade of the Fifth Corps in the Battle of Fredericksburg. In the Battle of Gettysburg as Chief Engineer of the Army of the Potomac he won the brevet of Colonel United States Army, for gallant and meritorious services, was made Major-General of Volunteers to date from Chancellorsville, and given on August 12 temporary command of the Second Corps, which at Briscoe Station, October 14, gained a brilliant success, for which he was brevetted Brigadier-General, United States Army. In 1864 he was given by the President command of the combined First and Fifth Corps, which he held till April, 1865, when he was placed in command of Petersburg. He received the brevet of Major-General, United States Army, for merit and gallantry during the war, after which he was engaged in the Engineer Corps on various harbor and fortification works, and resigned as Lieutenant-Colonel of Engineers March 4, 1879.

WEBB, ALEXANDER S., Brigadier-General, born in New York City, February 15, 1835, graduated at West Point in 1855, served in the Artillery on frontier duty; was Instructor in Mathematics at West Point, 1857-61. He served in the defence of Fort Pickens and in the first Battle of Bull Run; was made Major of Artillery serving in defence of Washington, and was with the Army of the Potomac in the Virginia Peninsula Campaign, April to August, 1862; was Chief of Staff, Fifth Corps, till November, when he was assigned to duty at Washington as Inspector of Artillery at Camp Barry. He was made Brigadier-General June 23, 1863, and assigned to the Second Corps. At Gettysburg General Webb's Brigade met the assault of the third day, where he displayed conspicuous bravery, was wounded and brevetted. He won another brevet for gallantry at Briscoe Station October 11, 1863. In the Richmond Campaign of 1864 he led a Brigade in the battles of the Wilderness and Spottsylvania, in which latter action, May 12, he was severely wounded. He served as Chief of Staff to General Meade, commanding the Army of the Potomac from January, 1865, till the surrender at Appomattox. He was appointed Lieutenant-Colonel 44th Infantry in 1866, and served at West Point until 1868. In 1871 he accepted the Presidency of the College of the City of New York. His highest brevet was that of Major-General, United States Army, for gallant and meritorious services during the Rebellion.

WEED, STEPHEN H., Brigadier-General, born in New York in 1834, graduated at West Point in 1854; served in artillery on frontier duty; appointed Captain 5th Artillery in 1861 on recruiting service; joined the Army of the Potomac and commanded his battery in the Peninsula Campaign of 1862; displayed great bravery and ability at Manassas, Antietam and Chancellorsville. After this latter action he was placed in command of the Artillery Brigade of the Fifth Corps, and in the terrible struggle for the possession of Little Round Top, July 2, 1863, he was instantly killed at the head of his command.

WHEATON, FRANK, Major-General, born in Providence, R. I., May 8, 1833, educated as Civil Engineer at Brown University; employed in the Mexican Boundary Survey 1850-55; appointed First Lieutenant 1st Cavalry, May 3, 1855; served on the frontier; appointed Lieutenant-Colonel 2d Rhode Island Volunteers, was engaged in the Battle of Bull Run, July 21, 1861, succeeding to the command on the fall of Colonel Slocum; led the regiment through the Peninsula Campaign at the second Battle of Bull Run, Chantilly, Antietam and Fredericksburg, and became Brigadier November 29, 1862. He commanded a Brigade Sixth Corps in the storming of Marye's Heights and Battle of Salem Heights, May 3-4, 1863; was in command of a Division at Gettysburg and of a Brigade in the Sixth Corps from the Wilderness Battle to the front of Petersburg; participated in the Shenandoah Campaign, and commanded a Division from September 20 to the close of the war. He won brevets from Lieutenant-Colonel to Major-General; was appointed Lieutenant-Colonel 39th Infantry and became Colonel 2d Infantry December 15, 1874.

WILLIAMS, ALPHEUS S., Major-General, was born at Saybrook, Ct., on September 20, 1810, graduated at Yale College in 1831, spent three years in European travel, after which he settled as a lawyer in Detroit, Mich., and secured an extensive practice. He was successively chosen Probate Judge, Alderman and Recorder, and subsequently became editor and proprietor of the Detroit *Daily Advertiser*. He served in the Mexican War as Lieutenant in a Michigan regiment, and on his return was appointed Postmaster of Detroit. In 1861 he went to the front as Brigadier-General of Volunteers. At the battles of South Mountain, Antietam and Gettysburg General Williams commanded the Twelfth Corps, and the Twentieth Corps during Sherman's "March to the Sea." He was known to his men by the affectionate title of "Pop" Williams. He received the brevet of Major-General. In 1866 President Johnson named him a Commissioner to Adjust the Military Claims of Missouri, and subsequent to that Minister Resident at the Republic of Salvador. He was elected to the Forty-fourth Congress, and re-elected to the Forty-fifth, serving on the Committee on Military Affairs and as Chairman of the Committee on the District of Columbia. He died from apoplexy at Washington, December 21, 1878.

WRIGHT, HORATIO GATES, Major-General, born at Clinton, Ct., March, 1820, graduated at West Point in 1841, assigned to Engineer duty, was an instructor in the Military Academy two years, engaged on defensive construction and harbor improvements and at Washington till the opening of the war. He was Chief Engineer of Heintzelman's Division in the first Battle of Bull Run; was made Brigadier-General September 14, 1861. In February, 1861, with a Brigade of Volunteers, he occupied the chief points in Florida, recapturing Fort Marion and Fort Clinch. He was promoted Major-General in July and commanded the Department of the Ohio. In May, 1863, he was assigned to command a Division of the Sixth Corps and engaged at Gettysburg on the second and third days of the battle and in the subsequent pursuit of Lee. In the spirited assault on Rappahannock Station he commanded the Corps and won a brevet. He led his Division in the severe fighting in May, 1864, in the Wilderness and at Spottsylvania, in which latter battle he succeeded to the command of the Corps after the death of Sedgwick, and he retained its command till its last battle and victory at Sailors' Creek, April 6, 1865. At Cedar Creek, October 19, 1864, he was in command of the Army of the Shenandoah, where after the surprise of the Eighth Corps he had reformed the line in a favorable position, when upon the arrival of Sheridan he resumed command of the Sixth Corps. His dispositions were approved and continued by Sheridan, and at the close of the day Early was hopelessly defeated and his army a wreck. At Petersburg his Corps was the first to pierce the Confederate lines and end the siege. He continued in the service after the war, and became Brigadier-General and Chief of Engineers, June 30, 1879.

ZOOK, SAMUEL K., Brigadier-General, born in Pennsylvania in 1823, became a practical telegrapher, and made important discoveries in the science of electricity; settled in New York City in 1848; went as a Lieutenant in the 6th New York Militia to Maryland in April, 1861; was Military Governor of Annapolis; raised and commanded the 57th New York Volunteers; commanded a Brigade on the Peninsula; was appointed Brigadier-General November 29, 1862; distinguished himself at Chancellorsville, and was killed during the first day's battle at Gettysburg.

MAJOR-GENERAL DANIEL BUTTERFIELD.
MAJOR-GENERAL RUFUS INGALLS.   MAJOR-GENERAL HENRY J. HUNT.

WARD, J. H. HOBART, Brigadier-General, born in the City of New York, June 17, 1823. At the age of eighteen he joined the 7th U. S. Infantry; after passing through the several grades was appointed Sergeant-Major in 1845. In the Mexican War participated in the Siege of Fort Brown, Monterey, Vera Cruz, Cerro Gordo and Huamantla. At the conclusion was appointed Assistant Commissary-General of New York, served five years, and promoted to be Commissary-General; retired by expiration of service. In the Civil War he recruited the 38th New York Volunteers, and was its first Colonel. Was engaged with his regiment at the first Bull Run, at all the battles of the Peninsula, including Yorktown, Williamsburg, Fair Oaks, Seven Pines, Glendale and Malvern Hill to James River, subsequently at second Bull Run, Groveton and Chantilly. October, 1862, promoted to be Brigadier-General. Commanded Second Brigade, First Division, Third Corps, at Fredericksburg, Chancellorsville, Auburn Mills and Gettysburg. Commanded First Division, Third Corps, on third day at Gettysburg, Kelly's Ford and Wapping Heights. Commanded Brigade at Mine Run, Locust Grove, Wilderness, up to and including Spottsylvania. Mustered out of service July 21, 1864. Wounded at Monterey, Mex., Gettysburg and Spottsylvania. For courage and capacity General Ward is frequently mentioned in the official reports of McClellan, Heintzleman, Kearny, Hooker, Sickles, Stoneman and French. He is now Clerk of the Superior Court in New York City.

MAURICE J. POWER,

No. 218 East 25th Street, New York City.   Office, 237 Broadway.

REAL · BRONZE · STATUARY ·

OF EVERY DESCRIPTION.

SOLDIERS' MONUMENTS IN GRANITE AND BRONZE.

Special Designs for Gettysburg Battlefield Free to Veteran Organizations.

This Establishment is recommended by the Gettysburg Monument Commission of the State of New York, of which General DANIEL E. SICKLES is President.

IX.

ORGANIZATION OF THE ARMY OF THE POTOMAC, WITH COMMANDING OFFICERS, DURING THE BATTLE OF GETTYSBURG.

MAJOR-GENERAL GEORGE GORDON MEADE COMMANDING THE ARMY.

Staff—Major-General Daniel Butterfield, Chief of Staff; Brigadier-General M. R. Patrick, Provost-Marshal-General; Brigadier-General Seth Williams, Adjutant-General; Brigadier-General Edward Schriver, Inspector-General; Brigadier-General Rufus Ingalls, Quartermaster-General; Colonel Henry F. Clarke, Chief Commissary of Subsistence; Major Jonathan Letterman, Surgeon-in-Chief of Medical Department; Brigadier-General G. K. Warren, Chief Engineer; Major D. W. Flagler, Chief Ordnance Officer; Major-General Alfred Pleasanton, Chief of Cavalry; Brigadier-General Henry J. Hunt, Chief of Artillery; Captain L. B. Norton, Chief Signal Officer.

SUBORDINATE SECTIONS.

Left Wing—The advance on July 1. Major-General John F. Reynolds (killed); Major-General O. O. Howard; Major-General W. S. Hancock.

Left Centre—July 2 and 3. Major-General W. S. Hancock (wounded on 3d).

Right Wing—July 2 and 3. Major-General Henry W. Slocum.

DETACHMENTS AT HEADQUARTERS.—*Command of the Provost Marshal.* 93d New York (not engaged), Colonel John S. Crocker; 8th United States (not engaged), Captain Edwin W. H. Read; 2d Pennsylvania Cavalry, Colonel R. Butler Price; E, 6th Pennsylvania Cavalry, Captain Emlen N. Carpenter; I, 6th Pennsylvania Cavalry, Captain James Starr; Detachment Regular Cavalry.

Engineer Brigade—Brigadier-General H. W. Benham. The 15th and 50th New York were ordered to Washington from Bear Dam Creek on July

1 and reached there on July 3. 15th New York (not engaged), Major Walter L. Cassin; 50th New York (not engaged), Colonel W. H. Pettes; Battalion United States (not engaged), Captain George H. Mendell.

Guards and Orderlies—Independent Company Oneida Cavalry, Captain D. P. Mann.

FIRST ARMY CORPS.

Major John F. Reynolds commanded left wing until killed July 1, leaving the Corps in command of Major-General Abner Doubleday on July 1, who in turn was succeeded by Major-General John Newton on the 2d and 3d. Headquarter Guard, L, 1st Maine Cavalry, Captain Constantine Tayler.

FIRST DIVISION—Brigadier James S. Wadsworth commanding.

First Brigade—Brigadier-General Solomon Meredith (wounded), Colonel Henry A. Morrow (wounded), Colonel W. W. Robinson. 19th Indiana, Colonel Samuel Williams; 24th Michigan, Colonel Henry A. Morrow (wounded), Lieutenant-Colonel Mark Flanigan (wounded), Major Edwin B. Wright (wounded), Captain Albert M. Edwards; 2d Wisconsin, Colonel Lucius Fairchild (wounded), Lieutenant-Colonel George H. Stevens (wounded), Major John Mansfield (wounded), Captain George H. Otis; 6th Wisconsin, Lieutenant-Colonel R. R. Dawes; 7th Wisconsin, Colonel W. W. Robinson, Major Mark Finnicum.

Second Brigade—Brigadier Lysander Cutter. 7th Indiana, Major Ira Grover; 76th New York, Major Andrew J. Glover (killed), Captain John E. Cook; 95th New York, Colonel George H. Biddle (wounded), Major Edward Pye; 147th New York, Lieutenant-Colonel F. C. Miller (wounded), Major George Harney; 14th New York State Militia, 84th New York Volunteers, Colonel E. B. Fowler; 56th Pennsylvania (9 companies), Colonel I. W. Hoffman.

SECOND DIVISION—Brigadier-General John C. Robinson.

First Brigade—Brigadier-General R. Paul (wounded), Colonel S. H. Leonard (wounded), Colonel Adrian R. Root (wounded), Colonel Richard Coulter (wounded), Colonel Richard Lyle, Colonel Richard Coulter. 16th Maine, Colonel Charles W. Tilden (captured), Lieutenant-Colonel N. E. Welch, Major Arch. D. Leavitt; 13th Massachusetts, Colonel S. H. Leonard (wounded), Lieutenant-Colonel N. Walter Balchelder; 94th New York, Colonel A. R. Root (wounded), Major S. H. Moffitt; 104th New York, Colonel Gilbert G. Prey; 107th Pennsylvania, Colonel T. F. McCoy (wounded), Lieutenant-Colonel James McThompson (wounded), Captain E. D. Roath 11th Pennsylvania (transferred to this Brigade from the second during the first day's fighting), Colonel Richard S. Coulter, Captain J. J. Bierer, Captain Benjamin F. Haines, Captain John B. Overmyer.

Second Brigade—Brigadier-General Henry Baxter. 12th Massachusetts, Colonel James L. Bates, Lieutenant-Colonel David Allen, Jr.; 9th New

York Militia (83d New York Volunteers), Lieutenant-Colonel Joseph R. Moesch ; 97th New York, Colonel Charles Wheelock, Major Charles Northrup ; 11th Pennsylvania (transferred to the Frst Brigade during the first day's fighting), Colonel Richard Coulter, Captain Benjamin F. Haines, Captain John B. Overmyer ; 88th Pennsylvania, Major Benezet F. Faust, Captain E. Y. Patterson, Captain Henry Whiteside ; 90th Pennsylvania, Colonel Peter Lyle, Major Alfred J. Sellers, Colonel Peter Lyle.

THIRD DIVISION—Major-General Abner Doubleday, who took command of the Corps during July 1 on the death of General Reynolds, resuming his position on the 2d and 3d. Brigadier-General Thomas A. Rowley commanded the Division during part of the first day's fighting.

First Brigade—Brigadier-General Thomas A. Rowley, July 2 and 3 ; Colonel Chapman Biddle, during part of July 1. 20th New York State Militia, Colonel Theodore B. Gates ; 121st Pennsylvania, Colonel Chapman Biddle, Major Alexander Biddle ; 142d Pennsylvania, Colonel Robert P. Cummings (killed), Lieutenant-Colonel A. B. McCalmont ; 151st Pennsylvania, Lieutenant-Colonel George F. McFarland (lost a leg), Captain Walter L. Owens, Colonel Harrison Allen.

Second Brigade—Colonel Rey Stone (wounded), Colonel Langhorne Wester (wounded), Colonel Edmund L. Dana. 143d Pennsylvania, Colonel Edmund L. Dana, Major John D. Musser ; 149th Pennsylvania, Lieutenant-Colonel Walton Dwight (wounded), Captain A. J. Sofield (killed), Captain John Irvin, Captain James Glenn ; 150th Pennsylvania, Colonel Langhorne Wister (wounded), Lieutenant-Colonel H. S. Hinedekoper (wounded), Major Thomas Chamberlain (wounded), Captain C. C. Widdis (wounded), Captain George W. Jones.

Third Brigade—Brigadier-General Stannard (wounded), Colonel Francis C. Randall. 12th Vermont, (not engaged), Colonel Asa P. Blunt ; 13th Vermont, Colonel Francis V. Randall ; Major Joseph J. Boynton ; Lieutenant-Colonel Wm. D. Munson ; 14th Vermont, Colonel William T. Nichols ; 15th Vermont (not engaged), Colonel Redfield Proctor ; 16th Vermont, Colonel Wheelock G. Veazey.

Artillery Brigade—Colonel Charles S. Wainwright. 2d Maine, Captain James A. Hall ; 5th Maine, Captain G. T. Stevens, Lieutenant Edward N. Whittier ; L, 1st New York, with E, 1st New York Heavy Artillery attached, Captain Gilbert H. Reynolds, Lieutenant George Breck ; B, 1st Pennsylvania, Captain J. H. Cooper ; B, 4th United States, Lieutenant James Stewart. Tidball's Battery, 2d United States, under Lieutenant John H. Calef also fought with the First Corps ; at times during the action, Lieutenant James Davis commanded detached section of Stewart's Battery, as did Lieutenants Benjamin W. Wilber and George Breck of Reynold's Battery.

SECOND ARMY CORPS.

Major-General Winfield S. Hancock took command of all the troops on the field immediately on his arrival, July 1, relieving Major-General O. O. Howard. Major-General John Gibbon of the Second Division assumed command of the Corps until the return of General Hancock. During the battle of the second day when General Hancock assumed command of the left centre General Gibbon again took command of the corps; when he was wounded Brigadier-General John C. Caludwell succeeded him.

Headquarters Guard—D & K, 6th New York Cavalry, Captain Riley Johnson.

FIRST DIVISION—Brigadier-General John C. Cauldwell, Colonel John R. Brooke (wounded).

First Brigade—Colonel Edward E. Cross (killed), Colonel H. B. McKeen. 5th New Hampshire, Colonel E. E. Cross, Lieutenant-Colonel C. E. Hapgood; 61st New York, Lieutenant-Colonel Oscar K. Broady; 81st Pennsylvania, Colonel H. Boyd McKeen, Lieutenant-Colonel Amos Stroh; 148th Pennsylvania, Lieutenant-Colonel Robert McFarland.

Second Brigade—Colonel Patrick Kelly. 28th Massachusetts, Colonel Richard Byrnes; 63d New York, Lieutenant-Colonel R. C. Bently (wounded), Captain Thomas Touhy; 69th New York, Captain Richard Moroney (wounded), Lieutenant James J. Smith; 88th New York, Colonel Patrick Kelly, Captain Dennis F. Burke; 116th Pennsylvania, Major St. Clair A. Mulholland.

Third Brigade—Brigadier-General S. K. Zook (killed), Lieutenant-Colonel John Frazer. 52d New York, Lieutenant-Colonel Charles G. Freudenberg (wounded), Captain William Scherrer; 57th New York; Lieutenant-Colonel Alfred B. Chapman; 66th New York, Colonel Orlando W. Morris (wounded), Lieutenant-Colonel John S. Hammell (wounded), Major Peter Nelson; 140th Pennsylvania, Colonel Richard P. Roberts (killed), Lieutenant-Colonel John Frazer.

Fourth Brigade—Colonel John R. Brooke (wounded). 27th Connecticut, Lieutenant-Colonel Henry C. Merwin (killed), Major James H. Coburn; 2d Delaware, Colonel William P. Bailey; 64th New York, Colonel Daniel G. Bingham; Major Leonard W. Bradley; 53d Pennsylvania, Colonel J. R. Brooke, Lieutenant-Colonel Richard McMichael; 145th Pennsylvania, Colonel Hiram L. Brown (wounded), Captain John W. Reynolds (wounded), Captain Moses W. Oliver.

SECOND DIVISION—Brigadier-General John Gibbon (wounded while commanding the Corps), Brigadier-General William Harrow.

First Brigade—Brigadier-General William Harrow, Colonel Francis E. Heath. 19th Maine, Colonel F. E. Heath, Lieutenant-Colonel Henry W.

Cunningham; 15th Massachusetts, Colonel George H. Ward (killed), Lieutenant-Colonel George C. Joslin; 1st Minnesota, Colonel William Colvill (killed), Captain N. S. Messick (killed), Captain Wilson B. Farrell, Captain Louis Muller, Captain Joseph Perram, Captain Henry C. Cortes; 82d New York, Colonel Henry W. Huston (killed), Captain John Darrow.

Second Brigade—Brigadier-General Alexander J. Webb (wounded). 69th Pennsylvania, Colonel Dennis O. Kane (killed), Lieutenant-Colonel M. Tschudy (killed), Major James Duffy (wounded), Captain William Davis; 71st Pennsylvania, Lieutenant-Colonel Richard Penn Smith; 72d Pennsylvania, Colonel De Witt C. Baxter, Lieutenant-Colonel Theodore Hesser; 106th Pennsylvania, Lieutenant-Colonel William L. Curry.

Third Brigade—Colonel Norman J. Hall. 19th Massachusetts, Colonel Arthur F. Devereux; 20th Massachusetts, Colonel Paul J. Revere (killed), Lieutenant-Colonel George N. Macy, Captain H. L. Abbott (wounded); 7th Michigan, Colonel N. J. Hall, Lieutenant-Colonel Amos E. Steele (killed), Major S. W. Curtis; 42d New York, Colonel James E. Mallon; 59th New York, Lieutenant-Colonel Max A. Thoman (killed), Captain William McFadden; Andrew's Massachusetts Sharpshooters (unattached); Captain William Plumer, Lieutenant Emerson L. Bicknell.

THIRD DIVISION—Brigadier-General Alexander Hayes.

First Brigade—Colonel Samuel S. Carroll. 14th Indiana, Colonel John Coons; 4th Ohio, Colonel James H. Godman, Lieutenant-Colonel L. W. Carpenter; 8th Ohio, Colonel S. S. Carroll, Lieutenant-Colonel Franklin Sawyer; 7th West Virginia, Colonel Joseph Snyder, Lieutanant-Colonel Jonathan H. Lockwood.

Second Brigade—Colonel Thomas A. Smyth (wounded), Lieutenant-Colonel T. E. Pierce; 14th Connecticut, Major Theodore G. Ellis; 1st Delaware, Colonel Thomas A. Smyth, Lieutenant-Colonel Edward P. Harris, Captain M. B. Ellgood (killed), Captain Thomas B. Hizar, Lieutenant William Smith (killed), Lieutenant John F. Dent; 12th New Jersey, Major John T. Hill; 10th New York (National Zouaves Battalion), Major George F. Hopper; 108th New York, Colonel Charles J. Powers, Lieutenant-Colonel F. E. Pierce.

Third Brigade—Colonel George L. Willard (killed), Colonel Eliakim, Sherrill (killed), Lieutenant-Colonel James M. Bull; 39th New York (four companies), Lieutenant-Colonel James G. Hughes, Major Hugo Hildebrandt; 111th New York, Colonel Clinton D. McDougall (wounded), Lieutenant-Colonel Isaac M. Lusk, Captain A. P. Seeley; 125th New York, Colonel George L. Willard (killed while commanding Brigade), Lieutenant-Colonel Levin Crandall; 126th New York, Colonel E. Sherrill (killed), Lieutenant-Colonel J. M. Bull.

Artillery Brigade—Captain J. G. Hazard. A, 1st Rhode Island, Lieutenant William A. Arnold; B, 1st Rhode Island, Lieutenant T. Fred Brown (wounded), Lieutenant Walter S. Perrin; I, 1st United States, Lieutenant G. A. Woodruff (killed), Lieutenant Tully McCrea; A, 4th United States, Lieutenant A. H. Cushing (killed), Sergeant Frederick Fuger; B, 1st New York Light, of the Reserve Artillery, was transferred here during July 3; Battery C, 4th United States, Lieutenant E. Thomas, was in the line of the Second Corps on July 3. The losses in this Brigade were so large that there were no officers to assume command at the close of the fight. Cavalry Squadron.

THIRD ARMY CORPS.

Major-General Daniel E. Sickles (wounded), Major-General David B. Birney.

FIRST DIVISION—Major-General D. B. Birney, Brigadier-General I. H. H. Ward.

First Brigade—Brigadier-General Charles R. Graham (wounded and captured), Colonel Andrew H. Tippin. 57th Pennsylvania, Colonel Peter Sides, Lieutenant-Colonel William P. Neeper (wounded), Captain A. H. Nelson; 63 Pennsylvania, Lieutenant-Colonel John A. Danks; 68th Pennsylvania, Colonel A. H. Tippin (all the field officers wounded), Captain Milton H. Davis; 105th Pennsylvania, Colonel Calvin A. Craig; 114th Pennsylvania, Lieutenant-Colonel Frederick K. Cavada (captured); men under Captain Edward R. Bowen fell in line of 141st Pennsylvania; 141st Pennsylvania, Colonel H. A. Madill. The 2d New Hampshire, 3d Maine, 7th New Jersey and 8th New Jersey formed part of General Graham's line on July 2.

Second Brigade—Brigadier-General I. H. H. Ward, Colonel H. Berdau. 1st United States Sharpshooters, Colonel H. Berdau, Lieutenant-Colonel C. Trapp; 2d United States Sharpshooters, Major H. H. Stoughton; 3d Maine, Colonel M. B. Lakeman (captured), Lieutenant-Colonel W. C. L. Taylor, Captain William C. Morgan; 4th Maine, Colonel Elijah Walker (killed), Major Ebenezer Witcomb (wounded), Captain Edwin Libby; 20th Indiana, Colonel John Wheeler (killed), Lieutenant-Colonel William C. L. Taylor; 99th Pennsylvania, Major John W. Moore; 86th New York, Lieutenant-Colonel Benjamin Higgins; 124th New York, Colonel A. Van Horn Ellis (killed), Lieutenant-Colonel Francis M. Cummings.

Third Brigade—Colonel Philip A. De Trobriand. 3d Michigan, Colonel Byron R. Pierce (wounded), Lieutenant-Colonel E. G. Pierce; 5th Michigan, Lieutenant-Colonel John Pulford (wounded), Major S. S. Matthews; 40th

New York, Colonel Thomas W. Egan; 17th Maine, Lieutenant Colonel Charles B. Merrill; 110th Pennsylvania, Lieutenant-Colonel David M. Jones (wounded), Major Isaac Rogers.

SECOND DIVISION—Brigadier-General Andrew A. Humphreys.

First Brigade—Brigadier-General Joseph B. Carr. 1st Massachusetts, Colonel N. B. McLaughlin, Lieutenant-Colonel Clark B. Baldwin; 11th Massachusetts, Lieutenant-Colonel Porter D. Trippe; 16th Massachusetts, Lieutenant-Colonel Waldo Merriam, Captain Matthew Donovan; 26th Pennsylvania, Major Robert L. Bodine, Captain George W. Tomlinson (wounded), Captain Henry Goodfellow; 11th New Jersey, Colonel Robert McAllister (wounded), Major Philip J. Kearney (killed), Captain W. B. Dunning, Lieutenant John Schoonover, Captain W. H. Lloyd, Captain Samuel T. Sleeper; 84th Pennsylvania (not engaged), Lieutenant-Colonel Milton Opp; 12th New Hampshire, Captain J. F. Langley.

Second Brigade—Colonel William A. Brewster. 70th New York, 1st Excelsior), Major Daniel Mahen, Colonel J. Egbert Farnum; 71st New York (2d Excelsior), Colonel Henry L. Potter; 72d New York (3d Excelsior), Colonel John J. Austin, Lieutenant-Colonel John Leonard; 73d New York (4th Excelsior), Colonel William R. Brewster, Major M. W. Burns; 74th New York (5th Excelsior), Lieutenant-Colonel Thomas Holt; 120th New York, Lieutenant-Colonel Cornelius D. Westbrook (wounded), Major J. R. Tappen, Captain A. L. Lockwood.

Third Brigade—Colonel George C. Burling. 5th New Jersey, Colonel W. J. Sewall (wounded), Captain Virgil M. Healey (wounded), Captain T. C. Godfrey, Captain A. H. Woolsey; 6th New Jersey, Colonel George C. Burling, Lieutenant-Colonel S. R. Gelkyson; 7th New Jersey, Colonel L. R. Francine (killed), Lieutenant-Colonel Francis Price, Major Frederick Cooper; 8th New Jersey, Colonel John Ramsey (wounded), Captain John G. Langton; 115th Pennsylvania, Lieutenant-Colonel John P. Dunne; 2d New Hampshire, Colonel Edward L. Bailey (wounded), Major Samuel P. Sayles (wounded).

Artillery Brigade—Captain George E. Randolph (wounded), Captain A. Judson Clark; E, 1st Rhode Island, Lieutenant John K. Bucklyn (wounded), Lieutenant Benjamin Freeborn; B, 1st New Jersey (Light), Captain A. J. Clark, Lieutenant Robert Sims; D, 1st New York, Captain George B. Winslow; K, 4th United States, Lieutenant F. W. Suley (wounded), Lieutenant Robert James; 4th New York, Captain James E. Smith.

FIFTH ARMY CORPS.

Major-General George Sykes, commanding Provost Guard, D and E, 12th New York, Henry W. Rider.

FIRST DIVISION—Brigadier-General James Barnes.

First Brigade—Colonel W. S. Tilton. 18th Massachusetts, Colonel Joseph Hayes ; 22d Massachusetts, Colonel William S. Tilton, Lieutenant-Colonel Thomas Sherwin, Jr.; 118th Pennsylvania, Colonel Charles M. Prevost, Lieutenant-Colonel James Gwyn : 1st Michigan, Colonel Ira C. Abbott (wounded), Lieutenant-Colonel W. A. Throop.

Second Brigade—Colonel J. B. Sweitzer. 9th Massachusetts, Colonel Patrick R. Guiney : 32d Massachusetts, Colonel George L. Prescott (wounded), Lieutenant-Colonel Luther Stephenson (wounded), Major J. Cushing Edwards ; 4th Michigan, Colonel Harrison H. Jeffords (killed), Lieutenant-Colonel George W. Lambard ; 62d Pennsylvania, Colonel J. B. Sweitzer, Lieutenant-Colonel James C. Hull.

Third Brigade—Colonel Strong Vincent (killed), Colonel James C. Rice. 20th Maine, Colonel Joshua L. Chamberlain ; 44th New York, Colonel James C. Rice, Lieutenant-Colonel Freeman Connor ; 83d Pennsylvania, Major William H. Lamont, Captain O. E. Woodward ; 16th Michigan, Lieutenant-Colonel N. E. Welch.

SECOND DIVISION—Brigadier-General Romay B. Ayres.

First Brigade—Colonel Hannibal Day. 3d United States (6 companies), Captain H. W. Freedly (wounded), Captain Richard G. Lay ; 4th United States (4 companies), Captain J. W. Adams ; 6th United States (5 companies), Captain Levi C. Bootes ; 12th United States (8 companies), Captain Thomas S. Dunn ; 14th United States (8 companies) Major G. R. Geddings.

Second Brigade—Colonel Sidney Burbank. 2d United States (6 companies), Major A. T. Lee (wounded), Captain S. A. McKee ; 7th United States (4 companies), Captain D. P. Hancock ; 10th United States (3 companies), Captain William Clinton ; 11th United States (6 companies), Major De L. Floyd-Jones ; 17th United States (7 companies), Lieutenant-Colonel J. Durrell Green.

Third Brigade—Brigadier-General S. H. Weed (killed), Colonel Kenner Garrard. 140th New York, Colonel Patrick H. O'Rourke (killed), Lieutenant Colonel Louis Ernst ; 146th New York, Colonel Kenner Garrard, Lieutenant-Colonel David T. Jenkins ; 91st Pennsylvania, Lieutenant-Colonel Joseph H. Sinex ; 155th Pennsylvania, Lieutenant-Colonel John H. Cain.

THIRD DIVISION—Brigadier-General S. Wiley Crawford. This Division joined the Corps on June 28, leaving its Second Brigade in the Department of Washington.

First Brigade—Colonel William McCandless. 1st Pennsylvania Rifles (Bucktail's), Colonel Charles J. Taylor (killed), Lieutenant-Colonel A. E.

Niles (wounded), Major William R. Hartshorne; 1st Pennsylvania Reserves (9 companies), Colonel William Cooper Talley; 2d Pennsylvania Reserves, Colonel William McCandless, Lieutenant-Colonel George A. Woodward; 6th Pennsylvania Reserves, Colonel Wellington H. Ent.

Third Brigade—Colonel Joseph W. Fisher. 5th Pennsylvania Reserves, Colonel J. W. Fisher, Lieutenant-Colonel George Dare; 9th Pennsylvania Reserves, Lieutenant-Colonel James McK. Snodgrass; 10th Pennsylvania Reserves, Colonel A. J. Warner; 11th Pennsylvania Reserves, Colonel S. M. Jackson; 12th Pennsylvania Reserves, Colonel M. D. Hardin.

Artillery Brigade—Captain A. P. Martin. D, 5th United States, Lieutenant Charles E. Hazlett (killed), Lieutenant B. F. Rittenhouse; I, 5th United States, Lieutenant Skalbone F. Watson, Lieutenant Charles C. MacConnell; C, 1st New York, Captain Albert Barnes; L, 1st Ohio, Captain Frank C. Gibbs; C, 3d Massachusetts, Captain A. P. Martin, Lieutenant Aaron F. Wolcott.

SIXTH ARMY CORPS.

Major-General John Sedgwick, commanding Headquarters Guard, L, 1st New Jersey Cavalry, and H, 1st Pennsylvania Cavalry, Captain William S. Croft.

FIRST DIVISION—Brigadier-General H. G. Wright. Provost Guard, 4th New Jersey (3 companies), Captain William R. Maxwell.

First Brigade—Brigadier-General A. T. A. Torbert. 1st New Jersey, Lieutenant-Colonel William Henry, Jr.; 2d New Jersey, Colonel Samuel L. Buck; Lieutenant-Colonel Charles Wiebecke; 3d New Jersey, Colonel Henry W. Brown, Lieutenant-Colonel Edward L. Campbell; 15 New Jersey, Colonel William H. Penrose.

Second Brigade—Brigadier-General J. J. Bartlett. 5th Maine, Colonel Clark G. Edwards; 121st New York, Colonel Emory Upton; 95th Pennsylvania, Lieutenant-Colonel Edward Carrol; 96th Pennsylvania, Major William H. Lessig.

Third Brigade—Brigadier-General A. D. Russell. 6th Maine, Colonel Hiram Burnham; 49th Pennsylvania (4 companies), Colonel William H. Irwin, Lieutenant-Colonel Thomas M. Hulings; 119th Pennsylvania, Colonel P. C. Ellmaker; 5th Wisconsin, Colonel Thomas S. Allen.

SECOND DIVISION—Brigadier-General A. P. Hare.

Second Brigade—Colonel A. L. Grant. 2d Vermont, Colonel J. H. Wallridge; 3d Vermont, Colonel T. O. Seaver; 4th Vermont, Colonel E. H. Stoughton; 5th Vermont, Lieutenant-Colonel John R. Lewis; 6th Vermont, Lieutenant-Colonel Elisha L. Barney.

Third Brigade—Brigadier-General T. A. Neill. 7th Maine, (6 companies), Lieutenant-Colonel Seldon Conner; 33d New York, Captain Henry J. Gifford; 43d New York (detachment), Colonel B. F. Baker, Lieutenant-Colonel John Wilson; 49th New York, Colonel D. D. Bidwell; 77th New York, Colonel J. B. McKean, Lieutenant-Colonel Winsor B. French; 61st Pennsylvania, Lieutenant-Colonel George F. Smith, Major George W. Dawson.

THIRD DIVISION—Major-General John Newton, Brigadier-General Frank Wheaton.

First Brigade—Brigadier-General Alexander Shaler. 65th New York, Colonel J. E. Hamblin; 67th New York, Colonel Nelson Cross; 122d New York, Colonel Silas Titus, Lieutenant-Colonel A. W. Dwight; 23d Pennsylvania, Lieutenant-Colonel John F. Glenn; 82d Pennsylvania, Colonel Isaac A. Bassett.

Second Brigade—Colonel H. L. Eustus. 7th Massachusetts, Lieutenant-Colonel Frank P. Harlow; 10th Massachusetts, Lieutenant-Colonel Joseph B. Parsons; 37th Massachusetts, Colonel Oliver Edwards; 2 l Rhode Island, Colonel Horatio Rogers.

Third Brigade—Brigadier-General F. Wheaton, Colonel David J. Nevin. 62d New York, Colonel D. L. Nevin, Lieutenant-Colonel Theodore B. Hamilton; 93d Pennsylvania, Colonel James M. McCarter; Major John I. Nevin; 98th Pennsylvania, Major John B. Kohler; 102d Pennsylvania (not engaged), Colonel John W. Patterson; 139th Pennsylvania, Colonel Fred H. Collier, Lieutenant-Colonel William H. Moody.

Artillery Brigade—Colonel C. H. Tompkins. A, 1st Massachusetts, Captain W. H. McCartney; D, 2d United States, Lieutenant E. B. Williston; G, 2d United States, Lieutenant John H. Butler; F, 5th United States, Lieutenant Leonard Martin; C, 1st Rhode Island, Captain Richard Waterman; G, 1st Rhode Island, Captain George W. Adams; 1st New York, Captain Andrew Cowan; 3d New York, Captain William A. Harn.

ELEVENTH ARMY CORPS.

Major-General O. O. Howard, Major-General Carl Schurz (July 1). After the death of General Reynolds, General Howard commanded all the troops in the field until relieved by General Hancock. Headquarters Guard, I and K, 1st Indiana Cavalry, Captain Abram Sharra; I, 8th New York Infantry, Lieutenant H. Foerster.

FIRST DIVISION—Brigadier-General Francis C. Barlow (wounded); Brigadier-General Adelbert Ames.

First Brigade—Colonel Leopold Von Gilsa. 41st New York, Colonel L. Von Gilsa, Lieutenant-Colonel Detleo Von Einsiedel; 54th New York, Colonel Eugene A. Kezley, Major Stephen Kovacs; 68th New York, Colonel Gotthilf Bourney de Ivernois; 153d Pennsylvania, Colonel Charles Glanz, Major John F. Frulaff.

Second Brigade—Brigadier-General Adelbert Ames, Colonel Andrew L. Harris. 17th Connecticut, Lieutenant-Colonel Douglas Fowler (killed), Major A. G. Brady; 25th Ohio, Lieutenant-Colonel Jeremiah Williams (captured), Lieutenant William Malaney (wounded), Lieutenant Israel White; 75th Ohio, Colonel Andrew L. Harris (wounded), Lieutenant-Colonel Benjamin Morgan (wounded), Major Charles W. Friend; 107th Ohio, Colonel Seraphim Meyer, Captain John M. Lutz.

SECOND DIVISION—Brigadier-General A. Von Steinwehr.

First Brigade—Colonel Charles R. Coster. 27th Pennsylvania, Lieutenant-Colonel Lorenz Cantador; 73d Pennsylvania, Captain Daniel F. Kelly; 134th New York, Colonel Charles R. Coster, Lieutenant-Colonel Allen H. Jackson; 154th New York, Colonel Patrick H. Jones, Lieutenant-Colonel Daniel B. Allen.

Second Brigade—Colonel Orlando Smith. 33d Massachusetts, Lieutenant-Colonel Adin R. Underwood; 136th New York, Colonel James Wood, Jr.; 55th Ohio, Colonel Charles B. Gambee; 73d Ohio, Colonel Orlando Smith, Lieutenant-Colonel Richard Long.

THIRD DIVISION—Major-General Carl Schurz, Brigadier-General Alexander Schimmelpfennig (July 1).

First Brigade—Brigadier-General Alexander Schimmelpfennig (captured), Colonel George Von Amsburg. 45th New York, Colonel G. Von Amsburg, Lieutenant-Colonel Adolphus Dobke; 157th New York, Colonel Philip P. Brown, Jr.; 74th Pennsylvania, Colonel Adolph Von Hartung (captured), Lieutenant-Colonel Von Mitzel (captured), Captain Gustav Schleiter, Captain Henry Krauseneck; 61st Ohio, Colonel S. J. McGroarty; 82d Illinois, Colonel J. Hecker; Lieutenant-Colonel Edward S. Salomon.

Second Brigade—Colonel Waldimir Kryzanowski. 58th New York, Colonel W. Kryzanowski, Lieutenant-Colonel August Otto, Captain Emil Koenig, Lieutenant-Colonel Frederick Gellman; 119th New York, Colonel John F. Lockman, Lieutenant-Colonel Edward F. Lloyd; 75th Pennsylvania, Colonel Francis Mahler (wounded), Major August Ledig; 82 Ohio, Colonel James S. Robinson (wounded), Lieutenant-Colonel D. Thomson; 26th Wisconsin, Colonel William H. Jacobs, Lieutenant-Colonel Hans Boebel, Captain John W. Fuchs.

Artillery Brigade—Major Thomas W. Osborn. I, 1st New York, Captain M. Wiedrick; I, 1st Ohio, Captain Hubert Dilger; K, 1st Ohio, Captain Lewis Heckman; G, 4th United States, Lieutenant Bayard Wilkeson (killed), Lieutenant A. E. Bancroft; 13th New York, Lieutenant William Wheeler.

TWELFTH ARMY CORPS.

Brigadier-General Alpheus S. Williams, commanding; General Henry W. Slocum, during the battle, commanding the right wing of the Army. Headquarter Guard, 10th Maine Battalion, Captain John D. Beardsley.

First Division—Brigadier-General Thomas H. Ruger.

First Brigade—Colonel Archibald L. McDougall. 5th Connecticut, Colonel Warren W. Packer; 20th Connecticut, Lieutenant-Colonel William B. Wooster; 123d New York, Colonel A. L. McDougall, Lieutenant-Colonel James C. Rogers, Captain Adolphus H. Tanner; 145th New York, Colonel E. L. Price; 46th Pennsylvania, Colonel James L. Selfridge; 3d Maryland, Colonel J. M. Sudsburg.

Second Brigade—(Unassigned during a portion of the battle, when they became this Brigade), Brigadier-General Henry H. Lockwood. 150th New York, Colonel John H. Ketcham; 1st Maryland (Potomac Home Brigade), Colonel William P. Maulsby; 1st Maryland (Eastern Shore), Colonel James Wallace.

Third Brigade—Colonel Silas Colgrove. 2d Massachusetts, Colonel Charles R. Mudge (killed), Lieutenant-Colonel Charles F. Morse; 107th New York, Colonel Myron M. Crane; 13th New Jersey, Colonel Ezra A. Carman (wounded), Lieutenant-Colonel John R. Fesler; 27th Indiana, Colonel Silas Colgrove; 3d Wisconsin, Colonel William Hawley, Lieutenant-Colonel Martin Flood.

Second Division—Brigadier-General John W. Geary.

First Brigade—Colonel Charles Candy. 28th Pennsylvania, Captain John Flynn; 147th Pennsylvania (8 companies), Lieutenant-Colonel Ario Pardu, Jr.; 5th Ohio, Colonel John H. Patrick; 7th Ohio, Colonel William R. Creighton; 29th Ohio, Captain W. F. Stevens (wounded), Captain Edward Hayes · 66th Ohio, Colonel C. Candy, Lieutenant-Colonel Eugene Powell.

Second Brigade—Colonel George A. Cobham, Jr., Brigadier-General Thomas L. Kane, Colonel George A. Cobham, Jr. 29th Pennsylvania, Colonel William Rickards, Jr.; 109th Pennsylvania, Captain Fred L. Gimber; 111th Pennsylvania, Lieutenant-Colonel Thomas M. Walker, Colonel George A. Cobham, Jr., Lieutenant-Colonel Thomas M. Walker.

Third Brigade—Brigadier-General George S. Greene. 60th New York, Colonel Abel Godard; 78th New York, Lieutenant-Colonel Herbert Von Hammerstein; 102d New York, Lieutenant-Colonel James C. Lane (wounded), Captain Lewis R. Stigman; 137th New York, Colonel David Ireland; 149th New York, Colonel Henry A. Barnum, Lieutenant-Colonel Charles B. Randall.

Artillery Brigade—Lieutenant Edward D. Muhlenberg. F, 4th United States, Lieutenant E. D. Muhlenberg, Lieutenant S. T. Rugg; K, 5th United States, Lieutenant D. H. Kinsie; M, 1st New York, Lieutenant Charles E. Winegar; Knapp's Pennsylvania, Lieutenant Charles Atwell.

CAVALRY CORPS.

Major-General Alfred Pleasanton, commanding.

FIRST DIVISION, Brigadier-General John Buford.

First Brigade—Colonel William Gamble. 8th New York, Colonel Benjamin F. Davis, Lieutenant-Colonel William L. Markell; 8th Illinois, Colonel William Gamble, Lieutenant-Colonel D. R. Clendennin, Major John L. Beveridge; 12th Illinois (detachment, 4 companies); 3d Indiana (detachment, 6 companies), Colonel George H. Chapman.

Second Brigade—Colonel Thomas C. Devin. 6th New York, Colonel Thomas C. Devin, Lieutenant-Colonel William H. Crocker, Major William E. Beardsley; 9th New York, Colonel William Sackett; 17th Pennsylvania, Colonel J. H. Kellogg; 3d Virginia (2 companies), Captain Seymour B. Conger.

Reserve Brigade—Brigadier-General Wisley Merritt. 1st United States, Captain R. S. C. Lord; 2d United States, Captain T. F. Rodenbough; 5th United States, Captain J. W. Mason; 6th United States, Major S. H. Starr (wounded), Lieutenant Louis H. Carpenter, Lieutenant Nicholas Nolan, Captain Ira W. Claflin; 6th Pennsylvania, Major James H. Hazeltine.

SECOND DIVISION—Brigadier-General D. McM. Gregg. Headquarter Guard, A, 1st Ohio, Captain Noah Jones.

First Brigade—Colonel J. B. McIntosh. 1st New Jersey, Major M. H. Beaumont; 1st Pennsylvania, Colonel John P. Taylor; 3d Pennsylvania, Lieutenant-Colonel Edward S. Jones; Pernell Legion (Maryland), A, Captain Robert E. Duvall; 1st Maryland (11 companies), Lieutenant-Colonel James M. Deems; 1st Massachusetts (detached from Brigade at Headquarters, Sixth Corps), Lieutenant-Colonel Greely S. Curtis; Section Battery, H, 3d Pennsylvania, Heavy Artillery (not engaged), Captain William D. Rank.

Second Brigade (Not engaged), Colonel Pennock Hoey. 2d New York (not engaged), Lieutenant-Colonel Otto Harhaus; 4th New York (not engaged), Lieutenant-Colonel Augustus Pruyn; 8th Pennsylvania (not engaged), Captain William Corrie; 6th Ohio (10 companies, not engaged), Major William Stedman.

Third Brigade—Colonel J. Irving Gregg. 1st Maine, Lieutenant-Colonel Charles H. Smith; 10th New York, Major M. Henry Avery; 4th Pennsylvania, Lieutenant-Colonel William E. Doster; 16th Pennsylvania, Lieutenant-Colonel John K. Robinson.

THIRD DIVISION—Brigadier-General Judson Kilpatrick. Headquarter Guard, C, 1st Ohio, Captain Samuel N. Stanford.

First Brigade—Brigadier-General E. J. Farnsworth (killed), Colonel N. P. Richmond. 5th New York, Major John Hammond; 18th Pennsylvania, Lieutenant-Colonel William P. Briston; 1st Vermont, Colonel E. D. Sawyer, Lieutenant-Colonel Addison W. Preston; 1st West Virginia (10 companies), Colonel N. P. Richmond, Major Charles E. Capehart.

Second Brigade—Brigadier-General George A. Custer. 1st Michigan, Colonel Charles H. Town; 5th Michigan, Colonel Russell A. Alger; 6th Michigan, Colonel George Gray; 7th Michigan (10 companies), Colonel William D. Mann.

HORSE ARTILLERY.

First Brigade—Captain James M. Robertson. B and L, 2d United States, Lieutenant Edward Heaton; M, 2d United States, Lieutenant A. C. M. Pennington; E, 4th United States, Lieutenant S. S. Elder; 6th New York, Lieutenant Joseph W. Martin; 9th Michigan, Captain J. J. Daniels.

Second Brigade—Captain John C. Tidball. G and E, 1st United States, Captain A. M. Randol; K, 1st United States, Captain William M. Graham; A, 2d United States, Lieutenant John H. Calef; C, 3d United States, Lieutenant W. D. Fuller.

ARTILLERY RESERVE—Brigadier-General R. O. Tyler (disabled) Captain John M. Robertson.

First Regular Brigade—Captain D. R. Ransom (wounded). H, 1st United States, Lieutenant C. P. Eakin (wounded), Lieutenant Philip D. Mason; F and K, 3d United States, Lieutenant J. G. Turnbull; C, 4th United States, Lieutenant Evan Thomas; C, 5th United States, Lieutenant G. V. Weir.

First Volunteer Brigade—Lieutenant-Colonel F. McGilvery. 15th New York, Captain Patrick Hart; C and F, Pennsylvania (Light), Captain

James Thompson; 5 Massachusetts (10th New York Battery attached), Captain C. A. Phillips; 9th Massachusetts, Captain John Bigelow, Lieutenant Richard S. Milton.

Second Volunteer Brigade—Captain E. D. Tafft. B, 1st Connecticut (not engaged), Captain Albert F. Brooker; M, 1st Connecticut (not engaged), Captain Franklin A. Pratt; 5th New York, Captain E. D. Tafft; 2d Connecticut, Lieutenant John W. Sterling.

Third Volunteer Brigade—Captain James F. Huntington. F and G, 1st Pennsylvania, Captain R. B. Ricketts; H, 1st Ohio, Captain James F. Huntington, Lieutenant George W. Norton; A, 1st New Hampshire, Captain F. M. Edgell; C, 1st West Virginia, Captain Wallace Hill.

Fourth Volunteer Brigade—Captain R. H. Fitzhugh; B, 1st New York, Captain James McK. Rorty (killed), Lieutenant A. S. Sheldon, Lieutenant Robert E. Rogers. This Battery served in line with Artillery Brigade, Second Corps, on July 3. G, 1st New York, Captain Albert N. Ames; K, 1st New York (with Eleventh Battery attached), Captain Robert H. Fitzhugh; A, 1st Maryland, Captain James H. Rigby; A, 1st New Jersey, Lieutenant Augustin N. Parsons; 6th Maine, Lieutenant Edwin R. Dow.

TRAIN GUARD—4th New Jersey Infantry (7 companies), Major Charles Ewing.

Headquarter Guard—C, 32d Massachusetts, Captain Josiah C. Fuller.

X.

LEE AND HIS COMMANDERS.

A SERIES OF BRIEF BIOGRAPHIES.

(WITH PORTRAITS.)

LEE, ROBERT EDWARD, Major-General, born at Stratford on the Potomac, in Westmoreland County, Va., January 19, 1807. He was the son of the Revolutionary general Henry Lee, known as "Light-Horse Harry," and was graduated from West Point in 1829, ranking second in a class of forty-six. At the beginning of the Mexican war he was Chief Engineer of the Army under General Wood, with the rank of Captain. He won several brevets and the special commendation of General Scott, who attributed the prompt capture of Vera Cruz to his skill. In 1852 he was assigned to the command of West Point, where he remained three years and effected great improvements. At the outbreak of the Rebellion, April 20, 1861, he resigned his commission. On this occasion he wrote his sister: "We are now in a state of war which yields to nothing. The whole South is in a state of revolution, into which Virginia, after a long struggle, has been drawn, and though I recognize no necessity for this state of things, and would have forborne and pleaded to the end for redress of grievances, real or supposed, yet in my own person I had to meet the question whether I should take part against my native State. With all my devotion to the Union, and the feeling of loyalty and duty of an American citizen, I have not been able to make up my mind to raise my hand against my relatives, my children, my home. I have, therefore, resigned my commission in the Army, and, save in defence of my native State—with the sincere hope that my poor services may never be needed—I hope I may never be called upon to draw my sword." He was made Commander-in-Chief of the Virginia State forces, and a General under the Confederate Government. In the autumn of 1861 Lee was sent to South Carolina, where he planned the defensive coast lines that successfully resisted all efforts directed against them until the very end of the war. On March 13, 1862, he was assigned to duty "under the direction of the President," and "charged with the conduct of military operation in the armies of the Confederacy. McClellan had reorganized the National Army, and transferring his base to Fort Monroe advanced upon Richmond by way of the peninsula, and reached a line near the city with more than 100,000 men. Under the mistaken impression that Johnston's opposing force outnumbered his own, he waited for McDowell with 40,000 men from Fredericksburg to join him. To prevent this Lee ordered Jackson to threaten Washington City, which task he executed with such celerity and success as to cause serious apprehension in the Federal Capital. McDowell was recalled, and McClellan established himself on the Chickahominy. Now, for the first time, General Lee had direct command of a great army confronting an enemy strongly posted, and his capacity as a strategist and commander was first demonstrated in that bloody and brilliant, but only in part successful, series of manœuvres and contests known as "the seven day's battle." He adopted that offensive defence which was always his favorite method. He attacked McClellan, and was, after very severe fighting, so far successful that McClellan transferred his base to James River. But Lee was convinced that he had had, and lost, an opportunity to compel the actual surrender of his enemy, though stronger than himself in numbers, and regarded McClellan's escape upon any terms as a partial failure of his plans, due to accidental miscarriages. General Lee's desire next was to transfer the scene of operations to a distance from the Confederate Capital by again threatening Washington. After many minor engagements this movement ended in the second battle of Bull Run, where on August 30 the Confederates succeeded in driving their enemy under General John Pope to Centreville. Lee turned the Federal position on September 1, and Pope retired toward Washington. The transfer of McClellan's force to Washington had been made imperative, and Lee's Army was again filled with confidence in itself and its leaders, who at once undertook to transfer the scene of operation to the enemy's territory. On September 5 the Confederate Army, 45,000 strong, crossed the Potomac and took up a position near Frederick, Md., from which it might move at will against Washington or Baltimore, or invade Pennsylvania. In the execution of Lee's designs his lieutenants captured Harper's Ferry after an obstinate resistance. This was followed by the desperate and bloody battle of Antietam, in which neither side gained a decided victory. Lee was able to save the remnant of his army by recrossing the Potomac and subsequently falling back to Winchester. His invasion of Union territory had brought no valuable result except in the

1. GENERAL ROBERT E. LEE.
2. LIEUT.-GENERAL JAMES LONGSTREET.
3. LIEUT GENERAL RICHARD S EWELL.
4. LIEUT GENERAL AMBROSE P. HILL.
5. MAJOR-GENERAL J. E. B STUART.

improved morale of his troops, who from this time onward placed the most implicit confidence in their chief commander. On December 13 General Burnside attacked Lee at Fredericksburg, where the latter held a naturally strong position. The day's fighting cost the Federal Commander a loss of 13,000 men, while the Confederate loss was but 5,000. Burnside withdrew on the 15th across the Rappahannock, and operations were suspended for the winter. General Joseph Hooker planned a spring campaign in 1863 to force Lee out of his intrenched position at Fredericksburg and overcome him in the field. This plan he executed with great vigor. With his main force he crossed above Fredericksburg, while Sedgwick threw a smaller corps across below. Lee, with 48,000 men, met Hooker at Chancellorsville with more than double his numbers. While Lee with 15,000 confronted Hooker's front he detached Jackson with the main body to strike his rear. The surprise was complete. In spite of a stubborn resistance Hooker was signally defeated. Sedgwick had succeeded in capturing the Confederate works at Fredericksburg, but after the disaster to his chief he was forced to abandon them, and the Union Army retired once more beyond the Rappahannock. Encouraged by the advantage gained over Hooker at Chancellorsville, and hoping to counteract the effect of important Union successes in Western fields, General Lee at once set about his second invasion of Northern territory. It ended ingloriously for him in the great Gettysburg fight with the Unionists under General Meade, July 1, 2 and 3, which is fully described in these pages, and which closed the campaign of 1863. In the spring of 1864 Lee, with less than 70,000 men, confronted Grant, whose force aggregated 120,000. Lee skilfully used his advantage of position, showed great strategic genius, and made all possible use of the alertness and gallantry of his generals and the bravery and loyalty of his men; but the continuous pounding of Grant told with great effect upon Lee's constantly diminishing force. Grant steadily pushed his columns south of Richmond to cut off the Confederate Capital from its lines of communication and supply, so as to insure in the end the evacuation of Virginia, while the Confederates should have no road open for retreat. There was good fighting all through the campaign on both sides, but the advantage uniformly showed to the credit of the Union commanders. Early in the spring of 1865 Grant opened the final campaign. Lee was forced to abandon Richmond and the strong fortifications of Petersburg and make a desperate effort to form a junction with Johnston in North Carolina. Meanwhile the victorious column of Sherman had crossed Georgia, from Atlanta to Savannah, and was menacing Johnston from the south. Grant finally corraled Lee's force, and on April 9 Lee practically ended the war by surrender at Appomattox. After the termination of the great struggle General Lee retired from public life, but he was soon made President of

Washington College, at Lexington, Va., now called Washington and Lee University. He devoted himself with great assiduity and success to the interests of education and of the institution over which he presided till his death at Lexington, October 12, 1870.

ANDERSON, RICHARD HENRY, Lieutenant-General, born in South Carolina in 1816, graduated at West Point in 1842, served in the Dragoons on the frontier and through the Mexican War, became Captain in 1855 and was an instructor at Carlisle Barracks. Resigning in March, 1861, he was commissioned Brigadier in the Confederate service, and in August, 1862, promoted to Major-General, commanding the 5th Corps of Bragg's Army. He commanded a Division at Gettysburg, and was made Lieutenant-General in May, 1864. His unexpected night march, in default of finding a desirable place to encamp, placed Lee's van at Spottsylvania ahead of Grant, and prolonged a campaign that might have otherwise ended in a decisive fight. He took a prominent part in the defence of Petersburg and in the actions which closed the struggle. He retired to private life, and died June 26, 1879, at Beaufort, S. C.

ARMISTEAD, LEWIS ADDISON, Brigadier-General, born February 18, 1817, at Newbern, N. C., son of General Walter K. Armistead, U. S. Army, was educated at West Point and appointed a Lieutenant of 6th Infanty in 1839, served gallantly in Mexico, and received the brevet of Captain for Contreras and Cherubses, and Major for Molino del Rey. At the opening of the Civil War he resigned with great reluctance and was made a Confederate Brigadier-General. He was wounded at Antietam. At Gettysburg he was one of the few in Pickett's Division who nearly reached the Federal lines in the desperate charge on the third day. He was mortally wounded, and died in captivity a few hours later.

BARKSDALE, WILLIAM, Brigadier-General, born in Rutherford County, Tenn., August 21, 1821, graduated at Nashville University, became a lawyer at Columbus, Miss., and the editor of the *Democrat* in that city. He served in a Mississippi volunteer regiment through the Mexican war. In 1853 he was elected to Congress, and at once became prominent as a pro-slavery Democrat. He left his Congressional seat after his State seceded, took command of the 13th Mississippi Confederate Volunteers, and was soon commissioned Brigadier-General. In the Gettysburg battle he commanded the 3d Brigade of Early's Division, and was killed on the second day while leading his men to an assault on the Federal left.

CHAMBLISS, JOHN RANDOLPH, Jr., Brigadier-General, born at Hicksford, Va., January 23, 1833, was graduated at West Point in 1853, assigned to Mounted Rifles, served at the Cavalry School, Carlisle, Pa., resigned in 1854, and became a Virginia planter. He joined the Confederate Army in

1861, commanded the 13th Cavalry, was subsequently promoted to Brigadier-General, and killed in action at Deep Bottom, near Richmond, Va., while leading a brigade of Cavalry, August 16, 1864.

DEARING, JAMES, Brigadier-General, born in Campbell County, Va., April 25, 1840, was a cadet at West Point, resigned in 1861, became a Colonel of Confederate Artillery, and was promoted Brigadier-General for gallantry in the Battle of Plymouth. He took part in the chief actions between the Army of Northern Virginia and the Army of the Potomac. On the retreat of the Confederates from Petersburg to Appomattox, April 5, 1865, he was fatally wounded by General Theodore Read of the Federal Army. The two met at the head of their forces at High Bridge, on opposite sides of the Creek, where in a duel between them with pistols Read was shot dead. Dearing died at Lynchburg, Va., a few days later.

DOLES, GEORGE PIERCE, Major-General, born May 14, 1830, at Milledgeville, Ga., where he was educated. When the war opened he was Captain of a Militia Company which volunteered. In May, 1862, he was made Colonel of the 4th Georgia Regiment. He fought in most of the actions of the Army of Northern Virginia, and at the Battle of Gettysburg succeeded to the Command of a Brigade, his commission being dated November 2, 1862. During the overland campaigns he commanded a Division in Ewell's Corps, and was killed in the Battle of Cold Harbor, June 2, 1864.

EARLY, JUBAL ANDERSON, Major-General, born November 3, 1816, in Franklin County, Va., was graduated at West Point in 1837, appointed Lieutenant of Artillery and served in the Seminole War, resigned, and was a lawyer in Virginia, being several years Commonwealth Attorney. In the Mexican War he commanded a Virginia Regiment. He entered the Confederate service in 1861 as Colonel, commanded a Brigade at Bull Run, and was severely wounded at Williamsburg, May 5, 1862. Made Brigadier-General in May, 1863, his command held the lines at Fredericksburg, while Lee fought the Battle of Chancellorsville. He commanded a Division at Gettysburg. In 1864 he gained the battle at Monocacy in July and threatened Washington, while a portion of his force captured and burned Chambersburg, Pa. He was defeated by Sheridan on the Opequan, September 19, and at Fisher's Hill three days later. He gained a surprise, October 19, over the Federal force at Cedar Creek, but after the arrival of Sheridan he was forced to retire, losing most of his guns and wagons. In March, 1864, he was totally routed by Custer at Waynesboro', and was soon after relieved of command. Since the war he has resided in New Orleans and Lynchburg.

EWELL, RICHARD STODDERT, Lieutenant-General, born in Georgetown, D. C., February 8, 1817, was graduated at West Point in 1840, fought reditably in the Mexican War, became Captain of Dragoons in 1849, and resigned in 1861. He was commissioned Major-General in the Confederate Army, and fought at Bull Run and Blackburn's Ford in July. In 1862 he lost a leg at Warrenton Turnpike, August 28. When Jackson was fatally wounded at Chancellorsville, Ewell, at his request, was made Lieutenant-General and given command of the 2d Corps, and led it gallantly at Winchester, Gettysburg and at the Wilderness on the Confederate left. He was captured by Sheridan at Sailor's Creek with his entire force, April 5, 1865. He retired to private life at the close of the war, and died at Springfield, Tenn., January 25, 1872. There are many anecdotes related of General Ewell, showing him, while a brave officer, to be the very opposite of Stonewall Jackson: the latter finding in every incident of battle, march or bivouac, a subject for devout and earnest prayer—Ewell looking upon the same matters as nothing but routine work often unworthy of comment.

GORDON, JOHN BROWN, Lieutenant-General, was born in Upson County, Ga., February 6, 1832. educated at the University of Georgia, studied law, and had begun its practice at the outbreak of the war. He entered the Confederate service as Captain of Infantry, and rose to the rank of Lieutenant-General, commanding one wing of General Lee's Army at Appomattox Court House. He was wounded in battle eight times during the war. The Democrats of Georgia supported him for Governor in 1868. In 1873, he was elected United States Senator and re-elected in 1879, but resigned in 1880. In 1886 he was elected Governor of Georgia, which place he now holds.

GARNETT, RICHARD BROOKE, Brigadier-General, born in Virginia in 1819, graduated at West Point in 1841, was assigned to the Infantry, served in Florida and on the Texas frontier, became Captain May 9, 1855, was engaged in Kansas in 1856-7, and in the Utah Expedition of 1858, and resigned May 17, 1861, to join the Confederate Army. He was engaged in many of the battles in Virginia, was afterwards attached to General Lee's Army with the rank of Brigadier-General, and fell in the Battle of Gettysburg.

HAMPTON, WADE, Lieutenant-General, born in Columbia, S. C., in 1818, was graduated at the University of South Carolina, and studied law. He served in the State Legislature as a Democrat, but was not popular, having delivered a strong speech against re-opening the slave trade. At the beginning of the Civil War he enlisted as a private in the Confederate service, but soon raised a force of infantry, cavalry and artillery known as Hampton's Legion, which won distinction for good conduct in the Battle of Bull Run and in the Peninsular campaign. At Seven Pines they lost half their number and Hampton was seriously wounded. He was soon made a Brigadier-General of Cavalry, serving under General J. E. B. Stuart with brilliant success. Hampton's force bore a conspicuous part at Gettysburg, where he was three times wounded, and twenty-one out of twenty-five field officers and more than half of his men were killed or wounded. He became a Major-General, August 3, 1863. In 1864 he checked Sheridan at Trevillian's Station, and in twenty-three days captured over 3,000 prisoners and valuable stores, with a loss of 719 men. In August he was made Lieutenant-General, commanding Lee's Cavalry. In September he struck the Union rear and captured 400 prisoners and 2,486 beeves, and soon after in another action he made 500 prisoners. In 1865 he commanded the Cavalry under General J. E. Johnston in the effort to check the advance of General Sherman northward from Savannah. After the war he accepted promptly the results of defeat and engaged in cotton planting. He was chosen Governor of South Carolina in 1876. In 1878 an accident deprived him of a leg, and while his life was still despaired of he was elected to the United States Senate, where he is still serving.

HETH, HENRY, Major-General, was born in Virginia in 1825, graduated at West Point in 1847, entered the 6th Infantry, and became Captain in the 10th Infantry March 3, 1855. He resigned from the Union Army in 1861 and became a Confederate Brigadier-General, and in May, 1863, a Major-General, commanding a Division in General A. P. Hill's Corps. He was in the contest at Gettysburg and in the subsequent campaigns. Since he has been engaged in business in South Carolina.

HILL, AMBROSE POWELL, Lieutenant-General, born in Culpeper County, Va., Nov. 9, 1825, graduated at West Point in 1847, and entering the 1st Artillery served in Mexico and in Florida, and became Captain of Artillery. In November, 1855, he was made an assistant on the coast survey. He resigned in 1861, and in the first battle of Bull Run commanded a Virginia regiment, winning promotion, and for gallantry in the battle of Williamsburg in May, 1862, he was made a Major-General. In the seven days' battles around Richmond he opened the fight by driving McClellan's forces from Meadow Bridge, clearing a way for Longstreet and D. H. Hill to advance. He was active in the succeeding campaign against General Pope and at the second battle of Bull Run, July 29 and 30, 1862. He received the surrender of the National troops at Harper's Ferry on September 17. 1862, and making a forced march arrived at Antietam in time to enable General Lee to maintain his ground. He was engaged in the action at Fredericksburg, December 13, 1862, and at Chancellorsville, May 5 and 6, 1863, his Corps participated in the flank movement that crushed Hooker's right. In the assault he was severely wounded. For gallantry in this battle he was promoted, May 20, 1863, to Lieutenant-General and given command of one of the three grand Corps into which the Army was divided. He led his Corps at Gettysburg, and in the affair at Bristow Station, October, 1863, while in command of two Brigades, was repelled with severe loss. On June 22, 1864, his Corps, with Longstreet's, repelled the attack on the Weldon Railroad. On Sunday morning, April 2, 1865, in the struggle for the possession of the works in front of Petersburg, he was shot from his horse dead by stragglers from the National Army.

HOOD, JOHN BELL, Major-General, was born at Owenville, Ky., June 1, 1831, graduated at West Point in 1853, served in the 2d Cavalry on the Indian frontier with Colonel Albert Sidney Johnson and Lieutenant-Colonel Robert E. Lee. In July, 1857, he was severely wounded by an Indian in a hand-to-hand fight. In 1858 he became 1st Lieutenant, and was Cavalry Instructor at West Point in 1859 and 1860. He resigned in 1861, and entering the Confederate Army as a Colonel was soon made Brigadier-General, commanding Texas troops. While leading his men at Gaine's Mills he was shot in the body, his Brigade lost more than half its number, and he was brevetted Major-General on the field. He served in both Maryland campaigns and in the battles of Second Bull Run, Boonesborough, Fredericksburg and Antietam. At Gettysburg he was again severely wounded, disabling his arm. During the second day's fight at Chickamauga, seeing his men waver he rode to the front and demanded the colors. His Texans rallied, and in the charge at the head of the column he was shot down, losing his right leg. He succeeded General Joseph E. Johnston in command in 1864, and after stubborn fighting was outflanked by General William T. Sherman and compelled to evacuate Atlanta, enabling the Union leader to make the march through Georgia to the sea. Hood began a counter-movement into Tennessee and compelled the evacuation of Decatur, but was defeated by General Thomas at Franklin, November 30, and again, December 16, by the same commander at Nashville, after which, at his own request, he was retired. He engaged in trade in New Orleans, and died there August 30, 1879.

IVERSON, ALFRED, Brigadier-General, born in Burke County, Ga., December 3, 1798, was graduated at Princeton, N. J., in 1820, and became a lawyer at Columbus, Ga. After serving in the Legislature several terms, in both branches, he was seven years a Judge of the Superior Court. He was elected to the National House of Representatives in 1846 and to the Senate in 1855. On the passage by his State of the Ordinance of Secession, he withdrew January 28, 1861, having been an open advocate of disunion and a leader of the Secession movement, and having announced in the United States Senate that slavery must be recognized with the right to carry slaves into the common territories, and to be assured full Congressional protection. He raised a Confederate Regiment, and in November, 1862, was commissioned Brigadier-General. He died at Macon, Ga., March 4, 1873.

JOHNSON, EDWARD, Major-General, was born in Chesterfield Co., Va., April 16, 1816, graduated at West Point in 1838, and assigned to the 6th Infantry, was in the Mexican War, and brevetted Captain for gallantry at Molino del Rey and Major for Chapultepec. At the end of the campain he was presented with swords by his native County and State. He became Captain in 1851 and resigned June 10, 1861. Entering the Confederate service as Colonel of the 12th Georgia Volunteers, he was promoted Brigadier-General in 1862 and Major-General the next year. At Gettysburg he commanded a Division. On May 12, 1864, he was captured with his entire force at Spottsylvania Court House. At the close of the war he retired to his Virginia farm, and died in Richmond, February 22, 1873.

JONES, JOHN MARSHALL, Brigadier-General, born at Charlottesville, Va., July 26, 1820, graduated at West Point in 1841, was an Instructor there several years, and later member of a Board to revise rifle and artillery practice, and was promoted Captain in 1855. He resigned in 1861, was appointed Colonel of a Virginia Confederate Regiment, and in 1863 promoted Brigadier-General. He was severely wounded at Gettysburg, took part in the siege of Knoxville, Tenn., and in the operations from the Wilderness to Spottsylvania, where he was killed May 10, 1864.

JONES, WILLIAM EDMONDSON, Major-General, born in Washington County, Va., in 1824, was graduated at West Point in 1848, assigned to Mounted Rifles, resigned in 1857, traveled abroad, and became a farmer at Gluch Spring, Va. He joined the Confederate service as a Captain in September, 1861, was made Colonel 1st Virginia Cavalry, promoted September 19, 1862, Brigadier-General, and commanded the Department of the Valley of Virginia. He was mas made Major-General in 1863, and had charge of Southwestern Virginia and Eastern Tennessee till he was ordered back to the Valley of Virginia to meet General Hunter, and was killed in action with the force under that General at New Hope, Va., June 5, 1864.

KEMPER, JAMES LAWSON, Brigadier-General, was born in Madison County, Va., June 11, 1823, graduated at Washington College, Lexington, Va., in 1842, served as a Captain in the Mexican War, was ten years in the Virginia Legislature, and its Speaker two years. In 1861 he became Colonel 2d Virginia Regiment, Confederate Army, Brigadier-General in 1862, and served with distinction on many fields. He was wounded and captured at Gettysburg and disabled for further military service. In 1874 he was Governor of Virginia, and on the expiration of his term devoted himself to agriculture in Orange County, Va.

KERSHAW, JOSEPH BREVARD, Major-General, was born in Camden, S. C., January 5, 1822, educated in South Carolina Academies, and became a lawyer. He was in the State Senate in 1852-7, and in the State Convention of 1860. He raised the 2d South Carolina Regiment for the Confederate Army, and commanded it in the first battle of Bull Run, was made Brigadier-General February 13, 1862, commanded a Brigade of McLaw's Division in the Peninsular Campaign of that year, and held the Sunken Road at Fredericksburg against the assault of the National Troops. He led Longstreet's attack at Gettysburg, and lost more than half of his Brigade. After the battle of Chickamauga and the Siege of Knoxville, in which he had a command, he commanded a Division in General Lee's final campaign. He held the Union forces in check at Spottsylvania, was in the action of Coldwater in Early's Valley Campaign, and in the rear of Lee's Army at Sailor's Creek, where he surrendered April 6, 1865. After the close of the war he resumed law practice at Camden, S. C., was in the State Senate in 1865, and its President in 1866. In 1870 he drew the resolutions adopted by the Conservative Convention recognizing the Federal Constitution Amendments, and in 1877 he was elected Judge of the Fifth Circuit of South Carolina.

LEE, FITZHUGH, Major-General, nephew of General R. E. Lee, was born at Clermont, Va., November 19, 1835, graduated at West Point in 1856, assigned to the Cavalry, and in 1860 made an Instructor at the Military Academy. He resigned in 1861, became Adjutant-General in the Confederate Army on the staff of General Ewell, and took part in all the campaigns of the Army of Northern Virginia. He was made Brigadier-General July 25, 1862, and Major-General September 3, 1863. Three horses were shot under him in the Battle of Winchester, September 19, 1864, and he was severely wounded. In March, 1865, he was given command of the whole Cavalry force in the Army of Northern Virginia. He surrendered to General Mead at Farmville County April 7, 1865, and retired to his home in Stafford County. His famous speech at Bunker Hill in 1874 attested the sincerity with which he accepted the results of the great struggle and his fidelity to the reconstructed Union. He was elected Governor of Virginia in 1885.

LONGSTREET, JAMES, Major-General, was born in Edgefield District, S. C., January 8, 1821, graduated at West Point in 1842, served in the Infantry on frontier duty, engaged in the Mexican War at Palo Alto, Resaca, Monterey, Vera Cruz, Cerro Gordo, Churubusco and Molino del Rey, winning brevets of Captain and Major. Resigning in 1861 he was made Brigadier-General in the Confederate Army. In the first Battle of Bull Run he led a Brigade on the right of the Confederate line, and prevented a large Union force from joining in McDowell's attempted flank attack. He was made Major-General, and commanded the Rear Guard in General Joseph E. Johnston's retreat before McClellan from Yorktown. On May 5, 1862, he attacked Hintzleman, Hooker and Kearney at Williamsburg, and held them engaged till they were reinforced. He bore a prominent part in the seven day's fight around Richmond, commanded the First Corps of the Army of Northern Virginia in the second Battle of Bull Run, coming to Jackson's relief when Pope was pressing him hard, and by a determined flank charge saved the fight. He commanded Lee's right wing at Gettysburg, and tried to dissuade him from the disastrous charge on the third day. He was sent to help Bragg at Chickamauga, and made a fruitless effort to capture Knoxville. Rejoining Lee in 1864 he was wounded by the fire of his own troops in the Wilderness fight, and was included in Lee's surrender. Known throughout the army as "Old Pete" he had the entire confidence of his men, and was considered the hardest fighter of the Confederate leaders. After the war he resided at New Orleans, where he held several Federal appointments. President Hayes made him Minister to Turkey.

MAHONE, WILLIAM, Major-General, born December 1, 1826, in Southampton County, Va., educated at the Virginia Military Institute, and became a civil engineer engaged in railroad construction. He joined the Confederate Army in 1861, helped to capture the Norfolk Navy Yard in April, raised and commanded the 6th Virginia Regiment, became known as a fighting commander, being present in most of the battles of the Peninusula, on the Rappahannock, and around Petersburg, in which latter locality he won the title of "Hero of the Crater." He was made Brigadier in March, 1864, and Major-General in August of that year, led a Division in A. P. Hill's Corps, and when Lee surrendered was posted a Bermuda Hundred. He became President of the Norfolk and Tennessee Railroad, was the leader of the Readjuster party, was elected United States Senator in 1880, and served as such till 1887.

McLAWS, LAFAYETTE, Major-General, born at Augusta, Ga., January 15, 1821, graduated at West Point in 1842, served on frontier posts, joined Tayler's Army at Corpus Christi, was in the capture of Monterey and Vera Cruz, and in 1851 became Captain of Infantry. He resigned in 1861, became a Confederate Brigadier, fought at Lee's Mill and Williamsburg, and was promoted to Major-General. His Division was in the fight at Malvern Hill, and joined in the march into Maryland. He was given command of a Corps, captured Harper's Ferry, and reached Sharpsburg in time to arrest the retreat of Hood and Jackson. At Fredericksburg his men from a sunken road on Marye's Hill drove back the Union troops. He commanded the Confederate right wing at Chancellorsville, and at Gettysburg he led a portion of Longstreet's force in its attack on Sickles' Corps in the second day's fight. He commanded the District of Georgia when General William T. Sherman moved on Savannah, and falling back attempted vainly at several places to check the northward march of the Union force. After the return of peace he engaged in business at Savannah, and was subsequently Postmaster there.

PEGRAM, WILLIAM JOHNSON, Brigadier-General, born at Petersburg, Va., in 1841, was a student in the University of Virginia at the beginning of the war, enlisted in a Confederate Artillery Regiment as a private, and won promotion for gallantry at Cedar Run, Chancellorsville and Gettysburg. Early in 1865 he was made Brigadier-General, and was killed in the seige of Petersburg, April 2, 1865.

PENDER, WILLIAM DORSEY, Major-General, born in Edgecombe County, N. C., February 6, 1834, was graduated at West Point in 1854, served on the frontier in the Dragoons until March, 1861, when he resigned and was commissioned Colonel of a North Carolina regiment, promoted Brigadier in June, 1862, and Major-General May 27, 1863. His Division was part of A. P. Hill's Corps in the Army of Northern Virginia. He died at Staunton, Va., July 18, 1863, from wounds received at Gettysburg.

PERRIN, ABNER M., Brigadier-General, born in Edgefield County, S. C., in 1827, was educated in Bothany Academy and served as Lieutenant of Volunteers in the Mexican War. He became a lawyer practicing till 1861, when he entered the Confederate Army as Captain in the 14th South Carolina Regiment, was promoted Colonel in 1863, and as Brigadier-General in May, 1864, with command of an Alabama Brigade.

PETTIGREW, JAMES JOHNSTON, Brigadier-General, born in Tyrrel County, N. C., July 4, 1828, was graduated at the University of North Carolina, and became a lawyer in Charleston, S. C., and a Captain of Militia. By order of Governor Pickens he demanded of Major Robert Anderson, United States Army, the evacuation of Fort Sumter. He was Colonel of the 12th North Carolina Regiment, and was promoted Brigadier-General in the Confederate Army in 1862. He was wounded at Seven Pines and taken prisoner. At Gettysburg he commanded Heth's Division on the third day, taking part in Pickett's charge, and was again wounded. On the retreat into Virginia he was surprised by National Cavalry, and received a wound from which he died near Winchester, Va., July 17, 1863.

PICKETT, GEORGE E., Major-General, born in Henrico County, Va., January 25, 1825, graduated at West Point in 1846; served in the war with Mexico as an Infantry officer under General Winfield Scott; was in the battles Contresas, Churubusco, Molino del Rey, and Chapultepec, winning two brevets for conspicuous gallantry. He accompanied his regiment, 9th Infantry, to the Pacific coast, and as Captain distinguished himself in holding the disputed island of St. Juan when threatened by British men-of-war. He resigned in 1861 and became a Confederate Colonel, and soon a Brigadier. His command did notable service at Yorktown, Williamsburg, Seven Pines, and in the seven days' fighting around Richmond. He was severely wounded at Gaines' Mills. Commissioned Major-General, his Division was daringly and actively engaged in nearly every action of the Army of Northern Virginia. In the Battle of Gettysburg he led his men in the desperate and memorable charge on the Union left centre at Cemetery Hill. He took part in the later battles in 1864 around Richmond, Petersburg, and at Five Forks ; and ended his military career in the fight at Sailor's Creek, April 6, 1865. After the war he retired to private life in Virginia, was engaged in the insurance business, and died at Norfolk July 30, 1875.

RAMSEUR, STEPHEN D., Major-General, born in South Carolina in 1837, graduated at West Point in 1860, and was assigned to the Artillery. He resigned in April, 1861, and was appointed Brigadier in the Confederate service. He served with distinction at Gettysburg, and was promoted Major-General. At the Battle of Cedar Creek, October 19, 1864, while in command of a Division, he was mortally wounded, and died October 21, 1864.

STUART, JAMES E. B., Major-General, born in Patrick County, Va., in 1833, graduated at West Point in 1854, and served on the frontier in the Dragoons. He resigned, was appointed May 14, 1861, a Colonel of Confederate Cavalry, and was Chief Cavalry Commander in the first battle of Bull Run. He was promoted Brigadier and early in 1862 Major-General, and served thenceforth with the Army of Northern Virginia. With 1,500 troops and four guns Stuart left Richmond June 13, 1862, and, reaching Hanover Court House, dispersed two squadrons of United States Cavalry at daybreak on the 15th : crossed the Chickahominy at Jones' Bridge next morning and was safe at Richmond that night, having made the circuit of McClellan's position with the loss of but one man. During Pope's campaign in command of the Union troops, Stuart surprised his headquarters at Catlett's Station August 25, 1862, captured Pope's personal baggage and correspondence, and the next night struck Manassas Junction capturing eight guns, many prisoners, ten locomotives, and great quantities of military stores. When Lee invaded Maryland in September Stuart covered the Confederate rear. With 1,500 cavalry he crossed the Potomac above Williamsport, crossed Maryland and occupied Chambersburg, Pa. His command formed the right of the Confederate line at Fredericksburg. At Chancellorsville May 3, 1863, after Jackson and A. P. Hill fell Stuart commanded the Corps, figting with great ability. In Lee's movement to invade Pennsylvania Stuart commanded a large Cavalry force to meet which Hooker sent two Cavalry Divisions and two Infantry Brigades. In the Cavalry fight which ensued 500 or 600 men were lost on each side. In the campaign of 1864 Stuart threw his troops between Richmond and Sheridan's threatening advance. He was attacked at Yellow Tavern. During the desperate fight Stuart was mortally wounded and died May 11, 1864, soon after reaching Richmond.

HOW WELL THEY FOUGHT.

"Say, Jim," he began, as they shook hands, "how do you stand on this Gettysburg dispute?"

"Well, I've favored Sickles all along."

"So have I. Now, see here. Right here on this paper is Gettysburg."

"Yes."

"Along this road is where Hancock came up."

"I see."

"Howard came up this road."

"He did."

"Sedgwick and his Sixth Corps travelled along right here, and swung into action over there on the second day."

"You just bet they did."

"Let's see? Sykes must have come up by this road."

"Yes, I'm certain of it."

"Now, then, Jim, where were you?"

"Well, our sutler wagon was away off here, say about twelve miles. Where were you?"

"I was with the wagon train off this way, about seven miles. Say, we've got this thing down to a dot, and we ought to write a letter to some newspaper."

"'Zactly, Jim, and we can't do it too soon. It's left to us to straighten out this tangle, and we are the men to do it."

XI.

ORGANIZATION OF THE ARMY OF NORTHERN VIRGINIA AT THE BATTLE OF GETTYSBURG.

GENERAL ROBERT E. LEE COMMANDING.

Staff—Colonel W. H. Taylor. Adjutant-General; Colonel C. S. Venable, A. D. C.; Colonel Charles Marshall, A. D. C.; Colonel James L. Corley, Chief Quartermaster; Colonel R. G. Cole, Chief Commissary; Colonel B. G. Baldwin, Chief of Ordnance ; Colonel H. L. Peyton, Assistant Inspector-General; General W. N. Pendleton, Chief of Artillery ; Dr. L. Guild, Medical Director; Colonel W. Proctor Smith, Chief Engineer ; Major H. E. Young, Assistant Adjutant-General ; Major G. B. Cook, Assistant Inspector-General.

FIRST CORPS.

LIEUTENANT-GENERAL JAMES LONGSTREET.

McLAWS'S DIVISION—Major-General Lafayette McLaws.

Kershaw's (1st) *Brigade*—Brigadier-General J. B. Kershaw. 2d South Carolina, Colonel John D. Kennedy ; 3d South Carolina, Colonel James D. Vance ; 7th South Carolina, Colonel D. Wyatt Aiken ; 8th South Carolina. Colonel J. W. Memminger ; 15th South Carolina, Colonel W. D. Saussure ; 3d South Carolina Battalion, ——.

Semmes (2d) *Brigade*—Brigadier-General P. J. Semmes (killed), Colonel Goode Bryan. 10th Georgia, Lieutenant-Colonel John B. Weems ; 50th Georgia, Colonel W. R. Manning ; 51st Georgia. Colonel W. M. Slaughter; 53d Georgia, Colonel James P. Semmes.

Barksdale's (3d) *Brigade*—Brigadier-General W. Barksdale (wounded). Colonel B. G. Humphreys. 13th Mississippi. Colonel J. W. Carter ; 17th Mississippi, Colonel W. D. Holder ; 18th Mississippi, Colonel Thomas M. Griffin ; 21st Mississippi, Colonel B. G. Humphries.

Wofford's (4th) Brigade—Brigadier-General W. T. Wofford. 16th Georgia, Colonel Goode Bryan; 18th Georgia, Major E. Griffs; 24th Georgia, Colonel Robert McMillan; Cobb's Georgia Legion, Lieutenant-Colonel L. D. Glenn; Phillips' Georgia Legion, Colonel W. M. Phillips.

Artillery—Colonel H. C. Cabell. Major Hamilton. Carlton's Georgia Battery (Troop Artillery); Fraser's Georgia Battery (Putaski artillery); McCarthy's Battery (1st Richmond Howitzers); Manly's North Carolina Battery.

PICKETT'S DIVISION—Major-General George E. Pickett.

Garnett's (1st) Brigade—Brigadier-General R. B. Garnett (killed), Major George C. Cabell. 8th Virginia, Colonel Eppa Hunton; 18th Virginia, Colonel R. E. Withers; 19th Virginia, Colonel Henry Gantt; 28th Virginia, Colonel R. C. Allen; 56th Virginia, Colonel W. D. Stewart.

Armistead's (2d) Brigade—Brigadier-General L. A. Armistead (killed), Colonel W. R. Aylett. 9th Virginia, Lieutenant-Colonel J. S. Gilliam; 14th Virginia, Colonel J. G. Hodges; 38th Virginia, Colonel E. C. Edmonds; 53d Virginia, Colonel John Grammer; 57th Virginia, Colonel J. B. Magruder.

Kemper's (3d) Brigade—Brigadier-General J. L. Kemper (wounded), Colonel Joseph Mayo, Jr. 1st Virginia, Colonel Lewis B. Williams, Jr; 3d Virginia, Colonel Joseph Mayo, Jr; 7th Virginia, Colonel W. T. Patton; 11th Virginia Colonel David Funston; 24th Virginia, Colonel W R. Terry.

Corse's (4th) Brigade (not engaged)—Brigadier-General M. D. Corse. The Brigade was encamped at Gordonsville, July 1–8. 15th Virginia, Colonel T. P. August; 17th Virginia, Colonel Morton Marye; 29th Virginia, Colonel James Giles; 30th Virginia, Colonel A. F Harrison; 32d Virginia, Colonel E. B. Montague.

Artillery—Major James Dearing. Blount's Virginia Battery; Caskie's Virginia Battery (Hampden Artillery); Macon's Battery (Richmond Fayette Artillery); Stubling's Virginia Battery (Farquhar Artillery).

HOOD'S DIVISION—Major-General John B. Hood (wounded).

Law's (1st) Brigade—Brigadier-General E. M. Law. Colonel James M. Sheffield. 4th Alabama, Colonel P. A. Bowls; 15th Alabama, Colonel James Canty; 44th Alabama, Colonel W. H. Perry; 47th Alabama. Colonel J. W. Jackson; 48th Alabama, Colonel J. F. Shepherd.

Anderson's (2d) Brigade—Brigadier-General Geo. T. Anderson (wounded), Colonel W. W. White. 7th Georgia, Colonel W. W. White; 8th Georgia. Lieutenant-Colonel J. B. Towers; 9th Georgia, Colonel B. F. Beck; 11th Georgia, Colonel F. H. Little; 59th Georgia.

Robertson's (3d) *Brigade*—Brigadier-General J. B. Robertson. 3d Arkansas, Colonel Van H. Manning; 1st Texas, Colonel A. T. Rainey: 4th Texas, Colonel J. C. G. Key; 5th Texas, Colonel R. M. Powell.

Benning's (4th) *Brigade*—Brigadier-General H. L. Benning. 2d Georgia, Colonel E. M. Butt; 15th Georgia, Colonel E. M. Dubose; 17th Georgia, Colonel W. C. Hodges; 20th Georgia, Colonel J. B. Cummings.

Artillery—Major M. W. Henry. Bachman's South Carolina Battery (German artillery); Gordon's South Carolina Battery (Palmetto Light Artillery): Latham's North Carolina Battery (Branch Artillery); Reilly's North Carolina Battery (Rowan Artillery).

RESERVE ARTILLERY (FIRST CORPS)—Colonel J. B. Walton. Chief of Artillery.

Alexander's Battalion—Colonel E. P. Alexander. Jordan's Virginia Battery (Bedford Artillery); Moody's Louisiana Battery (Madison Light Artillery); Parker's Virginia Battery; Rhett's South Carolina Battery (Brooks' Artillery); Taylor's Virginia Battery; Woolfolk's Virginia Battery (Ashland Artillery).

Washington (*La.*) *Artillery*—Major B. F. Eshleman. Miller's (3d) Company; Norcom's (4th) Company; Richardson's (2d) Company; Squire's (1st) Company.

SECOND CORPS.

LIEUTENANT-GENERAL RICHARD S. EWELL.

EARLY'S DIVISION—Major-General Jubal A. Early.

Hays' (1st) *Brigade*—Brigadier-General Harry T. Hays. 5th Louisiana, Colonel Henry Forno; 6th Louisiana, Colonel William Monaghan; 7th Louisiana, Colonel D. P. Penn; 8th Louisiana, Colonel Henry B. Keely; 9th Louisiana, Colonel A. L. Stafford.

Hoke's (2d) *Brigade*—Brigadier-General R. F. Hoke. Colonel Isaac E. Avery (wounded), Colonel A. C. Godwin. 6th North Carolina, Colonel J. E. Avery; 21st North Carolina, Colonel W. W. Kirkland; 54th North Carolina, Colonel J. T. C. McDowell; 57th North Carolina, Colonel A. C. Godwin; 1st North Carolina Battalion, ——.

Smith's (2d) *Brigade*—Brigadier-General William Smith, Colonel John S. Hoffman. 13th Virginia, Colonel J. A. Walker; 31st Virginia, Colonel John S. Hoffman; 49th Virginia, Colonel Gibson; 52d Virginia, Colonel Skinner; 58th Virginia, Colonel F. H. Board.

Gordon's (4th) *Brigade*—Brigadier-General J. B. Gordon. 13th Georgia, Colonel J. M. Smith; 26th Georgia, Colonel E. N. Atkinson; 31st Georgia, Colonel C. A. Evans; 38th Georgia, Major J. D. Matthews; 60th Georgia, Colonel W. H. Stiles; 61st Georgia, Colonel J. H. Lamar.

Artillery—Lieutenant-Colonel H. P. Jones. Carrington's Virginia Battery (Charlottesville Artillery); Gaiber's Virginia Battery (Staunton Artillery); Green's Battery (Louisiana Artillery); Tanner's Virginia Battery (Courtney Artillery).

JOHNSON'S DIVISION—Major-General Edward Johnson.

Steuart's (1st) *Brigade.*—Brigadier-General George H. Steuart. 1st Maryland Battalion; 1st North Carolina, Colonel J. A. McDowell; 3d North Carolina, Lieutenant-Colonel Thurston; 10th Virginia, Colonel E. T. H. Warren; 23d Virginia, Colonel A. G. Taliaferro; 37th Virginia, ——.

Nicholl's (2d) *Brigade*—Colonel J. M. Williams. 1st Louisiana, Colonel William R. Shirers; 2d Louisiana, Colonel J. M. Williams; 10th Louisiana, Colonel E. Waggerman; 14th Louisiana, Colonel Z. York; 15th Louisiana, Colonel Edward Pendleton.

Walker's "*Stonewall*" (3d) *Brigade*—Brigadier-General James A. Walker. 2d Virginia, Colonel J. Q. A. Nadenbousch; 4th Virginia, Colonel Charles A. Ronald; 5th Virginia, Colonel J. H. S. Funk; 27th Virginia, Colonel J. K. Edmondson; 33d Virginia, Colonel F. M. Holladay.

Jones's (4th) *Brigade*—Brigadier-General John M. Jones (wounded), Lieutenant-Colonel R. H. Dungan, Colonel B. T. Johnson. 21st Virginia, ——; 25th Virginia; 42d Virginia, Lieutenant-Colonel Withers; 44th Virginia, Colonel William C. Scott; 48th Virginia, Colonel T. S. Garnett; 50th Virginia, Colonel Vandeventer.

Artillery—Lieutenant-Colonel R. S. Andrews. Brown's Maryland Battery (Chesapeake Artillery); Carpenter's Virginia Battery (Allegheny Artillery); Dement's 1st Maryland Battery; Raine's Virginia Battery (Lee Battery).

RODES' DIVISION—Major-General R. E. Rodes.

Daniel's (1st) *Brigade*—Brigadier-General Junius Daniel. 32d North Carolina, Colonel E. C. Brabble; 43d North Carolina, Colonel Thomas S. Keenan; 45th North Carolina, Lieutenant-Colonel Samuel H. Boyd; 53d North Carolina, Colonel W. A. Owens; 2d Battalion North Carolina, Lieutenant-Colonel H. S. Andrew.

Iverson's (2d) *Brigade*—Brigadier-General Alfred Iverson. 5th North Carolina, Captain S. B. West; 12th North Carolina, Lieutenant-Colonel W. S. Davis; 20th North Carolina, Lieutenant-Colonel N. Slough; 23d North Carolina, Colonel D. H. Christie.

Doles' (3d) *Brigade*—Brigadier-General George Doles. 4th Georgia, Lieutenant-Colonel D. R. E. Winn; 12th Georgia, Colonel Edward Willis; 21st Georgia, Colonel John T. Mercer; 44th Georgia, Colonel S. P. Lumpkin.

Ramseur's (4th) *Brigade*—Brigadier-General J. D. Ramseur. 2d North Carolina, Major E. W. Hurtt; 4th North Carolina, Colonel Bryan Grimes; 14th North Carolina, Colonel R. T. Bennett; 30th North Carolina, Colonel F. M. Parker.

O'Neal's (5th) *Brigade*—Brigadier-General E. A. O'Neal, Colonel C. A. Battle. 3d Alabama, Colonel C. A. Battle; 5th Alabama, Colonel J. M. Hall; 6th Alabama, Colonel J. N. Lightfoot; 12th Alabama, Colonel S. B. Pickens; 16th Alabama, Lieutenant-Colonel J. C. Goodame.

Artillery—Lieutenant-Colonel Thomas H. Carter. Carter's Virginia Battery (King William Artillery); Fry's Virginia Battery (Orange Artillery); Pages' Virginia Battery (Morris Artillery); Reese's Alabama Battery (Jeff Davis Artillery.)

RESERVE ARTILLERY (SECOND CORPS)—Colonel J. Thompson Brown, Chief of Artillery.

Brown's Battalion—Captain Willis J. Dance. Dance's Virginia Battery (Powhattan Artillery); Hupp's Virginia Battery (Salem Artillery); Graham's Virginia Battery (Rockbridge Artillery); Smith's Battery (3d Richmond Howitzers); Watson's Battery (2d Richmond Howitzers).

Nelson's Battalion (1st Virginia Artillery)—Lieutenant-Colonel William Nelson. Kirkpatrick's Virginia Battery (Amherst Artillery); Massies Virginia Battery (Fluvania Artillery); Milledge's Georgia Battery.

THIRD CORPS.

LIEUTENANT-GENERAL AMBROSE P. HILL.

ANDERSON'S DIVISION—Major-General R. H. Anderson.

Wilcox's (1st) *Brigade*—Brigadier-General Cadmus M. Wilcox. 8th Alabama, Colonel T. L. Royster; 9th Alabama, Colonel S. Henry; 10th Alabama, Colonel W. H. Forney; 11th Alabama, Colonel J. C. C. Saunders; 14th Alabama, Colonel L. P. Pinkhard.

Mahone's (2d) *Brigade*—Brigadier-General William Mahone. 6th Virginia, Colonel G. T. Rodgers; 12th Virginia, Colonel D. A. Weisiger; 16th Virginia, Lieutenant-Colonel Joseph H. Ham; 41st Virginia, Colonel W. A. Parkham; 61st Virginia, Colonel V. D. Groner.

Wright's (3d) *Brigade*—Brigadier-General A. R. Wright, Captain E. H. Wright. 3d Georgia, Colonel E. J. Walker; 22d Georgia, Colonel R. H. Jones; 48th Georgia, Colonel William Gibson; 2d Georgia Battalion, Major G. W. Ross.

Perry's (4th) *Brigade*—Colonel David Long. Brigadier-General E. A. Perry. 2d Florida, Lieutenant-Colonel S. G. Pyles; 5th Florida, Colonel J. C. Hately; 8th Florida, Colonel David Long.

Posey's (5th) Brigade—Brigadier-General Carnot Posey. 12th Mississippi, Colonel W. H. Taylor ; 16th Mississippi, Colonel Samuel E. Baker ; 19th Mississippi, Colonel John Mullins ; 48th Mississippi, Colonel Joseph Jayne.

Artillery (Sumter's Battalion)—Major John Lane. Patterson's Georgia Battery, Ross' Georgia Battery, Wingfield's Georgia Battery (Irwin Artillery).

HETH'S DIVISION—Major-General Henry Heth, Brigadier-General J. J. Pettigrew.

Pettigrew's (1st) Brigade—Brigadier-General J. J. Pettigrew (wounded), Colonel J. K. Marshall, Colonel C. T. Singeltary. 11th North Carolina, Colonel W. J. Martin ; 26th North Carolina, Colonel Henry K. Burgwin ; 44th North Carolina, Colonel Thomas C. Singeltary (left at Hanover Junction and not engaged at Gettysburg) ; 47th North Carolina, Colonel George H. Faribault ; 52d North Carolina, Colonel James K. Marshall.

Field's (2d) Brigade—Brigadier-General Charles W. Field, Colonel J. M. Brockenbrough. 40th Virginia, Colonel J. M. Brockenbrough ; 47th Virginia, Colonel R. M. Mayo ; 55th Virginia, Colonel F. Mallory ; 22d Virginia Battalion, Major E. P. Taylor.

Archer's (3d) Brigade—Brigadier-General James J. Archer, Colonel B. D. Fry, Brigadier-General H. H. Walker. 13th Alabama, —— ; 5th Alabama Battalion, Major A. S. Van de Graaff ; 1st Tennessee (Prov. Army), Colonel P. Turney ; 7th Tennessee, Colonel John F. Goodner ; 14th Tennessee, Colonel William McComb.

Davis' (4th) Brigade—Brigadier-General Joseph R. Davis. 2d Mississippi, Colonel J. M. Stone ; 11th Mississippi, Major R. O. Reynolds ; 42d Mississippi, Lieutenant-Colonel A. M. Nelson ; 55th North Carolina, Captain R. W. Thomas.

Artillery—Lieutenant-Colonel John J. Garnet, Major Charles Richardson. Grandy's Virginia Battery (Norfolk Light Artillery Blues) ; Lewis' Virginia Battery ; Maurin's Louisiana Battery (Donaldson's Artillery) ; Moore's Virginia Battery.

PENDER'S DIVISION—Major-General William D. Pender (wounded), Brigadier-General James H. Lane.

McGown's (1st) Brigade—Brigadier-General S. McGown, Colonel Abner Perrin. 1st South Carolina (Orr's Rifles), Lieutenant-Colonel J. M. Perrin ; 12th South Carolina, Lieutenant-Colonel Calwalader Jones ; 13th South Carolina, Lieutenant-Colonel O. E. Edwards ; 14th South Carolina, Lieutenant-Colonel Samuel McGown.

Lane's (2d) Brigade—Brigadier-General James H. Lane, Colonel C. M. Avery. 7th North Carolina, Colonel E. G. Haywood ; 18th North Carolina, Lieutenant-Colonel T. J. Purdie ; 28th North Carolina, Lieutenant-Colonel S. D. Lowe ; 33d North Carolina, Colonel C. M. Avery ; 37th North Carolina, Colonel W. M. Barbour.

Thomas' (3d) *Brigade*—Brigadier-General E. L. Thomas. 14th Georgia, Colonel R. W. Folsom ; 35th Georgia, Colonel B. H. Holt ; 45th Georgia, Colonel T. J. Simmons ; 49th Georgia, Colonel A. J. Lane.

Scales' (4th) *Brigade*—Brigadier-General A. M. Scales (wounded), Colonel W. Lee Lowrance. 13th North Carolina, Colonel A. M. Scales ; 16th North Carolina, Colonel J. S. McElroy ; 22d North Carolina, Colonel James Conner ; 34th North Carolina, Colonel W. L. J. Lowrance ; 38th North Carolina, Colonel W. J. Hoke.

Artillery—Major William T. Poague. Brooke's Virginia Battery ; Graham's North Carolina Battery ; Ward's Mississippi Battery (Madison Light Artillery) ; Wyatt's Virginia Battery (Albemarle Artillery).

RESERVE ARTILLERY (THIRD CORPS)—Colonel R. L. Walker, Chief of Artillery.

McIntosh's Battalion—Major D. G. McIntosh. Hurt's Alabama Battery (Hardaway Artillery) ; Lusk's Virginia Battery ; Johnson's Virginia Battery ; Rice's Virginia Battery, Danville Artillery.

Pegram's Battalion—Major W. J. Pegram, Captain E. B. Brunson. Brander's Virginia Battery (Letcher Artillery) ; Brunson's South Carolina Battery (Pee Dee Artillery) ; Crenshaw's Virginia Battery ; McGraw's Virginia Battery (Purcell Artillery) ; Marye's Virginia Battery (Fredericksburg Artillery.)

CAVALRY.

MAJOR-GENERAL J. E. B. STUART.

Hampton's 1st *Brigade*—Brigadier-General Wade Hampton, Colonel L. S. Baker. 1st North Carolina, 1st and 2d South Carolina, Cobb's Georgia Legion, Jeff Davis Legion, Phillips' Georgia Legion.

Robertson's 2d *Brigade*—Brigadier-General B. H. Robertson, 4th and 5th North Carolina.

Fitz Lee's (3d) *Brigade*—Brigadier-General Fitz Hugh Lee, Colonel Thomas T. Munford. 1st Maryland Battalion, 1st, 2d, 3d, 4th and 5th Virginia.

Jenkins' 4th *Brigade*—Brigadier-General A. G. Jenkins. 14th, 16th, 17th, 34th and 36th Virginia.

Jones' 5th *Brigade*—Brigadier-General William E. Jones. 6th, 7th, 11th and 12th Virginia, 35th Virginia Battalion.

W. H. F. Lee's (6th) Brigade—Colonel J. R. Chambliss, Jr.   2d North Carolina, 9th, 10th, 13th and 15th Virginia.

NOT BRIGADED:

IMBODEN'S COMMAND.   43d Virginia (Mosby's) Battalion.

Stuart Horse Artillery—Major R. F. Beckham.   Breathed's Maryland Battery; Chew's Virginia Battery; Guffin's 2d Maryland Battery; Hart's South Carolina Battery (Washington Artillery); McGregor's Virginia Battery; Moorman's Virgina Battery.

[This table has been corrected by Colonel Charles T. Loehr, of Richmond, Va., Secretary of the Pickett's Division Association, by authority of General A. L. Long, General Lee's Private Secretary.]

XII.

DETAILED REPORT OF LOSSES IN EACH ARMY AT THE BATTLE OF GETTYSBURG, JULY 1-4, 1863

COMPILED FROM OFFICIAL REPORTS.

ARMY OF THE POTOMAC.

	Killed		Wounded		Capt'd or Missing		Aggregate.
	Officers.	Enlisted Men.	Officers.	Enlisted Men.	Officers.	Enlisted Men.	
General Headquarters—Staff.....	...	....	2	2	...	....	4
FIRST ARMY CORPS.							
Corps Headquarters—Staff.......	1	....	1	....	...	....	2
1st Maine Cavalry, Co. L.........	...	1	....	2	...	....	3
FIRST DIVISION.							
First Brigade.							
Staff..............................	...	....	1	....	...	....	1
19th Indiana.....................	2	25	12	121	4	46	210
24th Michigan...................	8	50	13	201	3	88	363
2d Wisconsin.....................	1	25	11	144	5	47	233
6th Wisconsin....................	2	28	7	109	...	22	168
7th Wisconsin....................	...	21	10	95	1	51	178
Total First Brigade...........	13	149	54	670	13	254	1,153
Second Brigade.							
7th Indiana.......................	...	2	....	5	...	3	10
76th New York...................	2	30	16	116	...	70	234
84th New York (14th Militia).....	...	13	6	99	...	99	217
95th New York...................	...	7	8	54	1	45	115
147th New York..................	3	40	9	125	...	92	269
56th Pennsylvania................	1	13	5	55	2	54	130
Total Second Brigade........	6	105	44	454	3	363	975
Total First Division..........	19	254	98	1,124	16	617	2,128
SECOND DIVISION.							
Staff..............................	...	....	1	....	...	....	1

SECOND DIVISION—CONTINUED.

	Killed Officers.	Killed Enlisted Men.	Wounded Officers.	Wounded Enlisted Men.	Capt'd or Missing Officers.	Capt'd or Missing Enlisted Men.	Aggregate.
First Brigade.							
Staff	...	....	1	1	2	1	5
16th Maine	2	7	5	54	11	153	232
13th Massachusetts	...	7	4	73	3	98	185
94th New York	...	12	6	52	8	167	245
104th New York	...	11	10	81	10	82	194
11th Pennsylvania	*...	1	2	12	...	...	15
107th Pennsylvania	...	11	8	48	6	92	165
Total First Brigade	2	49	36	321	40	593	1,041

*Transferred on afternoon of July 1st from Second to First Brigade; other losses reported in latter Brigade.

	Killed Officers.	Killed Enlisted Men.	Wounded Officers.	Wounded Enlisted Men.	Capt'd or Missing Officers.	Capt'd or Missing Enlisted Men.	Aggregate.
Second Brigade.							
Staff	...	....	....	....	1	....	1
12th Massachusetts	2	3	7	45	3	59	119
83d New York (9th Militia)	2	4	3	15	...	58	82
97th New York	2	10	9	27	3	75	126
11th Pennsylvania	*...	5	6	44	...	62	117
88th Pennsylvania	...	3	3	51	4	45	106
90th Pennsylvania	1	7	3	42	1	39	93
Total Second Brigade	7	32	31	224	12	338	644
Total Second Division	9	81	68	545	52	931	1,686

THIRD DIVISION.

	Killed Officers.	Killed Enlisted Men.	Wounded Officers.	Wounded Enlisted Men.	Capt'd or Missing Officers.	Capt'd or Missing Enlisted Men.	Aggregate.
Staff			1				9
First Brigade.							
Staff	...	....	1	....	...	....	1
80th New York (20th Militia)	3	32	15	95	1	23	170
121st Pennsylvania	...	12	5	101	1	60	179
142d Pennsylvania	3	10	11	117	2	68	211
151st Pennsylvania	2	29	7	195	2	100	335
Total First Brigade	8	83	39	509	6	251	896
Second Brigade.							
143d Pennsylvania	1	20	10	130	...	91	252
149th Pennsylvania	1	33	12	159	4	127	336
150th Pennsylvania	2	27	10	141	4	80	264
Total Second Brigade	4	80	32	430	8	298	852
Third Brigade.							
Staff	...	....	2	....	...	....	2
13th Vermont	...	10	4	99	...	10	123
14th Vermont	1	18	1	66	...	21	107
16th Vermont	...	16	5	97	...	1	119
Total Third Brigade	1	44	12	262	...	32	351
Total Third Division	13	207	84	1,201	14	581	2,100
Artillery Brigade.							
Maine Light 2d Battery	...	....	...	18	...	....	18
Maine Light 5th Battery	...	3	2	11	...	7	23
1st New York Light Battery L, 1st N. Y. H'y Artillery attached	...	1	1	14	...	1	17

THIRD DIVISION—CONTINUED.

	Killed Officers.	Killed Enlisted Men.	Wounded Officers.	Wounded Enlisted Men.	Capt'd or Missing Officers.	Capt'd or Missing Enlisted Men.	Aggregate.
1st Pennsylvania Light Battery B.	...	2	1	8	...	...	11
4th U. S. Battery B.	...	2	2	29	...	3	36
Total Artillery Brigade	...	8	6	80	...	11	105
Total First Army Corps	42	551	257	2,952	82	2,140	6,024

SECOND ARMY CORPS.

	Killed Officers.	Killed Enlisted Men.	Wounded Officers.	Wounded Enlisted Men.	Capt'd or Missing Officers.	Capt'd or Missing Enlisted Men.	Aggregate.
General Headquarters—Staff	...	...	3	...	...	...	3
6th New York Cavalry Companies D and K	...	1	...	3	...	...	4
FIRST DIVISION.							
First Brigade.							
Staff	...	...	1	...	...	...	1
5th New Hampshire	1	26	4	49	...	...	80
61st New York	...	6	6	50	...	...	62
81st Pennsylvania	...	5	5	44	...	8	62
148th Pennsylvania	1	18	6	95	...	5	125
Total First Brigade	2	55	22	238	...	13	330
Second Brigade.							
28th Massachusetts	...	8	1	56	...	35	100
63d New York	...	5	1	9	1	7	23
69th New York	...	5	1	13	...	6	25
88th New York	1	6	1	16	...	4	28
116th Pennsylvania	...	2	...	11	1	8	22
Total Second Brigade	1	26	4	105	2	60	198
Third Brigade.							
Staff	1	...	...	...	...	...	1
52d New York	1	1	3	23	...	10	38
57th New York	...	4	2	26	...	2	34
66th New York	2	3	5	24	1	9	44
140th Pennsylvania	3	34	8	136	3	57	241
Total Third Brigade	7	42	18	209	4	78	358
Fourth Brigade.							
27th Connecticut	2	8	4	19	...	4	37
2d Delaware	2	9	7	54	...	12	84
64th New York	4	11	7	57	...	19	98
53d Pennsylvania	...	7	11	56	...	6	80
145th Pennsylvania	1	9	8	58	...	8	84
Total Fourth Brigade	9	44	37	244	...	49	383
Total First Division	19	167	81	796	6	200	1,269
SECOND DIVISION.							
Staff	...	...	3				3
First Brigade.							
Staff	...	...	1	...	...	...	1
19th Maine	1	28	11	155	...	4	199
15th Massachusetts	3	20	8	89	...	28	148
1st Minnesota	3	47	14	150	...	1	224
82d New York (2d Militia)	3	42	12	120	1	14	192
Total First Brigade	10	137	46	522	1	47	764

SECOND DIVISION—CONTINUED.

	Killed		Wounded		Capt'd or Missing.		Aggregate.
	Officers.	Enlisted Men.	Officers.	Enlisted Men.	Officers.	Enlisted Men.	
Second Brigade.							
69th Pennsylvania	4	36	8	72	2	7	129
71st Pennsylvania	2	19	3	55	3	16	98
72d Pennsylvania	2	42	7	138	...	2	191
106th Pennsylvania	1	8	9	45	...	1	64
Total Second Brigade	9	105	27	310	5	26	482
Third Brigade.							
19th Massachusetts	2	7	9	52	...	7	77
20th Massachusetts	2	28	8	86	...	3	127
7th Michigan	2	19	3	41	...	....	65
42d New York	...	15	6	49	...	4	74
59th New York	...	6	3	25	...	....	34
Total Third Brigade	6	75	29	253	...	14	377
Unattached.							
1st Massachusetts Sharpshooters	...	2	....	6	...	....	8
Total Second Division	25	319	105	1,092	6	87	1,634
THIRD DIVISION.							
First Brigade.							
14th Indiana	...	6	3	22	...	....	31
4th Ohio	2	7	1	16	...	5	31
8th Ohio	1	17	10	73	...	1	102
7th West Virginia	...	5	1	40	...	1	47
Total First Brigade	3	35	15	151	...	7	211
Second Brigade.							
14th Connecticut	...	10	10	42	...	4	66
1st Delaware	1	9	10	44	1	12	77
12th New Jersey	2	21	4	79	...	9	115
10th New York (Battalion)	...	2	...	4	...	....	6
108th New York	3	13	10	76	...	....	102
Total Second Brigade	6	55	34	245	1	25	366
Third Brigade.							
39th New York	1	14	3	77	...	....	95
111th New York	3	55	8	169	...	14	249
125th New York	2	24	6	98	...	9	139
126th New York	5	35	9	172	...	10	231
Total Third Brigade	11	128	26	516	...	33	714
Total Third Division	20	218	75	912	1	65	1,291
Artillery Brigade.							
1st New York Light Battery B, 14th N. Y. Battery attached	1	9	1	15		....	26
1st Rhode Island Light Battery H	...	3	1	27	...	1	32
1st Rhode Island Light Battery B	1	6	1	18	...	2	28
1st U. S. Battery I	...	1	1	23	...	....	25
4th New York Battery A	1	5	1	31	...	....	38
Total Artillery Brigade	3	24	5	114	...	8	149
Total Second Army Corps	67	789	362	2,917	13	855	4,356

THIRD ARMY CORPS.

	Killed		Wounded		Capt'd or Missing		Aggregate.
	Officers.	Enlisted Men.	Officers.	Enlisted Men.	Officers.	Enlisted Men.	
Staff...........................	...	....	2	....	...	....	2

FIRST DIVISION.

First Brigade.							
Staff............................	...	....	3	....	...	....	3
57th Pennsylvania................	2	9	9	37	3	55	115
63d Pennsylvania.................	...	1	3	26	...	4	34
68th Pennsylvania................	3	4	9	117	...	19	152
105th Pennsylvania...............	1	7	14	101	...	9	132
114th Pennsylvania...............	...	8	1	85	3	57	154
141st Pennsylvania...............	...	25	6	97	...	21	149
Total First Brigade...........	6	54	45	463	6	165	739
Second Brigade.							
Staff............................	...	....	1	....	...	....	1
20th Indiana.....................	2	30	9	105	...	10	156
3d Maine.........................	1	17	2	57	...	45	122
4th Maine........................	2	9	3	56	4	70	144
86th New York....................	1	10	3	48	1	3	66
124th New York	4	24	3	54	...	5	90
99th Pennsylvania................	1	17	4	77	...	11	110
1st U. S. Sharpshooters..........	1	5	4	33	...	6	49
2d U. S. Sharpshooters...........	...	5	4	19	1	14	43
Total Second Brigade.........	12	117	33	449	6	164	781
Third Brigade.							
17th Maine.......................	1	17	7	105	...	3	133
3d Michigan......................	...	7	3	28	...	7	45
5th Michigan.....................	2	17	8	78	...	4	109
40th New York....................	1	22	4	116	...	7	150
110th Pennsylvania...............	...	8	6	39	...	....	53
Total Third Brigade	4	71	28	366	...	21	490
Total First Division...........	22	242	106	1,278	12	350	2,010

SECOND DIVISION.

Staff............................	...	2	2	7	...	....	11
First Brigade.							
Staff............................	...	....	2	....	...	....	2
61st Massachusetts...............	1	15	8	75	...	21	120
11th Massachusetts...............	1	22	7	89	2	8	129
16th Massachusetts...............	3	12	4	49	...	13	81
12th New Hampshire...............	1	13	5	62	...	11	92
11th New Jersey..................	3	14	9	115	...	12	153
26th Pennsylvania................	1	29	10	166	...	7	213
Total First Brigade...........	10	105	45	556	2	72	790
Second Brigade.							
Staff............................	...	..	2	....	...	..	2
70th New York....................	...	20	8	85	...	4	117
71st New York....................	1	9	6	62	...	13	91
72d New York.....................	...	7	7	72	...	28	114

SECOND DIVISION—CONTINUED.

	Killed Officers.	Killed Enlisted Men.	Wounded Officers.	Wounded Enlisted Men.	Capt'd or Missing Officers.	Capt'd or Missing Enlisted Men.	Aggregate.
73d New York	4	47	11	92	...	8	162
74th New York	...	12	6	68	..	?	89
120th New York	7	23	10	144	...	19	203
Total Second Brigade	12	118	50	523	...	75	778
Third Brigade. 2d New Hampshire	2	17	18	119	...	36	193
5th New Jersey	2	11	5	60	...	16	94
6th New Jersey	...	1	3	29	...	8	41
7th New Jersey	1	14	10	76	..	13	114
8th New Jersey	...	7	7	31	...	2	47
115th Pennsylvania	...	3	....	18	...	3	24
Total Third Brigade	6	53	43	333	...	78	513
Total Second Division	28	278	140	1,419	2	225	2,092
Artillery Brigade. New Jersey Light 2d Battery	...	1	....	16	...	3	20
1st New York Light Battery D	...	....	....	10	...	8	18
New York Light 4th Battery	...	2	....	10	...	1	13
1st Rhode Island Light Battery E	...	3	2	24	...	1	30
4th U. S. Battery K	...	2	1	18	...	4	25
Total Artillery Brigade	...	8	3	78	...	17	106
Total Third Army Corps	50	528	251	2,775	14	592	4,210

FIFTH ARMY CORPS.

FIRST DIVISION.

	Killed Officers.	Killed Enlisted Men.	Wounded Officers.	Wounded Enlisted Men.	Capt'd or Missing Officers.	Capt'd or Missing Enlisted Men.	Aggregate.
First Brigade. 18th Massachusetts	...	1	....	23	...	3	27
22d Massachusetts	...	3	3	24	...	1	31
1st Michigan	1	4	6	27	...	4	42
118th Pennsylvania	1	2	3	16	...	3	25
Total First Brigade	2	10	12	90	...	11	125
Second Brigade. 9th Massachusetts	...	1	....	6	...	....	7
32d Massachusetts	1	12	7	55	...	5	80
4th Michigan	1	24	9	55	1	75	165
62d Pennsylvania	4	24	10	97	...	40	175
Total Second Brigade	6	61	26	613	1	120	427
Third Brigade. Staff	...	....	1	....	...	....	1
20th Maine	...	29	6	85	...	5	125
16th Michigan	3	20	2	32	...	3	60
44th New York	2	24	5	77	...	3	111
83d Pennsylvania	1	9	3	42	...	....	55
Total Third Brigade	6	82	17	236	...	11	352
Total First Division	14	153	55	529	1	142	904

SECOND DIVISION.

	Killed Officers.	Killed Enlisted Men.	Wounded Officers.	Wounded Enlisted Men.	Capt'd or Missing Officers.	Capt'd or Missing Enlisted Men.	Aggregate.
First Brigade.							
Staff	...	....	....	1	...	....	1
3d United States	...	6	4	62	...	1	73
4th United States	...	10	2	28	...	....	40
6th United States	...	4	1	39	...	....	44
12th United States	1	7	4	67	...	13	92
14th United States	...	18	2	108	...	4	132
Total First Brigade	1	45	13	305	...	18	382
Second Brigade.							
2d United States	1	5	4	51	...	6	67
7th United States	1	11	3	42	...	2	59
10th United States	1	15	5	27	...	3	51
11th United States	3	16	7	85	...	9	120
17th United States	1	24	13	105	...	7	150
Total Second Brigade	7	71	32	310	...	27	447
Third Brigade.							
Staff	1	....	....	....	...	....	....
140th New York	1	25	5	84	...	18	133
146th New York	...	4	2	22	...	....	28
91st Pennsylvania	...	3	2	14	...	....	19
155th Pennsylvania	...	6	2	11	...	....	19
Total Third Brigade	2	38	11	131	...	18	200
Total Second Division	10	154	56	746	...	18	1,029
THIRD DIVISION.							
First Brigade.							
1st Pennsylvania Reserves	...	8	3	35	...	....	46
2d Pennsylvania Reserves	...	3	2	31	...	1	37
6th Pennsylvania Reserves	...	2	1	21	...	....	24
13th Pennsylvania Reserves, 1st Rifles	2	5	8	31	...	2	48
Total First Brigade	2	18	14	118	...	3	155
Third Brigade.							
5th Pennsylvania Reserves	...	....	....	2	...	....	2
9th Pennsylvania Reserves	...	....	....	2	...	....	5
10th Pennsylvania Reserves	...	2	....	3	...	....	5
11th Pennsylvania Reserves	1	2	3	35	...	....	41
12th Pennsylvania Reserves	...	1	....	1	...	....	2
Total Third Brigade	1	5	3	46	...	....	55
Total Third Division	3	23	17	164	...	3	210
Artillery Brigade.							
Mass. Light 3d Battery C	...	....	....	6	...	....	6
1st Ohio Light Battery L	...	....	....	2	...	....	2
5th United States Battery D	1	6	....	6	...	....	13
5th United States Battery I	...	1	1	18	...	2	22
Total Artillery Brigade	1	7	1	32	...	2	43
Ambulance Corps	...	....	....	1	...	....	1
Total Fifth Army Corps	28	337	129	1,482	1	210	2,187

SIXTH ARMY CORPS.

FIRST DIVISION.

	Killed		Wounded		Capt'd or Missing		Aggregate
	Officers	Enlisted Men	Officers	Enlisted Men	Officers	Enlisted Men	
First Brigade.							
2d New Jersey	...	....	....	6	...	....	6
3d New Jersey	...	....	....	2	...	....	2
15th New Jersey	...	....	....	3	...	....	3
Total First Brigade	...	....	....	11	...	....	11
Second Brigade.							
121st New York	...	....	....	2	...	....	2
95th Pennsylvania	...	1	....	1	...	....	2
96th Pennsylvania	...	....	....	1	...	....	1
Total Second Brigade	...	1	....	4	...	....	5
Third Brigade.							
119th Pennsylvania	...	....	....	2	...	....	2
Total Third Brigade	...	....	....	2	...	....	2
Total First Division	...	1	....	17	...	....	18

SECOND DIVISION.

	Officers	Enlisted Men	Officers	Enlisted Men	Officers	Enlisted Men	Aggregate
Second Brigade.							
4th Vermont	...	...	....	1	...	....	1
Total Second Brigade	...	....		1	...	....	1
Third Brigade.							
7th Maine	...	....		6	...	....	6
43d New York	1	1		2	...	1	5
49th New York	...	....		2	...	....	2
61st Pennsylvania	...	....	....	1	...	1	2
Total Third Brigade	1	1	....	11	...	2	15
Total Second Division	1	1	....	12	...	2	16

THIRD DIVISION.

	Officers	Enlisted Men	Officers	Enlisted Men	Officers	Enlisted Men	Aggregate
First Brigade.							
65th New York	...	4	....	5	...	....	9
67th New York	...	...	....	....	...	1	1
122d New York	...	10	2	30	...	2	44
23d Pennsylvania	1		1	12	...	....	14
82d Pennsylvania	...	....	....	6	...	....	6
Total First Brigade	1	14	3	53	...	3	74
Second Brigade.							
7th Massachusetts	...	....	....	6	...	....	6
10th Massachusetts	...	....	1	3	...	5	9
37th Massachusetts	...	2	1	25	...	19	47
2d Rhode Island	...	1	....	5	...	1	7
Total Second Brigade	...	3	2	39	...	25	69
Third Brigade.							
62d New York	...	1	1	10	...	....	12
93d Pennsylvania	...	....	1	9	...	....	10
98th Pennsylvania	...	....	2	9	...	..	11
139th Pennsylvania	...	1	3	16	...	....	20
Total Third Brigade	...	2	7	44	...	....	53
Total Third Division	1	19	12	136	...	28	196

SIXTH ARMY CORPS—CONTINUED.

	Killed		Wounded		Capt'd or Missing		Aggregate
	Officers	Enlisted Men	Officers	Enlisted Men	Officers	Enlisted Men	
Artillery Brigade.							
New York Light 1st Battery	...	4	2	6	...	....	12
Total Artillery Brigade	...	4	2	6	...	....	12
Total Sixth Army Corps	2	25	14	171	...	30	242

ELEVENTH ARMY CORPS.

	Killed		Wounded		Capt'd or Missing		Aggregate
	Officers	Enlisted Men	Officers	Enlisted Men	Officers	Enlisted Men	
General Headquarters—Staff			1		...	....	1
1st Indiana Cavalry Co's I and R.		....			...	3	3

FIRST DIVISION.

	Killed		Wounded		Capt'd or Missing		Aggregate
	Officers	Enlisted Men	Officers	Enlisted Men	Officers	Enlisted Men	
Staff			1				1
First Brigade.							
Staff	1	....	...	....	...	....	1
41st New York	1	14	8	50	...	2	75
54th New York	...	7	2	45	4	44	102
68th New York	1	7	4	59	2	65	138
153d Pennsylvania	1	22	7	135	...	46	211
Total First Brigade	4	50	21	289	6	157	527
Second Brigade.							
17th Connecticut	2	18	4	77	2	94	197
25th Ohio	1	8	5	95	3	72	184
75th Ohio	2	14	7	67	4	92	186
107th Ohio	...	23	8	103	...	77	211
Total Second Brigade	5	63	24	342	9	335	778
Total First Division	9	113	46	631	15	492	1,306

SECOND DIVISION.

	Killed		Wounded		Capt'd or Missing		Aggregate
	Officers	Enlisted Men	Officers	Enlisted Men	Officers	Enlisted Men	
Staff			1				1
First Brigade.							
134th New York	1	41	4	147	2	57	252
154th New York	...	1	1	20	9	169	200
27th Pennsylvania	2	3	3	26	1	76	111
73d Pennsylvania	...	7	....	27	...	....	34
Total First Brigade	3	52	8	220	12	302	597
Second Brigade.							
33d Massachusetts	...	7	....	38	...	....	45
136th New York	...	17	1	88	1	2	109
55th Ohio	...	6	1	30	1	11	49
73d Ohio	...	21	3	117	...	4	145
Total Second Brigade	...	51	5	273	2	17	348
Total Second Division	3	103	14	493	14	319	946

THIRD DIVISION.

	Killed		Wounded		Capt'd or Missing		Aggregate
	Officers	Enlisted Men	Officers	Enlisted Men	Officers	Enlisted Men	
First Brigade.							
82d Illinois	...	4	1	18	4	85	112
45th New York	...	11	1	34	14	164	224
157th New York	4	23	8	158	6	108	307
61st Ohio	2	4	6	30	2	10	54
74th Pennsylvania	2	8	4	36	2	58	110
Total First Brigade	8	50	20	276	28	425	807

THIRD DIVISION—CONTINUED.

	Killed		Wounded		Capt'd or Missing		Aggregate
	Officers	Enlisted Men	Officers	Enlisted Men	Officers	Enlisted Men	
Second Brigade.							
58th New York	1	1	2	13	...	3	20
119th New York	2	9	4	66	1	58	140
82d Ohio	4	13	14	71	2	77	181
75th Pennsylvania	3	16	5	84	...	3	111
26th Wisconsin	2	24	11	118	2	60	217
Total Second Brigade	12	63	36	352	5	201	669
Total Third Division	20	113	56	628	33	626	1,476
Artillery Brigade.							
1st New York Light Battery I	...	3	2	8	...	....	13
New York Light 13th Battery	...	....	....	8	...	3	11
1st Ohio Light Battery I	...	...	....	13	...	....	13
1st Ohio Light Battery K	...	2	1	10	...	2	15
4th United States Battery G	1	1	....	11	...	4	17
Total Artillery Brigade	1	6	3	50	...	9	69
Total Eleventh Army Corps	33	335	120	1,802	62	1,449	3,801

TWELFTH ARMY CORPS.

FIRST DIVISION.

	Killed		Wounded		Capt'd or Missing		Aggregate
	Officers	Enlisted Men	Officers	Enlisted Men	Officers	Enlisted Men	
First Brigade.							
5th Connecticut	...	....	....	2	...	5	7
20th Connecticut	...	5	....	22	...	1	28
3d Maryland	1	....	1	6	...	....	8
123d New York	...	3	1	9	1	....	14
145th New York	...	1	1	8	...	....	10
46th Pennsylvania	...	2	1	9	...	1	13
Total First Brigade	1	11	4	56	1	7	80
Second Brigade.							
1st Md. Potomac Home Brigade	3	20	3	77	...	1	104
1st Maryland Eastern Shore	...	5	....	18	...	2	25
150th New York	...	7	....	23	...	15	45
Total Second Brigade	3	32	3	118	...	18	174
Third Brigade.							
27th Indiana	...	23	8	78	...	1	110
2d Massachusetts	2	21	8	101	...	4	136
13th New Jersey	...	1	3	17	...	....	21
107th New York	...	....	....	2	...	....	2
3d Wisconsin	...	2	1	7	...	....	10
Total Third Brigade	2	47	20	205	...	5	279
Total First Division	6	90	27	379	1	30	533

SECOND DIVISION.

	Killed		Wounded		Capt'd or Missing		Aggregate
	Officers	Enlisted Men	Officers	Enlisted Men	Officers	Enlisted Men	
First Brigade.							
5th Ohio	1	1	1	15	...	....	18
7th Ohio	...	1	....	17	...	....	18
29th Ohio	2	5	....	31	...	....	38
66th Ohio	...	....	3	14	...	....	17
28th Pennsylvania	...	3	1	20	...	3	27
147th Pennsylvania	1	4	....	15	...	....	20
Total First Brigade	4	14	5	112	...	3	138

SECOND DIVISION — CONTINUED.

	Killed Officers.	Killed Enlisted Men.	Wounded Officers.	Wounded Enlisted Men.	Capt'd or Missing Officers.	Capt'd or Missing Enlisted Men.	Aggregate.
Second Brigade.							
29th Pennsylvania	2	13	....	43	...	2	66
100th Pennsylvania	...	3	....	6	...	1	10
111th Pennsylvania	...	5	1	16	...	....	22
Total Second Brigade	2	21	1	65	...	9	98
Third Brigade.							
60th New York	...	11	2	39	...	....	52
78th New York	...	6	1	20	1	2	30
102d New York	2	2	1	16	...	8	29
137th New York	4	36	3	84	...	10	137
149th New York	...	6	3	43	...	3	55
Total Third Brigade	6	61	10	202	1	23	303
Total Second Division	12	96	16	379	1	35	539
Artillery Brigade.							
Pennsylvania Light Battery E	...	....	....	3	...	....	3
4th United States Battery F	...	....	....	1	...	....	1
5th United States Battery K	...	....	....	5	...	....	5
Total Artillery Brigade	...	....	....	9	...	....	9
Total Twelfth Army Corps	18	186	43	767	2	65	1,081

CAVALRY CORPS.
FIRST DIVISION.

	Killed Officers.	Killed Enlisted Men.	Wounded Officers.	Wounded Enlisted Men.	Capt'd or Missing Officers.	Capt'd or Missing Enlisted Men.	Aggregate.
First Brigade.							
8th Illinois	...	1	1	4	...	1	7
12th Illinois (4 companies)	...	4	3	7	...	6	20
3d Indiana (6 companies)	1	5	1	20	...	5	32
8th New York	...	2	1	21	...	16	40
Total First Brigade	1	12	6	52	...	28	99
Second Brigade.							
6th New York	...	....	....	1	...	8	9
9th New York	...	2	....	2	...	7	11
17th Pennsylvania	...	....	....	....	...	4	4
3d West Virginia (2 companies)	...	....	....	....	...	4	4
Total Second Brigade	...	2	....	3	...	23	28
Reserve Brigade.							
6th Pennsylvania	...	3	....	7	...	2	12
1st United States	...	1	....	9	...	5	15
2d United States	...	3	1	6	1	6	17
5th United States	...	....	....	4	...	1	5
6th United States	...	6	5	23	5	203	242
Total Reserve Brigade	...	13	6	49	6	217	291
Total First Division	1	27	12	104	6	268	418

SECOND DIVISION.

	Killed Officers.	Killed Enlisted Men.	Wounded Officers.	Wounded Enlisted Men.	Capt'd or Missing Officers.	Capt'd or Missing Enlisted Men.	Aggregate.
First Brigade.							
1st Maryland	...	....	....	2	...	1	3
1st New Jersey	...	....	....	7	...	....	7
1st Pennsylvania	...	....	....	....	...	2	2
3d Pennsylvania	...	....	5	10	...	6	21
Total First Brigade	...	....	5	19	...	9	33

SECOND DIVISION—CONTINUED.

	Killed		Wounded		Capt'd or Missing		Aggregate
	Officers.	Enlisted Men.	Officers.	Enlisted Men.	Officers.	Enlisted Men.	
Third Brigade.							
1st Maine........................	...	1	....	4	...	....	5
10th New York..................	...	2	....	4	1	2	9
16th Pennsylvania.............	...	2	....	4	...	....	6
Total Third Brigade..........	...	5	....	12	1	2	20
Total Second Division........	...	5	5	31	2	11	53

THIRD DIVISION.

	Officers.	Enlisted Men.	Officers.	Enlisted Men.	Officers.	Enlisted Men.	Aggregate
First Brigade.							
Staff...............................	1	....	....	....	...	....	1
5th New York....................	...	1	....	1	...	4	6
18th Pennsylvania.............	...	2	....	4	...	8	14
1st Vermont......................	...	13	3	22	...	27	65
1st West Virginia...............	2	2	3	1	1	3	12
Total First Brigade...........	3	18	6	28	1	42	98
Second Brigade.							
1st Michigan.....................	...	10	6	37	...	20	73
5th Michigan....................	1	7	1	29	...	18	56
6th Michigan....................	...	1	2	24	...	1	28
7th Michigan....................	...	13	4	44	...	49	100
Total Second Brigade........	1	31	13	134	...	78	257
Total Third Division.........	4	49	19	162	1	120	355

HORSE ARTILLERY.

	Officers.	Enlisted Men.	Officers.	Enlisted Men.	Officers.	Enlisted Men.	Aggregate
First Brigade.							
9th Michigan....................	...	1	....	4	...	....	5
6th New York....................	...	....	....	1	...	....	1
2d United States Battery M....	...	....	1	....	...	...	1
4th United States Battery E....	...	1	....	....	...	....	1
Total First Brigade...........	...	2	1	5	...	....	8
Second Brigade.							
1st United States Battery K....	...	2	....	....	...	....	3
2d United States Battery A....	...	....	....	13	...	....	12
Total Second Brigade........	...	2	....	13	...	....	15
Total Cavalry Corps..........	5	85	37	315	8	399	849

ARTILLERY RESERVE.

	Officers.	Enlisted Men.	Officers.	Enlisted Men.	Officers.	Enlisted Men.	Aggregate
First Regular Brigade.							
1st United States Battery H.....	...	1	1	7	...	1	10
3d U. S. Batteries F and K......	1	8	....	14	...	1	24
4th United States Battery C.....	...	1	1	16	...	....	18
5th United States Battery C.....	...	2	2	12	...	....	16
Total First Regular Brigade..	1	12	4	49	...	2	68
First Volunteer Brigade.							
Mass. Light 5th Battery E, ⎫	...	2	1	13	...	.... ⎫	21
10th N. Y. Battery attached.. ⎭	...	2	....	3	...	.... ⎭	
Mass. Light 9th Battery.........	1	7	2	16	...	2	28
New York Light 15th Battery....	...	3	2	11	...	....	16
Penn. Light Battery C and F.....	...	1	5	18	...	4	28
Total 1st Volunteer Brigade..	1	15	10	61	...	6	93

ARTILLERY RESERVE—CONTINUED.

	Killed Officers.	Killed Enlisted Men.	Wounded Officers.	Wounded Enlisted Men.	Capt'd or Missing Officers.	Capt'd or Missing Enlisted Men.	Aggregate.
Second Volunteer Brigade.							
Connecticut Light 2d Battery	...	....	....	3	...	2	5
New York Light 5th Battery	...	1	....	2	...	2	3
Total 2d Volunteer Brigade	...	1	....	5	...	2	8
Third Volunteer Brigade.							
New Hampshire Light 1st Battery	...	....	...	5	...	....	5
1st Ohio Light Battery H	...	2	....	3	...	....	5
1st Penn. Light Battery F and G	...	6	1	13	...	3	23
West Virginia Light Battery C	...	2	....	2	...	....	4
Total 3d Volunteer Brigade	...	10	1	23	...	3	37
Fourth Volunteer Brigade.							
Maine Light 6th Battery		....		13			13
New Jersey Light 1st Battery		2		7			9
1st New York Light Battery G		....		7			7
4th New York Light Battery K, 11th N. Y. Battery attached	...			7	...	....	7
Total 4th Volunteer Brigade	...	2	....	34	...		36
Total Artillery Reserve	2	40	15	172	...	....	242

RECAPITULATION

	Killed Officers.	Killed Enlisted Men.	Wounded Officers.	Wounded Enlisted Men.	Capt'd or Missing Officers.	Capt'd or Missing Enlisted Men.	Aggregate.
General Headquarters	...	....	2	2	...	....	4
First Army Corps	42	551	257	2,952	82	2,140	6,024
Second Army Corps	67	729	269	2,917	13	355	4,356
Third Army Corps	50	528	251	2,775	14	592	4,210
Fifth Army Corps	28	337	129	1,482	1	210	2,187
Sixth Army Corps	2	25	14	171	...	30	242
Eleventh Army Corps	33	335	120	1,802	62	1,449	3,801
Twelfth Army Corps	18	186	43	767	2	65	1,081
Cavalry Corps	5	85	37	315	8	399	849
Artillery Reserve	2	40	15	172	...	13	242
Total Army of the Potomac	247	2,816	1,137	13,355	182	5,253	22,000

LIST OF CASUALTIES AT GETTYSBURG, SHOWING THE LOSS SUSTAINED BY EACH STATE.

	Killed Officers.	Killed Enlisted Men.	Wounded Officers.	Wounded Enlisted Men.	Capt'd or Missing Officers.	Capt'd or Missing Enlisted Men.	Aggregate.
Maine	7	117	40	585	16	301	1,066
New Hampshire	5	56	27	235	...	47	370
Vermont	1	57	13	285	...	59	415
Massachusetts	18	182	70	939	8	311	1,537
Rhode Island	1	13	4	74	...	5	97
Connecticut	4	41	18	165	2	110	340
New York	77	888	208	3,737	60	1,708	6,777
New Jersey	8	72	41	448	...	63	632
Pennsylvania	54	633	287	3,453	44	1,394	5,865
Delaware	3	18	17	98	1	24	161
Maryland	4	25	4	103	...	4	140

LIST OF CASUALTIES AT GETTYSBURG—CONTINUED.

	Killed		Wounded		Capt'd or Missing		Aggregate
	Officers	Enlisted Men	Officers	Enlisted Men	Officers	Enlisted Men	
Ohio	5	124	60	707	12	351	1,269
Indiana	5	91	33	351	4	68	562
Illinois	....	9	5	29	4	92	139
Wisconsin	5	100	40	473	8	180	806
Michigan	18	173	57	600	4	259	1,111
West Virginia	2	9	4	43	1	8	67
Minnesota	3	47	14	159	...	1	224
United States Regulars	12	159	62	860	6	268	1,367
Army Headquarters—Staff	...	....	3	2	...	....	4
Other Staffs	5	2	32	9	3	....	51
	247	2,816	1,137	13,355	182	5,253	22,990

LOSSES OF THE ARMY OF NORTHERN VIRGINIA.

This report is as perfect as it is possible to make it from all obtainable data. The disagreement in totals cannot be corrected, and the figures do not cover the real losses of the Confederate commands. The records of prisoners of war on file in Washington bear the names of 12,227 Confederate prisoners captured at and around Gettysburg from July 1 to 5 inclusive.

FIRST ARMY CORPS.

M'LAW'S DIVISION.

	Killed	Wounded	Captured or Missing	Aggregate
Kershaw's Brigade.				
2d South Carolina	27	125	2	154
3d South Carolina	18	63	2	83
7th South Carolina	18	85	7	110
8th South Carolina	21	79	....	100
15th South Carolina	21	98	18	137
3d South Carolina Battalion	10	33	3	46
Total	115	483	32	630
Semmes' Brigade.				
Staff	....	1	....	1
10th Georgia	9	77	....	86
50th Georgia	10	68	....	78
51st Georgia	8	47	....	55
53d Georgia	15	72	....	87
Total	55	284	91	430
Barksdale's Brigade.				
Staff	1	....		1
13th Mississippi	28	137		165
17th Mississippi	40	160		200
18th Mississippi	18	82		100
21st Mississippi	16	87	....	103
Total	105	530	92	747

M'LAW'S DIVISION—CONTINUED.

	Killed.	Wounded.	Captured or Missing.	Aggregate.
Wofford's Brigade.				
16th Georgia	9	52	....	61
18th Georgia	3	16	....	19
24th Georgia	4	32	....	36
Cobb's Legion	2	20	....	22
Phillips' Legion	4	24	....	28
Total	30	192	112	334
Artillery Battalion.				
Carlton's Georgia Battery	1	6	....	7
Fraser's Georgia Battery	4	14	....	18
McCarthy's Howitzers	2	3	....	5
Manly's North Carolina Battery	1	6	....	7
Total	8	29	....	37
Total McLaw's Division	313	1,538	327	2,178

PICKETT'S DIVISION.

	Killed.	Wounded.	Captured or Missing.	Aggregate.
Garnett's Brigade.				
Staff	1	....	....	1
8th Virginia	6	48	....	54
18th Virginia	10	77	....	87
19th Virginia	10	34	....	44
28th Virginia	19	58	....	77
56th Virginia	22	40	....	62
Total	78	324	539	941
Armistead's Brigade				
Staff	1	....	....	1
9th Virginia	....	71	....	71
14th Virginia	17	91	....	108
38th Virginia	23	147	....	170
53d Virginia	17	87	....	104
57th Virginia	26	95	....	121
Total	88	460	643	1,191
Kemper's Brigade.				
Staff	1	3	....	4
1st Virginia	2	62	....	64
3d Virginia	16	51	....	67
7th Virginia	15	79	....	94
11th Virginia	12	97	....	109
24th Virginia	17	111	....	128
Total	58	356	317	731
Artillery Battalion.				
Blount's Virginia Battery				
Caskies' Virginia Battery	No details obtained.			
Macon's Battery				
Stribling's Virginia Battery				
Total	8	17	....	25
Total Pickett's Division	232	1,157	1,499	2,888

HOOD'S DIVISION.

	Killed.	Wounded.	Captured or Missing.	Aggregate.
Law's Brigade.				
4th Alabama	17	49	....	87
15th Alabama	17	66	....	161
44th Alabama	24	64	....	94
47th Alabama	10	30	....	40
48th Alabama	8	67	....	102
Total	74	276	146	496
Anderson's Brigade.				
Staff	....	1	....	1
7th Georgia	....	15	....	15
8th Georgia	25	114	....	139
9th Georgia	28	115	....	189
11th Georgia	32	162	....	204
59th Georgia	18	92	....	116
Total	105	512	54	671
Robertson's Brigade.				
3d Arkansas	26	116	....	142
1st Texas	24	54	....	93
4th Texas	14	73	....	87
5th Texas	23	86	....	109
Total	84	396	120	597
Benning's Brigade.				
2d Georgia	25	66	....	91
15th Georgia	8	64	....	171
17th Georgia	15	75	....	90
20th Georgia	21	83	....	121
Total	76	299	122	497
Artillery Battalion.				
Bachman's South Carolina Battery	} No details obtained.			
Garden's South Carolina Battery				
Latham's North Carolina Battery				
Reilly's North Carolina Battery				
Total	4	23	....	27
Total Hood's Division	343	1,504	442	2,289

RESERVE ARTILLERY.

	Killed.	Wounded.	Captured or Missing.	Aggregate.
Alexander's Battalion.				
Jordan's Virginia Battery	} No details obtained.			
Moody's Louisiana Battery				
Parker's Virginia Battery				
Rhett's South Carolina Battery				
Taylor's Virginia Battery				
Woolfolk's Virginia Battery				
Total	19	114	6	139

RESERVE ARTILLERY—CONTINUED.

Washington (La.) Artillery.	Killed	Wounded.	Captured or Missing.	Aggregate.
1st Company				
2d Company				
3d Company	} No details obtained.			
4th Company				
Total	3	23	16	42
Total Reserve Artillery	22	137	22	181
Total First Army Corps	910	4,346	2,290	7,536

SECOND ARMY CORPS.

EARLY'S DIVISION.

	Killed	Wounded	Captured or Missing	Aggregate
Staff		1	....	1
Hays' Brigade.				
5th Louisiana	5	31	13	49
6th Louisiana	5	34	21	60
7th Louisiana	8	43	6	57
8th Louisiana	8	54	13	75
9th Louisiana	10	39	23	72
Total	36	201	76	313
Hoke's Brigade.				
6th North Carolina	20	131	21	172
21st North Carolina	9	65	37	111
57th North Carolina	6	20	36	62
Total	35	216	94	345
Smith's Brigade.				
31st Virginia	....	20	7	27
49th Virginia	12	78	10	100
52d Virginia	....	15	....	15
Total	12	113	17	142
Gordon's Brigade.				
13th Georgia	20	83	....	103
26th Georgia	2	4	5	11
31st Georgia	9	34	....	43
38th Georgia	12	51	29	92
60th Georgia	4	29	5	38
61st Georgia	24	69	....	93
Total	71	270	39	380
Artillery Battalion.				
Carrington's Virginia Battery	....	....	....	....
Garber's Virginia Battery	....	1	....	1
Green's Battery	2	5	....	7
Tanner's Virginia Battery	2	....	....	....
Total	2	6	....	8
Total Early's Division	156	806	226	1,188

JOHNSON'S DIVISION.

	Killed.	Wounded.	Captured or Missing.	Aggregate.
Staff	....	1	1	2
Stewart's Brigade.				
1st Maryland Battalion	25	119	....	144
1st North Carolina	4	48	....	52
3d North Carolina	29	127	....	156
10th Virginia	4	17	....	21
23d Virginia	4	14	....	18
37th Virginia	10	44	....	54
Total	83	409	190	682
Nicholl's Brigade.				
1st Louisiana	9	30	....	39
2d Louisiana	10	52	....	62
10th Louisiana	14	77	....	91
14th Louisiana	9	56	....	65
15th Louisiana	2	36	....	38
Total	43	309	36	388
Stonewall Brigade.				
2d Virginia	1	13	....	14
4th Virginia	8	78	....	86
5th Virginia	5	46	....	51
27th Virginia	7	34	....	41
33d Virginia	11	37	....	48
Total	35	208	87	330
Jones' Brigade.				
Staff	....	2	....	2
21st Virginia	2	29	....	50
25th Virginia	3	37	....	70
42d Virginia	8	48	....	56
44th Virginia	3	14	....	56
48th Virginia	15	43	....	76
50th Virginia	13	47	....	99
Total	58	302	61	421
Artillery Battalion.				
Staff	....	1	....	1
Brown's Maryland Battery	4	12	....	16
Carpenter's Virginia Battery	5	19	....	24
Dement's 1st Maryland Battery	1	4	....	5
Raines' Virginia Battery	....	4	....	4
Total	10	40	....	50
Total Johnson's Division	229	1,269	375	1,873

RODE'S DIVISION.

	Killed.	Wounded.	Captured or Missing.	Aggregate.
Daniels' Brigade.				
32d North Carolina	26	116	....	142
43d North Carolina	21	126	....	147
45th North Carolina	46	173	....	219
53d North Carolina	13	104	....	117
2d Battalion	29	124	....	153
Total	165	635	116	916

RODE'S DIVISION—CONTINUED.

	Killed.	Wounded.	Captured or Missing.	Aggregate.
Iverson's Brigade.				
5th North Carolina	31	112	....	143
12th North Carolina	10	46	....	56
20th North Carolina	29	93	....	122
23d North Carolina	41	93	....	134
Total	130	328	308	826
Dole's Brigade.				
4th Georgia	9	29	7	45
12th Georgia	4	35	10	49
21st Georgia	1	11	5	17
44th Georgia	10	49	9	68
Total	24	124	31	179
Ramseur's Brigade.				
2d North Carolina	4	27	1	32
4th North Carolina	8	24	24	56
14th North Carolina	5	37	2	44
30th North Carolina	6	34	5	45
Total	23	124	32	177
O'Neal's Brigade.				
3d Alabama	12	79	....	91
5th Alabama	21	109	....	209
6th Alabama	18	113	....	131
12th Alabama	13	65	....	83
26th Alabama	5	41	....	120
Total	73	450	193	696
Artillery Battalion.				
Carter's Virginia Battery				
Fry's Virginia Battery	} No details obtained.			
Page's Virginia Battery				
Reese's Alabama Battery				
Total	6	35	24	65
Total Rode's Division	421	1,728	704	2,853
RESERVE ARTILLERY.				
Brown's Battalion.				
Dance's Virginia Battery				
Hupp's Virginia Battery				
Graham's Virginia Battery	} No details obtained.			
Smith's Battery				
Watson's Battery				
Total	3	19	....	22
Nelson's Battalion.				
Kirkpatrick's Virginia Battery				
Massie's Virginia Battery	} No report obtained.			
Milledge's Georgia Battery				
Total	....	....	....	....
Total Reserve Artillery	3	19	....	22
Total Second Army Corps	809	3,823	1,305	5,937

THIRD ARMY CORPS.

ANDERSON'S DIVISION.

	Killed.	Wounded.	Captured or Missing.	Aggregate.
Wilcox's Brigade.				
8th Alabama	22	139	....	161
9th Alabama	3	55	....	58
10th Alabama	13	91	....	104
11th Alabama	6	69	....	75
14th Alabama	7	41	....	48
Total	51	469	257	777
Mahone's Brigade.				
6th Virginia	....	3	....	3
12th Virginia	2	12	....	14
16th Virginia	2	7	....	9
41st Virginia	1	11	....	12
61st Virginia	2	10	....	12
Total	8	55	39	102
Wright's Brigade.				
3d Georgia	....	100	....	100
22d Georgia	21	75	....	96
48th Georgia	16	74	....	90
2d Georgia Battalion	3	46	....	49
Total	40	295	333	668
Berry's Brigade.				
2d Florida	11	70	....	81
5th Florida	12	63	....	75
8th Florida	10	84	....	94
Total	33	217	205	455
Posey's Brigade.				
12th Mississippi	....	7	....	7
16th Mississippi	2	17	....	19
19th Mississippi	4	23	....	27
48th Mississippi	6	24	....	30
Total	12	71	....	83
Artillery (Sumter) Battalion.				
Company A	1	7	....	8
Company B	2	5	....	7
Company C	....	9	....	9
Total	3	21	6	30
Total Anderson's Division	147	1,128	840	2,115

HETH'S DIVISION.

	Killed.	Wounded.	Captured or Missing.	Aggregate.
Staff		1	....	1
First Brigade.				
11th North Carolina	50	159	....	209
26th North Carolina	86	502	....	588
47th North Carolina	21	140	....	161
52d North Carolina	33	114	....	147
Total	190	915	....	1,105

HETH'S DIVISION—CONTINUED.

	Killed.	Wounded.	Captured or Missing.	Aggregate.
Second Brigade.				
40th Virginia	4	38	....	42
47th Virginia	10	38	....	48
55th Virginia	8	26	....	34
22d Virginia	3	21	....	24
Total	25	123	....	148
Third Brigade.				
13th Alabama	6	36	....	42
5th Alabama Battalion	....	26	....	26
1st Tennessee P. A.	2	40	....	42
7th Tennessee	5	18	....	23
14th Tennessee	3	24	....	27
Total	16	144	517	677
Fourth Brigade.				
2d Mississippi	49	183	....	232
11th Mississippi	32	170	....	202
42d Mississippi	60	205	....	265
55th North Carolina	39	159	....	198
Total	180	717	....	897
Artillery Battalion.				
Grandy's Virginia Battery				
Lewis' Virginia Battery		No details obtained.		
Maurin's Louisiana Battery				
Moore's Virginia Battery				
Total	....	5	17	22
Total Heth's Division	411	1,905	534	2,850

PENDER'S DIVISION.

	Killed.	Wounded.	Captured or Missing.	Aggregate.
Staff	1	4	....	5
First Brigade.				
1st South Carolina	20	75	....	95
1st South Carolina Rifles	2	9	....	11
12th South Carolina	20	112	....	132
13th South Carolina	31	99	....	130
14th South Carolina	27	182	....	209
Total	100	477	....	577
Second Brigade.				
7th North Carolina	5	84	....	89
18th North Carolina	4	41	....	45
28th North Carolina	12	92	....	104
33d North Carolina	10	53	....	63
37th North Carolina	10	78	....	88
Total	41	348	....	389
Third Brigade.				
14th Georgia	5	27	....	32
35th Georgia	6	42	....	48
45th Georgia	....	35	....	35
49th Georgia	5	32	....	37
Total	16	136	....	152

PENDER'S DIVISION—CONTINUED.

	Killed.	Wounded.	Captured or Missing.	Aggregate.
Fourth Brigade.				
Staff	....	1	....	1
13th North Carolina	29	97	....	126
16th North Carolina	16	50	....	66
22d North Carolina	20	69	....	89
34th North Carolina	16	48	....	64
38th North Carolina	21	58	....	79
Total	102	323	110	535
Artillery Battalion.				
Brooks' Virginia Battery	} No details obtained.			
Graham's North Carolina Battery				
Ward's Mississippi Battery				
Wyatt's Virginia Battery				
Total	2	24	6	32
Total Pender's Division	262	1,312	116	1,690

RESERVE ARTILLERY.

	Killed.	Wounded.	Captured or Missing.	Aggregate.
McIntosh's Battalion.				
Hunt's Alabama Battery	} No details obtained.			
Lusk's Virginia Battery				
Johnson's Virginia Battery				
Rice's Virginia Battery				
Total	7	25	....	32
Pegram's Battalion.				
Brander's Virginia Battery	} No details obtained.			
Brunson's Virginia Battery				
Crenshaw's Virginia Battery				
McGraw's Virginia Battery				
Marye's Virginia Battery				
Total	10	37	1	48
Total Reserve Artillery	17	62	1	80
Total Third Army Corps	837	4,407	1,491	6,735

CAVALRY.

STUART'S DIVISION.

	Killed.	Wounded.	Captured or Missing.	Aggregate.
Hampton's Brigade.				
Staff	....	1	....	1
1st North Carolina	2	17	4	23
1st South Carolina	1	9	4	14
2d South Carolina	1	6	....	7
Cobb's Georgia Legion	8	6	7	21
Jeff Davis Legion	4	10	1	15
Phillips' Georgia Legion	1	9	....	10
Total	17	58	16	91

STUART'S DIVISION—CONTINUED.

	Killed	Wounded.	Captured or Missing.	Aggregate.
Fitz Lee's Brigade.				
1st Virginia	4	8	10	22
2d Virginia	1	3	1	5
3d Virginia	....	5	1	6
4th Virginia	....	....	17	17
5th Virginia	No report obtained.			
Total	5	16	29	50
W. H. F. Lee's Brigade.				
2d North Carolina	No report obtained.			
9th Virginia	....	6	6	12
10th Virginia	1	9	2	12
13th Virginia	1	11	5	17
Total	2	26	13	41
Jones' Brigade.				
6th Virginia	4	19	5	28
7th Virginia	8	21	1	30
11th Virginia	No report obtained.			
Total	12	40	6	58
Jenkins' Brigade.				
14th Virginia				
16th Virginia				
17th Virginia	No report obtained.			
34th Virginia Battalion				
35th Virginia Battalion				
Total	No report obtained.			
Stuart Horse Artillery.				
Breathed's Maryland Battery				
Griffin's 2d Maryland Battery	No report obtained.			
McGregor's Virginia Battery				
Total	No report obtained.			
Total Stuart's Division	36	140	64	240

RECAPITULATION.

	Killed.	Wounded.	Captured or Missing.	Aggregate.
First Army Corps	910	4,336	2,290	7,536
Second Army Corps	809	3,823	1,305	5,937
Third Army Corps	837	4,407	1,491	6,735
Stuart's Cavalry Division	36	140	64	240
Grand total as far as obtained	2,592	12,706	5,150	20,448

XIII.

DESCRIPTION OF THE GETTYSBURG BATTLEFIELD.

(WITH MAP.)

The Map of the Field of Gettysburg, which accompanies this number in the Souvenir Programme of the Re-union of the two armies who fought there twenty-five years ago, clearly points out the salient features of the ground, as well as the location of the Union Regiments during the battle, and the monuments which will be dedicated during this year.

A verbal description is, however, necessary to point out the striking features of the ground, that the map may be more thoroughly understood. Colonel Bachelder thus describes it : The country is generally open, and the surface rolling, though deep forests, high hills and rocky ravines are not infrequent. The geological formation in this section of the country consists of a succession of undulations, commencing with the Blue Ridge, eight or ten miles away, and running generally parallel with it in a northerly and southerly direction.

The next of importance east of the South Mountain, as affects the history of the battle, is Seminary Ridge, on which is situated the Lutheran Theological Seminary in the western suburbs of the town. Previous to the battle this was called Oak Ridge, a local name unknown to the soldiers who fought there. * * * They naturally called it Seminary Ridge. This name, christened with fire and baptized in blood, will be retained. * * * As a defensive military position this ridge possesses great advantages. * * * The altitude of Seminary Ridge is not as great as Cemetery Hill and Ridge, * * * but its extended position, admitting of a converging fire upon any desired locality, more than balanced this defect.

Cemetery Ridge, the next of importance towards the east, * * * seems to have been more capricious in its formation. This is marked by three distinct elevations, standing out in clear relief like bastions on a rampart. Round Top, its extreme southern terminus, is seven-eighths of a mile east from Seminary Ridge, and rises directly from the plains beyond, its wooded crest towering high above the surrounding country. From its northern face a bold shoulder protrudes, separated from the parent mount by a gentle depression, heavily wooded, * * * known as Little Round Top. * * * Returning from Little Round Top towards the larger hill is a rough stony ridge, * * * called " Vincent's Spur." Plumb Run, a small and unimportnant stream, flows along the western base of these hills and drains a marshy swale in front of Little Round Top. West of this is a stony, precipitous undulation called Houck's Ridge, along which the Third Corps line of battle ran. * * * The evidences are that by some mighty convulsion of nature this ridge was rent asunder at its intersection with the base of Round Top, thereby draining an extensive body of water in front of Little Round Top. The gorge thus produced is called the Devil's Den, and presents a scene of the wildest character. Huge syenitic boulders are crowded into this narrow ravine, through which struggles the waters of Plumb Run, while yawning chasms suggest to the visitor the haunts of the lurking sharpshooters who occupied them during the battle.

From Little Round Top the ridge, depressed yet well defined, rises gradually in its northern course to Cemetery Hill, where, obstructed by some unseen cause, it was hurled ruthlessly back to the east, and in convulsive throbs expended its force in the formation of Culp's Hill; thus leaving a broad extensive basin northward from the Cemetery Hill, in which, upon a gentle elevation, is situated the village of Gettysburg. * * * Culp's Hill * * * is irregular in shape, quite precipitous on its eastern face, and generally covered with a heavy open growth of hardy timber. Rock Creek separates it from Wolf's Hill. This, like the last, is wooded, but exceedingly rough, and formed the eastern boundary of the Infantry operations.

A half mile northeast from Culp's Hill, on the opposite side of Rock Creek, and a half mile east from the town, another elevation commences, called Benner's Hill. This hill continues several miles N. N. E. Its highest summit is called Hospital Hill, where a general hospital was located soon after the battle. Benner's Hill was occupied by Confederate Artillery. Turning back again to the south of the field we find an undulation (Houck's Ridge) intermediate between Cemetery and Seminary Ridges, yet parallel with either. It shoots off from Cemetery Hill, and, leading directly across the valley, intersects with Seminary Ridge at a distance of nearly three miles. The Emmettsburg Road is laid along this ridge. The historic Peach and Apple Orchards are here, and on it General Sickles formed his line of battle on the second day. The foregoing constitute the grand topographical features of the battlefield. These are again subdivided into minor irregularities, each bearing upon the general result of the battle; but it will be impossible to describe them in a book of this size.

RELATIVE ELEVATIONS ON GETTYSBURG BATTLEFIELD.

These elevations are calculated in feet from the level of the square within the town:

―――― Union Positions. ――――   ―――― Confederate Positions. ――――

[Chart showing elevations from Level of square in town up to 250 feet, with numbered markers 1–16 positioned at various heights]

LOCATION OF MONUMENTS TO BE DEDICATED IN 1888.

UNION POSITIONS.

	Elevation, feet.
1—Big Round Top	252
2—Little Round Top	136
3—Devil's Den Hill	28
4—Peach Orchard	52
5—Cemetery Hill	88
6—Culp's Hill	96
7—Power's Hill	44
8—Wolf's Hill	132

CONFEDERATE POSITIONS.

	Elevation, feet.
9—Opposite Big Round Top	52
10—P. Snyder's House	48
11—Opposite Peach Orchard	56
12—Opposite Codori's House	36
13—Opposite Cemetery Hill	52
14—Lutheran Cemetery	40
15—Oak Hill	88
16—Benner's Hill	46

LOCATION OF MONUMENTS TO BE DEDICATED IN 1888.

Upon the Map facing the next page will be found plainly marked the location of each Monument that will be dedicated during the Summer and Fall of the present year. If any are omitted it is because they have failed to report or a change in the intended arrangements has been made since June 1. A large number will be found marked for Pennsylvania; this arises from the fact that changes have been made where monuments have been already set up—some have been enlarged or new stones substituted.

The programme of exercises at many of the Memorials will be found elsewhere in this book, with pictures of the Memorials. The figures following the name of each organization is the number of the location as marked on the Map. Number 1 is on the extreme left of the Union Line, in front of Round Top, and at the bottom of the Map, and the numbers run in rotation around to the right of the line on or near the Baltimore Pike. The second series of figures, relating to the first day's fight, commences on the left of the line on Battle Avenue near the Fairfield Road.

MAINE MONUMENTS.

	No.		No.		No.		No.
2d Light Battery	127	3d Infantry	11	6th Infantry	117	16th Infantry	140
5th Light Battery	151	4th Infantry	12	7th Infantry	113	17th Infantry	87
6th Light Battery	66	5th Infantry	32	10th Infantry	114	19th Infantry	67

MARYLAND MONUMENTS.

	No.		No.		No.		No.
Rigby's Bat'y "A"	150	1st Potomac Home Brigade	111	1st Cavalry	150	1st E. S. Infantry	110
1st M'ryl'd Art'y	115			3d Infantry	97		

MICHIGAN MONUMENTS.

	No.		No.		No.		No.
1st Infantry	4	4th Infantry	64	7th Infantry	68	24th Infantry	—
3d Infantry	21	5th Infantry	10	16th Infantry	6		

NEW JERSEY MONUMENTS.

	No.		No.		No.		No.
N. J. Brigade, 6th Corps	50	6th Infantry	15	8th Infantry	27	12th Infantry	75
		1st Battery	47	Battery A	71	1st Cavalry	149
5th Infantry	56	7th Infantry	48	11th Infantry	55	13th Infantry	95

NEW YORK MONUMENTS.

	No.		No.		No.		No.
1st Ind'p't Battery	73	5th Battery	78	15th Battery	44-40	Battery B	70
4th Battery	13	13th Battery	144	Battery D	26	Light Battery I	82
5th Cavalry	3	6th Cavalry	134	9th Cavalry	135	10th Cavalry	151
39th Infantry	74	62d Infantry	63	86th Infantry	16	126th Infantry	77
40th Infantry	14	64th Infantry	17	94th Infantry	138	134th Infantry	79
41st Infantry	85	65th Infantry	100½	97th Infantry	139	137th Infantry	90
45th Infantry	143	67th Infantry	103	104th Infantry	142	140th Infantry	7
49th Infantry	112	68th Infantry	84	107th Infantry	102	145th Infantry	98
52d Infantry	36	73d Infantry	45	108th Infantry	76	146th Infantry	9
54th Infantry	80	76th Infantry	131	119th Infantry	145	147th Infantry	129
57th Infantry	33	78th and 102d Inf'y	86	122d Infantry	91	149th Infantry	89
60th Infantry	87	80th Inf'y (20th Mil)	119	123d Infantry	99	150th Infantry	107
61st Infantry	28	83d Inf'y (9th Mil.)	141	Greene's Brig. 60th, 78th, 102d & 137th Infantry	88	Shaler's Brigade, 65th, 67th & 122d Infantry	103
Irish Brigade, 63d, 69th and 88th Infantry	24	Excelsior Brig. 70th 71st, 72d, 73d and 74th Infantry	46				

*PENNSYLVANIA MONUMENTS.

	No.		No.		No.		No.
Battery C and F (Thompson's)	41	Shaler's Brig., 23d and 82d Inf'try	103	96th Infantry	30	11th Infantry	133
23d Infantry	104	16th Cavalry	108	17th Cavalry	137	139th Infantry	60
26th Infantry	58	68th Infantry	42	98th Infantry	65	140th Infantry	38
27th Infantry	81	73d Infantry	83	99th Infantry	72	141st Infantry	53
28th Infantry	106	75th Infantry	146	102d Infantry	62	142d Infantry	120
29th Infantry	93	81st Infantry	35	105th Infantry	52	143d Infantry	126
46th Infantry	96	82d Infantry	105	107th Infantry	139½	145th Infantry	20
53d Infantry	119	84th Infantry	57	109th Infantry	94	148th Infantry	34
56th Infantry	130	88th Infantry	134½	110th Infantry	18	150th Infantry	125
57th Infantry	51	90th Infantry	136	111th Infantry	93	151st Infantry	121
62d Infantry	23	93d Infantry	61	115th Infantry	22	153d Infantry	148
63d Infantry	43	95th Infantry	29	116th Infantry	39		
				121st Infantry	31-118		

* Includes changes, enlargements, substitutions and sometimes a second monument.

VERMONT MONUMENTS.

	No.		No.		No.		No.
State	69	Co's E & H U. S. Sharpshooters (Vt)	2	1st Brigade	5	Co. F U. S. Sharpshooters (Vt.)	54
				1st Cavalry	1		

WISCONSIN MONUMENTS.

	No.		No.		No.		No.
2d Infantry		fantry	109	5th Infantry	116	6th Infantry	128
7th Infantry						26th Infantry	147

MISCELLANEOUS MONUMENTS.

	No.		No.
Statue to General	9	First Army Corps	122

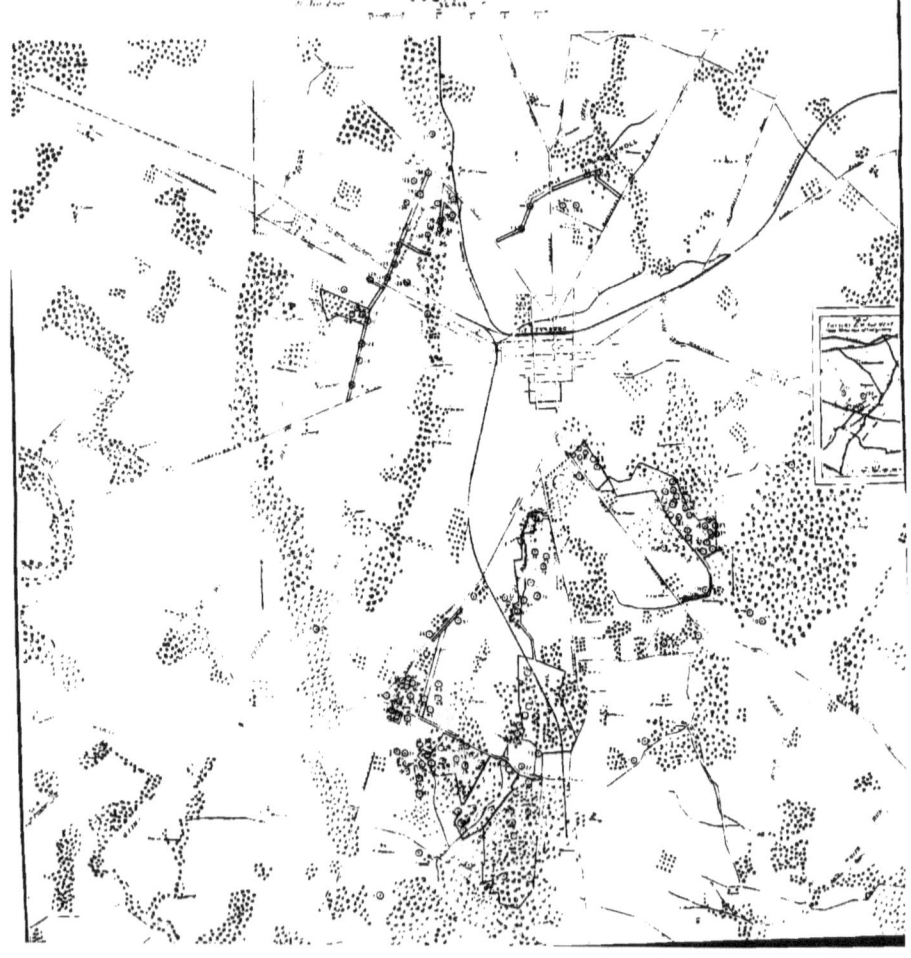

XIV.

DISTANCES TO ALL POINTS OF INTEREST ON THE BATTLEFIELD.

The routes of the following itineraries are those adopted by the various guides or vehicles in the town of Gettysburg. They all begin and end at the public square, in the centre of the town.

FIRST DAYS' BATTLE GROUND.

From Square in Town to	—Miles.—	From Square in Town to	—Miles.—	
Barlow Ave., Mummasburg Road.	1.23	Battle Avenue	.14	2.70
Chambersburg Pike	.83	2.06	Fairfield Road	.47	3.17
Reynold's Avenue	.18	2.24	Dr. Wolf's	.59	3.76
Springs Road	.32	2.56	Square	.71	4.47

SECOND AND THIRD DAYS' BATTLE GROUND.

From Square in Town to	—Miles.—	From Square in Town to	—Miles.—	
Peach Orchard, via Emmittsburg Road		2.34	Rosensteel's Hotel, near Sykes Avenue	.79	4.31
Devils Den, via Emmittsburg Road and Avenue	1.18	3.52	Square	2.73	7.04

From Square in Town to	—Miles.—	From Square in Town to	—Miles.—	
Rosensteel's Hotel		2.73	Peach Orchard	.35	4.70
Devil's Den	.79	3.52	Square	2.34	7.04
End of Avenue Cross Roads	.83	4.35			

From Square in Town to	—Miles.—	From Square in Town to	—Miles.—	
Cemetery Gate		.73	Local County Gate	.97	3.18
Culp's Hill Avenue	.16	.89	Battlefield Hotel	.25	3.43
Pike by Slocum Avenue	1.32	2.21	Square	.51	3.94

From Square in Town to	—Miles.—	
C. H. Buehler's Gate		.39

NOTE.—For this table, the table of elevations and the average of losses by Brigades in the Union Army we are indebted to Mr. J. R. Hill, Company B, 11th Massachusetts Infantry, detached to the 4th New York Independent Battery, in which latter organization he fought at Gettysburg.

194 Fifth Avenue,
Under Fifth Avenue Hotel.

212 Broadway,
Corner Fulton Street.

340 Fulton Street,
BROOKLYN, L. I.

AGENTS
In Every City in the
United States.

**STYLES
ALWAYS CORRECT.**

Quality the very BEST.

KNOX
THE HATTER'S
World Renowned
HATS
ARE FOR SALE
EVERYWHERE!

Martin's Umbrella

Foreign
Novelties

ENGLISH HATS
From the best known London Manufacturers,
NOT
from small Retail Dealers

All Hats manufactured by this House are the recognized standard of excellence throughout the World. None genuine without the Trade Mark.

EAGLE HOTEL
GETTYSBURG, PA.

H. YINGLING, - - - Proprietor.

HEADQUARTERS FOR INFORMATION IN
Connection with Battlefield
AND PLACE TO
Secure Reliable Guides

FREE 'BUS TO ALL TRAINS.

Two blocks from W. Md. R. R. Depot and one block from G. & H. R. R. Depot.

XV.

PROCEEDINGS OF THE LAST MEETING OF THE SOCIETY OF THE ARMY OF THE POTOMAC.

The eighteenth annual meeting of the Society of the Army of the Potomac took place at Saratoga Springs, New York, June 22d and 23d, 1887.

At the Re-union in San Francisco, August, 1886, the Society of the Army of the Potomac fixed upon Saratoga Springs as its next place of meeting. The members of the old army were a long distance from their base, and the usual invitation was not presented, but the members felt that the proverbial hospitality of Saratoga Springs was a sufficient guarantee of a cordial reception, and they were not disappointed.

As soon as notice was sent, a Local Executive Committee was appointed, as follows : General W. B. French, President ; Col. H. S. Clement, Col. D. F. Ritchie, Surg. W. H. Hall, Col. George H. Gillis, Lt. Com. A. R. McNair, Treasurer ; Capt. James M. Andrews, Jr., Secretary.

Hotel Accomodations—C. C. Wells, Maj. W. J. Riggs, E. R. Stevens, A. F. Mitchell, and J. Mingay.

Committee on Reception of Veteran Organizations—Maj.-Gen. S. G. Burbridge, Gen. Geo. S. Batcheller, and Com. E. T. Woodward.

Decoration Committee—A. A. Paterson, Capt. H. C. Rowland, J. W. Ehninger, S. G. Slocum, R. N. Breeze, B. F. Judson, Willard Lester, Hiram Hays, G. B. Croff, Chas. Mosher, D. Weatherwax, R. G. Smythe, C. F. Rich, F. G. Vaguhan, J. F. Case, A. R. Walker, and P. B. Liker.

Transportation—C. Durkee, T. F. Hamilton, and R. B. Beattie.

Excursions—Capt. Lewis Wood, R. F. Knapp, C. D. Thurber, and C. A. Coombs.

Militia Organizations—Capt. R. C. McEwen, W. L. Rich, and A. L. Hall.

Corps Headquarters—Maj. W. T. Rockwood, Geo. W. Blodgett, and W. H. Hull.

Invitations—Capt. E. P. Howe, Col. J. S. Fassett, and Charles H. Hodges.

Livery—Col. Wm. M. Searing, Capt. J. H. Robinson, and A. E. Carroll.

Reception Committee—Messrs. Henry Hilton, J. M. Marvin, J. R. Putnam, George West, S. Ainsworth, M. N. Nolan, Edward Kearney, John Foley, A. Bockes, J. S. L'Amoreaux, E. H. Peters, S. C. Medbury, W. A. Sackett, E. F. O'Connor, A. Pond, Judge Dillon, C. S. Lester, Wm. A. Shepard, Spencer Trask, W. J. Arkell, C. Sheehan, H. S. Leach, Wm. D. Ellis, E. C. Clark, J. A. Manning, W. A. Thompson, H. M. Ruggles, J. W. Drexel, J. W. Fuller, Chas. McLeod, Geo. S. Robinson, Edward Cluett, Geo. B. Cluett, Col. Lawton, I. N. Phelps, J. R. Chapman, J. M. Andrews, Sr.; A. Downing, J. L. Barbour, J. P. Butler, F. H. Hathorn, W. B. Gage, R. F. Milligan, Nathan Sheppard, Geo. L. Ames, Dr. S. S. Strong, Paul C. Grening, John M. Otter, D. Yuengling, Jr., John Cox, A. W. Shepherd, G. A. Farnham, W. W. Durant, L. A. Sharp, Drs. T. B. Reynolds, C. S. Grant, John A. Pearsall, Capt. W. W. Worden, Messrs. P. M. Suarez, C. P. Dowd, Revs. Chas. J. Young, W. R. Terrett, S. V. Leech, Dr. Joseph Carey, T. W. Jones, R. F. McMichael, John McMenomy, Messrs. W. C. Bronson, Geo. W. Langdon, J. T. Bryant, E. T. Brackett, L. W. James, I. Steinfeld, S. A. Sague, A. G. Hull, William Ingham, F. A. White, W. Hay Bockes, C. F. Fish, Davis Coleman, Le Grand Cramer, E. N. Jones, P. L. Brocklebank, Dr. E. H. Rockwood, Rev. Dr. B. Hawley, and Dr. Edward Clark.

Through the courtesy of the Legislature of the State and Governor Hill, its Executive, an appropriation of $7,500 was made to send two veteran regiments to Saratoga. The regiments selected by General Porter, the Adjutant-General, were the Sixty-ninth and the Fourteenth. The other veteran regiment, the Ninth, still in existence, was debarred from going because of its order to attend the State camp.

The headquarters of the Society and of the several corps were established at Congress Hall, under the management of Col. H. S. Clement, himself a member of the society, and a most genial and generous host.

The stillness of the evening of the 21st was broken by the sounds of martial music. The Sixty-ninth Regiment, with Colonel Jas. Cavanagh in command, came down the street in soldierly style, and were followed by the famous Brooklyn Fourteenth, under the command of Colonel Harry Michell.

The detachment was under the command of Brig.-Gen. James McLeer, 2d Brigade, N. G. S. N. Y., who was accompanied by the following staff:

Col. John B. Frothingham, Adjutant-General; Majors G. A. Jahn, A. F. Jenks, G. R. Fowler, G. Kindle, Jr., and Captains Fritz Broze and F. D. Beard.

Governor Hill, who arrived early in the day, was accompanied by Adjutant-General Josiah Porter, Generals George S. Field, J. D. Bryant, J. M. Varian, Jr., Charles F. Robbins, Col. Hilton and other members of his staff. They were handsomely entertained by ex-Judge Henry Hilton.

Generals W. T. Sherman, Henry W. Slocum, Calvin E. Pratt, Daniel E. Sickles, J. C. Robinson, J. C. Black, C. K. Graham, Daniel Butterfield, Lucius Fairchild, F. E. Pinto, F. T. Locke, J. B. Carr, G. H. Sharpe and N. Curtis, Colonels R. F. O'Beirne, Charles L. McArthur, and F. D. Grant, with a goodly company of veterans, were also on hand.

In the early morning of the 22d, the Seventh Regiment Uniformed Veterans, under command of General Henry E. Tremaine, some one hundred and fifty in number, arrived by train, and escorted the President, General M. T. McMahon, to Congress Hall, where, after giving him a marching salute, they were happily quartered.

The village was profusely and brilliantly decorated. Hotels and buildings, public and private, vied with each other in the ingenuity and beauty of their display. Congress Hall was a mass of shields and war and peace emblems, while the Grand Union, the Windsor, the United States, the Kensington, and other public houses were smothered under the wealth of decorative art. A grand triumphal arch, nearly opposite the office of the *Saratogian*, spanned the wide main street, and contained the portraits of Lincoln, Grant and other great celebrities, and the names of many of the heroes of the war, dead and living. Along the proposed line of march and stretching across the streets were a great number of banners containing the names of famous battlefields and distinguished officers. Nearly every dwelling bore testimonials to the memory of the men who wore the blue.

The meetings of the several corps societies were held at the Town Hall and Odd Fellows' Hall.

BUSINESS MEETING.

The business meeting of the Society of the Army of the Potomac was held at the Casino. There were about 1,000 persons present, including a row of ladies who occupied seats in front of the platform. General McMahon, President, presided, and on the platform, in addition to those previously named, were Generals Henry A. Barnum, Horatio C. King, Farnsworth, Fairchild, Burbridge and French, ex-United States Senator Warner Miller, State Senator Colonel Murphy, General Greely of the Signal Corps and Colonel D. F. Ritchie.

The President called the meeting to order at 2:30 p. m.

The Recording Secretary presented the last annual report as the minutes of the Society. On his motion the reading of the minutes was dispensed with, and the report was accepted and adopted.

The Treasurer then presented his annual report, which, on motion, was received and referred to an auditing committee.

General Locke, as chairman of the committee appointed at the last meeting, to prepare a suitable button or bow knot to be worn by members of the Society, presented the bow knot now in use, which, on motion, was adopted.

The next business being the selection of a place for the next meeting, communications were presented from the Mayor and New England Society of Orange, N. J., inviting the Society to hold its next annual re-union in that city.

DECIDING ON THE RE-UNION.

General Sickles offered the following resolutions:

Resolved, That a committee consisting of three representatives of each of the Army corps belonging to the Army of the Potomac be appointed by the President of this Society, which committee shall take such action as it shall deem expedient and proper to commemorate the twenty-fifth anniversary of the battle of Gettysburg, by a re-union of the survivors of the Army of the Potomac, on the battlefield, on the 1st, 2d and 3d days of July, 1888.

Resolved, That the committee representing this Society be instructed to tender to the survivors of the Army of Northern Virginia our cordial invitation to take part with us in the battlefield re-union of July, 1888, so that the survivors of both armies may on that occasion record in friendship and fraternity the sentiments of good will, loyalty and patriotism which now happily unite us all in sincere devotion to our beloved country.

General Fairchild seconded the resolutions.

The President appointed as the committee to report three places from which the place of meeting shall be selected, General Daniel E. Sickles, Captain A. M. Matthews, General C. A. Whittier, General J. J. Milhau, Lieutenant F. S. Halliday.

After consultation the committee reported the names of Gettysburg, Pa., Orange, N. J., and Boston, Mass.

Colonel R. F. O'Beirne and Private H. C. Larowe were appointed tellers. The ballot resulted as follows: Gettysburg, 138; Orange, 93; Boston, 58.

General Sickles' resolutions, already presented, were amended to include all the corps in the Army, and were adopted.

OFFICERS ELECTED.

General John C. Robinson was nominated for President by the Fifth Corps. The nomination was seconded by the First and Sixth Corps.

General F. C. Barlow was nominated by the Second Corps.

General C. E. Pratt, General H. C. King, General Geo. S. Greene, General J. B. Carr, were also nominated. General King requested that his name be withdrawn.

Corporal E. A. Dubey and Lieutenant W. H. Racey were appointed tellers.

General John C. Robinson having received a majority of all the votes cast, was declared to be elected President for the ensuing year.

Lieut.-Colonel Samuel Truesdell was nominated as Treasurer of the Society, General Horatio C. King as Recording Secretary, and General George H. Sharpe as Corresponding Secretary, and on motion the President was directed to cast the unanimous ballot of the Society for those officers, who were then declared elected. General King, who endeavored to decline a re-election, was overwhelmed by cries of "Out of order," in which the President joined, and declared the election carried.

The following resolutions, offered by Corporal James Tanner, were adopted:

Resolved, That the Society of the Army of the Potomac congratulates the country at large that, in obedience to a sentiment vastly dominant throughout the land, the battle banners wrested by the valor of our comrades, living and dead, from the hands of a gallant foe, are to remain, as the law of the land provides, forevermore under the protection of all the people, as represented by the constituted authorities of the nation.

Resolved, That while in the days when we kept step to the martial music of the Union, when the scenes of camp and field and all the dread accompaniments of deadly strife entered so largely into our daily life, these banners floated at the head of rebellious columns, they are nevertheless holy relics of our common people. Brave men died to keep them afloat. Brave men died to bring them down. They shall not be burned. They shall not be lightly given away by those who in no sense can enter into the feelings of either those who by the exercise of a heroism unexcelled were enabled to lay them as trophies at the feet of Abraham Lincoln, or of those who only surrendered them after a heroic defence which but enhanced the glory of the capture. For Northern man and Southern man—Union men all to-day—we demand for those flags such care as will insure their preservation, in order that generations yet to come may gaze upon them, not in humiliation or exultation, but to the end that such contemplation may produce reflections upon the awful sacrifice through which we have reached our high plane of national existence, and give them firm resolve that through all their lives this generation will stand solidly for Union, for Peace and for Fraternity.

The following resolutions offered by General King were unanimously adopted:

Resolved, That the Society extend its thanks to the Legislature of New York, and especially to Senators Sloan and Murphy, and to Governor Hill, the Executive of the State, for the generous appropriation of $7,500 for the purpose of sending two of the historic regiments of the National Guard, the 14th and 69th Regiments, to honor the re-union of the Army of the Potomac.

Resolved, That the thanks of the Society of the Army of the Potomac are hereby extended to the President and corporate authorities of Saratoga, to the Executive Committee, and to the citizens of this beautiful village, for the generous reception extended to the members of the Society; and also to the local and visiting military bodies and Grand Army Posts, which, by their presence, have made this one of the most successful re-unions of the Society in its history.

General Robinson presented an invitation from the Fairmount Park Art Association to the Society, to participate in the ceremony attending the dedication of the bronze equestrian statue of General George G. Meade, which was accepted.

Coporal Tanner: I move that this Society does not thank General McMahon for simply doing his duty, but we compliment him and congratulate ourselves that he has filled the chair with such marked ability, such courtesy and such conservatism of the rights of each individual.

The motion was unanimously carried by a rising vote.

The President: I thank you for your kind courtesy in adopting the motion of Coporal Tanner. I appreciate it fully, and I consider it the greatest honor I have ever achieved or hope to achieve to have been President of this Society.

On motion, the following named gentlemen were elected honorary members of the Society: Lieutenant Com. A. R. McNair, U. S. N.; Commander E. T. Woodward, U. S. N.; Lieutenant Loyal Farragut, U. S. A.; Lieutenant C. M. Depew, the Orator; Mr. Wallace Bruce, the Poet. Subsequently at the banquet, on motion of General King, General W. T. Sherman was also elected an honorary member.

At this moment General Sherman and Mr. Depew entered the hall, and each in turn was received with three cheers of welcome.

It was moved and carried that the Society be requested to attend the unveiling of the statue of General A. E. Burnside, at Providence, R. I., on the 4th of July, 1887.

On motion, it was resolved that a committee be appointed from each corps to take steps to prepare a suitable memorial in honor of General George B. McClellan, and report at the next meeting.

On motion, the meeting adjourned.

THE PROCESSION.

After the meeting the parade took place, in which the Society did not join because of the inclement weather.

The procession moved in the following order from Monument Square:

Platoon of police, 16 strong.

Major-General S. G. Burbridge, Grand Marshal.

Assistants, Capt. J. M. Andrews, Jr., Chief of Staff; Brt. Maj. Gen. W. L. McMillan, Col. C. L. McArthur, Maj. Eugene F. O'Connor, Maj. W. T. Rockwood, Maj. W. J. Riggs, Maj. C. A. Coombs, Capt. David C. King, Surg. C. C Wells, Capt. W. W. French, Capt. I. D. Clapp, Capt. John D. Rogers, Capt. T. F. Allen, Col. Edward R. Howe, Lt. A. Howland, Lt. Thomas Harris, Capt. Geo. D. Story, Lt. W. G. Ball, Lt. Job Spofford, Lt. A. J. Reid, Lt. Walter H. Bryant, Lt. C. F. Rich, Comrades A. F. Mitchell, Julius Case and J. R. Gibbs.

FIRST DIVISION.

General B. F. Baker, commanding.

Brigadier General McLeer and staff

Bayne's Sixty-ninth Regiment Band.

Sixty-ninth Regiment, N. G. S. N. Y., Colonel James Cavanagh commanding, 600 strong.

Fourteenth Regiment Band.

Fourteenth Regiment, N. G. S. N. Y., Colonel Harry Michell commanding, 400 strong.

SECOND DIVISION.

Lieutenant-Colonel John S. Fassett, commanding.

Doring's Band.

Twenty-second Separate Co., N. G. S. N. Y., 60 strong, Captain R. C. McEwen commanding (Saratoga Citizens Corps).

Post Wheeler, No. 92, G. A. R., as escort to Posts of G. A. R.

Post McConhie, No. 185, of Troy, 57 strong.

Representatives of Post Frank Norton, No. 116, of Schuylerville.

Post B. C. Butler, No. 316, of Luzerne.

Post B. Rice, No. 290, Corinth, Washington Co., Veteran Association.

Saratoga Co. Veteran Association.

Unorganized Veterans.

Sons of Veterans, 18 strong.

Numerous organizations which came to participate did not take part, owing to the weather and the muddy line of march; including the Veterans of the Seventh Regiment.

Notwithstanding the rain, the pavements of Broadway were thronged and every window was filled with enthusiastic spectators.

EVENING MEETING.

The vast Casino, with a capacity of four thousand people, was filled in every part. It was handsomely decorated with flags, bunting, emblematic devices and Chinese lanterns. At the end farthest from the entrance was a large canvas, upon which was painted a lifelike camp scene. Upon the platform, besides General Sherman and other distinguished ex-officers and citizens, were many of the wives of the visiting veterans. General McMahon presided, and after a spirited prelude by Doring's Band, in which were introduced many of the familiar songs of the war times, the President called the meeting to order, and requested the Rev. Dr. Joseph Carey of Saratoga Springs to offer prayer.

An address of welcome was next delivered by Rev. William R. Terry, acting for Captain Lewis R. Wood, a veteran and President of the village of Saratoga; the response being made by the President of the Society, General M. T. McMahon.

At the conclusion of his address the band struck up "Marching Through Georgia," and Secretary King, springing to his feet, lead the chorus, in which he was joined by the audience, and the grand melody rolled forth from thousands of throats. None sang with more enthusiasm than did the rugged old hero of that famous march to the sea; and the effect was electrical.

The President: Ladies and gentlemen, perhaps you are not aware that the Army of the Potomac, which was equipped in its day with everything necessary for a quiet life, now keeps a poet. I have the honor to introduce Mr. Wallace Bruce, of New York, the poet of the evening

Mr. Bruce then stepped forward, and delivered with brilliant and thrilling effect, the poem entitled "The Candle Parade," illustrating a most striking incident, at the close of the war, when the armies were encamped around Washington, waiting for the closing review in the streets of that city.

The poet was frequently interrupted by fervent demonstrations of appreciation, and at the close was greeted with prolonged applause.

The orator of the day, Lieutenant Chauncey M. Depew, was next introduced, and, as was anticipated, made a striking and masterly exhibition of his rhetorical powers.

The oration, during its delivery, was frequently interrupted with applause, and at its close three cheers were proposed for the orator, and given with enthusiasm.

At this point a number of young misses belonging to the High School of Saratoga, marshaled by their principal, sang one of the old army songs, after which two of them, bearing a large wreath of immortelles, came to the front of the stage, accompanied by their teacher, who addressed the President as follows:

General McMahon, on behalf of the young ladies of the High School of Saratoga, forty-two in number, I present to you, or the Army of the Potomac through you, this beautiful gift as their gift.

To which the President responded:

On behalf of the Society of the Army of the Potomac here and elsewhere, I accept this very beautiful gift from the very beautiful donors.

The class then sang the "Star Spangled Banner."

In response to loud calls and cheering, General Sherman made the next oration, and was followed by General H. W. Slocum, General Daniel E. Sickles and ex-Judge Henry D. Hilton.

THE BANQUET.

The second day opened with rain, and many who had intended to remain and participate in the banquet, were discouraged at the outlook and returned home.

The upper end of the immense dining room in Congress Hall was set apart for the banquet. Around the walls there was a liberal attendance of ladies, and immediately in the rear of the main table, on a raised dais, were seated a number of ladies, including Mrs. Colonel Grant, Mrs. General King, Mrs. Colonel Clement, Mrs. Colonel Church, Mrs. General Pinto, Mrs. General Whipple, Mrs. Wallace Bruce and Mrs. F. S. Halliday.

Promptly at half-past eight some two hundred and fifty members, preceded by the President and invited guests, marched into the room and took their seats.

The menu represented crossed flags, the one the faded and torn battle flag of the nation, and the other the white flag of peace, surmounted by a dove, and beneath was the embossed badge of the Society, a beautiful and exquisite bit of workmanship, the most tasteful of any of the menu cards at the banquets of the Society.

Grace was asked by the Rev. Joseph Carey, and the members then attacked the following bill of fare:

MENU.

SOUP.
Snapping Turtle.

FISH.
Sauterne.
Boiled Kennebec Salmon, Cardinal Sauce.
Cucumbers. Parisienne Potatoes.
Vino de Pasto.

RELEVE.
Sweetbread Patties, with Truffles.

ENTREES.
Tenderloin of Beef, A. of P. Style.
Potato Croquettes.
Stewed Terrapin, American Fashion.
Croquettes of Fowls, with New Peas.
St. Julien.
Roman Punch.

ROASTS.
Spring Turkeys Stuffed, Lettuce Sauce.
G. H. Mumm Extra Dry.

PASTRY.
Diplomatic Pudding, Chandeau Sauce.
Assorted Fancy Cakes and Candies.
Champagne Jelly.

DESSERT.
Fruit en Compote. Coffee a la Francaise.
Monongahela Monogram Whiskey.
Cigars.

After a lengthy and very satisfactory discussion of the viands, the President rapped for order, and said:

COMRADES: It now becomes my duty to announce the first regular toast, "The President of the United States," to which General John C. Black will respond.

The next toast, "The State of New York," was responded to by General Judge Calvin E. Pratt.

"Saratoga Springs," called forth a reply from Professor Nathan Sheppard, which was both amusing and witty.

The Orator of the Day, Chauncey M. Depew, was received with applause and three cheers, and that gentleman responded with his usual alacrity and humor.

To the next toast, "The Army of the Potomac," General Slocum responded.

"Our Sister Societies and Brothers in Arms," brought a reply from old man Sherman himself.

At the close of his speech, which was pathetic and humorous, and contained numerous telling hits at men and events, the Secretary, General King, moved that General Sherman be elected an honorary member of the Society, which motion was enthusiastically carried.

The next toast in order was the "Army and Navy," of which the President said, "I shall request General Whipple, of the army, to respond, although he has not had much experience of the navy, further than living on Governor's Island, whence he reaches the mainland in a tug boat."

The next toast, "The Volunteers," was responded to by General Sickles.

Three cheers were proposed for General Sickles at the close of his address, and were given with great warmth.

The next toast, "The Army of the James," called forth a response from Corporal James Tanner, who spoke in his usually effective manner.

To the next regular toast, "The National Guard," General Daniel Butterfield responded.

Mr. Wallace Bruce responded to the toast, "The Poet," with the following lines: It is said that when General Grant was dying, a ray of sunlight through the half-closed shutters fell upon Lincoln's picture, leaving the General's picture beside it in shadow. After lingering for a moment, it passed and fell upon the dying hero's face. Here are the lines I have written:

THE SILENT SOLDIER.

From gulf to lake, from sea to sea,
  The land is draped—a nation weeps;
And o'er the bier bows reverently,
  Whereon the silent soldier sleeps.

The mountain top is bathed in light,
  And eastern cliff with outlook wide;
Its name shall live in memory bright—
  The Mount McGregor, where he died!

A monument to stand for aye,
  In summer's bloom, in winter's snows,
A shrine where men shall come to pray
  While at its base the Hudson flows.

A humble room, the light burns low,
  The morning breaks on distant hill,
The failing pulse is beating slow,
  The group is motionless and still.

Two portraits hang upon the wall,
  Two kindred pictures side by side—
Statesmen and soldier, loved by all—
  Lincoln and Grant, Columbia's pride.

A single ray through lattice streams,
  And breaks in rainbow colors there;
On Lincoln's brow a glory gleams,
  As wife and children kneel in prayer.

A halo round the martyr's head,
  It lights the sad and solemn room;
Above the living and the dead,
  The soldier's portrait hangs in gloom.

In shadow one, and one in light:
  But look! the pencil ray has passed,
And on the hero's picture bright
  The golden sunlight rests at last.

And so, throughout the coming years,
  On both the morning beam shall play,
When the long night of bitter tears
  Has melted in the light away.

The President then said: "We have now reached the end of our regular toasts, but as I desire to preserve the continuity of the Society, I will ask and propose the health of my successor, General John C. Robinson;" and General Robinson replied : " I hope to meet you all again on the field of the greatest battle of modern times, where we helped to preserve the nation. We will not find there the palatial hotels nor the sparkling streams of Saratoga, but I shall ask of the Governor of Pennsylvania to have quarters and a commissariat, so that we will all be comfortable, and I hope every member will be there."

ON TO GETTYSBURG.

In connection with the re-union this year on the great battlefield the following sentiments were expressed by the several orators of the day and evening :

Go to Gettysburg next year and welcome heartily your " enemy " of that field, your enemy no more.

You have had here, I think, one of the most delightful meetings the Society has ever enjoyed. You will have one more, at which more members will be present, and to which more interest will be attached—the meeting next year on the battlefield of Gettysburg.

A correspondent in writing of the banquet, said : "The four years of the great war had their annals told anew, and their glories again lighted the eyes and flushed the cheeks of the heroes who fought and suffered through them. Then the parting till the next re-union, which, with the Army of Northern Virginia, shall be at Gettysburg."

THIRD CORPS SOCIETY.

The annual meeting of the surviving officers of Third Army Corps and the Twenty-fourth Anniversary Banquet of the Third Army Corps Union were held at the Windsor Hotel, New York City, on Thursday, May 5, at four o'clock p. m., Colonel A. Judson Clark, Vice-President, in the chair.

General Sickles moved : " That a committee of seven members of the Third Union Corps be appointed to take steps looking to a re-union of the Army of the Potomac and the Army of Northern Virginia, at Gettysburg, on the 1st, 2d and 3d of July, 1888 ; that said committee be authorized to correspond with the Society of the Army of the Potomac and the societies of the army corps belonging to the Army of the Potomac, and with the organizations of the Grand Army of the Republic ; likewise with the organizations, societies and officers of the Army of North Virginia, for the purpose of making proper arrangements for the re-union contemplated in this resolution ; and that such committee have power to unite with the organizations above named in taking such measures as may be agreed upon for the occasion ;" which resolution was passed unanimously.

Colonel McMichael moved, and it was so ordered, " That it be expressed as the sense of this Society, that nothing contained in General Sickles' resolution shall be construed as interfering with or changing the regular annual re-union of the Third Corps-Union for 1888."

Committee named under General Sickles' resolution were: Generals Sickles, Carr, Robinson, Graham, Sharpe, Colonels Macmichael and Clark.

Pursuant to notice given at last re-union, and which was inadvertently omitted in the minutes of said re-union, the following resolution was presented, and after some discussion was unanimously adopted:

"That the Constitution and By-Laws be and they are hereby so amended as to extend eligibility to membership to all non-commissioned officers and privates who have served in the Third Army Corps, or who have participated in any of the battles of the corps."

Colonel Macmichael, Major Fassitt, and Major Bullard were appointed a committee, who shall, in conjunction with the President, the Secretary and the Treasurer, make all proper arrangements for the annual re-union and the twenty-fifth anniversary banquet of the Society.

The following officers were then nominated and elected for the ensuing year: President, Colonel A. Judson Clark of New Jersey.

Vice-President, General C. H. T. Callis of Pennsylvania.

Secretary, Colonel Edward Welling of New Jersey.

Directors, General William J. Sewell of New Jersey; General George H. Sharpe of New York; Colonel Clayton Macmichael of Pennsylvania; General Joseph B. Carr of New York; Major J. Barclay Fassitt of District of Columbia; Colonel Joseph F. Tobias of Pennsylvania; Major William Plimley of New Jersey; Captain John G. Noonan of New York; Captain C. W. Wilson of New York.

Trustees, General Charles K. Graham of New York; Major Willard Bullard of New York.

At a subsequent meeting of the Board of Directors, Major William P. Shreve of Massachusetts, was re-elected Treasurer.

FIFTH CORPS SOCIETY.

Minutes of the annual meeting of the Society of the Fifth Army Corps, held in the Putnam Music Hall, Saratoga Springs, on Wednesday, June 22, 1887.

The President appointed the following committee to nominate officers of the Society for the ensuing year: General H. A. Barnum, Captain Van Read, and J. W. Webb. The committee reported as follows: For President, Major-General Fitz John Porter, U. S. Vols.; for First Vice-President, Colonel Richard F. O'Beirne, U. S. A.; for Second Vice-President, Colonel William D. Dickey, U. S. Vols.; for Secretary and Treasurer, General Fred T. Locke, U. S. Vols. For Executive Committee, General H. A. Barnum, U. S. Vols.; General Daniel Butterfield, U. S. Vols.; Captain John McGinlin, U. S. Vols.

The candidates named were unanimously elected.

General Locke reported, as chairman of the committee appointed at the meeting in Baltimore, to confer with a committee having in charge the erection of a monument to the late Major-General G. K. Warren, that, with the advice and consent of the President of the Society and the Executive Committee, he had paid the sum of $25 towards the erection of said monument, and, by the same authority, he had paid the sum of $25 towards the erection of a monument to the late Major-General George Sykes. He reported, also, that the monument to General Sykes was nearly completed, and would be erected over the General's grave in the cemetery at West Point by July 1, 1887.

It was resolved that the Executive Committee be authorized to make arrangements for the Society to meet at West Point at the ceremonies of unveiling the monument when completed.

On motion, the Secretary was directed to telegraph to General Porter the notice of his election as President of the Society.

General Barnum moved that the Society name for its choice as President of the Society of the Army of the Potomac Major-General John C. Robinson; carried unanimously. Major Joseph H. Stiner was elected Vice-President of the Society of the Army of the Potomac, to represent the Society of the Fifth Army Corps.

It was resolved that the Society hold its next annual meeting at the same time and place as the Army of the Potomac may select.

SIXTH CORPS SOCIETY.

The nineteenth annual re-union of the Sixth Army Corps was held in the rooms of Post Wheeler, No. 92, G. A. R., Department of New York, at Saratoga Springs, N. Y., on Wednesday, June 22, 1887.

The meeting was called to order by the President, General Francis E. Pinto.

A letter from Colonel S. W. Russell was read, inviting the Society to visit Salem, Washington Co., N. Y., and the last resting place of General David A. Russell, who was killed at Winchester, Va., September 19, 1864. The invitation was accepted, and the letter ordered to be spread in full upon the minutes.

Colonel Russell, who was present, exhibited the old headquarters flag of the First Division of the Corps, and promised a soldier's welcome to all who might find it convenient to visit Salem.

The following officers for the ensuing year were nominated and duly elected: President, General Charles A. Whittier; Vice-Presidents, Colonel S. W. Russell, Colonel August Belknap, Major R. Q. Anuersley, Colonel I. W. Cronkhite; Recording Secretary, Captain George B. Fielder;

Corresponding Secretary, Sergeant H. C. Larowe; Treasurer, Colonel S. Truesdell; Vice-President of the Society of the Army of the Potomac, representing the Sixth Corps, General Francis E. Pinto.

The meeting then adjourned, to meet on the same day and at the same place with the Society of the Army of the Potomac.

SOCIETY OF THE BURNSIDE EXPEDITION, AND NINTH ARMY CORPS.

The meeting of this Society was held in Odd Fellows' Hall, Saratoga Springs, N. Y., June 22, 1887, commencing at 11 a. m.

In the absence of the President—who sent a letter stating that he was detained by illness—Major John S. Koster was elected President *pro tem*.

The Secretary presented an obituary sketch of General Robert B. Potter, the only member of the Society known to have died during the year.

A communication was read from the Secretary of the committee in charge of the ceremonies at the unveiling of the Burnside equestrian statue at Providence, R. I., inviting this Society to participate in the exercises on the 4th day of July next. On motion the invitation was unanimously accepted.

The Committee on Nominations reported the following ticket, and it was unanimously elected—President, General Gilbert H. McKibben of New York; Vice-President, Colonel Robert H. I. Goddard of Rhode Island; Secretary and Treasurer, General C. H. Barney of New York; Vice-President of the Society of the Army of the Potomac, Major John S. Koster of Lyons Falls, N. Y.

It was voted that the Secretary send a cheering telegram to comrade General Edward Jardine, who had been confined to his bed for many weeks by a painful, and at one time dangerous, illness.

TWELFTH CORPS SOCIETY.

The Society of the Twelfth Army Corps met in Odd Fellows' Hall, June 22, at 11 o'clock a. m.

The President, Captain A. M. Matthews, formerly Thirteenth N. J. Vols., called the meeting to order.

The Nominating Committee reported as follows: For President of the Society. Lieutenant-Colonel William Fox, 107th New York; for Secretary and Treasurer, John J. H. Love; for Vice-President Society Army Potomac, General James C. Rogers of New York.

The committee also recommended the presentation to the Society of the Army of the Potomac of the name of General George S. Greene, as a suitable candidate for President of that Society.

NINETEENTH ARMY CORPS SOCIETY.

The seventh annual re-union of the Society of the Nineteenth Army Corps was held in the Town Hall, Saratoga Springs, New York, June 22, 1887, at 10:30 a. m.

The Society was called to order by the second Vice-President, General Nicholas W. Day.

The following officers for the ensuing year were nominated and duly elected: President, General William H. Emory, Washington, D. C.; First Vice-President, General Nicholas W. Day, New York City; Second Vice-President, Colonel O. W. Leonard, Massachusetts; Third Vice-President, Captain John J. Buchanan, Johnstown, New York; Secretary, Major Thomas B. Odell, New York City; Treasurer, Major Charles Appleby, New York City; Historian, Colonel Richard B. Irwin, Philadelphia, Pa.; Vice-President of the Society of the Army of the Potomac representing the Society of the Nineteenth Army Corps, General A. W. Greely, Washington, D. C.; Executive Committee, General E. L. Molineux, Captain William H. Jewell, Major A. C. Tate, Major W. Frank Tiemann, and Captain Emmett M. Fitch.

THE CAVALRY SOCIETY.

Society met pursuant to call at the Worden Hotel, at 3:30 p. m., June 21, 1887, and proceeded by special train to Mt. McGregor, where after a visit to the Drexel Cottage, they convened in business session, President Taylor in the chair.

The election of officers being the next order of business, resulted as follows: For President, Brevet Brigadier General Samuel E. Chamberlain; for First Vice-President, Major Henry E. Farnsworth; for Second Vice-President, Colonel John A. Richardson; for Third Vice-President, Major Henry A. Penfield; for Fourth Vice-President, Major F. R. Shattuck; for Fifth Vice-President, Colonel Floyd Clarkson; for Sixth Vice-President, Colonel A. J. Morrison; for Seventh Vice-President, Surgeon P. O'Meara Edson; for Treasurer, Major Gerrard Irvin Whitehead; for Secretary, Brevet Major L. L. Barney; for Vice-President of the Army of the Potomac, Private Henry T. Bartlett.

The following was adopted:

Resolved, That the name of the Society be changed from "The Cavalry Corps Society of the Armies of the United States" to that of the Cavalry Society of the Armies of the United States."

XVI.

PROCEEDINGS OF THE LAST MEETING OF THE SOCIETY OF THE ARMY OF NORTHERN VIRGINIA.

The annual gathering of the veterans of the Army of Northern Virginia in the State Capitol, at Richmond, always attracts a crowd of interested auditors, and this was no exception. At an early hour on Friday, October 28, 1887, the audience began to assemble, and a time was spent by the veterans in cordial greetings, the revival of old memories, and in the recognition and applause of well-known Confederates. Governor Lee, General J. E. Johnston, General Hampton, General Early, General Taliaferro, and others, were loudly applauded as they came into the hall. General Taliaferro, the President, called the Association to order, and the Chaplain, Dr. J. William Jones, led in prayer.

General Taliaferro then cordially congratulated the Association on the numbers present. He alluded in fitting phrase to the visit of President Cleveland to Richmond, and to the fact that the Southern veterans, while true to the Union, had not forgotten the memories of other days, the cause for which they fought, or their great commander, R. E. Lee. General Taliaferro warmly congratulated the Association on the presence of the first great commander of the Army of Northern Virginia, General J. E. Johnston; the great son of South Carolina (Hampton), who rode with the Cavalry Corps; the distinguished Lieutenant-General (J. A. Early), who was the first President of this Association; the son of our great commander (General W. H. F. Lee), who won his spurs in the Cavalry; our own distinguished Governor (General Fitz Lee), and other soldiers worthy of companionship with these; and then in fitting phrase he introduced the orator of the evening, Colonel A. M. Waddell, of North Carolina.

THE ORATION.

Colonel Waddell was warmly received by the Association and the audience, and was loudly applauded. With graceful and eloquent allusion to the memories of the occasion, and some very fine satire on the changes in the opinions held by certain so-called statesmen of the present, Colonel Waddell quoted from Colonel Charles Marshall's speech before the Association some years ago, as to the very great difficulty of giving accurately historic facts. Among other illustrations of this Colonel Waddell cited the mistakes that had been made in the accounts of Pettigrew's Division at Gettysburg. He eloquently insisted, amid the loud applause of the audience, that while he would not detract from the honor that justly belongs to Pickett's Division, yet it was due to Pettigrew's Division of North Carolinians and Archer's Tennessee Brigade to say that on that last day at Gettysburg they went as far and stayed as long as any other troops, and are entitled to equal honor with Pickett's men.

He introduced as his theme "The Last Year of the War in North Carolina," giving a very vivid account of the capture of Plymouth; an account of the bombardment and final capture of Fort Fisher, with a very amusing account of Butler's powder-ship and its explosion. He told an anecdote given him by Admiral Porter, which brought down the house in rapturous applause. His description of the final assault and capture of Fort Fisher and the gallant defence of the heroic garrison was very fine.

Colonel Waddell next spoke of the assuming of command by General J. E. Johnston, and the ability with which he conducted his operations; paid a tribute to General Hampton's operations, both of which elicited loud applause.

His contrast between the conduct of Cornwallis' Army in their march through North Carolina in the first Revolution and that of Sherman's "bummers," was very striking and certainly not to the credit of the latter. Colonel Waddell complimented General Taliaferro on his splendid fight at Averasboro; then gave a very interesting account of the Confederate victory at Bentonville; closing with a description of the final catastrophe, and an eloquent tribute to Virginia and to Lee, which was loudly applauded. Colonel Waddell enlivened his speech with keen wit, humor, and well-told anecdotes, which brought down the house in applause. The whole speech was an admirable one.

On motion of General Early, the officers of the Association were re-elected, the name of General J. R. Cooke being substituted for that of General Smith.

On motion of the Hon. George L. Christian, feeling resolutions on the death of General William Smith were adopted.

THE BANQUET.

After the addresses at the hall there was a banquet at Pizzini's. General Taliaferro presided, and there were present Generals Hampton, Early, W. H. F. Lee, B. T. Johnson, R. Ransom, William McComb, and T. T. Mumford, Colonel Waddell, Colonel R. T. W. Duke, Colonel Randolph Harrison, Colonel John B. Cary, Rev. Dr. Dame of Baltimore, Gardiner Tyler, Esq., Rev. Dr. Goodwin, E. V. Valentine, Esq., Judge Theodore S. Garnett, Judge George L. Christian, Captain W. Gordon McCabe, Professor J. M. Garnett, and a number of other good old Confederates, who greatly enjoyed the opportunity of mingling together in pleasant social intercourse. It had been determined to have no regular toasts or set speeches at this meeting, and so there was ample time to discuss the bill of fare as the old soldiers fought their battles over again, and compared the rations with those they were wont to "draw from the Commissary."

XVII.

OFFICERS OF EACH SOCIETY AND COMMITTEES HAVING THE REUNION IN CHARGE.

SOCIETY OF THE ARMY OF THE POTOMAC.
OFFICERS FOR 1888.

PRESIDENT:
  Major-General John C. Robinson, U. S. A.
VICE-PRESIDENTS:
  First Corps—Brigadier-General Lucius Fairchild, U. S. V.
  Second Corps—Corporal Edward A. Dubey, U. S. V.
  Third Corps—Brevet Colonel A. Judson Clarke, U. S. V.
  Fourth Corps—Brevet Brigadier-General Thomas Wilson, U. S. A.
  Fifth Corps—Major Joseph H. Stiner, U. S. V.
  Sixth Corps—Brevet Brigadier-General Francis E. Pinto, U. S. V.
  Ninth Corps—Sergeant John S. Koster, U. S. V.
  Eleventh Corps—Brevet Lieutenant-Colonel Henry Root, U. S. V.
  Twelfth Corps—Brevet Brigadier-General James C. Rogers, U. S. V.
  Eighteenth Corps—Major E. C. Ford, U. S. V.
  Nineteenth Corps—Brigadier-General Adolphus W. Greely, U. S. V.
  General Staff—Brevet Major-General Stewart Van Vliet, U. S. V.
  Cavalry Corps—Bugler Henry T. Bartlett, U. S. V.
  Artillery Corps—Brevet Lieutenant-Colonel J. A. Tompkins, U. S. V.
  Signal Corps—Brevet Major Bradford R. Wood, Jr., U. S. V.
TREASURER:
  Brevet Lieutenant-Colonel Samuel Truesdell, U. S. V., 93 Nassau street, New York.
RECORDING SECRETARY:
  Brevet Colonel Horatio C. King, U. S. V., 38 Park Row, New York.
CORRESPONDING SECRETARY:
  Brevet Major-General George H. Sharpe, U. S. V., Rondout, New York.

SOCIETY OF THE ARMY OF NORTHERN VIRGINIA.

OFFICERS FOR 1888.

PRESIDENT:
 Major-General William B. Taliaferro, Wareneck, Gloucester County, Va.
VICE-PRESIDENTS:
 Colonel Charles Marshall, Baltimore, Md.
 Colonel James H. Skinner, Staunton, Va.
 Brigadier-General T. T. Mumford, Lynchburg, Va.
 Brigadier-General John R. Cooke, Richmond, Va.
 Captain P. M. McKinney, Farmville, Va.
TREASURER:
 Robert S. Pooser, Richmond, Va.
SECRETARY:
 Carlton McCarthy, Richmond, Va.
EXECUTIVE COMMITTEE:
 Colonel Archer Anderson, Judge George L. Chushanson, John S. Ellett, Major Thomas A. Brader, Colonel W. H. Palmer.

COMMITTEES ON RE-UNION OF UNION AND CONFEDERATE VETERANS AT GETTYSBURG, JULY 2 AND 3, 1888.

ARMY OF THE POTOMAC.

First Corps—Generals Abner Doubleday and John C. Robinson.
Second Corps—General F. C. Barlow, Colonel W. L. Tidball.
Third Corps—Generals D. C. Sickles, J. B. Carr, C. K. Graham.
Fourth Corps—Colonel W. C. Church, Generals E. D. Keys and D. N. Couch.
Fifth Corps—Generals Daniel Butterfield, Fitz John Porter, G. W. Crawford.
Sixth Corps—Generals M. T. McMahon, C. A. Whittier and T. W. Hyde.
Ninth Corps—Generals John F. Hartranft and John G. Parke, Major Barker.
Eleventh Corps—Generals O. O. Howard, Charles Devens and Carl Schurz.
Twelfth Corps—Generals H. W. Slocum, Henry A. Barnum and G. S. Greene.
Cavalry Corps—Generals A. Pleasonton, J. B. McIntosh and Hammond.
Artillery Corps—General H. J. Hunt, Colonel Gowan.
Nineteenth Corps—Generals N. P. Banks, W. H. Emery and H. A. Williams.

Army of the James—Generals B. F. Butler, N. M. Curtis and Joseph R. Hawley.

General Staff—Generals George H. Sharpe. H. A. Tremaine, Major L. H. Fassitt.

Secretary—Major George W. Cooney.

ARMY OF NORTHERN VIRGINIA.

Not yet obtained.

EXECUTIVE COMMITTEE OF THE ARMY OF THE POTOMAC.

General H. W. Slocum, Chairman, 465 Washington avenue, Brooklyn, N. Y.; General Daniel Butterfield, 60 Fifth avenue, N. Y.; General E. L. Molineux, 106 Fulton street, N. Y.; General C. H. T. Collis, 19 New street, Y. Y.; General M. T. McMahon, United States Marshal's Office, N. Y.; General S. L. Woodford, 1 Broadway, N. Y.; Colonel W. C. Church, 240 Broadway, N. Y.; General C. H. Barney, 32 Nassau street, N. Y.; Colonel Floyd Clarkson, 35 Broadway, N. Y.; General John C. Robinson, Binghamton, N. Y.; General J. G. Farnsworth, Albany, N. Y.; General J. F. Hartranft, Philadelphia, Pa.; Colonel Samuel Truesdell, 18 Broadway, N. Y., and General George H. Sharpe, Kingston, N. Y.

EXECUTIVE COMMITTEE OF THE ARMY OF NORTHERN VIRGINIA.

Not yet received.

CITIZENS' COMMITTEES OF GETTYSBURG.

COMMITTEE OF THE BOARD OF TRADE.—Burgess W. H. Tipton, Dr. William H. O'Neal, Major F. W. Coleman and Hon. David Wills.

Reception Committee for the Re-Union.—Chairman, Hon. Edward McPherson; First Vice-Chairman, Hon. William McClean; Second, Hon. David Wills; Third, Hon. John A. Swope; Fourth, Colonel C. H. Buehler; Secretary, Martin Winter.

Committee.—R. D. Armor, Jacob Anghinbaugh, Samuel M. Bushman, Professor E. S. Breidenbaugh, Rev. H. L. Baugher, D.D.; J. Emory Bair, Guyon H. Buehler, Rev. P. M. Bikle, Ph. D.; F. C. Brinkerhoff, Rev.

Joseph A. Boll, Rev. T. J. Barkley, Major H. S. Benner, George J. Benner, Esq., H. J. Brinkerhoff, Jr.; Major F. W. Coleman, Simon J. Codori, Rufus E. Culp, Professor L. H. Croll, S. C. D.; William H. Culp, S. G. Cook, William Chritzman, H. B. Danner, Rev. J. K. Demarest, Simon J. Diller, Charles S. Duncan, Dr. H. L. Diehl, Rev. J. R. Dunkerly, Captain George A. Earnshaw, Amos Eckert, Frank Eberhart, R. M. Elliott, Dr. C. E. Eckenrode, F. A. Elliott, Edgar S. Faber, Dr. J. C. Felty, A. W. Fleming, Captain Calvin Gilbert, J. William Garlach, Levi Gross, William H. Gelbach, Samuel Herbst, John M. Huber, Dr. Charles Horner, Dr. Robert Horner, Sergeant W. D. Holtzworth, Dr. J. L. Hill, J. L. Hill, Jr.; Dr. James M. Hill, Professor John A. Himes. Professor Calvin Hamilton, R. L. Harnish, Captain James Hersh, Rev. C. A. Hay, D. D.; David Kendlehart, J. A. Kitzmiller, Calvin P. Krise, John M. Krauth, George W. Kirk, John A. Livers, Captain J. T. Long, Colonel J. H. McClellan, William Arch McLean, Nathaniel Miller, William N. Miller, Charles H. Miller, E. H. Minnigh, David McConaughy, William McSherry, Jr.; David McCleary, Charles M. McCurdy, Rev. H. W. McKnight, D. D.; Rev. A. Martin, D. D.; Captain William J. Martin, William S. McCreary, J. C. Neely, Dr. J. W. C. O'Neal, Dr. W. H. O'Neal, W. P. Quimby, Charles H. Ruff, Hon. S. R. Russell, F. S. Ramer, William H. Rupp, H. J. Stahle, J. Stahle, Rev. Joel Swartz, D. D.; W. C. Stallsmith. H. D. Scott, S. McC. Swope, J. H. Stine, J. L. Schick, D. A. Skelly, George E. Stock, Dr. J. B. Scott. William Spangler, Professor Aaron Sheely, W. C. Sheely, W. S. Schroder, G. W. Spangler, A. P. Seilhamer, Peter Sheads, George H. Swope, Burgess W. H. Tipton, Sheriff Jacob W. Faukinbaugh, David Troxel, John W. Tipton, Dr. T. T. Tate, George D. Thorn, Rev. M. Valentine, D. D.; Rev. C. H. Van Dyne, Rev. W. S. Van Cleve, Sergeant N. G. Wilson, H. T. Weaver, Jesse M. Walter, James S. Welty, John M. Warner, J. Nevin Wolf, J. E. Wible, Rev. E. J. Wolf, D. D.; Edward A. Weaver, **Henry Yingling**, William T. Zeigler. E. M. Zeigler, I. H. Zonn.

PRESS COMMITTEE FOR THE RE-UNION.

John Tregaskis, 5th New York Duryee Zouaves and 146th New York Volunteers, New York *Herald*, Chairman; William J. Starks, 104th New York Volunteers, New York *Herald*; Lewis R. Stegman, Major 102d and 78th New York Volunteers, Brooklyn *Citizen*; E. S. Brooks. General Staff Confederate Army, Baltimore *Sun*; George H. Carson. Major, General Staff, Philadelphia *Ledger*; Joseph Atkinson, U. S. S. Hendrick Hudson. *New Jersey Unionist*, Newark N. J.; J. Madison Drake, 9th N. J. Vols., *Sunday Leader*, Elizabeth, N. J.; James F. Farrell, 5th N. Y. Artil., Atlanta *Constitution*; Felix Agnes, General U. S. Vols., Baltimore *American*.

XVIII.

PROVISION MADE FOR THE ACCOMMODATION OF ALL WHO ATTEND THE RE-UNION..

The lack of shelter in the immediate vicinity of the Battlefield has, heretofore, been the one great drawback to the enjoyment of visitors to Gettysburg, who arrive there in large parties or on special occasions which attract many persons at the same time. To obviate this inconvenience, on the great occasion to which the eyes and best wishes of the country are directed, an appropriation of $25,000 was requested of the National Congress—not to pay railroad fares or any incidental expenses—but to put up barracks to shelter the thousands of Veterans of both Armies who will make the *fraternal pilgrimage*—to put up field kitchens and provide caterers, that everyone on the National camping ground may obtain good meals at a reasonable figure. Veterans are expected to bring their own blankets, and their expenses will be only $1 per day—for three good substantial meals, as good, if not better, than can be obtained in New York for the same money.

The Gettysburg and Harrisburg Railroad will run trains morning and evening to Carlisle sufficient to accommodate all those who desire to stop in the hotels and boarding houses along the line on the mountains between Carlisle and Gettysburg. Three or four thousand people can be accommodated in this way at Golden, Table Rock, Biglerville, Sunnyside, Bendersville, Gardner's, Idaville, Stainer's, Zion Church, Pine Grove Park, Laurel Forge, Hunter's Run, Mt. Holly Springs, Craighead, Bonny Brook and Carlisle. The trip forth and back is through a most picturesque and beautiful country and the noise and confusion of the nights in Gettysburg are avoided.

Tents will be provided by Governor James A. Beaver of Pennsylvania for 8,000 men; these will all be floored and nicely bedded with straw. The State of New Jersey will provide tents for the shelter of every man who leaves that State to participate in the dedication of her monuments. The New Jersey Camp will be pitched on the historic Wheat Field. The Grand Army of the Republic and Sons of Veterans of Pennsylvania will provide their own quarters as of yore. From New York but one regiment of the National Guard will represent the State and they, like the New Jersey troops, will encamp in their own establishment, bringing their own equipage.

Many of the Veteran Associations took time by the forelock and secured accommodations months ago, but the general mass of visitors will find that by application at the office of the Burgess, Mr. William H. Tipton, all vacant places can be obtained.

Several parties chartering special trains will sleep in them during the Re-Union, and for their accommodation a side track three-quarters of a mile in length has been constructed within the limits of the borough by Mr. William H. Woodward of the Gettysburg and Harrisburg Railroad. Still other parties have hotel cars and sleeping cars placed on a siding and shedded over; so that they have all the accommodations of home, with the additional facility of changing its location when inclination or necessity requires.

The people of Gettysburg generally are throwing their entire energies into providing for the many thousand strangers who will visit them, and every house will be a lodging house during the Re-Union.

W. H. TIPTON,

THE

Battlefield Photographer,

I have devoted my personal attention to photographing the field ever since the great battle in July, '63.

Over 5,000 negatives, of all sizes.

Photographs, Guide-Books, Souvenir Albums, etc., mailed anywhere.

XIX.

HOTELS AND BOARDING-HOUSES IN AND AROUND GETTYSBURG

HOTELS.

Name.	Location.	Room for	Name.	Location.	Room for
Springs Hotel	Springs	300	Keystone Hotel	Chambersburg St.	150
Eagle Hotel	Chambersburg St.	200	Washington Hotel	Carlisle St.	100
McClennen Hotel	Square	150	Central Hotel	Baltimore St.	100
Globe Hotel	York St.	125	Battle Field Hotel	Baltimore St.	75

BOARDING-HOUSES

Name.	Location.	Room for	Name.	Location.	Room for
Eli Little	Chambersburg St.	50	Mrs. Winebernner	Baltimore St	50
J. E. Pitzer	Chambersburg St.	75	Mrs. Tawney	Baltimore St	50
Mrs. Holtzworth	Chambersburg St.	40	Peter Culp	Water St	40
Mrs. Walter	Chambersburg St.	40	Captain J. T. Long	Baltimore St	50
Mrs. Currens	Chambersburg St.	30	Mrs. Stinaker	Breckenridge St.	40
Mrs. Gilbert	Middle St.	40	Mrs. T. S. Wible	High St	30
Mrs. Hummelbaugh	Middle St.	50	Mrs. Myers	Carlisle St	30
Mrs. Fromyers	Washington St	40	Mrs. Creighton	High St	40
Mrs. Garlach	Baltimore St	40	Mrs. C. E. Armor	Middle St.	25
Mrs. Gintling	High St	75	Mr. Erter	Emmetsburg Road.	30
Mrs. Warren	Baltimore St.	50	Mr. Patterson	Emmetsburg Road.	25
Mrs. Monfort	York St	30	Mr. Detrow	Emmetsburg Road.	25
Mrs. Rupps	Carlisle St.	40	Mrs. Cumford (1)	Emmetsburg Road.	25
Mrs. Freeman	Baltimore St	50	Mrs. Cumford (2)	Emmetsburg Road.	25

In addition to the above every house in the town will take boarders during the Re-Union, and all the hotels will prepare meals for many hundred more persons than they have sleeping accommodations for.

The following is a list of the principal hotels in the neighborhood of Gettysburg from which easy access can be obtained to and from the Battlefield at low rates during the Re-Union, from June 25 to July 7. The hotels, though first-class, are also put at low figures, and round trip tickets will be sold from Gettysburg, the train leaving there at 10:20 P. M., returning at 6:50 and 10:00 A. M.:

Name.	Location.	Room for	Name.	Location.	Room for
Central Hotel	Biglerville	25	Franklin	Carlisle	60
Central Hotel	Mount Holly Springs	65	Pennsylvania	Carlisle	50
Mount Holly Inn	Mount Holly Springs	150	Thudium	Carlisle	60
United States	Mount Holly Springs	42	Miller	Carlisle	120
Mansion	Carlisle	150	Valley	Carlisle	60
Florence	Carlisle	150	Garber	Carlisle	50
Washington	Carlisle	40			

For time table of trains see Article III. of this book.

SUBSCRIBE FOR
THE GETTYSBURG TRUTH
An Eight-Page Weekly Independent Journal.
PUBLISHED ON THE GREAT BATTLEFIELD.

Every Issue contains Interesting Matter relating to the Historic Field. Full Reports of Dedications, Excursions, etc., with ILLUSTRATIONS and Descriptions of Monuments, Distinguished People, etc. Our Pictorial Department is a Special Feature. Accurate Illustrations of every Monument erected on the field. All old soldiers ought to subscribe.

ONLY $1.50 PER ANNUM.

Address all communications to

TRUTH, Gettysburg, Adams Co., Pa.

OSBORN MANUFACTURING CO.,
SOLE MANUFACTURERS OF
The Celebrated Osborn Cages,
PLATED AND BRIGHT METAL.

No. 79 Bleecker Street,
Three Doors West of Broadway.
New York.

Edward P. Allis and Company,
Milwaukee, Wisconsin.

Reliance Works.

Machinists and Founders.

MANUFACTURERS OF

The Celebrated Reynolds' Improved Corliss Engines, High Duty Pumping Machinery, Blowing Engines for Bessemer Steel Plants, Rolling Mill Engines, Hoisting Plants and High Service Power Outfits of all kinds, Mining Machinery, Saw Mill Machinery, Flour Mill Machinery, and Mill and Engine Supplies.

☞ WRITE FOR OUR CATALOGUES.

XX.

THE BLUE AND THE GRAY

RE-UNION OF THE SURVIVORS OF THE PHILADELPHIA BRIGADE AND PICKETT'S DIVISION, JULY 1, 2 AND 3, 1887.

THE PRELIMINARIES.

The memorable and chivalric re-union of the Blue and Gray at Gettysburg, July 1, 2 and 3, 1887, at which three hundred survivors of Pickett's renowned division were the guests of the " Philadelphia Brigade," although a matter of interesting history, yet the causes which led to that three days' fraternizing of the bravest of Confederate forces with the Union troops, which met and repelled the most heroic charge recorded during the late war, have never been published. They are now given to the public for the first time.

The " Philadelphia Brigade," which was officially the Second Brigade, Second Division, Second Corps of the Army of the Potomac, was comprised of Colonel E. D. Baker's California Regiment, the 71st of the Pa. line; Baxter's Philadelphia Fire Zouaves, the 72d P. V.; " Paddy Owen's Regulars," the 69th P. V.; and the 106th Pa. Volunteer Regiment. Previous to 1887 the 72d and 106th erected monuments to mark their locations in the Gettysburg battle, and it was the intention of the 69th to dedicate its monument early in 1887, but owing to the fact that the 71st intended to unveil its monument on July 3d of that year, the 69th generously postponed its dedication until that date.

In the meantime, about February, 1887, the four regiments forming the Philadelphia Brigade came together and formed a Brigade Association with Colonel Charles H. Banes of the 72d as Commander, Lieutenant William S. Simpson of the 71st as Quartermaster, and Sergeant John W. Frazier of the

71st as Adjutant, but who resigned previous to the re-union, and Captain James M. Whitecar of the 69th was elected to fill the vacancy.

While the 69th and 71st P. V. Regiments were engaged in constructing their monuments, word reached them that the surviving members of Pickett's Division intended to erect a monument to mark the spot where General Armistead was killed, at the head of his Brigade, within the Union lines—about 150 feet inside the stone wall of Cemetery Ridge, and in consequence a good deal of correspondence passed between individual members of the two regiments named and of Pickett's Division, carried on mainly by Comrades William S. Stockton and John W. Frazier on the part of the 71st, and A. W. McDermott of the 69th P. V., and Sergeant William T. Loehr of Richmond, Va., on behalf of Pickett's Division, but nothing definite was concluded further than that the 71st and 69th P. V. would meet the men of Pickett's Division in a spirit of "Fraternity, Charity and Loyalty."

After the organization of the Philadelphia Brigade Association, Comrades Frazier and Stockton of the 71st, and McDermott and McKeever of the 69th, agreed that their Regimental Associations should extend an invitation to the Brigade Association to be present at the dedication of their monuments. The invitation was informally accepted, and immediately Comrades Frazier and Stockton planned to have the Brigade Association take the place of the two individual regiments in whatever action was to be had looking to a fraternal meeting with Pickett's Division, to which Comrades McDermott and McKeever gave reluctant but kindly assent, owing to the fact that they had already invited Colonel A. K. McClure of the Philadelphia *Times*, to become their orator of the day, and to ex-Governor Curtin to extend a welcome, on behalf of the State of Pennsylvania, to the men of Pickett's Division.

The 69th's position was embarrassing, but inasmuch as Colonel McClure had formally accepted, and no reply had been received from Governor Curtin, it was tacitly agreed by all parties in interest, upon the suggestion of Comrade Frazier, that in the event of Pickett's men being present, a soldier's welcome should be extended them by Colonel Charles H. Banes, on behalf of the Philadelphia Brigade, and that Colonel McClure should give them a hearty welcome on behalf of the people of Pennsylvania generally and of the city of Philadelphia particularly. That programme was carried out, and Comrades McDermott and McKeever did noble work in securing the great success achieved.

PICKETT'S MEN IN LINE.

About the middle of February, 1887, a meeting of the surviving members of Pickett's Division was held in Richmond, and it was determined to hold

a re-union of the whole Division at Gettysburg, July 3, 1887, and a Re-union Committee consisting of Judge William G. Clopton, Chairman; Major Charles Pickett, Captain A. R. Woodson, Major Joseph V. Bidgood and Sergeant Charles T. Loehr, Secretary, was appointed.

Correspondence with the Gettysburg Memorial Association resulted in the Committee receiving information that it was a rule not to allow Confederate monuments within the Federal lines; thereupon a committee consisting of Colonel J. L. Maury, Judge Clopton and Captain E. P. Reeve, visited Gettysburg, and, after a lengthy conference with the Gettysburg Memorial Association, were informed that monuments must be on original lines of battle and not in temporary positions, but that they were willing to allow a "marker" to be placed where General Armistead was shot—the extreme point of the charge.

Colonel Batchelder of the Gettysburg Commission, informed the Pickett's Committee that he had received bushels of letters from the North in regard to Pickett's Division, and intimated that many of the writers were bitterly opposed to their proposed visit to Gettysburg.

A meeting of the Executive Committee of Pickett's Division was held in Richmond, May 7, 1887, and when the Committee concluded its report, the Committee, on motion of Mr. Bidgood, unanimously adopted the following resolutions:

Resolved, That the Committee, having heard the report of the Sub-Committee sent to Gettysburg to confer with the Committee of the Gettysburg Memorial Association, and having learned that they will not be allowed to locate their proposed monument upon the spot to which the Division penetrated within the Federal lines in their charge, therefore,

Resolved, That it is inexpedient to erect their monument upon the Gettysburg Battlefield.

Resolved, That a copy of these resolutions be sent the Secretary of the Gettysburg Memorial Association.

The Committee unanimously resolved to hold no reunion at Gettysburg that summer.

THE PHILADELPHIA BRIGADE TAKE ACTION.

At a meeting of the Philadelphia Brigade Association held May 4, 1887, Comrade John W. Frazier moved that a committee of 9—two from each regiment, with Colonel Banes as Chairman—be appointed to make all the arrangements necessary to extend a fitting welcome to Pickett's Division at Gettysburg. The motion being adopted, Comrade Frazier was made Secretary, and having been informed of the action of the Executive Committee of Pickett's Division, held on May 7, called a meeting of his own Committee in Colonel A. K. McClure's editorial parlors—which had kindly been offered for the Philadelphia Brigade Committee's use—on the 10th of May, at which he was instructed to further communicate with the Pickett people, using every means in his power to secure their presence at Gettysburg. The following from the Philadelphia *Press* of May 12, headlines and all, tells its own story:

PICKETT'S DIVISION.

URGENT LETTER FROM PHILADELPHIA ADVOCATING THE RE-UNION AT GETTYSBURG.

At a meeting of the Committee of Reception of the Philadelphia Brigade to Pickett's Division on Tuesday, Secretary John W. Frazier was instructed to communicate with Pickett's Division Association and express the regret of the Brigade at the possibility of the re-union not taking place at Gettysburg on July 3, as was proposed. He was also instructed to extend an invitation to Pickett's men, inviting them to become the guests of the Philadelphia Brigade. Mr. Frazier's letter was read at the monthly meeting of the California Regiment last evening, and at the suggestion of Colonel R. Penn Smith, who commanded that regiment at Gettysburg, and on motion of Major John Lockhart, the letter was unanimously approved and Secretary Frazier advised to forward it to Richmond. The letter is as follows:

Sergeant Charles T. Loehr, Secretary Pickett's Division Association, Richmond, Va.

MY DEAR COMRADE: The very agreeable duty of communicating with your Association relative to the re-union at Gettysburg has been assigned to me.

At a meeting of the Philadelphia Brigade held May 4 a Committee of nine—two from each regiment—with Colonel Charles H. Banes, Commander of the Brigade Association, as Chairman, was appointed to make all the arrangements necessary to extend a fitting welcome to Pickett's Division Association at Gettysburg. At a meeting of that Committee held on May 10 I was directed to officially inform your Association of our deep regret at the possibility of the contemplated re-union between your Division and our Brigade Association not taking place in July next at Gettysburg.

We regret this all the more because we who witnessed it had intended on behalf of the State of Pennsylvania, and the city of Philadelphia particularly, to extend such a welcome as your unsurpassed bravery merited, and I was further instructed to earnestly request you not to forego your intention to hold your first re-union at Gettysburg July 3, but to meet there as the guests of the Philadelphia Brigade, to enjoy the hospitality that we will extend to you, and upon that occasion, with the fraternal feelings created by that re-union, the first of the kind held since the war, and with our sincere sympathy and aid, to complete the arrangements you have begun towards dedicating an imperishable monument to commemorate American heroism, of which none are prouder than they who withstood the shock of your charge—a charge not surpassed in its grandeur and unfaltering courage in the annals of war since time began.

Please lay this letter before your Association at its meeting on Saturday next, and urge your comrades—the brave men of Pickett's renowned Division—to meet us at Gettysburg July 3, and assure them for me and the Brigade I have the honor to represent that we will be more than pleased to greet as many as will meet with us, whether it be 100 or 1,000, or more, and that great good to all concerned will result from that re-union.

Please let me hear from you at the earliest moment, as your acceptance will necessitate some immediate and pleasant labor on our part. With renewed assurance of soldierly regard. believe me, yours very truly,

JOHN W. FRAZIER,
Secretary *pro tem.* Philadelphia Brigade.

Philadelphia, May 11.

Under date of May 14, Secretary Charles T. Loehr thus wrote to Secretary Frazier:

John W. Frazier, Esq., Secretary of the Philadelphia Brigade Association.

DEAR SIR: The cordial invitation extended to our Division by your Brigade Association was laid before our Committee. In reply I am requested to tender you our sincere and grateful thanks for the fraternal welcome and the very flattering terms therein contained, to express to your Association the assurance that while this Committee does not feel itself now authorized to accept the invitation so generously tendered, for the reason that their functions have ceased, when at their last meeting they decided not to hold their re-union at Gettysburg, they deeply feel and appreciate all your kind intentions and efforts for friendship sake.

We hope and trust that the day may come when all lines between us shall have forever faded, that the survivors of our old Division and those of your gallant Brigade will meet at Gettysburg to dedicate a Union monument (not for what was once called the Union side), a memorial to the gallant men of both sides, expressive of the true American motto, "A large Country and a large Heart," remembering only the devotion and courage of the men who dared to sacrifice their lives and limbs for their principle and their country.

Undaunted by reverses Comrade Frazier was more than ever determined that the re-union should take place, and under date of May 23, 1887, wrote the following letter to Sergeant Charles T. Loehr, who was personally doing almost superhuman service to bring the men of Pickett's Division Association to a reconsideration of the action of their Executive Committee :

MY DEAR COMRADE : In your letter of the 16th instant you state that a permanent Association of the survivors of Pickett's Division will be organized, and that a meeting for that purpose has been called for June 1 next. That being the case, I write to kindly ask you to present at that meeting my letter of May 11, officially inviting the brave men of Pickett's Division to become the guests of the Philadelphia Brigade at Gettysburg on the 2d, 3d and 4th of July next.

Writing as an individual member of the Brigade Association I do not hesitate to say that I am sure every member of our Association would gladly and earnestly co-operate with your Association in securing the location of a monument on the spot where the brave General Armistead fell, and I believe that your Association will yet determine to place one there to mark the spot not only where General Armistead laid down his life, but to indicate for all time to come on the historic grounds of Gettysburg the position reached by Pickett's Division in the face of a hail of musket balls, solid shot, and shell, more terrible, perhaps, than was hurled against any body of men on either side during the late war.

We have been so long anticipating, with so much pleasure, the renewal of an acquaintance begun and ended so unceremoniously twenty-four years ago that we know not how to take any disappointment of our hopes and plans, and if not all your Association, we still hope a goodly committee—not less than one hundred strong—will be appointed at your meeting on June 1 to represent your Association at Gettysburg as the honored guests of the Philadelphia Brigade.

If your Association could understand how very anxious we are to meet and welcome you, I am sure you would not fail in coming.

Please let me hear favorably from you. Very truly yours, JOHN W. FRAZIER.

The responses to the invitation of the Philadelphia Brigade Association, and to Comrade Frazier's unofficial letter of May 23, were as follows :

OFFICERS.	EXECUTIVE COMMITTEE.	
Gen. WM. R. TERRY, President.	Capt. WM. J CLOPTON.	Capt. JAS. E. PHILLIPS.
Maj. CHARLES PICKETT, V. Pres't.	Sergt. WM. HARPER DEAN.	Col. R.L. MAURY.
Maj. JOSEPH V. BIDGOOD, Treas.	Capt. E. P REEVE.	Capt. H. B. TALIAFERRO.
Sergt. CHARLES T. LOEHR Sec'y.		

PICKETT'S DIVISION ASSOCIATION,

RICHMOND, Va., May 26, 1887.

John W. Frazier, 3812 Spruce St., Philadelphia.

DEAR COMRADE : I took the liberty of giving your letter to the *Dispatch*, and, from the calls I have had to-day, I am almost sure that when your fraternal invitation is submitted at our general meeting on June 1, we shall succeed in getting at least a respectable delegation to join you in revisiting the spot where more history was made in three days than we can now possibly make in thirty years. Very truly yours, C. T. LOEHR.

PICKETT'S DIVISION ASSOCIATION,

RICHMOND, Va., June 2, 1887.

John W. Frazier, Esq., Secretary of the Philadelphia Brigade Association.

DEAR SIR AND COMRADE: Your fraternal invitation of 11th ultimo was submitted to our permanent Association last night. In reply thereto it was resolved that our members be at once notified that this Association recommends to all the members of Pickett's Division to accept your kind invitation to attend your Re-Union on the 2d, 3d and 4th of July next, at Gettysburg ; also to extend to your Association our heartfelt thanks for the considerate and friendly expressions conveyed by your invitation.

With fraternal greetings to all the Comrades of your Brigade, I am yours very truly,

C. T. LOEHR,

Sec'y Pickett's Division Association.

Immediately upon the receipt of the resolution of Pickett's Division to accept the invitation of the Philadelphia Brigade Association to become their guests, Secretary Frazier made a call upon a few of the leading citizens of Philadelphia for funds to enable them to hospitably entertain the brave Virginians, the result of which was a generous and patriotic response to the extent of about $1,500, and from Saturday evening, July 2, until Tuesday morning, July 5, the gallant boys of General E. D. Baker's Philadelphia Brigade left nothing undone to make the visit of Pickett's bronzed and grizzled veterans agreeable.

THE RE-UNION.

The news that the survivors of Pickett's Division of the Confederate Army would be the guests of the Veterans who had met them on the bloody field of Gettysburg in July, 1863, drew an immense number of visitors to that town, and every train brought its quota. They had read of the battle, had seen and heard of the G. A. R., but they had never seen the gallant, though mistaken, men who had opposed the Boys in Blue on the field. Hence they were anxious to see the Boys in Gray first and then applaud them afterwards. The sentiments raised by the Re-Union were of friendship and unity. Entire Posts of the Grand Army, detachments of regiments from various States, some accompanied by field music, helped to swell the numbers, so that when the Veterans of the two Armies were on parade the streets of the quaint and normally quiet town resembled the streets of New York during some great pageant.

The great pressure on the railroad delayed everything, and the trains were generally late. The weather was very sultry, and despite the hurrah business visible everywhere, there was much discomfort.

The last train from the North arrived in four sections, with the Philadelphia Brigade, and there was one train from the South. The latter brought a delegation from the Third and Seventh Virginia of Kemper's Brigade, forty men who came by steamer from Portsmouth to Baltimore, and from there acted as escort for Mrs. Pickett and her son. At the depot the men were quietly received, told to go to supper and then come down and join in the general reception.

This done, Captain Hicks, Chairman of the Committee of Arrangements, was invited into the presence of the widow of the Confederate General who had commanded the forces that were to-day the guests of their bygone enemies. When presented the Captain cordially invited her to become the guest of the Philadelphia Brigade. Signifying her assent, Mrs. Pickett was escorted through the ladies' room to avoid the crowd, and thence to an open barouche and to the Springs Hotel.

The last train arrived at nine o'clock and again the old time "yell" and the bold hurrah resounded in the streets of Gettysburg. "Pickett's Men" were there.

Shouting and yelling, amid a throng of people clasping hands and waving handkerchiefs, the united forces—Yankee and Southern—marched to a medley of airs through the streets to "The Diamond," or public square. The line halted. The Southoners marched up to the head of the Yankee line. An order was given—"Right and left face!" and the men in two lines faced each other, looking into each other's eyes. There was a blaze of fireworks. Someone shouted "Advance!" There was a general charge on the Southern line, and as the band started "Dixie" hands were clasped, greetings exchanged, and in not a few instances old acquaintances greeted each other.

This informal hearty welcome was totally unexpected and unlooked for, but it was heartfelt on both sides. The hand-shaking over, the column resumed its march to the Court House where the first camp fire of the Blue and the Gray upon the historic field of Gettysburg was held.

The scene in the court room was a remarkable one. In the front seats were the tall forms of the "Johnnies," and seated among them were a few ladies; the central seats were filled by a delegation of the white helmetted Philadelphians; behind them the citizens of Gettysburg and visiting Grand Army men, while on the platform and within the bar were the officers and orators of both Armies, public officials, and last, but not least, the band.

John W. Frazier, Secretary of the Philadelphia Brigade Association, called the meeting to order, and with a few words of cordial greeting presented, as presiding officer, W. S. Stockton.

Colonel Charles H. Banes, President of the Philadelphia Brigade Association, extended a soldier's welcome to the men who had been their foes in war, now warm and devoted friends in peace.

Captain Reeve of Richmond responded on behalf of Pickett's Veterans, returning hearty thanks for the welcome they had received.

The welcome to the ex-Confederates on behalf of the State of Pennsylvania was delivered by Colonel Alexander K. McClure of Philadelphia, who eulogized the memory of General Grant, and in concluding, said: " Free Government is stronger at home and mightier abroad to-day because of the wounds of the Civil War, and our children and our children's children will turn to its sacrifices, its sorrows, and its irrevocable judgments as the surest guarantee that ' Government of the People, by the People, and for the People' shall not perish from the earth."

Colonel William R. Aylett, who succeeded General Armistead as Commander of the Brigade after the latter's death, responded on behalf o. the State of Virginia. Colonel Aylett called attention to the picture of Chief Justice Marshall, a son of Virginia, which graced the wall, and in eloquent terms reminded those present that the picture was there when the battle was fought, and then, as now, the Sons of Pennsylvania honored the Sons of Virginia. He spoke of the glorious destiny of a re-united country, of the lives and deaths of Lincoln and Grant, and then paid a tribute to the noble self-sacrificing women of the North and South. "Why," said he "the bravest woman I ever saw was a Pennsylvania girl, who defied Pickett's whole Division while we marched through a little town called Greencastle. She had on a United States flag as an apron, which she defiantly waved up and down as our columns passed by her and dared us to take it from her. And there was not one man of us who dared do so. Struck by her courage and loyalty, Pickett, with hat off, gave her a military salute, my regiment presented arms, and we cheered her with a good, old-fashioned rebel yell, which some of you boys here have doubtless heard."

Letters of regret at their absence were then read from President Cleveland, Senator John Sherman and others. Chief Burgess Tipton then, in behalf of the citizens of Gettysburg, welcomed all the visitors, and Colonel Banes requested all to withdraw that Pickett's Men could be assigned to quarters and get that refreshment which a day's journey without intermission made absolutely necessary.

The Philadelphia Brigade—69th, 71st, 72d and 106th Pennsylvania Infantry—was organized by Senator E. D. Baker, who, authorized to rasie a regiment, kept on till he had a Brigade. The battle record of these commands as inscribed on their colors is Munson's Hill, Ball's Bluff, Yorktown, Fair Oaks, Garnett's Farm, Peach Orchard, Savage Station, Glendale, Malvern Hill, Harrison's Landing, Antietam, Fredericksburg, Chancellorsville, Gettysburg, Mine Run, The Wilderness, Spottsylvania, Cold Harbor and Petersburg.

Pickett's Division on the great day of his historic charge was composed of the Brigades of Kemper, Armistead, and Garnett, all Virginia troops; and representatives of each regiment were in the company which visited Gettysburg in 1887 to shake hands and say Godspeed to the sentiment of re-union which had called the old foes together on the platform for all the future—" One Country and One flag."

The limits of this pamphlet will not allow the pleasant task of recording all the incidents of one of the most striking events in the world's history—contestants in one of the most momentous of recorded battles, meeting on the scene of conflict, to compare notes, greet each other as friends, and pledge each other from thenceforth to stand shoulder to shoulder for weal or woe against all foes—whether internal or external. Some incidents are, however, too significant to leave unnoticed.

MAJOR-GENERAL GEORGE E. PICKETT.

Mrs. George E. Pickett, widow of the Commanding Officer of the Confederate Veterans, was the honored guest of both parties to the Re-Union, and in company with her son George took part in all the observances of the Re-Union. Mrs. Pickett bears the credit of having been the first woman who welded the Blue and the Gray together. She was married to General Pickett during the war and there are veterans here who remember when she was first brought to camp, a beautiful and girlish bride. In 1868 she had engraved on the case of her husband's watch the Confederate an' Federal flags.

At the dedication of the monuments, which took place on July 3, she was presented with a floral emblem, the trefoil badge of the Second Corps. Adjutant Alexander McDermott said, in presenting it: "Mrs. Pickett, we should have been happy to greet your gallant husband here to-day, but an Allwise Providence has prevented that; therefore, as his representative, the survivors of the 69th Regiment desire to present to you this token of our esteem and beg that you will accept it in the spirit in which it is given." He handed her at the same moment a ribbon badge of Blue and Gray. Mrs. Pickett, who was deeply affected even to tears, bowed in acknowledgement of this, and said in a broken voice: "My heart alone must answer." Then while still under the influence of the strong emotion kindled by the unexpected and singular tribute, she pinned the badge upon her breast and sank back in her seat as the gray-headed veterans sent up an old-fashioned cheer for the lady.

The public exercises of that Sunday afternoon consisted of the dedication of the monuments of the dead of the 69th and 71st Pennsylvania Volunteers, the stone marking the spot where the gallant Lieutenant Cushing died, and the monument for the losses in Cowan's New York Battery.

At the dedication of the latter, two remarkable incidents occurred. One was the placing of a sword by Captain Cowan into the hands of Pickett's Men "for the purpose of finding to whom it had belonged and restoring it to his family." Captain Cowan said that during the battle it had been wielded by a young Virginian officer who fell dead in front of his guns. The other was the passage of a resolution to erect a stone to General Armistead, Commander of the Brigade that actually pierced the Union lines.

On Monday morning Mrs. Pickett held a reception on the line on Seminary Ridge from which her husband started with his Division to make the celebrated charge of twenty-four years before. The scene was a most affecting one. The position occupied by each regiment was next located and the changes made in the direction of the charge pointed out for use of the historian; a ride over the entire field followed.

THE HAND-SHAKE AT THE WALL.

When the "Boys" reached the Bloody Angle all left the carraiges—the spot where they met in the actual tug of war was before them.

The erstwhile foes looked about them for a few moments—they are all goods friends now—the wall was before them: in a moment each had taken their own sides of "Auld Lang Syne," and they were shaking hands across it. No more fighting now. Silence, dead silence, fell upon them, and then one mighty cheer rose upon the air, repeated again. Changing individual positions up and down the line, the warm clasps were repeated and the cheering was resumed. The scene was a memorable one. The field of battle under a clear sky looked beautiful. It is said by those who frequently visit the ground, that it never looked more picturesque. While a great many visitors were at this time distributed over every portion of the field, the largest gathering assembled near the stone wall to witness the fraternal greetings, on the scene of death and suffering, of combatants in a civil war, that reached a magnitude unknown to the nations of an older world. The spectacle was caught on the camera and is engraved for our book so that the scene is imperishable.

The influences of that day drove all idea of sleep from the minds of the Veterans.

Mrs. Pickett came into town from the Springs Hotel in the evening and held a reception, the townspeople extending cordial greeting and sympathy, the band serenaded her, and after she had retired the Veterans of both Armies started a camp fire at the Washington Hotel which was maintained all night. Most of the speakers were Virginians, and one after the other they told of the feelings that possessed them. The general idea was tersely conveyed by Chaplain Ferguson at the close of his address: "I am the most conquered man you ever met—conquered here by love;" and then, with uplifted hand, he called the assemblage to prayer and invoked divine blessings on the actions of the great gathering on this scene of former strife. With this most appropriate ending the camp fire was closed, to allow the men to prepare for their departure.

Escorted to the train by the members of the 69th and 71st Veterans, good-bys were exchanged, and the parting words, in instances where the meeting had been the renewal of acquaintanceship, were touching. All seemed loath to part, and two or three were carried some distance away as the train moved out, so closely were hand-clasps maintained. Then, with a unanimous yell on the one hand and a hurrah on the other, the Veterans parted, hoping to meet again.

The cordial fraternization of the Blue and the Gray on the field during those three days, and the prospect during the three days of the coming July, seems to be a realization of Lincoln's prophetic utterance in his first inaugural, in his touching appeal to the South. "We are not enemies, but friends. We must not be enemies. Though passion may have strained, it must not break, our bonds of affection. The mystic chords of memory, stretching from every battlefield and patriot grave to every living heart and hearthstone all over this broad land, will yet swell the chorus of the Union when again touched, as surely they will be, by the better angels of our nature."

CIGARS. CIGARS.

THE PLACE TO BUY THEM IS
PERRY'S,
164 Nassau Street, Tribune Building,
NEW YORK.

Veterans, Tourists and Lovers of a Good Cigar can always find the article they need at that number.
Choicest Brands of Imported Cigars constantly on hand.

JAMES C. PERRY,

Late of Astor House, and Fourteen Years corner Park Place and Broadway.

STOCK AND NEWS TICKER.

H. POPPER,
MANUFACTURER OF

Fine Gold and Silver
Medals and Badges,

91 ESSEX ST.,
NEW YORK.

I would respectfully call attention to the fact that I have catered to the wants of the G.A.R. for the past twenty years, and pride myself as being one of the oldest and ablest manufacturers of G.A.R. and Military Presentation Badges, Rank and Corps Badges, and miniature vest or scarf pins. Am sole proprietor and originator of the celebrated Canteen Charm. Prisoner of War, Woman's Relief Corps, Sons of Veterans, and all other Badges and Medals connected with the G.A.R. Have also on hand and make to order Shooting, Sporting, Bowling, Boating, and in fact all varieties, for all known organizations, either Solid Gold, Silver or Plated.

XXI.

THE HAND-CLASP AT THE WALL.
SUBJECT OF ILLUSTRATION.

With heart to heart and hand to hand,
  Gettysburg! At Gettysburg!
An emblem of united land,
  Gettysburg! At Gettysburg!
The arms that waved the blade of steel
The earnest grasp of friendship feel;
While valor makes for peace appeal.
  Gettysburg! At Gettysburg!

No more the death-shots rattle fast,
  Gettysburg! At Gettysburg!
Nor cannon belch their fiery blast,
  Gettysburg! At Gettysburg!
But orchards show their summer bloom,
And flowers shed their sweet perfume
O'er many a fallen warrior's tomb,
  Gettysburg! At Gettysburg!

To joys like these let all awake,
  Gettysburg! At Gettysburg!
Our Union for the Union's sake,
  Gettysburg! At Gettysburg!
Though Peace again displays her charms,
We will not dread grim War's alarms,
But join against a world in arms,
  Gettysburg! At Gettysburg!

"Shake, Johnnie, shake!" "Shake, Yankee, shake!"
  Gettysburg! At Gettysburg!
The ties we bind no foe shall break,
  Gettysburg! At Gettysburg!
From every mountain top and lake,
From Northern wood and Southern brake,
"Shake, Yankee, shake!" "Shake, Johnnie, shake!"
  Gettysburg! At Gettysburg!

        FRANKLIN W. FISH,

LARGEST! BEST!

THE

MUTUAL ⋆ LIFE

INSURANCE CO.

OF NEW YORK.

RICHARD A. McCURDY, President.

Assets Over **$118,000,000.**

ISSUES EVERY DESIRABLE FORM OF POLICY.

IT HAS PAID MEMBERS SINCE ITS ORGANIZATION
Over $257,000,000.

Its NEW Distribution Policy is the Most Liberal ever offered by any Insurance Company.

The following figures show the growth of the Assets of The Mutual Life Insurance Company of New York

From 1845 to 1888,

RECKONING A PERIOD OF EVERY TEN YEARS FROM 1845:

1845	$97,490.34
1855	2,850,077.56
1865	12,235,407.86
1875	72,446,970.06
1885	103,876,178.51
Jan. 1, 1886	108,908,967.51
" 1, 1887	114,181,963.24
" 1, 1888	118,806,851.88

XXII.

PROPOSED MONUMENT TO GENERAL ARMISTEAD.

The efforts made by Pickett's Division Association to dedicate a monument to the memory of General Armistead, and to be located where he fell, mortally wounded, inside the Unions lines, were at the re-union of the Philadelphia Brigade and Pickett's Division strengthened by a united effort on the part of the Philadelphia Brigade and Cowan's New York Battery.

That action originated thus: Immediately after the ceremonies dedicating the monument of Cowan's First New York Battery had been concluded, Colonel Cowan, holding a most beautiful sword in his hand, stated that he had read in the newspapers that the Philadelphia Brigade intended to return to Pickett's Division the war flags captured from them by that Brigade at Gettysburg in 1863; and, while he considered that the crowning act of reconciliation, he regretted that his Battery had no flags to return to them.

On the afternoon of July 3, 1863, however, while his Battery was pouring grape and canister into the ranks of Pickett's Division, at ten paces, a handsome young Confederate officer fell, with his grasp almost on his (Cowan's) guns. There was nothing about his person to indicate who he was; but this beautiful and costly sword, inlaid with pearl, seemed to indicate that its owner was a young man of high social standing in Virginia; and he, Colonel Cowan, while having no captured flags to return, did desire to place this sword in the custody of Pickett's Division Association, with the request that they would make every effort to ascertain to whom it belonged, and from whose body it was taken; and restore it to the relatives or friends of the young man.

The scene was deeply impressive, and while Colonel Crocker, of Pickett's Division, to whom the sword was handed, was making a fitting reply to Colonel Cowan, Sergeant John W. Frazier, of Baker's California Regiment—the 71st of the Pennsylvania line—and the ranking regiment of the Philadelphia Brigade—hastily wrote a resolution, passed it to Colonel William R. Aylett and Colonel Andrew Cowan for their perusal, and upon their approval handed it to General W. W. Burns, of Governor's Island, New York Harbor, who commanded the Philadelphia Brigade upon the death of General Baker—with the request that he submit it for the consideration of those present. General Burns offered the resolution, immediately upon the conclusion of Colonel Crocker's speech, and Colonel Cowan put it to the meeting in this way:

"All who are in favor of that resolution please hold up their right hand."

Instantly 500 hands rose high in the air.

"All who are opposed to it will please hold their right hand."

Not a hand went up in opposition.

That resolution read as follows:

Resolved: By the members of the Philadelphia Brigade Association, Cowan's First New York Battery, Pickett's Division Association, and others here present, that the Gettysburg Memorial Association be asked to grant to the organizations named, the privilege of erecting a monument commemorative of American Heroism. The farthest point reached by Pickett's Division inside the Union lines, near the "Bloody Angle," is suggested as the spot for the erection of said monument.

The matter has been progressing steadily during the year, and on Wednesday, May 2, Colonel W. R. Aylett, who took command of General Armistead's Brigade, after the fall of the latter on the field on that fated July 3, 1863, lectured to a hearty, generous and enthusiastic audience at the Academy of Music in Philadelphia. The lecture on "Gettysburg" was delivered under the auspices of the Philadelphia Brigade, for the purpose of raising funds with which to erect the proposed monument.

A Philadelphia paper, speaking of the lecture and the audience, said that it was a fitting sequence to the re-union of the Philadelphia Brigade and Pickett's Division in the "Bloody Angle" of the battle of Gettysburg on the 3d of July, of 1887. All around the stage were grouped the veterans of the Philadelphia Brigade, officers and privates, who had initiated and carried to successful conclusion the re-union which Colonel Aylett graphically described as a scene never before witnessed in the history of the human race, and an event which "Heaven saw and God and the angels approved."

Mrs. General George E. Pickett and her son, Miss Aylett, Colonel Charles H. Barnes and wife, Mrs. Whitacre, wife of the Secretary of the Philadelphia Brigade, and Mrs. Wilkinson, wife of Mayor Wilkinson, of West Point, Va., occupied the Prince of Wales box. When Colonel Aylett expressed

the thanks of General Pickett's widow and the Virginians for the hospitality extended to them during their visit to Philadelphia the audience gave fresh proofs of enthusiasm.

The vast building resounded with applause as General W. F. ("Baldy") Smith took his seat on one side of the Virginian and General W. W. Burns, of the Philadelphia Brigade, was seated upon the other. When General S. Wylie Crawford, who fought from the first gun fired at Fort Sumter until the surrender at Appomattox, hobbled down upon crutches he was met with a storm of cheers.

Scattered throughout the auditorium were many citizens of prominence. Among them were President of Common Council William M. Smith, Thomas Cochran of the Union League, United States District Attorney John R. Read, John Y. Huber, Postmaster William F. Harrity, John H. Michener, John L. Grim, W. W. Goodman, Councilmen Andrew J. Maloney and J. Fred Loeble of the First Ward, Major Roberts of the Seventy-second Regiment, Representative John E. Faunce, W. W. Alcorn, Major John H. Weeks, John Huggard, George D. McCreary, Colonel Robert P. Dechert, Hibbert P. John, Colonel James O. Reilly, Ex-Councilman Joseph Hancock, Charles S. Keyser, James Butterworth, Colonel Joseph T. Tobias, and large delegations wearing the buttons of the Grand Army of the Republic and the Loyal Legion.

At the conclusion of the lecture, which was constantly interrupted by applause, Mrs. Pickett and the ladies held an impromptu reception in the green room, while Colonel Aylett dined with the Committee of the Brigade. John W. Frazier called the meeting to order, and Secretary Whitacre read letters of regret from Generals William T. Sherman and Joseph E. Johnston.

The prospect now is that the monument will be dedicated during 1889.

XXIII.

THE NATIONAL CEMETERY AT GETTYSBURG.

After the Battle of Gettysburg the herculean task of burying the dead was rapidly attended to, the hot weather and rapid decomposition rendering that duty imperative. Shallow ditches—and they were shallow—were dug, the bodies laid therein and a little dirt thrown over them. This imperfect burial, in fact scarce burial at all, horrified visitors to the battlefield and those who came seeking for the remains of their loved ones. The matter was laid before Governor Andrew Curtin, and that patriotic old war Governor set the "ball rolling." He appointed a number of citizens of Gettysburg to purchase ground and provide for the proper interment of the dead. Seventeen acres on the Baltimore Turnpike, adjoining the Cemetery of the Evergreens, were obtained, each of the States whose troops had served on the Union line in the battle paying a proportion of the expense. The title was vested in the State of Pennsylvania in trust for the nation, and the Battlefield Memorial Association was created, consisting of one member from each State, to whose care it was given.

William Saunders laid out the ground, the dead were taken from all parts of the battlefield, and conveyed to the enclosure. Many of the Union dead were removed to the North by their relatives, but still there remains in the National Cemetery and near where the centre of the Union line rested during the battle 3,575 bodies, of which 1,608 are "unknown."

Within the Cemetery the statue of Major-General Reynolds, the fated leader of the first day's fight, is erected—the Monument of the First Corps is to occupy the spot where he fell. There, also, is the National Monument, the allegorical figures of which are depicted on the illuminated covers of this pamphlet. The National Monument, which is not the artistic structure it might be, was designed by Mr. J. G. Batterson of Hartford, Ct., who thus explains his ideas.

> The whole rendering of the design is purely historical. * * * The superstructure is sixty feet high, having a massive pedestal, twenty-five feet square at the base, and is crowned with a colossal statue representing the Genius of Liberty. Standing upon a three-quarter globe she raises in her right hand the victor's wreath of laurel, while with the left she gathers up the folds of our national flag, under which the victory was won. Projecting from the angles of the pedestal are four buttresses, supporting an equal number of allegorical statues representing respectively War, History, Peace and Plenty. War is personified by a statue of the American soldier, who, resting from the conflict, relates to History the story of the battle which this monument is intended to commemorate. History in listening attitude records with stylus and tablet the achievments of the field and the names of the honored dead. Peace is symbolized by a statue of the American mechanic, characterized by appropriate accessories. Plenty is represented by a female figure, with a sheaf of wheat and fruits of the earth, typifying peace and abundance as the soldier's crowning triumph. The main die of the pedestal is octagonal in form, paneled upon each face. The cornice and plinth above are also octagonal and are heavily moulded. Upon this plinth rests an octagonal moulded base bearing upon its face, in high relief, the national arms. The upper die and cap are circular in form, the die being encircled by stars equal in number with the States whose sons contributed their lives as the price of the victory won at Gettysburg.

At the consecration of the Cemetery, November 19, 1864, President Abraham Lincoln delivered his matchless oration. The monument was completed in 1868, and after the addition of that address cast in bronze, to the design, it was dedicated July 1, 1869.

From the Cemetery superb views of the battlefield and the surrounding country may be obtained, and this, with the care taken of the grounds and the perfect repose of its situation, makes it a fitting resting place for the Nation's Dead.

XXIV.

NATIONAL CEMETERIES OF THE UNITED STATES.

The necessity for the Government to exclusively own the grounds in which deceased soldiers and sailors of the late war should be buried was demonstrated early in the struggle, and laws were passed empowering the purchase of lands for such purpose. Enactments to preserve the graves of soldiers from desecration and to secure the remains a permanent resting place, to be kept sacred forever, were also passed, and now every veteran of the late war can be interred, if his family choose, in Government reservations secure from removal, and under the daily care and supervision of United States officials, with the flag they defended floating over them every day from sunrise to sunset.

The following table of interments in the various National Cemeteries was furnished us by the Quartermaster-General of the United States Army, May 22, 1888:

INTERMENTS IN THE NATIONAL CEMETERIES TO APRIL 30, 1888.

	Known.	Un-known.	Total.		Known.	Un-known.	Total.
Annapolis, Md	2,288	204	2,492	Camp Nelson, Ky	2,455	1,189	3,644
Alexandria, La	520	789	1,309	Cave Hill, Ky	3,354	583	3,937
Alexandria, Va	3,401	123	3,524	Chalmette, La	6,863	5,734	12,597
Andersonville, Ga	12,779	943	13,722	Chattanooga, Tenn	8,057	4,963	13,000
Antietam, Md	2,854	1,829	4,683	City Point, Va	3,719	1,438	5,157
Arlington, Va	11,903	4,349	16,252	Cold Harbor, Va	672	1,286	1,958
Balls Bluff, Va	1	24	25	Corinth, Miss	1,782	3,937	5,719
Barrancas, Fla	843	711	1,554	Crown Hill, Ind	680	32	712
Baton Rouge, La	2,485	532	3,017	Culpeper, Va	456	912	1,368
Battle Ground, D. C	43	....	43	Custer Battlefield, M.T.	261	....	261
Beaufort, S. C	4,757	4,493	9,250	Cypress Hills, N. Y	4,418	366	4,784
Beverly, N. J	157	7	164	Danville, Ky	349	8	357
Brownsville, Tex	1,443	1,379	2,822	Danville, Va	1,175	153	1,328
Camp Butler, Ill	1,008	354	1,362	Fayetteville, Ark	438	776	1,214

INTERMENTS IN NATIONAL CEMETERIES—CONTINUED.

	Known.	Un-known.	Total.		Known.	Un-known.	Total.
Finn's Point, N. J	106	2,539	2,645	Mound City, Ill.......	2,473	2,762	5,235
Florence, S. C........	206	2,799	3,005	Nashville, Tenn.......	11,831	4,701	16,532
Fort Donelson, Tenn..	158	511	669	Natchez, Miss.........	308	2,780	3,088
Fort Gibson, I. T.....	233	2,212	2,445	New Albany, Ind.....	2,152	676	2,828
Fort Harrison, Va....	242	575	817	New Berne, N. C.....	2,185	1,091	3,276
Fort Leavenworth, Kan	1,161	1,060	2,221	Philadelphia, Pa......	1,967	223	2,190
Fort McPherson, Neb.	257	293	550	Pillsbury Land'g, Tenn	1,234	2,362	3,596
Fort Smith, Ark......	740	1,150	1,890	Poplar Grove, Va.....	2,198	4,001	6,199
Fort Scott, Kan	429	161	590	Port Hudson, La......	588	3,239	3,827
Fredericksburg, Va...	2,488	12,785	15,273	Quincy, Ill............	167	55	222
Gettysburg, Pa.......	1,974	1,611	3,585	Raleigh, N. C.........	626	571	1,197
Glendale, Va.........	235	961	1,196	Richmond, Va........	842	5,700	6,542
Grafter, W. Va.......	634	620	1,254	Rock Island, Ill.......	288	20	308
Hampton, Va.........	5,507	493	6,000	Salisbury, N. C.......	97	12,035	12,132
Jefferson Barracks, Mo.	8,715	2,906	11,621	San Antonio, Tex.....	702	225	927
Jefferson City, Mo....	475	334	809	San Francisco, Cal...	286	11	297
Keokuk, Ia...........	622	33	655	Seven Pines, Va......	150	1,218	1,368
Knoxville, Tenn... ..	2,109	1,046	3,155	Soldiers' Home, D. C..	5,388	288	5,676
*Laurie, Md..........	....	....	....	Springfield, Mo.......	873	734	1,607
Lebanon, Ky.........	592	277	869	Staunton, Va	234	523	757
Lexington, Ky	840	112	952	St. Augustine, Fla....	1,470	....	1,470
Little Rock, Ark.....	3,303	2,354	5,657	Stone River, Tenn....	3,811	2,334	6,145
†Logan's Cross Rds, Ky	346	366	712	Vicksburg, Miss......	3,899	12,716	16,615
London Park, Md.....	1,898	208	2,106	Wilmington, N. C....	713	1,577	2,290
Marcella, Ga.........	7,195	2,963	10,158	Winchester, Va.......	2,098	2,382	4,480
Memphis, Tenn.......	5,163	8,818	13,981	Woodl'n, Elmira, N.Y.	3,068	7	3,075
Mexico City	384	750	1,134	Yorktown, Va........	748	1,435	2,183
Mobile, Ala..........	764	113	877				
Total................					176,313	148,830	325,143

* Removed to London Park in 1884.
† Now Mill Springs, Ky.

These figures include a number of civilians and Confederates, known and unknown, buried during the existence of hostilities; and the cemetery at the City of Mexico contains the bodies of all Americans who died there entitled to the right of burial therein.

XXV.

ORGANIZATIONS MUSTERED INTO THE UNITED STATES SERVICE DURING THE REBELLION.

States and Territories.	CAVALRY.		ARTILLERY.			INFANTRY.		TOTALS.		
	Regiments.	Companies.	Regiments.	Companies.	Batteries.	Regiments.	Companies.	Regiments.	Companies.	Batteries.
Maine............	2	..	1	3	7	30	22	33	25	7
New Hampshire..	1	..	1	..	1	17	4	19	4	1
Vermont.........	1	..	1	1	3	17	..	19	1	3
Massachusetts....	5	4	4	8	19	68	47	77	59	19
Rhode Island.....	3	2	3	..	1	8	1	14	3	1
Connecticut......	1	..	2	..	3	21	..	30	..	3
New York........	27	10	15	..	35	252	15	294	25	35
New Jersey......	3	..	..	..	5	38	4	41	4	5
Pennsylvania.....	23	28	4	5	19	227	62	254	95	19
Delaware........	..	8	..	1	1	9	4	9	13	1
Maryland........	4	4	..	..	6	20	1	24	5	6
Dist. of Columbia.	1	1	..	..	..	2	33	3	34	..
West Virginia....	7	2	..	..	8	17	2	24	4	8
Virginia.........	..	..	..	..	..	..	1	..	1	..
North Carolina...	2	..	..	..	..	2	..	4	..	..
Georgia..........	..	..	..	..	..	..	2	..	2	..
Florida..........	2	..	..	..	..	..	..	2	..	..
Alabama.........	1	5	..	..	..	..	..	1	5	..
Mississippi......	..	2	..	..	..	..	..	..	2	..
Louisiana........	2	..	..	..	..	3	..	5	..	..
Texas............	1	9	..	..	..	..	..	1	9	..
Arkansas........	4	..	..	..	1	3	2	7	2	1
Tennessee.......	21	7	..	..	5	9	..	30	7	5
Kentucky........	16	10	..	..	7	45	1	61	11	7
Ohio.............	13	18	3	..	27	218	11	234	29	27
Michigan........	12	2	2	..	11	36	7	50	9	11
Indiana..........	13	1	1	..	26	123	16	137	17	26
Illinois..........	17	..	2	..	8	157	9	176	9	8
Missouri.........	30	26	..	..	6	64	20	94	46	6
Wisconsin........	4	..	1	..	12	53	..	58	..	12
Iowa.............	9	..	..	..	4	46	..	55	..	4
Minnesota.......	2	10	1	..	3	11	..	14	10	3
California.......	2	4	..	..	..	9	..	11	4	..
Kansas...........	9	..	..	..	3	10	5	19	5	3
Oregon...........	1	..	..	..	..	1	..	2	..	..
Nevada..........	..	6	..	..	..	..	3	..	9	..
Washington Ter..	..	..	..	..	..	1	..	1	..	..
New Mexico Ter..	2	5	..	..	..	6	11	8	16	..
Nebraska Ter.....	2	4	..	..	..	..	2	2	6	..
Colorado Ter.....	3	..	..	..	1	..	2	3	2	1
Dakota Ter......	..	2	..	..	..	..	..	..	2	..
U. S. V. V. Inf't'y.	..	..	..	..	..	10	..	10	..	..
U. S. Vol. Inf't'y..	..	..	..	..	..	6	1	6	1	..
U. S. Col. Troops.	6	..	11	4	10	102	18	119	22	10
U. S. A. Regulars.	6	..	5	..	..	19	..	30	..	..
Totals.........	258	170	57	22	232	1,666	306	1,981	498	232

XXVI.

TOTAL NUMBER OF TROOPS FURNISHED BY EACH STATE AND TERRITORY.

There were nine calls for volunteers issued during the rebellion; besides which, men were furnished by special authority during 1862 for three months, the militia were called out for six months during 1863, for one hundred days in 1864; and still other troops were furnished at various times without special calls from the General Government.

The following tables will show the total number of men furnished at each of these calls, by States and Territories, as well as the aggregate of men furnished during the war:

1.—CALL OF APRIL 15, 1861, FOR 75,000 MILITIA FOR THREE MONTHS.

	Quota.	Men Furnished.		Quota.	Men Furnished.
Maine	780	771	Ohio	10,153	12,357
New Hampshire	780	779	Indiana	4,683	4,686
Vermont	780	782	Illinois	4,683	4,820
Massachusetts	1,560	3,736	Michigan	780	781
Rhode Island	780	3,147	Wisconsin	780	817
Connecticut	780	2,402	Minnesota	780	930
New York	13,280	13,906	Iowa	780	968
New Jersey	3,123	3,123	Missouri	3,123	10,591
Pennsylvania	12,500	20,175	Kentucky	3,123	....
Delaware	780	775	Kansas	....	650
Maryland	3,123	....	Tennessee	1,560	....
West Virginia	2,340	900	Arkansas	780	....
District of Columbia	....	4,720	North Carolina	1,560	....

Totals—Quota, 73,391; Men furnished, 91,816.

II.—CALL OF MAY 3, 1861, FOR 500,000 MEN.

	Quota.	Men Furnished for				Total.
		Six Months.	One Year.	Two Years.	Three Years.	
Maine...................	17,560	....	....	....	18,104	18,104
New Hampshire..........	9,234	....	....	....	8,358	8,358
Vermont.................	8,950	....	....	....	9,508	9,508
Massachusetts...........	34,868	....	....	....	32,177	32,177
Rhode Island............	4,955	....	....	....	6,286	6,286
Connecticut.............	13,057	....	....	....	10,865	10,865
New York...............	109,056	....	....	30,950	89,281	120,231
New Jersey..............	19,152	....	....	....	11,523	11,523
Pennsylvania............	82,825	....	....	....	85,160	85,160
Delaware................	3,145	....	....	....	1,826	1,826
Maryland................	15,578	....	....	....	9,355	9,355
West Virginia...........	8,497	....	....	....	12,757	12,757
District of Columbia....	1,627	....	....	....	1,795	1,795
Ohio....................	67,365	....	863	....	83,253	84,116
Indiana.................	38,832	....	1,608	....	59,643	61,341
Illinois................	47,785	....	....	....	81,952	81,952
Michigan................	21,357	....	....	....	23,546	23,546
Wisconsin...............	21,758	....	....	....	25,499	25,499
Minnesota...............	4,809	....	1,167	....	5,770	6,937
Iowa....................	19,316	....	....	....	21,987	21,987
Missouri................	31,544	2,715	199	....	22,324	25,238
Kentucky................	27,237	....	5,129	....	29,966	35,095
Kansas..................	3,235	....	....	....	6,953	6,953
Nebraska Territory......	....	....	91	....	....	91
Totals.................	611,827	2,715	9,147	30,950	657,868	700,680

III.—MEN FURNISHED IN MAY AND JUNE, 1862, FOR THREE MONTHS, WITHOUT A CALL, AND UNDER SPECIAL AUTHORITY.

New York................	8,588	Illinois................	4,696
Indiana.................	1,723		
Total..			15,007

IV.—CALL OF JULY 2, 1862, FOR 300,000 MEN FOR THREE YEARS.

	Quota.	Men Furnished.		Quota.	Men Furnished.
Maine...................	9,630	6,644	District of Columbia...	890	1,167
New Hampshire..........	5,053	6,390	Ohio....................	36,858	58,325
Vermont.................	4,898	4,369	Indiana.................	21,250	30,359
Massachusetts...........	19,080	16,519	Illinois................	26,148	58,689
Rhode Island............	2,712	2,742	Michigan................	11,686	17,656
Connecticut.............	7,145	9,195	Wisconsin...............	11,904	14,472
New York...............	59,705	78,904	Minnesota...............	2,681	4,626
New Jersey..............	10,478	5,499	Iowa....................	10,570	24,438
Pennsylvania............	45,321	30,891	Missouri................	17,269	28,324
Delaware................	1,720	2,508	Kentucky................	14,905	6,463
Maryland................	8,532	3,586	Kansas..................	1,771	2,936
West Virginia...........	4,650	4,925	Nebraska Territory.....	....	1,838

Totals—Quota, 334,885; Men furnished, 421,465.

V.—CALL OF AUGUST 4, 1862, FOR 300,000 MILITIA FOR NINE MONTHS.

	Quota.	Men Furnished.		Quota.	Men Furnished.
Maine	9,609	7,620	District of Columbia	890	....
New Hampshire	5,053	1,736	Ohio	36,858	....
Vermont	4,898	4,781	Indiana	21,250	337
Massachusetts	19,080	16,685	Illinois	26,148	....
Rhode Island	2,712	2,059	Michigan	11,686	....
Connecticut	7,145	5,602	Wisconsin	11,904	958
New York	59,705	1,781	Minnesota	2,681	....
New Jersey	10,478	10,787	Iowa	10,570	....
Pennsylvania	45,321	32,215	Missouri	17,269	....
Delaware	1,720	1,799	Kentucky	14,905	....
Maryland	8,532	....	Kansas	1,771	....
West Virginia	4,650	....	Nebraska Territory	....	1,228

Totals—Quota, 334,835 ; Men furnished, 87,588.

VI.—MEN FURNISHED UNDER PROCLAMATION OF JUNE 15, 1863, FOR MILITIA FOR SIX MONTHS.

Massachusetts	103	Ohio		2,736
Pennsylvania	3,708	Indiana		3,767
Maryland	1,615	*Missouri		3,284
West Virginia	1,148			
Total				16,361

* Furnished in November, 1864.

VII.—CALLS OF OCTOBER 17, 1863, (INCLUDING MEN RAISED BY DRAFT) AND FEBRUARY 1, 1864, FOR 500,000 MEN FOR THREE YEARS.

	Quota.	Men Furnished.	Paid Commutation.	Total.
Maine	11,803	11,958	1,986	13,944
New Hampshire	6,469	6,406	571	6,977
Vermont	5,751	6,726	1,885	8,611
Massachusetts	26,597	17,711	3,703	21,414
Rhode Island	3,469	3,223	463	3,686
Connecticut	7,919	10,326	1,513	11,839
New York	81,993	59,839	15,912	75,751
New Jersey	16,759	9,187	....	9,187
Pennsylvania	64,979	36,723	17,672	54,395
Delaware	2,463	2,138	425	2,573
Maryland	10,794	6,244	1,106	7,350
West Virginia	5,127	3,988	....	3,988
District of Columbia	4,256	4,570	318	4,888
Ohio	51,465	32,809	....	32,809
Indiana	32,521	23,023	....	23,023
Illinois	46,309	28,818	....	28,818
Michigan	19,553	17,686	1,644	19,330
Wisconsin	19,852	10,389	5,080	15,469
Minnesota	5,451	3,054	....	3,054
Iowa	16,097	8,292	....	8,292
Missouri	9,813	3,823	....	3,823
Kentucky	14,471	4,785	....	4,785
Kansas	3,523	5,374	....	5,374
Totals	467,434	317,092	52,288	369,380

VIII.—CALL OF MARCH 14, 1864, FOR 200,000 MEN FOR THREE YEARS.

	Quota.	Men Furnished.	Paid Commutation.	Total.
Maine	4,721	7,042	....	7,042
New Hampshire	2,588	2,844	121	2,965
Vermont	2,300	1,601	89	1,690
Massachusetts	10,639	17,322	1,615	18,937
Rhode Island	1,388	1,906	....	1,906
Connecticut	3,168	5,294	....	5,294
New York	32,794	41,940	2,267	44,207
New Jersey	6,704	9,550	4,170	13,720
Pennsylvania	25,993	35,036	10,046	45,082
Delaware	985	652	951	1,603
Maryland	4,317	9,365	2,538	11,903
West Virginia	2,051	3,857	....	3,857
District of Columbia	1,702	1,142	....	1,142
Ohio	20,595	31,193	6,290	37,483
Indiana	13,008	14,862	....	14,862
Illinois	18,524	25,055	....	25,055
Michigan	7,821	7,341	325	7,666
Wisconsin	7,941	10,314	....	10,314
Minnesota	2,180	2,469	1,027	3,496
Iowa	6,439	11,579	....	11,579
Missouri	3,925	*10,137	....	10,137
Kentucky	5,789	6,448	3,241	9,689
Kansas	1,409	2,563	....	2,563
Totals	186,981	259,515	32,678	292,193

*Includes militia furnished for six months, 5,679; for nine months, 2,311; for one year, 1,954—credited as 2,174 three years' men.

IX.—MILITIA MUSTERED INTO SERVICE FOR ONE HUNDRED DAYS BETWEEN APRIL 23 AND JULY 18, 1864.

	Quota.	Men Furnished.		Quota.	Men Furnished.
New Hampshire	*....	167	Ohio	30,000	36,254
Massachusetts	4,000	6,809	Indiana	20,000	7,197
New York	12,000	5,640	Illinois	20,000	11,328
New Jersey	....	769	Wisconsin	5,000	2,134
Pennsylvania	12,000	7,675	Iowa	10,000	3,901
Maryland	....	1,297	Kansas	....	441

Totals—Quota, 113,000; men furnished, 83,612.
*Furnished for three months.

X.—CALL OF JULY 18, 1864, FOR 500,000 MEN (QUOTAS REDUCED BY EXCESS ON PREVIOUS CALLS.)

	Quota.	Men Furnished for				Paid Commutation.	Total.
		One Year	Two Years.	Three Years.	Four Years.		
Maine	11,116	8,320	131	2,590	1	11	11,053
New Hampshire	4,648	1,921	25	4,027	...	...	5,973
Vermont	2,665	1,861	18	2,081	11	...	3,971
Massachusetts	21,065	6,990	108	24,641	...	...	31,739
Rhode Island	1,423	1,223	196	891	...	...	2,310
Connecticut	5,583	493	20	10,318	24	2	10,857

X.—CONTINUED.

	Quota.	Men Furnished for				Paid Commutation.	Total.
		One Year.	Two Years.	Three Years.	Four Years.		
New York	77,539	45,089	2,128	36,547	74	5	83,843
New Jersey	14,431	9,587	1,184	4,337	...	11	15,119
Pennsylvania	49,986	44,489	433	10,416	198	171	55,707
Delaware	2,184	1,558	9	593	15	...	2,175
Maryland	10,947	6,198	246	3,727	64	31	10,266
West Virginia	2,717	1,726	28	202	...	...	1,956
District of Columbia	2,386	979	59	937	343	19	2,337
Ohio	27,001	25,431	748	4,644	...	176	30,999
Indiana	25,662	18,099	597	7,158	...	690	26,544
Illinois	21,997	12,558	535	2,323	...	49	15,465
Michigan	12,098	5,960	57	6,492	...	23	12,532
Wisconsin	17,590	10,995	86	5,832	...	16	16,839
Minnesota	4,018	2,791	205	239	...	3	3,238
Iowa	5,749	3,995	60	168	...	67	4,290
Missouri	25,569	7,782	1,295	14,430	...	...	23,507
Kentucky	9,871	5,060	169	10,137	...	24	15,390
Kansas	....	29	3	319	...	...	351
Totals	357,152	223,044	8,340	153,049	730	1,298	386,461

XI.—CALL OF DECEMBER 19, 1864, FOR 300,000 MEN

	Quota.	Men Furnished for				Paid Commutation.	Total.
		One Year.	Two Years.	Three Years.	Four Years.		
Maine	8,587	4,898	141	1,884	3	10	6,936
New Hampshire	2,072	492	9	775	28	...	1,304
Vermont	1,832	962	29	550	9	...	1,550
Massachusetts	1,306	1,535	43	2,349	2	...	3,929
Rhode Island	1,459	739	92	732	...	...	1,563
Connecticut	....	34	7	1,282	2	...	1,325
New York	61,076	9,150	1,645	23,321	67	13	34,196
New Jersey	11,695	6,511	1,075	3,527	155	15	11,283
Pennsylvania	46,437	26,666	204	3,903	44	282	31,099
Delaware	338	376	5	30	...	...	411
Maryland	9,142	3,236	430	1,275	...	3	4,944
West Virginia	4,431	2,114	8	415	...	...	2,537
District of Columbia	2,222	692	12	116	2	1	823
Ohio	26,027	21,712	641	2,214	..	13	24,580
Indiana	22,582	20,642	243	2,329	...	94	23,308
Illinois	32,902	25,940	356	2,022	..	6	28,324
Michigan	10,026	6,767	41	1,034	...	18	7,860
Wisconsin	12,356	9,066	15	240	..	1	9,322
Minnesota	3,636	2,689	12	68	...	2	2,771
Iowa	....	772	15	67	...	...	854
Missouri	13,984	3,161	44	1,002	...	...	4,207
Kentucky	10,481	1,987	7	5,609	...	...	7,603
Kansas	1,222	622	36	223	...	2	883
Totals	284,215	151,363	5,110	54,967	312	460	212,212

XII.—VOLUNTEERS AND MILITIA FURNISHED AT VARIOUS TIMES.

	Sixty Days.	Three Months.	One Hundred Days.	Four Months.	Six Months.	Eight Months.	One Year.	Three Years.	Total.
Tennessee	..	....	739	..	....	....	6,039	24,314	31,092
Arkansas	..	....	....	..	374	....	213	7,702	8,289
North Carolina	..	....	....	..	....	....	....	3,156	3,156
California	..	....	....	..	....	....	....	15,724	15,725
Nevada	..	....	....	..	....	....	....	1,080	1,080
Oregon	..	....	....	42	....	....	....	1,768	1,810
Washington Territory	..	....	....	..	....	....	....	964	964
Colorado Territory	..	....	1,156	..	186	....	....	3,561	4,903
Dakota Territory	..	....	....	..	....	....	....	206	206
New Mexico Territory	..	1,593	....	..	803	....	...	4,165	6,561
Alabama	..	....	....	..	....	....	1,447	1,129	2,576
Florida	..	....	....	..	....	....	....	1,290	1,290
Louisiana	296	....	....	..	....	373	....	4,555	5,224
Mississippi	..	....	....	..	....	....	....	545	545
Texas	..	....	....	..	....	....	499	1,466	1,965
Indian Nations	..	....	....	..	....	....	....	3,530	3,530
Totals	296	1,593	1,895	42	1,363	373	8,198	75,156	88,916

XIII.—AGGREGATES.

	Quota.	Men Furnished.	Paid Commutation.	Total.
Maine	73,587	70,107	2,007	72,141
New Hampshire	35,897	33,937	692	34,629
Vermont	*32,074	33,288	1,974	35,262
Massachusetts	*139,095	146,730	5,318	152,048
Rhode Island	*18,898	23,236	463	23,699
Connecticut	*44,797	55,864	1,515	57,379
New York	507,148	448,850	18,197	467,047
New Jersey	92,820	76,814	4,196	81,010
Pennsylvania	385,869	337,936	28,171	366,107
Delaware	13,935	12,284	1,386	13,670
Maryland	70,965	46,638	3,678	50,316
West Virginia	34,463	32,068	....	32,068
District of Columbia	*13,973	16,534	338	16,872
Ohio	*306,322	313,180	6,479	319,659
Indiana	199,788	196,363	784	197,147
Illinois	*244,496	259,092	55	259,147
Michigan	95,007	87,364	2,008	89,372
Wisconsin	109,080	91,327	5,097	96,424
Minnesota	26,326	24,020	1,032	25,052
Iowa	79,521	76,242	67	76,309
Missouri	122,496	109,111	....	109,111
Kentucky	100,782	75,760	3,265	79,025
Kansas	*12,931	20,149	2	20,151
Tennessee	*1,560	31,092	....	31,092
Arkansas	780	8,289	....	8,289
North Carolina	*1,560	3,156	....	3,156
California	....	15,725	....	15,725
Nevada	....	1,080	....	1,080
Oregon	....	1,810	....	1,810
Washington Territory	....	964	....	964

XIII.—CONTINUED.

	Quota.	Men Furnished.	Paid Commutation.	Total.
Nebraska Territory	....	3,157	....	3,157
Colorado Territory	....	4,903	....	4,903
Dakota Territory	....	206	....	206
New Mexico Territory	....	6,561	....	6,561
Alabama	....	2,576	....	2,576
Florida	....	1,290	....	1,290
Louisiana	....	5,224	....	5,224
Mississippi	....	545	....	545
Texas	....	1,965	....	1,965
Indian Nations	....	3,530	....	3,530
Totals	2,763,670	2,678,967	86,724	2,765,691

*Furnished more than their quota.

TOTAL NUMBER OF TROOPS FURNISHED, REDUCED TO A THREE YEARS' STANDARD.

	Aggregate Men Furnished.	Aggregate Reduced to a Three Years' Standard.		Aggregate Men Furnished.	Aggregate Reduced to a Three Years' Standard.
Maine	72,114	56,776	Missouri	109,111	86,530
New Hampshire	34,629	30,849	Kentucky	79,025	70,832
Vermont	35,262	29,068	Kansas	20,151	18,706
Massachusetts	152,048	124,104	Tennessee	31,092	26,394
Rhode Island	23,699	17,866	Arkansas	8,289	7,836
Connecticut	57,379	50,623	North Carolina	3,156	3,156
New York	467,047	392,270	California	15,725	15,725
New Jersey	81,010	57,908	Nevada	1,080	1,080
Pennsylvania	366,107	265,517	Oregon	1,810	1,773
Delaware	13,670	10,322	Washington Territory	964	964
Maryland	50,316	41,275	Nebraska Territory	3,157	2,175
West Virginia	32,068	27,714	Colorado Territory	4,903	3,697
District of Columbia	16,872	11,506	Dakota Territory	206	206
Ohio	316,650	240,514	New Mexico Territory	6,561	4,432
Indiana	197,147	153,576	Alabama	2,576	1,611
Illinois	259,147	214,133	Florida	1,290	1,290
Michigan	89,372	80,111	Louisiana	5,224	4,654
Wisconsin	96,424	79,260	Mississippi	545	545
Minnesota	25,052	19,693	Texas	1,965	1,632
Iowa	76,309	68,630	Indian Nations	3,530	3,530

Totals—2,765,691 Men furnished; 2,228,483, reduced to Three Years' basis. Calls reduced to Three Years' basis, 2,391,532.

XXVII.

AVERAGE OF LOSSES IN THE UNION ARMY, BY BRIGADES, AT GETTYSBURG.

Army Corps.	Officers Killed.	Men Killed.	Officers Wound.	Men Wound.	Officers Missing.	Men Missing.	Total Loss.
1st Corps—7 Brigades.	42	551	257	2,952	82	2,140	6,024
Artillery Losses......	....	8	6	80	....	11	105
Less Artillery Losses.	42	543	251	2,872	82	2,129	5,919
Average to Brigade.	6	77 4-7	35 6-7	410 2-7	11 5-7	304 1-7	845 4-7
2d Corps—10 Brigades.	67	729	269	2,917	13	355	4,350
Artillery Losses......	3	24	5	114	....	3	149
Less Artillery Losses.	64	705	264	2,803	13	352	4,201
Average to Brigade.	6 2-5	70 1-2	26 2-5	280 3-10	1 3-10	35 1-5	420 1-10
3d Corps—6 Brigades..	50	528	251	2,775	14	592	4,210
Artillery Losses......	....	8	3	78	....	17	106
Less Artillery Losses.	50	520	248	2,697	14	575	4,104
Average to Brigade.	8 1-3	86 2-3	41 1-3	449 1-2	2 1-3	95 5-6	684
5th Corps—8 Brigades.	28	337	129	1,482	1	210	2,187
Artillery Losses......	1	7	1	32	....	2	43
Less Artillery Losses.	27	330	128	1,450	1	208	2,144
Average to Brigade.	3 3-8	41 1-4	16	181 1-4	0 1-8	26	268
6th Corps—8 Brigades.	2	25	14	171	....	30	242
Artillery Losses......	....	4	2	6	....	....	12
Less Artillery Losses.	2	21	12	165	....	30	230
Average to Brigade.	0 1-4	2 5-8	1 1-2	20 5-8	....	3 3-4	28 3-4
11th Corps—6 Brigades	33	335	120	1,802	62	1,449	3,801
Artillery Losses......	1	6	3	50	....	9	69
Less Artillery Losses.	32	329	117	1,752	62	1,440	3,732
Average to Brigade.	5 1-3	54 5-6	19 1-2	292	10 1-3	240	622
12th Corps—6 Brigades	18	186	43	767	2	65	1,081
Artillery Losses......	....	....	....	9	....	....	9
Less Artillery Losses.	18	186	43	758	2	65	1,072
Average to Brigade.	3	31	7 1-6	126 1-3	0 1-3	10 5-6	278 1-3

XXVIII.

TOTAL CASUALTIES DURING THE WAR.

Causes.	Regulars.		White Volunteers.		Colored Troops.		Aggregate.		Total.
	Officers.	Enlisted Men.	Officers.	Enlisted Men.	Officers.	Enlisted Men.	Officers.	Enlisted Men.	
Killed in battle	157	1,800	3,345	54,056	124	1,380	3,626	57,236	61,862
Died of wounds	....	1,505	1,505	32,405	46	1,067	1,641	33,132	34,773
Died of disease	83	2,739	2,141	153,013	90	26,211	2,314	180,963	183,287
Accidentally killed	....	....	12	354			12	354	366
Executed by sentence	....	1	....	6				6	7
Missing in action	33	1,356	72	4,085	18	1,265	123	6,626	6,749
Honorably discharged	2	1,301	10,805	150,764	427	2,377	11,234	163,345	174,577
Discharged for disability	2	5,089	3,028	209,102	165	6,889	3,225	221,080	224,306
Dishonorably discharged	....	275	183	2,423	18	191	204	2,889	3,026
Dismissed	122	....	2,143		158		2,423		2,423
Cashiered	6		252		16		274		274
Resigned	330	....	21,000		801		22,131		22,131
Deserted	5	16,366	187	170,029	24	12,440	216	198,829	199,045
Total	800	29,831	44,886	783,467	1,888	52,211	47,574	864,509	912,083

NOTE.—This does not include men mustered out at expiration of term of service.

The total number of deaths reported by the Adjutant-General of the United States Army as having occurred in the Union Army from April 15, 1861, to August 1, 1865, including, however, those which occurred in the Volunteer troops who remained in the service after the cessation of hostilities, as guards, etc., up to December 20, 1867, when the last regiment was mustered out, is given below. The official declaration is made, however, that even this list is incomplete:

	Officers.	Men.		Officers.	Men.
Killed in action	4,142	62,916	Committed suicide	26	365
Died of wounds received in action	2,223	40,789	Executed by United States military authorities	....	267
Died of disease	2,795	221,791	Executed by enemy	4	60
Accidental deaths (except drowned)	142	3,972	Died from sunstroke	5	308
Drowned	106	4,838	Other known causes	62	1,972
Murdered	37	483	Causes not stated	28	12,093
Killed after capture	14	90			
Total				9,584	349,944

Aggregate—359,528.

While these figures seem to contradict the table on the preceding page, it will make but little difference in the grand total of casualties.

CHRONOLOGICAL LIST OF BATTLES AND SKIRMISHES IN THE UNITED STATES, 1861 to 1865.

1861.

APRIL 12.—Bombardment of Fort Sumter, S. C.   Battery E. 1st U. S. Artillery.   No casualties.
    15.—Evacuation of Fort Sumter, S. C.   Union 1 killed, 3 wounded.   By premature explosion of cannon in firing a salute to the United States flag.
    18.—Harper's Ferry, Va.   Ordnance men U. S. Army.
    19.—Riots in Baltimore, Md.   6th Mass., 26th Penna.   Union 4 killed, 30 wounded. Confed. 9 killed.
MAY 10.—Camp Jackson, Mo.   1st, 3d and 4th Mo.   Reserve Corps, 3d Mo.   Confed. 639 prisoners.
    —Riots in St. Louis, Mo.   5th Mo., U. S. Reserves.   Union 4 killed.   Confed. 27 killed.
JUNE 1.—Fairfax C. H., Va.   Co. B. 2d U. S. Cav.   Union 1 killed, 4 wounded.   Confed. 1 killed, 14 wounded.
    3.—Phillippi, W. Va.   1st W. Va., 14th and 16th Ohio, 7th and 9th Ind.   Union 2 wounded.   Confed. 16 wounded.
    10.—Great Bethel, Va.   1st, 2d, 3d, 5th and 7th N. Y., 4th Mass. Detachment of 2d U. S. Artil.   Union 16 killed, 34 wounded.   Confed. 1 killed, 7 wounded.
    11.—Romney, W. Va.   11th Ind.   Union 1 wounded.   Confed. 2 killed, 1 wounded.
    17.—Vienna, Va.   1st Ohio.   Union 5 killed, 6 wounded.   Confed. 6 killed.
    —Booneville, Mo.   2d Mo. (three months'), Batteries H. and L. Mo. Light Artil.   Union 2 killed, 19 wounded.   Confed. 15 killed, 20 wounded.
    —Edwards' Ferry, Md.   1st Penn.   Union 1 killed, 4 wounded.   Confed. 15 killed.
    —Independence, Mo.   Detachment Missouri Volunteers.
    —New Creek, W. Va.   Local Militia.
    18.—Camp Cole, Mo.   Home Guards.   Union some say 15, and some 25 killed, 25 to 52 wounded.   Confed. 4 killed, 20 wounded.
    26.—Patterson Creek or Kelley's Island, Va.   11th Ind.   Union 1 killed, 1 wounded.   Confed. 7 killed, 2 wounded.
    27.—Matthias' Point, Va.   Gunboats Pawnee and Freeborn.   Union 1 killed, 4 wounded.
JULY 2.—Falling Waters, Md., also called Haynesville or Martinsburg, Md. 1st Wis., 11th Penn.   Union 8 killed, 15 wounded.   Confed. 31 killed, 50 wounded.
    5.—Carthage or Dry Forks, Mo.   3d and 5th Mo., one battery of Mo. Artil.   Union 13 killed, 31 wounded.   Confed. 30 killed, 125 wounded, 45 prisoners.
    —Newport News, Va.   One Co. 9th N. Y.   Union 6 wounded.   Confed. 3 wounded.
    6.—Middle Creek Fork or Buckhannon, W. Va.   One Co. 3d Ohio.   Union 1 killed, 6 wounded.   Confed. 7 killed.
    7.—Great Falls, Va.   8th N. Y.   Union 2 killed.   Confed. 12 killed.
    8.—Laurel Hill or Bealington, W. Va.   14th Ohio, 9th Ind.   Union 2 killed, 6 wounded.

JULY 10.—Monroe Station, Mo. 16th Ill., 3d Ia., Hannibal, (Mo.) Home Guards. Union 3 killed. Confed. 4 killed, 29 wounded, 75 prisoners.
11.—Rich Mountain, Va. 8th, 10th and 13th Ind., 19th Ohio. Union 11 killed, 35 wounded. Confed. 60 killed, 140 wounded, 100 prisoners.
12.—Barboursville or Red House, Va. 2d Ky. Union 1 killed. Confed. 10 killed.
—Beverly, W. Va. 4th and 9th Ohio. Confed. 600 prisoners.
14.—Carrick's Ford, W. Va. 14th Ohio, 7th and 9th Ind. Union 13 killed, 40 wounded. Confed. 20 killed, 10 wounded, 50 prisoners.
16.—Millsville or Wentzville, Mo. 8th Mo. Union 7 killed, 1 wounded. Confed. 7 killed.
17.—Fulton, Mo. 3d Mo. Reserves. Union 1 killed, 15 wounded.
—Scarytown, W. Va. 2d Ky., 12th and 21 Ohio, 1st Ohio Battery. Union 9 killed, 38 wounded.
—Martinsburg, Mo. One Co. of 1st Mo. Reserves. Union 1 killed, 1 wounded.
—Bunker Hill, Va. Detachment of General Patterson's command. Confed. 4 killed.
18.—Blackburn's Ford, Va. 1st Mass., 2d and 3d Mich., 12th N. Y., Detachment of 2d. U. S. Cav., Batterry E 3d U. S. Artil. Union 19 killed, 38 wounded. Confed. 15 killed, 53 wounded.
18 and 19.—Harrisonville and Parkersville, Mo. Van Horne's (Mo.) Battalion, Cass Co. Home Guards. Union 1 killed. Confed. 14 killed.
21.—Bull Run or Manassas, Va. 2d Me., 2d N. H., 2d Vt., 1st, 4th and 5th, Mass., 1st and 2d R. I., 1st, 2d and 3d Ct., 8th, 11th, 12th, 13th, 16th, 18th, 27th, 29th, 31st. 32d, 35th, 38th, 39th N. Y., 2d, 8th, 14th, 69th, 71st and 79th N. Y. Militia, 27th Penn., 1st 2d and 3d Mich., 1st and 2d Minn., 1st and 2d Ohio., Detachments of 2d, 3d and 8th U. S. Regulars, Battalion of Marines, Batteries D, E, G and M, 2d U. S. Artil., Battery E, 3d Artil., Battery D, 5th Artil., 2d R. I. Battery, Detachments of 1st and 2d Dragoons. Union 481 killed, 1,011 wounded, 1,460 missing and captured. Confed. 269 killed, 1,483 wounded. Confederate Brigadier-Generals Bee and Barton killed.
22.—Forsyth, Mo. 1st Ia., 2d Kan., Stanley Dragoons, Totten's Battery. Union 3 wounded. Confed. 5 killed, 10 wounded.
—Ætna, Mo , 21st Missouri Vols.
24.—Blue Mills, Mo. 5th Mo. Reserves. Union 1 killed, 12 wounded.
26.—Lane's Prairie, near Rolla, Mo. Home Guards. Union 3 wounded. Confed. 1 killed, 3 wounded.
—Harrisonville, Mo. Missouri Horse Guards and 5th Kansas Cavalry.
27.—Fort Filmore, N. Mex. 7th U. S. Infantry and U. S. Mounted Rifles, in all, 426 men, captured by Confederates.
AUG. 2.—Dug Springs, Mo. 1st Ia., 3d Mo., five batteries of Mo. Light Artil. Union 4 killed, 37 wounded. Confed. 40 killed, 44 wounded.
3.—Messilla, N. Mex. 7th U. S. Infantry and U. S. Mounted Rifles. Union 3 killed, 6 wounded. Confed. 12 killed.
5.—Athens, Mo. Home Guards, 21st Mo. Union 3 killed, 8 wounded. Confed. 14 killed, 14 wounded.
—Point of Rocks, Md. 28th N. Y. Confed. 3 killed, 2 wounded.
7.—Hampton, Va. 20th N. Y. Confed 3 killed, 6 wounded.
8.—Lovettsville, Va. 19th N. Y. Confed. 1 killed, 5 wounded.
10.—Wilson's Creek, Mo , also called Springfield and Oak Hill. 6th and 10th Mo. Cav., 2d Kan. Mounted, one Co. of 1st U. S. Cav., 1st Ia., 1st Kan., 1st, 2d, 3d and 5th Mo., Detachments of 1st and 2d U. S. Regulars, Mo. Home Guards, 1st Mo. Light Artil , Battery F, 2d U. S. Artil. Union 223 killed, 721 wounded, 291 missing. Confed. 265 killed, 800 wounded, 30 missing. Union Brigadier-General Nathaniel Lyon killed.
—Potosi, Mo. Mo. Home Guards. Union 1 killed. Confed. 2 killed, 3 wounded.
13.—Grafton, Va. One Co. W. Va. Vols.
17.—Brunswick, Mo. 5th Mo. Reserves. Union 1 killed, 7 wounded.
19.—Charleston or Bird's Point, Mo. 22d Ill. Union 1 killed, 6 wounded. Confed. 40 killed.
20.—Hawk's Nest, W. Va. 11th Ohio. Union 3 wounded. Confed. 1 killed, 3 wounded.
—Lookout Station, Mo. Mo. Home Guards.
21.—Jonesboro, Mo. Missouri Home Guards.
26.—Cross Lanes or Summerville, W. Va. 7th Ohio. Union 5 killed, 40 wounded, 200 captured.
27.—Ball's Cross Roads, Va. Two Co's 23d N. Y. Union 1 killed, 2 wounded.
—Wayne's Court House, W. Va. 5th W. Va.
28 and 29.—Fort Hatteras, N. C. 9th, 20th and 99th N. Y. and Naval force. Union 1 killed, 2 wounded. Confed. 5 killed, 51 wounded, 715 prisoners.
29.—Lexington, Mo. Mo. Home Guards. Confed. 8 killed.

31.—Munson's Hill, Va. Two Co's 23d N. Y. Union 2 killed, 2 wounded.

SEPT 1.—Bennett's Mills, Mo. Mo. Home Guards. Union 1 killed, 8 wounded.
—Boone C. H., W. Va. 1st Ky Union 6 wounded. Confed. 30 killed.
2.—Dallas, Mo. 11th Mo. Union 2 killed.
—Worthington, W. Va.
—Dry Wood or Fort Scott, Mo. 5th and 6th Kan, one Co. 9th Kan. Cav., 1st Kan. Battery. Union 4 killed, 9 wounded.
Behor's Mills. 13th Mass. Confed. 3 killed, 5 wounded.
4.—Shelbina, Mo. 3d Iowa.
7.—Petersburg, W. Va. Three Co's 4th Ohio.
10.—Carnifex Ferry. 9th, 10th, 12th, 13th, 28th and 47th Ohio. Union 16 killed, 103 wounded.
11.—Lewinsville, Va. 19th Ind., 3d Vt., 65th N. Y., 79th N. Y. Militia. Union 6 killed, 8 wounded.
—Elkwater W. Va. 3d Ohio, 15th and 17th Ind.
12.—Black River, near Ironton, Mo. Three Co's 1st Ind. Cav. Confed. 5 killed.
12 and 13.—Cheat Mountain, W. Va. 13th, 14th, 15th and 17th Ind., 3d, 6th, 24th and 25th Ohio, 2d W. Va. Union 9 killed, 12 wounded. Confed. 80 wounded.
13.—Booneville Mo. Mo. Home Guards. Union 1 killed, 4 wounded. Confed. 12 killed, 30 wounded.
14.—Confederate Privateer Judah destroyed near Pensacola, Fla., by the U. S. Flag-ship Colorado. Union 3 killed, 15 wounded.
15.—Pritchard's Mills, or Darnestown, Va. 28th Penn., 13th Mass. Union 1 killed. Confed. 8 killed, 75 wounded.
12 to 20.—Lexington, Mo. 23d Ill., 8th, 25th and 27th Mo., 13th and 14th Mo. Home Guards, Berry's and Van Horne's Mo. Cav. 1st Ill. Cav. Union 42 killed, 108 wounded, 1,624 missing and captured. Confed. 25 killed, 75 wounded.
17.—Morristown, Mo. 5th, 6th and 9th Kan. Cav., 1st Kan. Battery. Union 2 killed, 6 wounded. Confed. 7 killed.
—Blue Mills, Mo. 3d Ia. Union 11 killed, 39 wounded. Confed. 10 killed, 60 wounded.
18.—Barbourville, W. Va. Ky. Home Guards. Union 1 killed, 1 wounded. Confed. 7 killed.
21 and 22.—Papinsville or Osceola, Mo. 5th, 6th and 9th Kan. Cav. Union 17 killed.
22.—Elliotts' Mill or Camp Crittenden, Mo. 7th Ia. Union 1 killed. 5 wounded.
23.—Romney or Hanging Rock, W. Va. 4th and 8th Ohio. Union 3 killed, 50 wounded. Confed. 35 killed.
25.—Chapmansville, W. Va. 1st Ky., 34th Ohio. Union 4 killed, 9 wounded. Confed. 20 killed, 50 wounded.
26.—Lucas Bend, Ky. Stewart's Cavalry. Confed. 4 killed.
27.—Shanghai, Mo. Mo. Home Guards.
29.—Camp Advance, Munson Hill, Va. 69th Pa., through mistake, fire into the 71st Pa., killing 9 and wounding 25.

OCT. 3.—Greenbrier, W. Va. 24th, 25th and 32d Ohio, 7th, 9th, 13th, 14th, 15th and 17th Ind., Battery G 4th U. S. Artil., Battery A 1st Mich. Artil. Union 8 killed, 32 wounded. Confed. 100 killed, 75 wounded.
4.—Alamosa, near Fort Craig, N. Mex. Mink's Cav. and U. S. Regulars. Confed. 11 killed, 30 wounded.
—Buffalo Hill, Ky. Union 20 killed. Confed. 50 killed.
5.—Chicanuicomico, N. C. 20th Ind.
8.—Hillsboro, Ky. Home Guards. Union 3 killed, 2 wounded. Confed. 11 killed, 29 wounded.
9.—Santa Rosa, Fla. 6th N. Y., Co. A. 1st U. S. Artil., Co. H 2d U. S. Artil., Co.'s C and E. 3d U. S. Infantry. Union 14 killed, 20 wounded. Confed. 350 wounded.
12.—Cameron, Mo. James' Cav. Union 1 killed, 4 wounded. Confed. 8 wounded.
—Upton Hill, Ky. 39th Ind. Confed. 5 killed, 3 wounded.
—Bayles' Cross Roads, La. 79th N. Y., Union 4 wounded.
13.—Beckwith Farm (12 miles from Birds' Point), Mo. Tuft's Cav. Union 2 killed, 5 wounded. Confed. 1 killed, 2 wounded.
—West Glaze, also called Shanghai, or Henrytown, or Monday's Hollow, Mo. 6th and 10th Mo. Cav. Fremont's Battalion Cav. Confed. 62 killed.
15.—Big River Bridge, near Potosi, Mo. Forty men of the 38th Ill. Union 1 killed, 6 wounded, 33 captured. Confed. 5 killed, 4 wounded.
—Lime Creek, or Linn, Mo. 13th Ill. Infantry, 6th Mo. Cav. Confed. 63 killed, 40 wounded.
16.—Bolivar Heights, Va. Parts of 26th Pa., 3d Wis., 13th Mass. Union 4 killed, 7 wounded.
—Warsaw, Mo. Confed. 3 killed.

OCT. 17 to 21.—Fredericktown and Ironton, Mo. 17th, 20th, 21st, 33d and 38th Ill., 8th Wis., 1st Ind. Cav., Co. A 1st Mo. Light Artil. Union 6 killed, 60 wounded. Confed. 200 wounded.
   19.—Big Hurricane Creek, Mo. 18th Mo. Union 2 killed, 14 wounded. Confed. 14 killed.
   21.—Ball's Bluff, also called Edward's Ferry, Harrison's Landing, Leesburg, Va. 15th, 20th Mass., 40th N. Y., 71st Pa., Battery B R. I. Artil. Union 223 killed, 226 wounded. Confed. 36 killed, 264 wounded. 445 Union captured and missing. Union Acting Brigadier-General E. D. Baker killed.
   —Wildcat, Ky. 33d Ind., 14th and 17th Ohio, 1st Ky. Cav. and 1st Ohio Battery.
   22.—Buffalo Mills, Mo. Confed. 17 killed.
   23.—West Liberty, Ky. 2d Ohio, 1st and Loughlin's Ohio Cav., 1st Ohio Artil. Union 2 wounded. Confed. 10 killed, 5 wounded.
   —Hodgeville, Ky. Detachment 6th Ind. Union 3 wounded. Confed. 3 killed, 5 wounded.
   25.—Zagonyi's Charge, Springfield, Mo. Fremont's Body Guard and White's Prairie Scouts. Union 18 killed, 37 wounded. Confed. 106 killed.
   26.—Romney or Mill Creek Mills, W. Va. 4th and 8th Ohio, 7th W. Va., Md. Volunteers, 2d Regt. of Potomac Home Guards and Ringgold (Pa.) Cav. Union 2 killed, 15 wounded. Confed. 20 killed, 15 wounded, 50 captured.
   —Saratoga, Ky. 9th Ill. Union 4 wounded. Confed. 8 killed, 17 wounded.
   27.—Plattsburg, Mo. Confed. 8 killed.
   —Spring Hill, Mo. One Co. of 7th Mo. Cav. Union 5 wounded.
   29.—Woodbury and Morgantown, Ky. 17th Ky., 3d Ky. Cav. Union 1 wounded.

NOV. 1.—Renick, Randolph Co., Mo. Union 14 wounded.
   6.—Little Santa Fe, Mo. 4th Mo., 5th Kan. Cav., Kowald's Mo. Battery. Union 2 killed, 6 wounded.
   7.—Belmont, Mo. 22d, 27th, 30th and 31st Ill., 7th Ia., Battery B 1st Ill. Artil., two Co's 15th Ill. Cav. Union 90 killed, 173 wounded, 235 missing. Confed. 261 killed, 427 wounded, 278 missing.
   —Galveston Harbor, Tex. U. S. Frigate Santee burned the Royal Yacht. Union 1 killed, 8 wounded. Confed. 3 wounded.
   —Port Royal, S. C. Bombardment by U. S. Navy. Union 8 killed, 23 wounded. Confed. 11 killed, 39 wounded.
   9.—Piketown or Fry Mountain, Ky. 2d, 21st, 33d and 59th Ohio, 16th Ky. Union 4 killed, 26 wounded. Confed. 18 killed, 45 wounded, 200 captured.
   10.—Guyandott, W. Va. Recruits of 9th W. Va. Union 7 killed, 20 wounded. Confed. 3 killed, 10 wounded.
   —Gauley Bridge, W. Va. 11th Ohio, 2d Ky. Cav. Union 2 killed, 16 wounded.
   —Taylor's Ford, Wantanga River, Tenn. Loyal Citizens.
   11.—Little Blue, Mo. 110 men of 7th Kan. Cav. Union 7 killed, 9 wounded.
   12.—Occoquan Creek, Va. Detachment 1st N. Y. Cav. Union 3 killed, 1 wounded.
   17.—Cypress Bridge, Ky. Union 10 killed, 15 wounded.
   18.—Palmyra, Mo. Detachment 3d Mo. Cav. Confed. 3 killed, 5 wounded.
   19.—Wirt C. H., W. Va. Detachment 1st W. Va. Cav. Confed. 1 killed, 5 wounded.
   23.—Fort Pickens, Pensacola, Fla. Co's C and E 3d U. S. Infantry, Co's G and I 6th N. Y., Batteries A, F and L 1st U. S. Artil. and C, H and K 2d U. S. Artil. Union 5 killed, 7 wounded. Confed. 5 killed, 23 wounded.
   24.—Lancaster, Mo. 21st Mo. Union 1 killed, 2 wounded. Confed. 13 killed.
   —Johnstown, Mo. Mo. Home Guard.
   26.—Little Blue, Mo. 7th Kan. Cav. Union 1 killed, 1 wounded.
   —Drainesville, Va. 1st Pa. Cav. Confed. 2 killed.
   —Hunter's Mills, Va. 3d Pa. Cav.
   29.—Black Walnut Creek, near Sedalia, Mo. 1st Mo. Cav. Union 15 wounded. Confed. 17 killed.

DEC. 1.—Morristown, Tenn.
   3.—Salem, Mo. Detachment 10 Mo. Cav. Union 6 killed, 10 wounded. Confed. 16 killed, 20 wounded.
   —Vienna, Va. Detachment 3d Pa. Cav. Union all captured. Confed. 1 killed.
   4.—Anandale, Va. 30 men of 3d N. J. Union 1 killed. Confed. 7 killed.
   —Dunksburg, Mo. Citizens repulse raiders. Confed. 7 killed, 10 wounded.
   9.—Bushy Creek, Ark. Union Indians under Opotheyholo.
   11.—Bertrand, Mo. 2d Ill. Cav. Union 1 wounded.
   —Dam No. X., Potomac, Va. 12th Ind.
   12.—Bagdad, Ky. 6th Ky.
   13.—Camp Allegheny or Buffalo Mountain, W. Va. 9th and 13th Ind., 25th and 32d Ohio, 2d W. Va. Union 20 killed, 107 wounded. Confed. 20 killed, 96 wounded.
   17.—Rowlett's Station, also called Munfordsville or Woodsonville, Ky. 32d Ind. Union 10 killed, 22 wounded. Confed 33 killed, 50 wounded.

DEC. 18.—Milford, also called Shawnee Mound, or Blackwater, Mo. 27th Ohio, 8th, 18th, 22d and 24th Ind., 00st Kan., 1st Ia. Cav., Detachment U. S. Cav., two Batteries of 1st Mo. Light Artil. Union 2 killed, 8 wounded. Confed. 1,300 captured.
20.—Drainsville, Va. 1st, 6th, 9th, 10th and 12th Pa. Reserve Corps, 1st Pa. Artil., 1st Pa. Cav. Union 7 killed, 61 wounded. Confed 43 killed, 143 wounded.
21.—Hudson, Mo. Detachment 7th Mo. Cav. Union 5 wounded. Confed. 10 killed.
22.—Newmarket Bridge, near Newport News, Va. 20th N. Y. Union 6 wounded. Confed. 10 killed, 20 wounded.
24.—Wadesburg, Mo. Mo. Home Guards. Union 2 wounded.
28.—Sacramento, Ky. 3d Ky. Cav. Union 1 killed, 8 wounded. Confed. 30 killed.
—Mt. Zion, Mo. Birge's Sharpshooters, 3d Mo. Cav. Union 5 killed, 63 wounded. Confed. 25 killed, 150 wounded.

1862.

JAN. 1.—Port Royal, S. C. 3d Mich., 47th, 48th and 79th N. Y., 50th Pa. Union 1 killed, 10 wounded.
3.—Hunnewell, Mo. 4 Co's 10th Mo. Cav.
4.—Huntersville, Va. Detachments of 25th Ohio, 2 W. Va. and 1st Ind. Cav. Union 1 wounded. Confed. 1 killed, 7 wounded.
—Bath, Va., also including skirmishes at Great Cacapon Bridge, Alpine Station and Hancock. 39th Ill. Union 2 killed, 2 wounded. Confed. 30 wounded.
—Calhoun, Mo. Union 10 wounded. Confed. 30 wounded.
7.—Blue Gap, near Romney, Va. 4th, 5th, 7th and 8th Ohio, 14th Ind., 1st W. Va. Cav. Confed. 15 killed.
—Jennies' Creek, Ky., also called Paintsville. Four Co's 1st W. Va. Cav. Union 3 killed, 1 wounded. Confed. 6 killed, 14 wounded.
8.—Charleston, Mo. 10th Ia. Union 8 killed, 16 wounded.
—Dry Forks, Cheat River, W. Va. One Co. of 2d W. Va Cav. Union 6 wounded. Confed 6 killed.
—Silver Creek, Mo., also called Sugar Creek, and Roan's Tan Yard. Detachments of 1st and 2d Mo., 4th Ohio, 1st Ia. Cav. Union 5 killed, 6 wounded. Confed. 80 wounded.
9.—Columbus, Mo. 7th Kan. Cav. Union 5 killed.
10.—Middle Creek and Prestonburg, Ky. 40th and 42d Ohio, 14th and 22d Ky. Union 2 killed, 25 wounded. Confed. 40 killed.
19 and 20.—Mills Springs, Ky., also called Logan's Cross Roads, Fishing Creek, Somerset and Beach Grove. 9th Ohio, 2d Minn., 4th Ky., 10th Ind., 1st Ky. Cav. Union 38 killed, 194 wounded. Confed. 190 killed, 160 wounded. Confed. General F. K. Zollikoffer killed.
22.—Knob Noster, Mo. 2d Mo. Cav. Union 1 killed.
29.—Occoquan Bridge, Va. Detachments of 37th N. Y. and 1st N. J. Cav. Union 1 killed, 4 wounded. Confed. 10 killed.

FEB. 1.—Bowling Green, Ky. One Co. of 2d Ind. Cav. Confed. 3 killed, 2 wounded.
2.—Morgan, Tenn.
6.—Fort Henry, Tenn. U. S. Gunboats Essex, Carondolet, St. Louis, Cincinnati, Conestoga, Tyler and Lexington. Union 40 wounded. Confed. 5 killed, 11 wounded.
8.—Linn Creek, Va. Detachment of 5th W. Va. Union 1 killed, 1 wounded. Confed. 8 killed, 7 wounded.
—Roanoke Island. N. C. 21st, 23d, 24th, 25th and 27th Mass., 10 Ct., 9th, 51st and 53d N. Y., 9th N. J., 51 Pa., 4th and 5th R. I., U. S. Gunboats Southfield, Delaware, Star and Stripes, Louisiana, Hetzel, Commodore Perry, Underwriter, Valley City, Commodore Barney, Hunchback, Ceres, Putnam, Morse, Lockwood, J. N. Seymour, Granite, Brinker, Whitehead, Shawseen, Picket, Poineer, Hussar, Videtle, Chasseur. Union 35 killed, 200 wounded. Confed. 16 killed, 39 wounded, 2,527 taken prisoners.
10.—Elizabeth City, or Cobb's Point, N. C. U. S. Gunboats Delaware, Underwriter, Louisiana, Seymour, Hetzel, Shawseen, Valley City, Putnam, Commodore Perry, Ceres, Morse, Whitehead and Brinker. Union 3 killed.
13.—Blooming Gap, Va. 8th Ohio, 7th W. V., 1st W. Va. Cav. Union 2 killed, 5 wounded. Confed. 13 killed.
14.—Flat Lick Fords, Ky. 49th Ind., 6th Ky Cav Confed. 4 killed, 4 wounded.
—Marshfield, Mo. 6th Mo. and 3d Ill. Cav.
14, 15 and 16.—Fort Donnelson, Tenn. 17th and 25th Ky., 11th, 25th, 31st and 44th Ind., 2d, 7th, 12th and 14th Ia., 1st Neb., 58th and 76th Ohio, 8th and 13th Mo., 8th Wis., 8th, 9th, 11th, 12th, 17th, 18th, 20th, 28th, 29th, 30th, 31st, 41st, 45th, 46th, 48th, 49th, 57th and 58th Ill., Batteries B and D 1st Ill. Artil., D and E 2d Ill. Artil., four

Co's Ill. Cav., Birge's Sharpshoots and six gunboats.   Union 446 killed, 1,735 wounded, 150 missing. Confed. 231 killed, 1,007 wounded, 13,829 prisoners. Union Major-General John A. Logan wounded.

15.—Bowling Green, Ky.   Occupied by General D. C. Buell's Army.
17.—Sugar Creek, or Pea Ridge, Mo.   1st and 6th Mo., 3d Ill. Cav.   Union 5 killed, 9 wounded.
18.—Independence Mo.   2d Ohio Cav.   Union 1 killed, 3 wounded.   Confed. 4 killed, 5 wounded.
21.—Fort Craig, or Valverde, N. Mex.   1st N. Mex. Cav., 2d Col. Cav., Detachments of 1st, 3d and 5th N. Mex. and of 5th, 7th and 10th U. S. Infantry, Hall's and McRae's Batteries.   Union 62 killed, 140 wounded.   Confed. 150 wounded.
24.—Mason's Neck, Occoquan, Va.   37th N. Y.   Union 2 killed, 1 wounded.
26.—Keytesville, Mo.   6th Mo. Cav.   Union 2 killed, 1 wounded.   Confed. 1 killed.

MAR. 1.—Sykestown, Mo.   7th Ill. Cav. and 10th Ill. Infantry.
2.—Pittsburg Landing, Tenn.   32d Ill. and U. S. Gunboats Lexington and Tyler.   Union 5 killed, 5 wounded.   Confed. 20 killed, 200 wounded.
3.—New Madrid, Mo.   5th Ia., 59th Ind., 39th and 63d Ohio, 2d Mich. Cav., 7th Ill. Cav.   Union 1 killed, 3 wounded.
5.—Occoquan, Va.   Detachment of 63d Pa.   Union 2 killed, 2 wounded.
6, 7 and 8.—Pea Ridge, Ark., including engagements at Bentonville, Leetown and Elkhorn Tavern.   25th, 35th, 36th, 37th, 44th and 59th Ill., 2d, 3d, 12th, 15th, 17th, 24th and Phelps Mo., 8th, 18th and 22d Ind., 4th and 9th Ia., 3d In. Cav., 3d and 15th Ill. Cav., 1st, 4th, 5th and 6th Mo. Cav., Batteries B and F 2d Mo. Light Artil., 2d Ohio Battery, 1st Ind. Battery, Battery A 2d Ill. Artil.   Union 203 killed, 972 wounded, 174 missing.   Confed. 1,100 killed, 2,500 wounded, 1,600 missing and captured.   Union Brigadier-General Asboth and Acting Brigadier-General Carr wounded.   Confed. Brigadier-General B. McCulloch and Acting Brigadier-General James McIntosh killed.
7.—Fox Creek, Mo.   4th Mo. Cav.   Union 5 wounded.
8.—Near Nashville, Tenn.   1st Wis., 4th Ohio Cav.   Union 1 killed, 2 wounded.   Confed. 4 killed.
—Mississippi City, Miss.   26th Mass.
9.—Mountain Grove, Mo.   10th Mo. Cav.   Union 10 killed, 2 wounded.
—Hampton Roads, Va.   20th Ind., 7th and 11th N. Y., U. S. Gunboats Monitor, Minnesota, Congress and Cumberland.   Union 261 killed, 108 wounded.   Confed. 7 killed, 17 wounded.
10.—Burke's Station, Va.   One Co. 1st N. Y. Cav.   Union 1 killed.   Confed. 3 killed, 5 wounded.
—Jacksboro', Big Creek Gap, Tenn.   2d Tenn.   Union 2 wounded.   Confed. 2 killed, 4 wounded.
11.—Paris, Tenn.   Detachments of 5th Ia. and 1st Neb. Cav., Battery K 1st Mo. Artil.   Union 5 killed, 5 wounded.   Confed. 10 wounded.
12.—Lexington, Mo.   1st Ia. Cav.   Union 1 killed, 1 wounded.   Confed. 9 killed, 3 wounded.
—Near Lebanon, Mo.   Confed. 13 killed, 5 wounded.
13.—New Madrid, Mo.   10th and 16th Ill., 27th, 39th, 43d and 63d Ohio, 3d Mich. Cav., 1st U. S. Infantry, Bissell's Mo. Engineers.   Union 50 wounded.   Confed. 100 wounded.
14.—Newberne, N. C.   51st N. Y., 8th, 10th and 11th Ct., 21st, 23d, 24th, 25th and 27th Mass., 9th N. J., 51st Pa., 4th and 5th R. I.   Union 91 killed, 466 wounded.   Confed. 64 killed, 106 wounded, 413 captured.
—Pound Gap, or Sounding Gap, Tenn.   Detachments of 22d Ky., 40th and 42d Ohio, and 1st Ohio Cav.
16.—Black Jack Forest, Tenn.   Detachments of 4th Ill. and 5th Ohio Cav.   Union 4 wounded.
—Acquia Creek Batteries, Va.   U. S. Gunboats Yankee and Anacostra.
18.—Salem, or Spring River, Ark.   Detachments of 6th Mo. and 3d Ia. Cav.   Union 5 killed, 10 wounded.   Confed. 100 killed, wounded and missing.
21.—Mosquito Inlet, Fla.   U. S. Gunboats Penguin and Henry Andrew.   Union 8 killed, 5 wounded.
22.—Independence, or Little Santa Fe, Mo.   2d Kan.   Union 1 killed, 2 wounded.   Confed. 7 killed.
23.—Carthage, Mo.   6th Kan. Cav.   Union 1 wounded.
—Winchester or Kearnstown, Va.   1st W. Va., 84 and 110th Pa., 5th, 7th, 8th, 29th, 62d and 67th Ohio, 7th, 13th and 14th Ind., 39th Ill., 1st Ohio Cav., 1st Mich. Cav., 1st W. Va. Artil., 1st Ohio Artil., Co. E 4th U. S. Artil.   Union 103 killed, 440 wounded, 24 missing.   Confed. 80 killed, 342 wounded, 269 prisoners.
26.—Warrensburg, or Briar, Mo.   Sixty men of 7th Mo. Militia Cav.   Union 7 killed, 23 wounded.   Confed. 9 killed, 17 wounded.

MAR. 26.—Hummonsville, Mo. Co. B 8th Mo. Militia Cav. Union 5 wounded. Confed. 15 wounded.
    26, 27 and 28.—Apache Canon or Glorietta, near Santa Fe, N. Mex. 1st and 2d Col. Cav. Union 32 killed, 75 wounded, 35 missing. Confed. 36 killed, 60 wounded, 93 missing.
    27.—Strasburg, Va. Portion of General Banks' command.
    28.—Warrensburg, Mo. 1st Ill. Cav. Union 3 killed, 1 wounded. Confed. 15 killed.
    —Middleburg, Va. 28 Pa.
    30.—Union City, Tenn. 2d Ill. Cav.

APRIL 2.—Putnam's Ferry, near Doniphan, Mo. 21st and 38th Ill., 5th Ill. Cav., 16th Ohio Battery and Colonel Carlin's Brigade. Confed. 3 killed.
    —Thoroughfare Gap, Va. 28th Pa.
    4.—Great Bethel, Va. Advance of 3d Corps Army of Potomac. Union 4 killed, 10 wounded.
    —Crump's Landing, or Adamsville, Tenn. 48th, 70th and 72d Ohio, 5th Ohio Cav. Union 2 wounded. Confed. 20 wounded.
    —Pass Christian, Miss. 9th Ct. and 6th Mass. Artil.
    5 to May 3.—Seige of Yorktown, 2d, 3d and 4th Corps Army of Potomac.
    6 and 7.—Shiloh or Pittsburg Landing, Tenn. Army of Western Tennessee, commanded by Major-General U. S. Grant, as follows : 1st Div., Major-General J. A. McClernand; 2d Div., Major-General C. F. Smith; 3d Div., Brigadier-General Lew Wallace; 4th Div., Brigadier-General S. A. Hurlburt ; 5th Div., Brigadier-General W. T. Sherman; 6th Div., Brigadier-General B. M. Prentiss. Army of the Ohio commanded by Major-General D. C. Buell, as follows : 2d Div., Brigadier-General A. M. D. Cook ; 4th Div., Brigadier-General W. Nelson ; 5th Div., Brigadier-General T. L. Crittenden, 21st Brigade of the 6th Div., Gunboats Tyler and Lexington. Union 1,735 killed, 7,882 wounded, 3,956 captured. Confed. 1,728 killed, 8,012 wounded, 959 captured. Union Brigadier-Generals W. T. Sherman and W. H. L. Wallace wounded, and B. M. Prentiss captured. Confed. Major-General A. S. Johnson, commander-in-chief, and Brigadier-General A. H. Gladden killed; Major-General W. S. Cheatham and Brigadier-Generals C. Clark, B. R. Johnson and J. S. Bowen wounded.
    8.—Island No. 10, Tenn. Major-General Pope's command, and the Navy under Flag-officer Foote. Confed. 17 killed, 3,000 prisoners.
    —Near Corinth, Miss. 3d Brigade 5th Div. Army of Western Tenn. and 4th Ill. Cav. Confed. 15 killed, 25 wounded, 200 captured.
    9.—Owen's River, Cal. 2d Cal. Cav. Union 1 killed, 2 wounded.
    10.—Fort Pulaski, Ga. 6th and 7th Ct., 3d R. I., 46th and 48th N. Y., 8th Maine, 15th U. S. Infantry, crew of U. S. S. Wabash. Union 1 killed. Confed. 4 wounded, 360 prisoners.
    11.—Huntsville, Ala. Army of the Ohio, 3d Div. Confed. 200 prisoners.
    —Yorktown, Va. 12th N. Y., 57th and 63d Pa. Union 2 killed, 8 wounded.
    12.—Little Blue River, Mo. Confed. 5 killed.
    —Monterey, Va. 75th Ohio, 1st W. Va. Cav. Union 3 wounded.
    14.—Pollocksville, N. C. Confed. 7 wounded.
    —Diamond Grove, Mo. 6th Kan. Cav. Union 1 wounded.
    —Walkerville, Mo. 2d Mo. Militia Cav. Union 2 killed, 3 wounded.
    —Montavallo, Mo. Two Co's 1st Ia. Cav. Union 2 killed, 6 wounded. Confed. 2 killed, 10 wounded.
    —Fort Pillow, Tenn. Bombarded by U. S. Navy.
    15.—Pechacho Pass, Ariz. 1st Cal. Cav. Union 3 killed, 3 wounded.
    —Peralto, N. Mex.
    16.—Savannah, Tenn. Confed. 5 killed, 65 wounded.
    —White Marsh, or Wilmington Island, Ga. 8th Mich. Battery of R. I. Light Artil. Union 10 killed, 35 wounded. Confed. 5 killed, 7 wounded.
    Lee's Mills, Va. 3d, 4th and 6th Vt., 3d N. Y. Battery and Battery of 5th U. S. Artil. Union 35 killed, 129 wounded. Confed. 20 killed, 75 wounded, 50 captured.
    17.—Holly River, W. Va. Union 3 wounded. Confed. 2 killed.
    18.—Falmouth, Va. 3d N. Y. Cav. Union 5 killed, 10 wounded. Confed. 19 captured.
    —Edisto Island, S. C. 55th Pa., 3d N. H., U. S. S. Crusader. Union 3 wounded.
    18 to 28.—Forts Jackson and St. Philip, and the capture of New Orleans, La. Commodore Farragut's fleet of war vessels and mortar boats, under Commander D. D. Porter. Union 36 killed, 193 wounded. Confed. 185 killed, 197 wounded, 400 captured.
    19.—Talbot's Ferry, Ark. 4th Ia. Cav. Union 1 killed. Confed. 3 killed.
    —Camden, N. C., also called South Mills. 9th and 89th N. Y., 21st Mass., 51st Pa., 6th N. H. Union 12 killed, 98 wounded. Confed. 6 killed, 19 wounded.
    23.—Grass Lick, W. Va. 3d Md., Potomac Home Brigade. Union 3 killed.

APRIL 25.—Fort Macon, N. C. U. S. Gunboats Daylight, Georgia, Chippewa, the bark Gemsbok and General Parkes' Division. Union 1 killed, 11 wounded. Confed. 7 killed, 18 wounded, 450 captured.
26.—Turnback Creek, Mo. 5th Kan. Cav. Union 1 killed.
—Neosha, Mo. 1st Mo. Cav. Union 3 killed, 3 wounded. Confed. 30 wounded, 62 prisoners.
—In front of Yorktown, Va. Three Co's 1st Mass. Union 3 killed, 16 wounded.
—Lick Creek, Miss. Troops under General A. J. Smith.
—Redoubt before Yorktown. Three Co's 1st Mass.
27.—Horton's Mills, N. C. 103d N. Y. Union 1 killed, 6 wounded. Confed. 3 wounded.
28.—Paint Rock Railroad Bridge. Twenty-two men of 10th Wis. Union 7 wounded.
—Cumberland Mountain, Tenn. 16th and 42d Ohio, 22d Ky.
—Montery, Tenn. 2d Ia. Cav. Union 1 killed, 3 wounded. Confed. 5 killed.
29.—Bridgport, Ala. 3d Div. Army of the Ohio. Confed. 72 killed and wounded, 350 captured.
30.—Siege of Corinth. Major-General H. W. Halleck's Army.

MAY 1.—Clarke's Hollow, W. Va. Co. C 23d Ohio. Union 1 killed, 21 wounded.
3.—Farmington, Miss. 10th, 16th, 22d, 27th, 42d and 51st Ill., 10th and 16th Mich., Yates' (Ill.) Sharpshooters, 2d Mich Cav., Battery C 1st Ill. Artil. Union 2 killed, 12 wounded. Confed. 30 killed.
4.—Licking, Mo. 24th Mo., 5th Mo. Militia Cav. Union 1 killed, 2 wounded.
—Cheese Cake Church, Va. 3d Pa., 1st and 6th U. S. Cav.
5.—Lebanon, Tenn. 1st, 4th and 5th Ky. Cav., Detachment of 7th Pa. Union 6 killed, 25 wounded. Confed. 66 prisoners.
—Lockringe Mills, or Dresden, Ky. 5th Ia. Cav. Union 4 killed, 16 wounded, 68 missing.
—Williamsburg, Va. 3d and 4th Corps. Army of the Potomac. Union 456 killed, 1,400 wounded, 372 missing. Confed. 1,000 killed, wounded and captured.
7.—West Point or Eltham's Landing, Va. 16th, 31st and 32d N. Y., 95th and 96th Pa., 5th Maine, 1st Mass. Artil., Battery D 2d U. S. Artil. Union 49 killed, 104 wounded, 41 missing.
—Somerville Heights, Va. 13th Ind. Union 2 killed, 7 wounded, 24 missing.
8.—McDowell, or Bull Pasture, Va. 25th, 32d, 75th and 82d Ohio, 3d W. Va., 1st W. Va. Cav., 1st Ct. Cav., 1st Ind. Battery. Union 28 killed, 225 wounded. Confed. 100 killed, 200 wounded.
—Glendale, near Corinth, Miss. 7th Ill. Cav. Union 1 killed, 4 wounded. Confed. 30 killed and wounded.
9.—Elkton Station, near Athens, Ala. Co. E. 37th Ind. Union 5 killed, 43 captured. Confed. 13 killed.
—Slatersville, or New Kent C. H., Va. 98th Pa., 2d R. I., 6th U. S. Cav. Union 4 killed, 3 wounded. Confed. 10 killed, 14 wounded.
—Farmington, Miss. Two Brigades Army of Mississippi.
10.—Fort Pillow, Tenn. U. S. Gunboats Cincinnati and Mound City. Union 3 wounded. Confed. 2 killed, 1 wounded.
—Norfolk, Va. 10th, 20th and 99th N. Y., 1st Del., 58 Pa., 20 Ind., 16th Mass., Battery D 4th U. S. Artil. and first N. Y. Mounted Rifles.
11. Bloomfield, Mo. 1st Wis. Cav. Confed. 1 killed.
13.—Montery, Tenn. Part of Brigadier-General M. L. Smith's Brigade. Union 2 wounded. Confed. 3 killed, 3 wounded.
—Reedy Creek, W. Va. Brigadier-General B. F. Kelley's command.
—Rodgersville, Ala. 1st Wis., 38th Ind and Starkweather's Cav.
14.—Trenton Bridge, N. C. 17th, 25th and 27th Mass., Battery B 3d N. Y. Artil. and two troops 3d N. Y. Cav.
15.—Linden, Va. One Co. of 28th Pa. Union 1 killed, 3 wounded, 14 missing.
—Darling, James Rives, Va. U. S. Gunboats Galena, Port Royal, Naugatuck, Monitor and Aristook. Union 12 killed, 14 wounded. Confed. 7 killed, 8 wounded.
—Chalk Bluffs, Mo. 1st Wis. Cav. Union 1 killed, 3 wounded.
—Butler, Bates Co., Mo. 1st Ia. Cav. Union 3 killed, 1 wounded.
15, 16 and 18.—Princeton, W. Va. General J. D. Cox's Division. Union 30 killed, 70 wounded. Confed. 2 killed, 14 wounded.
17.—Russell's house, in front of Corinth, Miss. Brigadier-General L. M. Smith's Brigade. Union 10 killed, 31 wounded. Confed. 12 killed.
19.—Searcy Landing, Ark. Detachments of 3d and 17th Mo. and 4th Mo. Cav., Battery B. 1st Mo. Light Artil. Union 18 killed, 27 wounded. Confed. 150 killed, wounded and missing.
—Clinton, N. C. Union 5 wounded. Confed. 9 killed.
21.—Phillip's Creek, Miss 2d Div. Army of Tennessee. Union 3 wounded.
22.—Florida, Mo. Detachment 3d Ia. Cav. Union 2 wounded.
—Near New Berne, N. C. Co. I 17th Mass. Union 3 killed, 8 wounded.

MAY 23.—Lewisburg, Va. 36th and 44th Ohio, 2d W. Va. Cav. Union 14 killed, 16 wounded. Confed. 40 killed, 66 wounded, 100 captured.
—Front Royal, Va. 1st Md., Detachments of 29th Pa., Captain Mape's Poineers, 5th N. Y. Cav. and 1st Pa. Artil. Union 32 killed, 122 wounded, 750 missing.
—Buckton Station, Va. 3d Wis., 27th Ind. Union 2 killed, 6 wounded. Confed. 12 killed.
—Ft. Craig, N. Mex. 3d U. S. Cav. Union 3 wounded.
24.—New Bridge, Va. 4th Mich. Union 1 killed, 10 wounded. Confed. 60 killed and wounded. 27 captured.
—Chickahominy, Va. Davidson's Brigade of 4th Corps. Union 2 killed, 4 wounded.
—Middleton, Va. 46th Pa., 28th N. Y., 1st Maine and Va. Cav. Battery, N. Y. Artil.
—Newtown, Va. 28th N. Y., 2d Mass., 29th Pa., 27th Ind. and 3d Wis., 2 Batteries Artil.
—New Bridge, Va. 4th Mich.
—Chickahominy, Va. Davidson's Brigade, 4th Corps.
25.—Winchester, Va. 2d Mass., 29th and 46th Pa., 27th Ind., 3d Wis., 28th N. Y., 5th Ct., Battery M 1st N. Y. Artil., 1st Vt. Cav., 1st Mich. Cav., 5th N. Y. Cav. Union 38 killed, 155 wounded, 711 missing.
27.—Hanover C. H., Va. 12th, 13th, 14th, 17th, 25th and 44th N. Y., 62d and 83d Pa., 16th Mich., 9th and 22d Mass., 5th Mass. Artil., 2d Maine Artil., Battery F 5th U. S. Artil., 1st U. S. Sharpshooters. Union 53 killed, 344 wounded. Confed. 200 killed and wounded, 730 prisoners.
—Big Indian Creek, near Searcy Landing, Ark., 1st Mo. Cav. Union 3 wounded. Confed. 5 killed, 25 wounded.
—Osceola, Mo. 1st Ia. Cav. Union 3 killed, 2 wounded.
28.—Wardensville, Va. 3d Md., Potomac Home Brigade, 3d Ind. Cav. Confed. 2 killed, 3 wounded.
—Charlestown and Harper's Ferry. Brigadier-General R. Saxton's Command.
—Cache River Bridge. Ark. 9th Ill. Cav.
28 and 29.—Sylamore, Ark. 10th Mo. and 3d Ia. Cav.
29.—Pocataligo, S. C. 50th Pa., 79th N. Y., 8th Mich., 1st Mass. Cav. Union 2 killed, 9 wounded.
30.—Booneville, Miss. 2d Ia. Cav., 2d Mich. Cav. Confed. 2,000 prisoners.
—Front Royal, Va. 1st R. I. Cav. Union 5 killed, 8 wounded. Confed. 156 captured.
31.—Neosha, Mo. 10th Ill. Cav., 14th Mo. Cav. (Militia). Union 2 killed, 3 wounded.
—Near Washington, N. C. 3d N. Y. Cav. Union 1 wounded. Confed. 3 killed, 2 wounded.
31 and June 1.—Seven Pines and Fair Oaks, Va. 2d Corps, 3d Corps and 4th Corps Army of the Potomac. Union 890 killed, 3,627 wounded, 1,222 missing. Confed. 2,800 killed, 3,897 wounded, 1,300 missing. Union Brigadier-Generals O. O. Howard, Naglee and Wessells wounded. Confed. Brigadier-General Hatton killed, General J. E. Johnson and Brigadier-General Rhodes wounded, Brigadier-General Pettigrew captured.

JUNE 1 and 2.—Strasburg and Staunton Road, Va. 8th W. Va., 60th Ohio, 1st N. J. Cav., 1st Pa. Cav. Union 2 wounded.
—Legare's Point, S. C. 28th Mass., 100th Pa. Union 5 wounded.
4.—Jasper, Sweden's Cove, Tenn. 79th Pa., 5th Ky. Cav., 7th Pa. Cav., 1st Ohio Battery. Union 2 killed, 7 wounded. Confed 20 killed, 20 wounded.
—Blackland, Miss. 2d Ia. Cav., 2d Mich. Cav. Union 5 killed.
—Fort Pillow or Fort Wright, Tenn. Mississippi Flotilla.
5.—Tranter's Creek, N. C. 24th Mass., Co. I 3d N. Y. Cav., Marine Artil. Union 7 killed, 11 wounded.
6.—Memphis, Tenn. U. S. Gunboats Benton, Louisville, Carondelet, Cairo and St. Louis, and Rams Monarch and Queen of the West. Confed. 80 killed and wounded, 100 captured.
—Harrisonburg, Va. 1st N. J. Cav., 1st Pa. Rifles, 60th Ohio, 8th W. Va. Union 63 missing. Confed. 17 killed, 50 wounded. Confed. General Ashby killed.
8.—Cross Keys, or Union Church, Va. 8th, 30th, 41st, 45th, 54th and 58th N. Y., 2d, 3d, 5th and 8th W. Va., 25th, 32d, 55th, 60th, 73d, 75th and 82d Ohio, 1st and 27th Pa., 1st Ohio Battery. Union 125 killed, 500 wounded. Confed. 42 killed, 230 wounded. Confed. Brigadier-Generals Stewart and Elzey wounded.
9.—Port Republic, Va. 5th, 7th, 29th and 66th Ohio, 84th and 110th Pa., 7th Ind., 1st W. Va., Batteries E 4th U. S. and A and L 1st Ohio Artil. Union 67 killed, 361 wounded, 574 missing. Confed. 88 killed, 535 wounded, 34 missing.
—Baldwin, Miss. 2d Ia. and 2d Mich. Cav.
10.—James Island, S. C. Union 3 killed, 13 wounded. Confed. 17 killed, 30 wounded.

JUNE 11.—Montery, Owen Co., Ky. Captain Blood's Mounted Provost Guards, 13th Ind. Battery. Union 2 killed. Confed. 100 captured.
　　12.—Waddell's Farm, near Village Creek, Ark. Detachment of 9th Ill. Cav. Union 12 wounded. Confed. 28 killed and wounded.
　　13.—Old Church, Va. 5th U. S. Cav. Confed 1 killed.
　　　—James Island, S. C. Union 3 killed, 19 wounded. Confed. 19 killed, 6 wounded.
　　14.—Tunstall Station, Va. Union 4 killed, 8 wounded. Bushwhackers fire into railway train.
　　16.—Secessionville, or Fort Johnson, James Island, S. C. 46th, 47th and 79th N. Y., 3d R. I., 3d N. H., 45th, 97th and 100th Pa., 6th and 7th Ct., 8th Mich., 28th Mass, 1st N. Y. Engineers, 1st Ct. Artil., Battery E 3d U. S. and I, 3d R. I. Artil., Co. H. 1st Mass. Cav. Union 85 killed, 472 wounded, 128 missing. Confed. 51 killed, 144 wounded.
　　17.—St. Charles, White River, Ark. 43d and 46th Ind., U. S. Gunboats Lexington, Mound City, Conestoga and St. Louis. Union 105 killed, 30 wounded. Confed. 155 killed, wounded and captured.
　　　—Warrensburg, Mo. 7th Mo. Cav. (Militia). Union 2 killed, 2 wounded.
　　　—Smithville, Ark. Union 2 killed, 4 wounded. Confed. 4 wounded, 15 prisoners.
　　18.—Williamsburg Road, Va. 16th Mass. Union 7 killed, 57 wounded. Confed. 5 killed, 9 wounded.
　　　—Cumberland Gap, Va., occupied by General George Morgan.
　　21.—Battle Creek, Tenn. 2d and 33d Ohio, 10th Wis., 24th Ill., 4th Ohio Cav., 4th Ky. Cav. and Edgarton's Battery. Union 4 killed, 3 wounded.
　　22.—Raceland, near Algiers, La. 8th Va. Union 3 killed, 8 wounded.
　　23.—Raytown, Mo. 7th Mo. Cav. Union 1 killed, 1 wounded.
　　25.—Oak Grove, Va., also called King School House and The Orchards. Hooker's and Kearney's Division of the Third Corps, Palmer's Brigade of the Fourth Corps and part of Richardson's Division of the Second Corps. Union 51 killed, 401 wounded, 64 missing. Confed. 65 killed, 465 wounded, 11 missing.
　　　—Germantown, Tenn. 56th Ohio. Union 10 killed.
　　　—Little Red River, Ark. 4th Ia. Cav. Union 2 wounded.
　　26 to 29.—Vicksburg, Miss. U. S. Fleet, under command of Commodore Farragut. No casualties recorded.
　　26 to July 1.—The Seven Days' Retreat. Army of the Potomac, Major-General George B. McClellan commanding, including engagements known as Mechanicsville or Ellison's Mills on the 26th, Gaines' Mills or Cold Harbor and Chickahominy on the 27th, Peach Orchard and Savage Station on the 29th, White Oak Swamp, also called Charles City Cross Roads, Glendale, Nelson's Farm, Frazier's Farm, Turkey Bend and New Market Cross Roads on the 30th and Malvern Hill on July 1. Union—First Corps, Brigadier-General McCall's Div., 253 killed, 1,240 wounded, 1,581 missing; Second Corps, Major-General E. V. Sumner, 187 killed, 1,076 wounded, 848 missing; Third Corps, Major-General Heintzleman, 189 killed, 1,051 wounded, 833 missing; Fourth Corps, Major-General E. D. Keyes, 69 killed, 507 wounded, 201 missing; Fifth Corps, Major-General Fitz John Porter, 620 killed, 2,460 wounded, 1,198 missing; Sixth Corps, Major-General Franklin, 245 killed, 1,313 wounded, 1,179 missing; Cavalry, Brigadier-General Stoneman, 19 killed, 60 wounded, 97 missing; Engineer Corps, 2 wounded, 21 missing; Total 1,582 killed, 7,709 wounded, 5,958 missing. (Major-General Sumner and Brigadier-Generals Mead, Brook and Burns, wounded.) Confed. Major-General Hager's Div., 187 killed, 803 wounded, 360 missing; Major-General Magruder's Div., 258 killed, 1,495 wounded, 30 missing; Major-General Longstreet's Div., 763 killed, 3,929 wounded, 239 missing; Major-General Hill's Div., 619 killed, 3,251 wounded; Major-General Jackson's Div., 966 killed, 4,417 wounded, 63 missing; Major-General Holmes' Div., 2 killed, 52 wounded; Major-General Stuart's Cav., 15 killed, 30 wounded, 60 missing; Artillery, Brigadier-General Pendleton, 10 killed, 34 wounded; Total 2,820 killed, 14,-011 wounded, 752 missing. Brigadier-Generals Griffith, killed, and Anderson, Featherstone and Pender, wounded.
　　27.—Williams Bridge, Amite River, La. 21st Ind. Union 2 killed, 4 wounded. Confed. 4 killed.
　　　—Village Creek, Ark. 9th Ill. Cav. Union 2 killed, 30 wounded.
　　　—Waddell's Farm, Ark. Detachment 3d Ia. Cav. Union 4 killed, 4 wounded.
　　29.—Willis Church, Va. Cav. advance of Casey's Div., Fourth Corps. Confed. 2 killed, 15 wounded, 46 captured.
　　30.—Luray, Va. Detachment of Cavalry of Brigadier-General Crawford's Command. Union 1 killed, 3 wounded.

JULY 1.—Booneville, Miss. 2d Ia. Cav., 2 Mich. Cav. Union 45 killed and wounded. Confed. 17 killed, 65 wounded.
　　　—Morning Sun, Tenn. 57th Ohio. Union 4 wounded. Confed. 11 killed, 26 wounded.
　　　—Russelville, Tenn. 1st Ohio Cav., 2d Milford, Va., 1st Maine Cav.

JULY 3.—Haxals or Elvington Heights, Va. 14th Ind., 7th W. Va., 4th and 8th Ohio. Union 8 killed, 32 wounded. Confed. 100 killed and wounded.
4.—Grand Haze, Ark. 13th Ill. Cav.
5.—Springville, Va. 1st Maine Cav.
6.—Grand Prairie, near Aberdeen, Ark. 24th Ind. Union 1 killed, 21 wounded. Confed. 84 killed and wounded.
7.—Bayou Cache, also called Cotton Plant, Round Hill, Hill's Plantation and Bayou de View. 11th Wis., 32d Ill., 8th Ind., 1st Mo. Light Artil., 1st Ind. Cav., 5th and 13th Ill. Cav. Union 7 killed, 57 wounded. Confed. 110 killed, 200 wounded.
8.—Black River, Mo. 5th Kan. Cav. Union 1 killed, 3 wounded.
—Lot Peach Farm, Mo. One Co. 1st Ia. Cav.
9.—Hamilton, N. C. 9th N. Y., and Gunboats Perry, Ceres and Shawseen. Union 1 killed, 20 wounded.
—Aberdeen, Ark. 24th. 34th, 43d and 46th Ind. Casualties not recorded.
—Tompkinsville, Ky. 3d Pa. Cav. Union 4 killed, 6 wounded. Confed. 10 killed and wounded.
10.—Scatterville, Ark. 1st Wis. Cav.
11.—Williamsburg, Va. Confed. 3 killed.
—Pleasant Hill, Mo. 1st Ia. Cav., Mo. Militia. Union 10 killed, 19 wounded. Confed. 6 killed, 5 wounded.
—New Hope, Ky. 33d Ohio.
12.—Lebanon, Ky. 28th Ky., Lebanon Home Guards (Morgan's Raid). Union 2 killed, 65 prisoners.
—Near Culpeper, Va. 1st Md., 1st Vt., 1st W. Va., 5th N. Y. Cav. Confed. 1 killed, 5 wounded.
13.—Murfreesboro', Tenn. 9th Mich., 3d Minn., 4th Ky. Cav.; 7th Pa. Cav., 1st Ky. Battery. Union 33 killed, 62 wounded, 800 missing. Confed. 50 killed, 100 wounded.
—Fairfax, Va. 1st Md. Cav.
14.—Batesville, Ark. 4th Ia. Cav. Union 1 killed, 4 wounded.
15.—Attempt to destroy 4th Wis., Gunboats Carondolet, Queen of the West, Tyler and Essex. Union 13 killed, 36 wounded. Confed. 5 killed, 9 wounded.
—Apache Pass, Ariz. 2d Cal. Cav. Union 1 wounded.
—Fayetteville, Ark. Detachment of Cavalry, under command of Major W. H. Miller. Confed. 150 captured.
—Near Decatur, Tenn. Detachment of 1st Ohio Cavalry. Union 4 wounded.
17.—Cynthiana, Ky. 18th Ky., 7th Ky. Cav., Cynthiana, Newport, Cincinnati and Bracken Co. Home Guards (Morgan's Raid). Union 17 killed, 34 wounded. Confed. 8 killed, 29 wounded.
18.—Memphis, Mo. 2d Mo. Cav., 9th and 11th Mo. State Militia. Union 13 killed, 35 wounded. Confed. 23 killed.
20 to September 20.—Guerilla Campaign in Missouri. General Schofield's Command. Union 77 killed, 156 wounded, 347 missing. Confed. 500 killed, 1,800 wounded, 500 missing.
20.—Turkey Island Bridge, Va. 8th Pa, Cav.
—Pittman's Ferry. Ark. 13th Ill. Cav.
21.—Nashville, Tenn. 2d Ky.
23.—Florida, Mo. Two Co's 3d Ia. Cav. Union 22 wounded. Confed. 3 killed.
—Columbus, Mo. 7th Mo. Cav. Union 2 wounded.
—North Anna River, Va. 2d N. Y. and 3d Ind. Cav.
24.—Trinity, Ala. Co. E. 31st Ohio. Union 2 killed, 11 wounded. Confed. 12 killed, 30 wounded.
—Bott's Farm, near Florida, Mo. 3d Ia. Cav. Union 1 killed, 2 wounded. Confed. 1 killed, 12 wounded.
24 and 25.—Santa Fe, Mo. 3d Ia. Cav. Union 2 killed, 13 wounded.
25.—Courtland Bridge, Ala. Two Co's 10th Ky., two Co's 1st Ohio Cav. Union 100 captured.
—Orange C. H., Va. General Gibson's reconnaisance.
25 and 26.—Mountain Store and Big Piney, Mo. Three Co's 3d Mo. Cav., Battery L 2d Mo. Artil. Confed. 5 killed.
26.—Young's Cross Roads, N. C. 9th N. J., 3d N. Y. Cav. Union 7 wounded. Confed. 4 killed, 18 wounded.
—Patten, Mo. Mo. Militia.
—Greenville, Mo. 3d and 12th Mo. Militia Cav. Union 2 killed, 5 wounded.
27.—Brownsprings, Mo. 2d Ia. Cav.
28.—Bayou Barnard, Ind. Ter. 1st, 2d and 3d Kan. Indian Home Guards, 1st Kan. Battery. No casualties recorded.
—Moore's Mills, Mo. 9th Mo., 3d Ia. Cav., 2d Mo. Cav., 3d Ind. Battery. Union 19 killed, 21 wounded. Confed. 30 killed, 100 wounded.
29.—Bollinger's Mills, Mo. Two Co's 13th Mo. Confed. 10 killed.
—Russelville, Ky. 7th Ind., Russelville Home Guards. Union 1 wounded.

JULY 29.—Mount Sterling, Ky. 18th Ky. and Home Guards.
—Brownsville, Tenn. One Co. 15th Ill. Cav. Union 4 killed, 6 wounded. Confed. 4 killed, 6 wounded.
30.—Paris, Ky. 9th Pa. Cav. Confed. 27 killed, 39 wounded.
31.—Coggin's Point, opposite Harrison's Landing, Va. U. S. Gunboat Fleet. Union 10 killed, 15 wounded. Confed. 1 killed, 6 wounded.

AUG. 1.—Newark, Mo. Seventy-three men of 11th Mo. State Militia. Union 4 killed, 4 wounded, 60 captured. Confed. 73 killed and wounded.
2.—Ozark, or Forsythe, Mo. 14th Mo. State Militia. Union 1 wounded. Confed. 3 killed, 7 wounded.
—Orange C. H., Va. 5th N. Y. Cav., 1st Vt. Cav. Union 4 killed, 12 wounded. Confed. 11 killed, 52 captured.
—Clear Creek, or Taberville, Mo. Four Co's 1st Ia. Cav. Union 5 killed, 11 wounded. Confed. 11 killed.
—Coahomo Co., Miss. 11th Wis. Union 5 wounded.
—Austin, Miss. 8th Ind.
3.—Sycamore Church, near Petersburg Va. 3d Pa. Cav., 5th U. S. Cav. Union 2 wounded. Confed. 6 wounded.
—Chariton Bridge, Mo. 6th Mo. Cav. Union 2 wounded. Confed. 11 killed, 14 wounded.
—Jonesboro', Ark. 1st Wis. Cav. Union 4 killed, 2 wounded, 21 missing.
Lnnnguelle Ferry, Ark. 1st Wis. Cav. Union 17 killed, 38 wounded.
4.—Sparta, Tenn. Detachments of 4th Ky. and 7th Ind Cav. Union 1 killed.
—White Oak Swamp Bridge, Va. 3d Pa. Cav. Confed. 10 wounded, 28 captured.
5.—Baton Rouge, La. 14th Maine, 6th Mich., 7th Vt., 21st Ind., 30 Mass., 9th Ct., 4th Wis., 2d, 4th and 6th Mass. Batteries. Union 82 killed, 255 wounded, 34 missing. Confed. 84 killed, 316 wounded, 78 missing. Union Brigadier-General Thomas Williams killed.
5.—Malvern Hill, Va. Portion of Hooker's Div., Third Corps, and Richardson's Div., Second Corps and Cavalry, Army of the Potomac. Union 3 killed, 11 wounded. Confed. 100 Captured.
6.—Montavallo, or Church in the Woods, Mo. 3d Wis. Union 1 wounded, 3 missing.
—Beach Creek, W. Va. 4th W. Va. Union 3 killed, 8 wounded. Confed. 1 killed, 11 wounded.
Kirksville, Mo. Mo. State Militia. Union 28 killed, 60 wounded. Confed. 128 killed, 200 wounded.
—Matapony, or Thornburg, Va. Detachment of King's Division. Union 1 killed, 12 wounded, 72 missing.
—Tazewell, Tenn. 16th and 42d Ohio, 14th and 22d Ky., 4th Wis. Battery. Union 3 killed, 23 wounded, 50 missing. Confed. 9 wounded, 40 wounded.
7.—Trenton, Tenn. 2d Ill. Cav. Confed. 30 killed, 20 wounded.
—Fort Fillmore N. Mex. California troops under General Canby.
8.—Panther Creek, Mo. 1st Mo. Militia Cav. Union 1 killed, 4 wounded.
9.—Stockton, Mo. Colonel McNeil's command of Mo. State Militia. Confed. 13 killed, 36 missing.
—Cedar Mountain, Va., also called Slaughter Mountain, Southwest Mountain, Cedar Run and Mitchell's Station. Second Corps, Major-General Banks ; Third Corps, Major-General McDowell. Army of Virginia, under command of Major-General Pope. Union 450 killed, 660 wounded, 290 missing. Confed. 229 killed, 1,047 wounded, 31 missing. Union Brigadier-Generals Augur, Carroll and Geary wounded. Confed. Brigadier-General C. S. Winder killed.
10.—Nueces River, Tex. Texas Loyalists. Union 40 killed. Confed. 8 killed, 14 wounded.
10 to 13.—Grand River, Lee's Ford, Chariton River, Walnut Creek, Compton Creek, Switzler's Mills and Yellow Creek, Mo. 9th Mo. Militia. Union 100 killed and wounded.
11.—Independence, Mo. 7th Militia Cav. Union 14 killed, 18 wounded, 312 missing.
—Helena, Ark. 2d Wis. Cav. Union 1 killed, 2 wounded.
—Wyoming C. H., W. Va. Detachment of 37th Ohio. Union 2 killed.
—Kinderhook, Tenn. Detachments of 3d Ky. and 1st Tenn. Cav. Union 3 killed. Confed. 7 killed.
—Taberville, Ark. 1 Mo. and 3d Wis. Cav.
—Salisbury, Tenn. 11th Ill. Cav.
—Williamsport, Tenn. General Negley's command.
12.—Galatin, Tenn. 2d Ind., 4th and 5th Ky., 1st Pa. Cav. Union 30 killed, 50 wounded, 200 captured. Confed. 6 killed, 18 wounded.
13.—Galatin, Tenn. 13th and 69th Ohio, 11th Mich., drove the Confederates from the town with slight loss.

AUG. 13—Clarendon, Ark. Brigadier-General Hovey's Div. of the 13th Corps. Confed. 700 captured.
 15.—Merriweather's Ferry, Tenn. One Co. 2d Ill. Cav. Union 3 killed, 6 wounded. Confed. 20 killed.
 16.—Lone Jack, Mo. Mo. Militia Cav. Union 60 killed, 100 wounded. Confed. 110 killed and wounded.
 18.—Capture of Rebel steamer Fairplay, near Milliken's Bend, La. 58th and 76th Ohio. Confed. 40 prisoners.
 —Redwood, Minn. One Co. of 5th Minn. massacred by Indians.
 19.—Clarkville, Tenn. 71st Ohio. Union 200 captured.
 —White Oak Ridge, near Hickman, Ky. 2d Ill. Cav. Union 2 wounded. Confed. 4 killed.
 20.—Brandy Station, Va. Cavalry of Army of Virginia Confed. 3 killed, 12 wounded.
 —Edgefield Junction, Tenn. Detachment of 50th Ind. Confed. 8 killed, 18 wounded.
 —Union Mills, Mo. 1st Mo. Cav., 13th Ill. Cav. Union 4 killed, 3 wounded. Confed. 1 killed.
 20 and 22.—Fort Ridgely, Minn. Co's B and C 5th Minn., and Bienville Rangers.
 21.—Pinckney Island, S. C. Union 3 killed, 3 wounded.
 —Kellysford, Va. Cav. Corps.
 22.—Courtland, Tenn. 42d Ill. Union 2 wounded. Confed. 8 killed.
 —Crab Orchard, Ky. 9th Pa. Cav.
 23.—Big Hill, Madison Co., Ky. 3d Tenn., 7th Ky. Cav. Union 10 killed, 40 wounded and missing. Confed. 25 killed.
 —Catlett's Station, Va. Purnell Legion, Md. and 1st Pa.
 23 to 25.—Skirmishes on the Rappahannock at Waterloo Bridge, Lee Springs, Freeman's Ford and Sulphur Springs, Va. Army of Virginia, under Major-General Pope. Confed. 27 killed, 94 wounded. Union Brigadier-General Bowlen killed.
 24.—Dallas, Mo. 12th Mo. Militia Cav. Union 2 killed, 1 wounded.
 24.—Coon Creek or Lamar, Mo. Union 2 killed, 22 wounded.
 25 and 26.—Fort Donelson and Cumberland Iron Works, Tenn. 71st Ohio, 5th Ia. Cav. Union 31 killed and wounded. Confed. 30 killed and wounded.
 —Bloomfield, Mo. 13th Ill. Cav. Confed. 20 killed and wounded.
 26.—Rienzi and Kossuth, Miss. 2d Ia. Cav., 7th Kan. Cav. Union 5 killed, 12 wounded.
 27.—Bull Run Bridge, Va. 11th and 12th Ohio, 1st, 2d, 3d and 4th N. J. Union Brigadier-General G. W. Taylor mortally wounded.
 —Kettle Run, Va. Major-General Hooker's Div. of Third Corps. Union 300 killed and wounded. Confed. 300 killed and wounded.
 28.—Readyville, or Round Hill, Tenn. 10th Brigade Army of Ohio. Union 5 wounded.
 28 and 29.—Groveton and Gainesville, Va. First Corps, Major-General Sigel; Third Corps, Major-General McDowell, Army of Virginia; Hooker's and Kearney's Divisions of Third Corps and Reynold's Div. of First Corps, Army of the Potomac; Ninth Corps, Major-General Reno. Union 7,000 killed, wounded and missing. Confed. 7,000 killed, wounded and missing.
 29.—Manchester, Tenn. Two Co's 10th Ohio, one Co. 9th Mich. Confed. 100 killed and wounded.
 30.—Second Battle of Bull Run, or Manassas, Va. Same troops as engaged at Groveton and Gainesville on the 28th and 29th, with the addition of Porter's Fifth Corps. Union 800 killed, 4,000 wounded, 3,000 missing. Confed. 700 killed, 3,000 wounded.
 —Bolivar, Tenn. 20th and 78th Ohio, 2d and 11th Ill. Cav., 9th Ind. Artil. Union 54 killed, 18 wounded, 64 missing. Confed. 100 killed and wounded.
 —McMinnville, or Little Pond, Tenn. 26th Ohio, 17th and 58th Ind., 8th Ind. Battery. Confed. 1 killed, 20 wounded.
 —Richmond, Ky. 12th, 16th, 55th, 66th, 69th and 71st Ind., 95th Ohio, 18th Ky., 6th and 7th Ky., Cav., Batteries D and G Mich. Artil. Union 200 killed, 700 wounded, 4,000 missing. Confed. 250 killed, 500 wounded.
 31.—Medon Station, Tenn. 45th Ill., 7th Mo. Union 3 killed, 13 wounded, 43 missing.
 —Yates' Ford, Ky. 94th Ohio. Union 3 killed, 10 wounded.

SEPT. 1.—Britton's Lane, Tenn. 20th and 30th Ill., 4th Ill. Cav., Foster's (Ohio) Cav., Battery A 2d Ill. Artil. Union 5 killed, 51 wounded, 52 missing. Confed. 179 killed, 100 wounded.
 —Chantilly, or Ox Hill, Va. McDowell's Corps, Army of Virginia. Hooker's and Kearney's Divisions of Third Corps, Army of Potomac, Reno's Corps. Union 1,300 killed, wounded and missing. Confed. 800 killed, wounded and missing. Union Major-General Kearney and Brigadier-General Stevens killed.
 2.—Vienna, Va. 1st Minn. Union 1 killed, 5 wounded.

SEPT. 2.—Plymouth, N. C.   Co. F 9th N. Y., and 1st N. C.
—3.—Slaughterville, Ky.   Foster's (Ohio) Cav.   Confed. 3 killed, 2 wounded, 25 captured.
—6.—Washington, N. C.   24th Mass., 1st N. C., 3d N. Y. Cav.   Union 8 killed, 36 wounded.   Confed. 30 killed, 100 wounded.
—Beacon Bridge, Va.   1st N. Y. Cav.
—7.—Poolesville, Md.   3 Ind. and 8th Ill. Cav.   Union 2 killed, 6 wounded.   Confed. 3 killed, 6 wounded.
—Clarksville or Rickett's Hill, Tenn.   11th Ill., 13th Wis., 71st Ohio, 5th Ia. Cav. and two Batteries.   No Casualties recorded.
—9.—Columbia Tenn.   42d Ill.   Confed. 18 killed, 45 wounded.
—Des Allemands, La.   21st Ind., 4th Wis.   Confed. 12 killed.
—Nolanville, Md.   3d Ind. and 8th Ill. Cav.
—Williamsburg, Va.   5th Pa. Cav.
—10.—Coldwater, W. Va.   6th Ill. Cav.   Confed. 4 killed, 80 wounded.
—Fayetteville, W. Va.   34th and 37th Ohio, 4th W. Va.   Union 13 killed, 80 wounded.
—Sugar Loaf Mountain, Md.   6th U. S. Cav.
—11.—Cotton Hill, W. Va.   34th and 37th Ohio and 4th W. Va,
—11 to 13.—Bloomfield, Mo.   Battery E and Mo. Artil., 13th Ill., 1st Wis. Cav. and Mo. Militia.
—12.—Charlestown, W. Va.   34th Ohio and 4th W. Va.
—12 to 15.—Harper's Ferry, Va.   39th, 111th, 115th, 125th and 126th N. Y., 12th N. Y. Militia, 32d, 60th and 87th Ohio, 9th Vt., 65th Ill., 15th Ind., 1st and 3d Md. Home Brigade, 8th N. Y. Cav., 12th Ill. Cav., 1st Md. Cav., four Batteries of Artil.   Union 80 killed, 120 wounded, 11.583 missing and captured.   Confed. 500 killed and wounded.
—14.—Ponchelonta, La.   12th Maine, 26th Mass. and 13th Ct.
—Turner's and Crampton's Gap, South Mountain, Md.   First Corps, Major-General Hooker ; Sixth Corps, Major-General Franklin ; Ninth Corps Major-General Reno.   Union 443 killed, 1.806 wounded.   Confed. 500 killed, 2,343 wounded, 1,500 captured.   Union Major-General Reno killed.   Confed. Brigadier-General Garland killed.
—14 to 16.—Mumfordsville, Ky.   18th U. S. Infantry, 28th and 33d Ky., 17th, 50th, 60th, 67th, 68th, 74th, 78th and 89th Ind., Conkle's Battery, 13th Artil. and Louisville Provost Guard.   Union 50 killed, 3,566 captured and missing.   Confed. 714 killed and wounded.
—15.—Boonsboro', Md.   Cav. Army of Potomac.
—17.—Durhamville, Tenn.   Detachment of 52d Ind.   Union 1 killed, 10 wounded.   Confed. 8 killed, 10 wounded.
—Goose Creek and Leesburg Road, Va.   Reconnaisance Kilpatrick's Cav.
—Antietam, or Sharpsburg, Md.   First Corps, Major-General Hooker ; Second Corps, Major-General Sumner ; Fifth Corps, Major-General Fitz-John Porter ; Sixth Corps, Major-General Franklin ; Ninth Corps, Major-General Burnside ; Twelfth Corps, Major-General Williams; Couch's Div., Fourth Corps; Pleasonton's Div. of Cavalry.   Union 2,010 killed, 9,416 wounded, 1,043 missing.   Confed. 3,500 killed, 16,389 wounded, 6,000 missing.   Union Brigadier-General Mansfield killed, Major-Generals Hooker and Richardson and Brigadier-Generals Rodman, Weber, Sedgwick, Hartsuff, Dana and Meagher wounded.   Confed. Brigadier-Generals Branch, Anderson and Starke killed, Major-General Anderson, Brigadier-Generals Toombs, Lawton, Ripley, Rodes, Gregg, Armistead and Ransom wounded.
—19 and 20.—Iuka, Miss.   Stanley's and Hamilton's Divisions, Army of the Mississippi, under Major-General Rosecrans.   Union 144 killed, 598 wounded.   Confed. 263 killed, 692 wounded, 561 captured.   Confed. Brigadier-Generals Little killed and Whitfield wounded.
—20.—Blackford's Ford, Shepherdstown, Va.   Fifth Corps, Griffith's and Barne's Brigades.   Union 92 killed, 131 wounded, 103 missing.   Confed. 33 killed, 231 wounded.
—Williamsport, Md.   Couch's Div.
—22.—Ashby's Gap, Va.   2d Pa. and 1st W. Va. Cav.
—26.—Warrenton Junction, Va.   Cavalry under Colonel McLean.
—27.—Buffalo, W. Va.   34th Ohio.
—28.—Blackwater, Va.   1st N. Y. Mounted Rifles.
—30.—Newtonia, Mo.   1st Brigade Army of Kansas, 4th Brigade Mo. Militia Cav.   Union 50 killed, 80 wounded, 150 missing.   Confed. 220 killed, 280 wounded.

OCT 1.—Floyd's Fork, Ky.   34th Ill., 77th Pa., 4th Ind. Cav.   No casualties recorded.
—Shepherdstown, Va.   8th Ill., 7th Pa., 3d Ind. Cav., Pennington's Battery.   Union 12 wounded.   Confed. 60 killed.

OCT. 3 and 4.—Corinth, Miss. McKean's, Davies', Hamilton's and Stanley's Division, Army of the Miss. Union 315 killed, 1,812 wounded, 232 missing. Confed. 1,423 killed, 5,692 wounded, 2,248 missing. Union Brigadier-Generals Hackleman killed and Oglesby wounded.

 5.—Metamora, on Big Hatchie River, Miss. Hurlburt's and Ord's Divisions. Union 500 killed and wounded. Confed. 400 killed and wounded.

 6.—Charleston, Va. 6th U. S. Cav.

 7.—La Vergne, Tenn. Palmer's Brigade, Union 5 killed, 9 wounded. Confed. 80 killed and wounded, 175 missing.

 8.—Perryville, Ky. First Corps, Army of the Ohio, Major-General McCook, and Third Corps, Brigadier General Gilbert. Union 916 killed, 2,943 wounded, 489 missing. Confed. 2,500 killed, wounded and missing. Union Brigadier-Generals J. S. Jackson and Terrill killed. Confed. Brigadier-Generals Cleburne, Wood and Brown wounded.

—Lawrenceburg, or Dogwalk, Ky. 15th and 19th U. S. Infantry, 1st and 49th Ohio, Battery H 5th U. S. Artil. and 9th Ky. Cav.

 10.—Harrodsburg, Ky. Union troops, commanded by Lieutenant-Colonel Boyle, 9th Ky. Cav. Confed. 1,000 captured.

 11.—La Grange, Ark. Detachment 4th Ia. Cav. Union 4 killed, 13 wounded.

—Cape Fear River, N. C. U. S. Gunboat Maratanza.

Mouth of Monocacy, Md. 3d and 4th Me.

 15.—Darnsville, Va. 7th Pa. Cav.

 17.—Lexington, Ky. Detachment 3d and 4th Ohio Cav. Union 4 killed, 24 wounded, 350 missing.

 19.—Haymarket, Va. Detachment 6th Ia. Cav. Union 1 killed, 6 wounded, 23 captured.

 22.—Pocotaligo, or Yemassee, S. C. 47th, 55th and 76th Pa., 48th N. Y., 5th and 7th Ct., 3d and 4th N. H., 3d R. I., 1st N. Y. Engineers, 1st Mass. Cav., Batteries D and M 1st U. S. Artil. and E 3d U. S. Artil. Union 43 killed, 258 wounded. Confed. 14 killed, 102 wounded.

 23.—Waverly, Tenn. 83d Ill. Union 1 killed, 2 wounded. Confed. 40 killed and wounded.

 24.—Grand Prarie, Mo. Two Battalions Mo. Militia Cav. Union 3 wounded. Confed. 8 killed, 20 wounded.

—Blackwater, Va. 1st N. Y. Mounted Rifles, 39th Ill., 62d Ohio and other troops under General Terry.

 27.—Pittman's Ferry, Mo. 23d Ia., 24th and 25th Wis., 1st Mo. Militia, 12th Mo. Cav.

—Labadieville, or Thebodeauxville, or Georgia Landing, La. 8th N. H., 12th and 13th Ct., 75th N. Y., 1st La. Cav. and 1st Me. Battery.

 28.—Clarkson, Mo. Detachment 2d Ill. Artil. Confed. 10 killed, 2 wounded.

 31.—Aldie, Va. 1st N. J. Cav., 2d N. Y. Cav.

NOV. 1.—Philomont, Va. Pleasonton's Cav. Union 1 killed, 14 wounded. Confed. 5 killed, 10 wounded.

 2 and 3.—Bloomfield and Union, London Co., Va. Pleasonton's Cav. Union 2 killed, 10 wounded. Confed. 3 killed, 15 wounded.

 3.—Harrisonville, Mo. 5th and 6th Mo. Cav. Union 10 killed, 3 wounded. Confed. 6 killed, 20 wounded.

—Rawle's Mills and Little Creek, Williamstown, N. C. 24th and 44th Mass. and 9th N. J.

—Bayou Teche, Gunboats Kinsman, Estrella, St. Mary, Calhoun, Diana and 21st Ind.

 5.—Barbee's Cross Roads and Chester Gap, Va. Pleasonton's Cav. Union 5 killed, 10 wounded. Confed. 30 killed.

—Nashville, Tenn. 16th and 51st Ill., 69th Ohio, 14th Mich, 78th Pa., 5th Tenn. Cav., 7th Pa. Cav. Union 26 wounded. Confed. 25 captured.

 6.—Garrettsburg, Ky. 8th Ky. Cav. Confed. 17 killed, 85 wounded.

 7.—Big Beaver Creek, Mo. 10th Ill., two Co's Mo. Militia Cav. Union 300 captured.

—Marianna, or La Grange, Ark. 3d and 4th Ia., 9th Ill. Cav. Union 3 killed, 20 wounded. Confed. 50 killed and wounded.

 8.—Hudsonville, or Coldwater, Miss. 7th Kan. Cav., 2d Ia. Cav. Confed. 10 killed, 185 captured.

 17.—Gloucester, Va. 104th Pa. Union 1 killed, 3 wounded.

 18. Rural Hills, Tenn. 8th Ky. Cav. Confed. 16 killed.

 24. Beaver Creek, Mo. 21st Ia., 3d Mo. Cav. Union 6 killed, 10 wounded. Confed. 5 killed, 20 wounded.

 26.—Summerville, Miss. 7th Ill. Cav. Confed. 28 captured.

 28.—Cane Hill, Boston Mountain, and Boonsboro', Ark. 1st Div. Army of the Frontier. Union 4 killed, 36 wounded. Confed. 75 killed, 300 wounded.

—Hartwood Church, Va. 3d Pa. Cav. Union 4 killed, 9 wounded, 200 missing.

DEC. 1.—Charleston and Berryville, Va. 2d Div. 12 Corps. Confed. 5 killed, 18 wounded.

5.—Coffeeville, Miss. 1st, 2d and 3d Cav. Brigades, Army of the Tennessee. Union 10 killed, 54 wounded. Confed. 7 killed, 43 wounded.
—Helena, Ark. 30th Ia. 29th Wis. Confed. 8 killed.

7.—Prairie Grove, or Fayetteville, Ark. 1st, 2d and 3d Divisions Army of the Frontier. Union 167 killed, 798 wounded, 183 missing. Confed. 300 killed, 1,200 wounded and missing.
—Hartsville, Tenn. 106th and 108th Ohio, 104th Ill., 2d Ind. Cav., 11 Ky. Cav., 13th Ind. Battery. Union 55 killed, 1,800 captured. Confed. 21 killed, 114 wounded.

9.—Dobbin's Ferry, Tenn. 33d Ind., 51st Ohio, 8th and 21st Ky., 7th Ind. Battery. Union 5 killed, 48 wounded.

12.—Little Bear Creek, Ala. 52d Ill. Union 1 killed, 2 wounded. Confed. 11 killed, 30 wounded.

12 to 18.—Foster's expedition to Goldsboro', N. C. 1st, 2d and 3d Brigades of First Division and Wessell's Brigade of Peck's Division, Dept of North Carolina. Union 90 killed, 487 wounded. Confed. 71 killed, 268 wounded. 400 missing.

13.—Fredericksburg, Va. Army of the Potomac, Major-General Burnside ; Second Corps, Major-General Couch ; Ninth Corps, Major-General Wilcox ; Right Grand Div., Major-General Sumner ; First Corps, Major-General Reynolds ; Sixth Corps, Major-General W. F. Smith. Left Grand Div., Major-General Franklin ; Fifth Corps, Major-General Buttterfield ; Third Corps, Major-General Stoneman. Centre Grand Div., Major-General Hooker. Union 1,180 killed, 9,028 wounded, 2,145 missing. Confed. 579 killed, 3,870 wounded, 127 missing. Union Brigadier-Generals Jackson and Bayard killed and Gibbons and Vinton wounded. Confed. Brigadier-Generals T. R. R. Cobb killed and Maxey Gregg wounded.

14.—Kingston, N. C. 1st, 2d and 3d Brigade First Div. and Wessell's Brigade of Peck's Division, Depart. of North Carolina. Union 40 killed, 120 wounded. Confed. 50 killed, 75 wounded, 400 missing.

18.—Lexington, Tenn. 11th Ill. Cav., 5th Ohio Cav., 2d Tenn. Cav. Union 7 killed, 10 wounded, 124 missing. Confed. 7 killed, 28 wounded.

20.—Holly Springs, Miss. 2d Ill. Cav. Union 1,000 captured.
—Trenton, Tenn. Detachments 122d Ill. 7th Tenn. Cav. and convalescents. Union 1 killed, 250 prisoners. Conted. 17 killed, 50 wounded.

21.—Davis' Mills, Miss. Six Co's 25th Ind., two Co's 5th Ohio Cav. Union 3 wounded. Confed. 22 killed, 50 wounded, 20 missing.

24.—Middleburg, Miss. 115 men of 12th Mich. Union 9 wounded. Confed. 9 killed, 11 wounded.
—Glasgow, Ky. Five Co's 2d Mich. Cav. Union 1 killed, 1 wounded. Confed. 3 killed, 3 wounded.

25.—Green Chapel, Ky. Detachment of 4th and 5th Ind. Cav. Union 1 killed. Confed. 9 killed, 22 wounded.

26.—Bacon Creek, Ky. Detachment of 2d Mich. Cav. Union 23 wounded.

27.—Elizabethtown, Ky. 91st Ill., 500 men captured by Morgan.
—Dumfries, Va. 5th, 7th and 66th Ohio, 12th Ill Cav., 1st Md. Cav., 6th Me. Battery. Union 3 killed, 8 wounded. Confed. 25 killed, 40 wounded.

28.—Elk Fort, Tenn. 6th and 10th Ky. Cav. Confed. 30 killed, 176 wounded, 51 missing.

28 and 29.—Chickasaw Bayou, Vicksburg, Miss. Army of Tennessee, Major-General W. T. Sherman—Brigadier-Generals G. W. Morgan's, Frederick Steele's, M. L. Smith's and A. J. Smith's divisions of the right wing. Union 191 killed, 982 wounded, 756 missing. Confed. 207 wounded. Union Major-General M. L. Smith wounded.

30.—Wautauga Bridge and Carter's Station, Tenn. 7th Ohio Cav., 9th Pa. Cav. Union 1 killed, 2 wounded. Confed. 7 killed, 15 wounded, 273 missing.
—Jefferson, Tenn. Second Brigade 1st Division Thomas' Corps. Union 20 killed, 40 wounded. Confed. 15 killed, 50 wounded.
—Parker's Cross Roads, or Red Mound, Tenn. 18th, 106th, 110th and 122d Ill., 27th, 39th and 63d Ohio, 50th Ind., 39th Ia., 7th Tenn., 7th Wis. Battery. Union 23 killed, 139 wounded, 58 missing. Confed. 50 killed, 150 wounded, 300 missing.

31 to Jan. 2.—Murfreesboro', or Stone River, Tenn. Army of the Cumberland, Major-General Rosecrans. Right Wing, McCook's Corps ; Centre, Thomas' Corps ; Left Wing, Crittenden's Corps. Union 1,533 killed, 7,245 wounded, 2,800 missing. Confed. 14,560 killed, wounded and missing. Union Brigadier-Generals Sill killed and Kirk wounded. Confed. Brigadier-Generals Raines and Hanson killed, and Chalmers and Davis wounded.

1863.

JAN. 1.—Galveston, Tex. Three Co's 42d Mass., U. S. Gunboats Westfield, Harriett Lane, Owasco, Sachem, Clifton and Coryphæus. Union 600 killed, wounded and missing. Confed. 50 killed and wounded.
    7 and 8.—Springfield, Mo. Mo. Militia, convalescents and citizens. Union 14 killed, 144 wounded. Confed. 40 killed, 200 wounded and missing. Union Brigadier-General Brown wounded.
    11.—Fort Hindman, Ark. Thirteenth Corps, Major-General McClernand; Fifteenth Corps, Major-General Sherman and gunboats Mississippi squadron. Union 129 killed, 831 wounded. Confed. 100 killed, 400 wounded, 5,000 prisoners.
    —Hartsville, or Wood's Fork, Mo. 21st Ia., 99th Ill., 3d Ia. Cav., 3d Mo. Cav., Battery L 2d Mo. Artil. Union 7 killed, 64 wounded. Confed. 300 killed and wounded. Confed. Brigadier-General McDonald killed.
    14.—Bayou Teche, La. 8th Vt., 16th and 75th N. Y., 12th Ct., 6th Mich., 21st Ind., 1st La. Cav., 4th and 6th Mass. Battery, 1st Maine Battery and U. S. Gunboats Calhoun, Diana, Kinsman and Estrella. Union 10 killed, 27 wounded. Confed. 15 killed. Union Commodore Buchanan killed. Confed. Gunboat Cotton destroyed.
    24—Woodbury, Tenn. Second Division Crittenden's Corps. Union 2 killed, 1 wounded. Confed. 35 killed, 100 missing.
    30.—Deserted House, or Kelly's Store, near Suffolk, Va. Portion of Major-General Peck's forces. Union 24 killed, 80 wounded. Confed. 50 wounded.
    31.—Rover, Tenn. 4th Ohio Cav. Confed. 12 killed, 12 wounded, 300 captured.

FEB. 3.—Fort Donnelson, or Cumberland Iron Works, Tenn. 83d Ill., 2d Ill. Artil., one Battalion 5th Ia. Cav. Union 16 killed, 60 wounded, 50 missing. Confed. 140 killed, 400 wounded, 130 missing.
    14.—Brentville, Va. 1st Mich. Cav. Union 15 wounded.
    16.—Near Romney, W. Va. Detachments 116th and 122d Ohio. Union 72 wounded and captured.
    21.—Prairie Station, Miss. 2d Ia. Cav. Union 1 killed, 3 wounded
    24.—Mississippi River below Vicksburg. U. S. Gunboat Indianola. Union 1 killed, 1 wounded. Confed. 35 killed.

MAR. 1.—Bradyville, Tenn. 3d and 4th Ohio Cav., 1st Tenn. Cav. Union 1 killed, 6 wounded. Confed. 5 killed, 25 wounded, 100 captured.
    4.—Skeet, N. C. 3d N. Y. Cav. Union 3 killed, 15 wounded. Confed. 28 wounded.
    4 and 5.—Thompson's Station, also called Spring Hill and Unionville, Tenn. 33d and 85th Ind., 22d Wis., 19th Mich., 124th Ohio, 18th Ohio Battery, 2d Mich. Cav., 9th Pa. Cav., 4th Ky. Cav. Union 100 killed, 300 wounded, 1,306 captured. Confed. 150 killed, 450 wounded.
    8—Fairfax C. H., Va. Brigadier-General Stoughton and 33 men captured by Mosby in his midnight raid.
    10.—Covington, Tenn. 6th and 7th Ill. Cav. Confed. 25 killed.
    13 to April 5.—Fort Pemberton. Miss. Thirteenth Corps, Brigadier-General Ross; Seventeenth Corps, Brigadier-General Quimby, U. S. Gunboats Chillicothe and DeKalb. Casualties not recorded.
    14.—Port Hudson, La. Major-General Banks' troops and Admiral Farragut's fleet. Union 65 wounded.
    16 to 22.—Expedition up Steele's Bayou and Deer Creek, Miss. 2d Div. Fifteenth Corps, Major-General Sherman, gunboat fleet, Admiral Porter. Casualties not recorded.
    17.—Kelly's Ford, Va. 1st and 5th U. S. Regulars, 3d, 4th and 16th Pa., 1st R. I., 6th Ohio, 4th N. Y. Cav., 5th U. S. Battery. Union 9 killed, 35 wounded. Confed. 11 killed, 88 wounded.
    20.—Vaught's Hill, near Milton, Tenn. 105th Ohio, 101st Ind., 80th and 123d Ill., 1st Tenn. Cav., 9th Ind. Battery. Union 7 killed, 48 wounded. Confed. 63 killed, 300 wounded.
    23.—Mt. Sterling, Ky. 10th Ky. Cav. Union 4 killed, 10 wounded. Confed. 8 killed, 13 wounded.
    24.—Danville, Ky. 18th and 22d Mich., 1st Ky. Cav., 2d Tenn. Cav., 1st Ind. Battery.
    —Ponchatoula, La. 127th and 165th N. Y., 9th Ct., 14th and 24th Maine, 6th Mich. Union 6 wounded. Confed. 3 killed, 11 wounded.
    25.—Brentwood, Tenn. Detachment 22d Wis. and 19th Mich. Union 1 killed, 4 wounded, 300 prisoners. Confed. 1 killed, 5 wounded.
    —Franklin and Little Harpeth, Tenn. 4th and 6th Ky. Cav., 9th Pa. Cav., 2d Mich. Cav. Union 4 killed, 19 wounded, 40 missing.
    28—Pattersonville, La. Gunboat Diana, with Detachment of 12th Ct. and 106th N. Y. on board. Union 4 killed, 14 wounded, 90 missing.
    29.—Somerville, Tenn. 6th Ill. Cav. Union 9 killed, 20 wounded.

MAR. 30.—Dutton's Hill, or Somerset, Ky. 1st Ky. Cav., 7th Ohio Cav., 44th and 45th Ohio Mounted. Union 10 killed, 25 wounded. Confed. 290 killled, wounded and missing.
—Point Pleasant, W. Va. One Co. 13th W. Va. Union 1 killed, 3 wounded. Confed. 20 killed, 25 wounded,
30 to April 4.—Washington and Rodman's Point, N. C. Major-General Foster's Command.

APRIL 2 and 3.—Woodbury and Snow Hill, Tenn. 3d and 4th Ohio Cav. Union 1 killed, 8 wounded. Confed. 50 killed and wounded.
7.—Bombardment of Fort Sumter, S. C. South Atlantic squadron ; Keokuk, Weehawken, Passaic, Rontauk, Patapsco, New Ironsides, Catskill, Nantucket and Nahant. Union 2 killed, 20 wounded. Confed. 4 killed, 10 wounded.
10.—Franklin and Harpeth River, Tenn. 40th Ohio and portion of Granger's Cav. Union 100 killed and wounded. Confed. 19 killed, 35 wounded, 83 missing.
—Antioch, Tenn. Detachment 10th Mich. Union 8 killed, 12 wounded.
12 to 14.—Irish Bend and Bisland, La., also called Indian Ridge and Centreville. Nineteenth Corps, Grover's, Emory's and Weitzel's Divisions. Union 350 killed, wounded and missing. Confed. 400 wounded, 200 missing and captured.
12 to May 4.—Seige of Suffolk, Va. Troops, Army of Virginia and Department of North Carolina. Union 44 killed, 202 wounded. Confed. 500 killed and wounded, 400 captured.
15.—Dunbar's Plantation, La. 2d. Ill Cav. Union 1 killed, 2 wounded.
17 to May 2.—Grierson's expedition from Le Grange, Tenn., to Baton Rouge, La. 6th and 7th Ill. Cav., 2d Ia. Cav. Confed. 100 killed and wounded, 500 prisoners.
18 and 19.—Hernando and Coldwater, Miss. Portion of Sixteenth Corps, detachment of Artil., 2d Brigade Cav. Div. Casualties not recorded.
20.—Patterson, Mo. 3d Mo. Militia Cav. Union 12 killed, 7 wounded, 41 missing.
24.—Tuscumbia, Ala. Sixteenth Corps, 2d Div., Major-General Dodge.
—White Water, Mo. 1st Wis. Cav. Union 2 killed, 6 wounded.
26.—Cape Girardeau, Mo. 32d Ia., 1st Wis. Cav., 2d Mo. Cav., Batteries D and L 1st Mo. Light Artil. Union 6 killed, 6 wounded. Confed. 60 killed, 275 wounded and missing.
27 to May 3. Streight's Raid, Tuscumbia, Ala., to Rome, Ga., including skirmishes at Day's Gap, April 30. Black Warrior Creek, May 1st and Blount's Farm May 2d. 3d Ohio, 51st and 73d Ind , 80th Ill., Mounted Infantry, two Co's 1st Ala. Cav. Union 12 killed, 69 wounded, 1,466 missing and captured.
27 to May 8.—Stoneman's Cavalry Raid in Virginia.
29.—Fairmont, W. Va. Detachments 106th N. Y., 6th W. Va. and Va. Militia. Union 1 killed, 6 wounded. Confed. 100 killed and wounded.
—Grand Gulf, Miss. Gunboat fleet. Union 26 killed, 54 wounded.
30.—Spottsylvania C. H., Va. 6th N. Y. Cav. Union 58 killed and wounded.
30 and May 1.—Chalk Bluff and St. Francois River, Mo. 2d Mo. Militia, 3d Mo. Cav., 1st Ia. Cav., Battery E 1st Mo. Light Artil. Union 2 killed, 11 wounded.

MAY 1.— Port Gibson, Miss. (the first engagement in Grant's Campaign against Vicksburg). Thirteenth Corps, Major-General McClernand and 3d Div. Seventeenth Corps, Major-General McPherson. Union 130 killed, 718 wounded. Confed. 1,150 killed and wounded, 500 missing. Confed. Brigadier-General Tracy killed.
1.—La Grange, Ark. 3d Ia. Cav. Union 3 killed, 9 wounded, 30 missing.
—Monticello, Ky. 2d Tenn. Cav., 1st Ky. Cav., 2d and 7th Ohio Cav., 45th Ohio and 112th Ill. Mounted Infantry.
1 to 4.—Chancellorsville, Va., including battles of Sixth Corps at Fredericksburg and Salem Heights. Army of the Potomoc, Major-General Hooker; First Corps, Major-General Reynolds , Second Corps, Major-General Couch ; Third Corps, Major-General Sickles, Fifth Corps, Major-General Meade ; Sixth Corps, Major-General Sedgwick; Eleventh Corps, Major-General Howard; Twelfth Corps, Major-General Slocum. Union 1,512 killed, 9,518 wounded, 5,000 missing. Confed. 1,581 killed, 8,700 wounded, 2,000 missing. Union Major-General Berry and Brigadier-General Whipple killed, Devan and Kirby wounded. Confed. Brigadier-General Paxton killed, Lieutenant-General J. S. Jackson, Major-General A. P. Hill, Brigadier-Generals Hoke, Nichols, Ramseur, McGown, Heth and Pender wounded.
3.—Warrenton Junction, Va. 1st W. Va. Cav., 5th N. Y. Cav. Union 1 killed, 16 wounded. Confed. 15 wounded.
11.—Horseshoe Bend, Ky. Detachment Commanded by Colonel R. T. Jacobs. Union 10 killed, 20 wounded, 40 missing. Confed. 100 killed, wounded and missing.
12.—Raymond, Miss. Seventeenth Corps, Major-General McPherson. Union 69 killed, 341 wounded. Confed. 969 killed and wounded. Confed. General Telghman killed.
13.—Hall's Ferry. 2d Ill. Cav. Confed. 12 killed.

MAY 14.—Jackson, Miss. Fifteenth Corps, Major-General Sherman ; Seventeenth Corps, Major-General McPherson. Union 40 killed, 240 wounded. Confed. 450 killed and wounded.
16.—Champion Hills, Miss. Hovey's Div. Thirteenth Corps and Seventeenth Corps. Union 426 killed, 1,842 wounded, 189 missing. Confed. 2,500 killed and wounded, 1,800 missing.
17.—Big Black River, Miss. Carr's and Osterhaus's Division Thirteenth Corps. Major-General McClernand. Union 29 killed, 242 wounded. Confed. 600 killed and wounded, 2,500 captured.
18 to July 4.—Siege of Vicksburg. Thirteenth Corps, Fifteenth Corps and Seventeenth Corps, commanded by Major-General U. S. Grant, and gunboat fleet, commanded by Admiral Porter. Assault on Fort Hill on May 19th and general assault on the 20th, in which Confed. Brigadier-General Green was killed. Three Divisions of the Sixteenth Corps, and two Divisions of the Ninth Corps, and Major-General Herron's Division were then added to the besieging forces. Union 545 killed, 3,688 wounded, 303 missing. Confed. 31,277 killed, wounded and prisoners.
20 to 28.—Clendenin's raid, below Fredericksburg, Va. 8th Ill. Cav. Confed. 100 prisoners.
21.—Middleton, Tenn. 4th Mich., 3d Ind., 7th Pa., 3d and 4th Ohio and 4th U. S. Cav., 39th Ind. Mounted Infantry. Casualties not recorded.
25.—Near Helena, or Polk's Plantation, Ark. 3d Ia. and 5th Kan. Cav. Union 10 killed, 14 wounded.
27.—Lake Providence, La. 47th U. S. Colored. Union 1 killed, 1 wounded.
27 to July 9.—Siege of Port Hudson, La. Union 500 killed, 2,500 wounded. Confed. 100 killed, 700 wounded, 6,408 prisoners. Union Brigadier-Generals W. T. Sherman and H. E. Paine wounded.

JUNE 4.—Franklin, Tenn. 85th Ind., 7th Ky. Cav., 4th and 6th Ky. Cav., 9th Pa. Cav., 2 Mich. Cav. Union 25 killed and wounded. Confed. 200 killed and wounded.
5.—Franklin's Crossing, Rappahannock River, Va. 26th N. J., 5th Vt., 15th and 50th N. Y. Engineers, supported by 6th Corps. Union 6 killed, 35 wounded.
6 to 8.—Milliken's Bend, or Ashland, Wis. 23d Ia. and three regiments colored troops. (No quarter shown.) Union 154 killed, 223 wounded, 115 missing. Confed. 125 killed, 400 wounded, 200 missing.
9.—Monticello and Rocky Gap, Ky. 2d and 7th Ohio Cav., 1st Ky. Cav., 45th Ohio and 2d Tenn. Mounted Infantry. Union 4 killed, 26 wounded, Confed. 20 killed, 80 wounded.
—Beverly Ford and Brandy Station, Va. 2d, 3d and 7th Wis., 2d and 33d Mass., 6th Maine, 86th and 104th N. Y., 1st, 2d, 5th and 6th U. S. Cav., 3d, 6th, 8th, 9th and 10th N. Y. Cav. 1st, 6th and 17th Pa. Cav., 1st Md., 8th Ill., 3d Ind., 1st N. J., 1st Cav. and 3d W. Va. Cav. Union 500 killed, wounded and missing. Confed. 700 killed, wounded and missing.
11.—Middleton, Va. 87th Pa., 13th Pa. Cav., Battery L, 5th U. S. Artil. Confed. 8 killed, 42 wounded.
13 and 15.—Winchester, Va. 2d, 67th and 87th Pa., 18th Ct., 12th W. Va., 110th, 116th, 122d and 123d Ohio, 3d, 5th and 6th Md., 12th and 13th Pa. Cav., 1st N. Y. Cav., 1st and 3d W. Va. Cav., Battery L, 5th U. S. Artil., 1st W. Va. Battery, Baltimore Battery, one Co. 14th Mass. Heavy Artil. Union 3,000 killed, wounded and missing. Confed. 850 killed, wounded and missing.
14.—Martinsburg, Va. 106th N. Y., 126th Ohio, W. Va. Battery. Union 200 missing. Confed. 1 killed, 2 wounded.
16.—Triplett's Bridge, Ky. 15th Mich., 10th and 14th Ky. Cav., 7th and 9th Mich. Cav., 11th Mich. Battery. Union 15 killed; 18 wounded.
17.—Aldie, Va. Kilpatrick's Cav. Union 24 killed, 41 wounded, 89 missing. Confed. 100 wounded.
—Westport, Mo. Two Co's 9th Kan. Union 14 killed, 6 wounded.
—Capture of Rebel Gunboat Atlanta by U. S. ironclad Weehawken. Confed. 1 killed, 17 wounded, 145 captured.
20.—Rocky Crossing, Miss. 5th Ohio Cav., 9th Ill. Mounted Infantry. Union 7 killed, 28 wounded, 30 missing.
20 and 21.—La Fourche Crossing, La. Detachments 23d Ct., 176th N. Y., 26th, 42d 47th Mass., 21st Ind. Union 8 killed, 40 wounded. Confed. 53 killed, 150 wounded.
21.—Upperville, Va. Pleasonton's Cavalry. Union 94 wounded. Confed. 20 killed, 100 wounded, 60 missing.
22.—Hill's Plantation, Miss. Detachment of 4th Ia. Cav. Union 4 killed, 10 wounded, 28 missing.
23.—Brashear City, La. Detachments of 114th and 176th N. Y., 23d Ct., 42d Mass., 21st Ind. Union 46 killed, 40 wounded, 300 missing. Confed. 3 killed, 18 wounded.
23 to 30.—Rosecran's Campaign. Murfreesboro' to Tullahoma, Tenn., including Middleton, Hoover's Gap, Beech Grove, Liberty Gap and Gray's Gap. Army of the

Cumberland: Fourteenth, Twentieth and Twenty-first Corps, Granger's Reserve Corps and Stanley's Cav. Union 85 killed, 462 wounded. Confed. 1,634 killed, wounded and captured.

JUNE 28.—Donaldsonville, La. 28th Maine and convalescents, assisted by gunboats. Confed. 39 killed, 112 wounded, 150 missing.

29.—Westminster, Md. Detachment 1st Del. Cav. Union 2 killed, 7 wounded. Confed 3 killed, 15 wounded.

30.—Hanover, Pa. Cav. Corps. Union 12 killed, 43 wounded. Confed. 75 wounded, 60 missing.

JULY 1 to 3.—Gettysburg. Pa. Army of the Potomac, Major-General George G. Meade; First Corps, Major-General Reynolds; Second Corps, Major-General Hancock; Third Corps, Major-General Sickles; Sixth Corps, Major-General Sedgwick; Eleventh Corps, Major-General Howard; Twelfth Corps, Major-General Slocum; Cavalry Corps, Major-General Pleasonton. Union 2,834 killed, 13,709 wounded, 6,643 missing. Confed. 3,500 killed, 14,500 wounded, 13,621 missing. Union Major-General Reynolds, Brigadier-Generals Weed, Zook and Farnsworth killed, Major-Generals Sickles and Hancock, Brigadier-Generals Paul, Rowley, Gibbons and Barlow wounded. (General Lucius Fairchild, Commander-in-Chief Grand Army of the Republic, lost his arm on the first day.) Confed. Major-General Pender, Brigadier-Generals Garnett, Barksdale and Semmes killed, Major-Generals Hood, Trimble and Heth, Brigadier-Generals Kemper, Scales, Anderson, Hampton, Jones, Jenkins, Pettigrew and Posey wounded.

1 to 26.—Morgan's raid into Kentucky, Indiana and Ohio finally captured at New Lisbon, Ohio by Brigadier-General Shackleford's Cavalry. Union 22 killed, 80 wounded, 700 missing. Confed. 86 killed, 385 wounded, 3,000 captured.

4.—Helena, Ark. Major-General Prentiss' Division of Sixteenth Corps and Gunboat Tyler. Union 57 killed, 117 wounded, 32 missing. Confed. 173 killed, 687 wounded, 776 missing.

4 and 5.—Bolton and Birdsong Ferry, Miss. Major-General Sherman's forces. Confed. 2,000 captured.

4 and 5.—Montery Gap and Smithsburg, Md., and Fairfield, Pa. Kilpatrick's Cav. Union 30 killed and wounded. Confed. 30 killed and wounded, 100 prisoners.

5.—Lebanon, Ky. 20th Ky. Union 9 killed, 15 wounded, 400 missing. Confed. 3 killed, 6 wounded.

—.Quaker's Bridge, N. C. 17th, 23d and 27th Mass., 9th N. J., 81st and 158th N. Y., Belger's and Angel's Batteries.

—Hagerstown and Williamsport, Md. Kilpatrick's Cav.

7 and 9.—Iuka, Miss. 10th Mo. and 7th Kan. Cav. Union 5 killed, 3 wounded.

7 to 9.—Boonsboro, Md. Buford's and Kilpatrick's Cavalry. Union 9 killed, 45 wounded.

9 to 16.—Jackson, Miss., including engagements at Rienzi, Bolton Depot, Canton and Clinton. 9th, 13th, 15th and part of the 16th Corps. Union 100 killed, 800 wounded, 100 missing. Confed. 71 killed, 504 wounded, 764 missing.

20 to Sept. 6.—Siege of Fort Wagner, Morris Island, S. C. Troops Department of the South, under command of Major-General Gilmore and U. S. Navy, under Admiral Dahlgreen. Union 1,757 killed, wounded and missing. Confed. 561 killed, wounded and missing.

12.—Ashby Gap, Va. 2d Mass. Cav. Union 2 killed, 8 wounded.

13.—Yazoo City, Miss. Major-General Herron's Division and three gunboats. Confed. 250 captured.

—Jackson, Tenn. 9th Ill., 3d Mich. Cav., 2d Ia. Cav. and 1st Tenn. Cav. Union 2 killed, 20 wounded. Confed. 38 killed, 150 wounded.

—Donaldsonville, La. Portions of Weitzel's and Grover's Divisions, Nineteenth Corps. Union 450 killed, wounded and missing.

13 to 15.—Draft riots in New York City, in which over 1,000 rioters were killed.

14.—Falling Waters, Md. 3d Cav. Division Army of the Potomac. Union 20 killed, 30 wounded. Confed. 125 killed and wounded, 1,500 prisoners. Confed. Major-General Pettigrew killed.

14.—Elk River, Tenn. Advance of the Fourteenth Corps Army of the Cumberland. Union 10 killed, 30 wounded. Confed. 60 killed, 24 wounded, 100 missing.

—Near Bolivar Heights, Va. 1st Ct. Cav. Confed. 25 killed.

15.—Pulaski, Ala. 3d Ohio and 5th Tenn. Cav. Confed. 3 killed, 50 missing.

—Halltown, Va. 16th Pa. and 1st Maine Cav. Union 55 killed and wounded. Confed. 20 killed and wounded.

16.—Sheppardstown, Va. 1st, 4th and 16th Pa., 10th N. Y. and 1st Maine Cav. Confed. 25 killed, 75 wounded.

17.—Honey Springs, Ind. Ter. 2d, 6th and 9th Kan' Cav., 2d and 3d Kan. Batteries, 2d and 3d Kan. Indian Home Guards. Union 17 killed, 60 wounded. Confed. 150 killed, 400 wounded.

JULY 17.—Wytheville, W. Va.   34th Ohio, 1st and 2d W. Va. Cav.   Union 17 killed, 61 wounded.   Confed. 75 killed, 125 missing.
—Canton, Miss.   76th Ohio, 25th and 31st Ia., 3d, 13th and 17th Mo., 2d Wis., 5th Ill. Cav., 3d and 4th Ia. Cav., one battery of artillery.   Casualties not recorded.
18 to 21.—Potter's Cav. Raid to Tar River and Rocky Mount, N. C.   3d and 12th N. Y. Cav., 1st N. C. Cav.   Union 60 wounded.
1 to 26.—Morgan's Raid into Kentucky, Indiana and Ohio pursued and captured by Brigadier-General Hobson's and Shackleford's Cav., including skirmishes at Burkesville, Columbia, Green River Bridge, Lebanon and Bradenbug, Ky., Corydon and Vernon, Ind., capture of the larger part of Buffington Island, Ohio, and final capture at New Lisbon, Ohio, on the 26th.   Union 83 killed, 97 wounded, 805 missing.   Confed. 765 killed and wounded, 4,104 captured.
21 to 23.—Manassas Gap and Chester Gap, Va.   Cavalry advance and Third Corps, Army of the Potomac.   Union 35 killed, 102 wounded.   Confed. 300 killed and wounded.
26.—Pattacassey Creek, N. C.   Brigadier-General Heckman's Troops.   Union 3 killed, 17 wounded.
30.—Irvine, Ky.   14th Ky. Cav.   Union 4 killed, 5 wounded.   Confed. 7 killed, 18 wounded.

AUG. 1 to 3.—Rappahannock Station, Brandy Station and Kelly's Ford, Va.   Brigadier-General Buford's Cav.   Union 16 killed, 134 wounded.
3.—Jackson, La. 73d, 75th and 78th U. S. Colored Troops.   Union 2 killed, 2 wounded, 27 missing.
5.—Dutch Gap, James River, Va.   U. S. Gunboats Commodore, Barney and Cohassett.   Union 3 killed, 1 wounded.
7.—New Madrid, Mo.   One Co. 24th Mo.   Union 1 killed, 1 wounded.
9.—Sparta, Tenn.   Cavalry Army of the Cumberland.   Union 6 killed, 25 wounded.
13.—Grenada, Miss.   9th Ill., 2d Ia. Cav., 3d Mich. Cav., 3d, 4th 9th and 11th Cav. Casualties not recorded.
—Pineville, Mo.   6th Mo. Militia Cav.   Confed. 65 wounded.
14.—West Point, White River, Ark.   32d Ohio, with Gunboats U. S. Lexington, Cricket and Mariner.   Union 2 killed, 7 wounded.
21.—Quantrell's plunder and massacre of Lawrence, Kan., in which 140 citizens were killed and wounded.   Confed. 40 killed.
—Coldwater, Miss.   3d and 4th Ia. Cav., 5th Ill. Cav.   Union 10 wounded.
24.—Coyle's Tavern, near Fairfax C. H., Va.   2d Mass. Cav.   Union 2 killed, 3 wounded.   Confed. 2 killed, 4 wounded.
25 to 30.—Averill's Raid in W. Va.   Union 3 killed, 10 wounded, 60 msssing.
26.—Rocky Gap, near White Sulphur Springs, Va.   3d and 8th W. Va., 2d and 3d W. Va. Cav., 14th Pa. Cav.   Union 16 killed, 113 wounded.   Confed. 156 killed and wounded.
25 to 31.—Brownsville, Bayou Metoe and Austin, Ark.   Davidson's Cav.   Union 13 killed, 72 wounded.

SEPT. 1.—Barbee's Cross Roads, Va.   Detachment 6th Ohio Cav.   Union 2 killed, 4 wounded.
—Devil's Back Bone, Ark.   1st Ark., 6th Mo. Militia, 2d Ind. Battery.   Union 4 killed, 12 wounded.   Confed. 25 killed, 40 wounded.
5.—Limestone Station, Tenn.   Five Co's 100th Ohio.   Union 12 killed, 20 wounded, 240 missing.   Confed. 6 killed, 10 wounded.
8.—Night attack on Fort Sumter, S. C.   Four hundred and thirteen marines and sailors, commanded by Commander Stevens, U. S. N.   Union 3 killed, 144 wounded.
9.—Cumberland Gap, Tenn.   Shackleford's Cav.   Confed. 2,000 captured.
10.—Little Rock, Ark.   Major-General Steele's troops and Davidson's Cav.
11.—Ringgold, Ga.   Advance of 21st Corps.   Union 8 killed, 19 wounded.   Confed. 3 killed, 18 missing.
12.—Sterling's Plantation, La.   Battery E 1st Mo. Artil.   Union 3 killed, 3 wounded.
13.—Culpeper, Va.   1st, 2d and 3d Divisions, Cav. Corps Army of the Potomac.   Union 3 killed, 40 wounded.   Confed. 10 killed, 40 wounded, 75 missing.
—Lett's Tan Yard, near Chickamauga, Ga.   Wilder's Mounted Brigade.   Union 50 killed and wounded.   Confed. 10 killed, 40 wounded.
14.—Rapidan Station, Raccoon Ford, Va.   Cav. Army of the Potomac.   Union 8 killed, 40 wounded.
—Vidalia, La.   3d Mo.   Union 2 killed, 4 wounded.   Confed. 6 killed, 11 wounded.
19.—Rapidan Station, Va.   Buford's Cav.   Union 4 killed, 19 wounded.
19 and 20.—Chickamauga, Ga. Army of the Cumberland, Major-General Rosecrans ; Fourteenth Corps, Major-General Thomas: Twentieth Corps, Major-General McCook ; Twenty-first Corps, Major-General Crittenden, and Reserve Corps, Major-General Granger.   Union 1,644 killed, 9262 wounded, 4,945 missing.   Confed. 2,389

killed, 13,412 wounded, 2,003 missing. Union Brigadier-General Lytle killed, and Starkweather, Whittaker and King wounded. Confed. Brigadier-Generals Preston, Smith, Deshler and Helm killed, and Major-General Hood, Brigadier-Generals Adams, Gregg, Brown, McNair, Bunn, Preston, Cleburne, Benning and Clayton wounded.

SEPT. 21.—Bristol, Tenn. Shackleford's and Foster's Cavalry. Casualties not recorded.
22.—Madison C. H., Tenn. 1st Division Buford's Cavalry. Union 1 killed, 20 wounded.
—Blountsville, Tenn. Foster's 2d Brigade Cav. Union 5 killed, 22 wounded. Confed. 15 killed, 50 wounded, 100 missing.
—Rockville, Md. 11th N. Y. Cav. Confed. 34 killed and wounded.
26.—Calhoun, Tenn. Cavalry Army of the Ohio. Union 6 killed, 20 wounded, 40 missing.
27.—Moffat's Station, Ark. Detachment 1st Ark. Union 2 killed, 2 wounded. Confed. 5 killed, 20 wounded.
29.—Near Morganzia, La. 19th Ia., 26th Ind. Union 14 killed, 40 wounded, 400 missing.

OCT. 1.—Anderson's Gap, Tenn. 21st Ky. Union 38 killed and wounded.
2.—Anderson's Cross Roads, Tenn. McCook's Cav. Corps. Union 70 killed and wounded. Confed. 200 killed and wounded.
3.—McMinnville, Tenn. 4th Tenn. Union 7 killed, 31 wounded, 350 missing. Confed. 23 killed and wounded.
4.—Neosho, Mo. Three Co's 6th Mo. Militia Cav. Union 1 killed, 14 wounded, 43 missing.
5.—Stockade at Stone River, Tenn. One Co. 19th Mich. Union 6 wounded, 44 captured.
—Glascow, Ky. 37th Ky. Mounted Infantry. Union 3 wounded, 100 missing. Confed. 13 wounded.
6.—Quantrell's attack on the escort of Major-General Blunt, at Baxter Springs, Ark. robbing and murdering the prisoners. Union 54 killed, 18 wounded, 5 missing.
7.—Near Farmington, Tenn. 1st, 3d and 4th Ohio Cav., 2d Ky. Cav., Long's 2d Cav Div. and Wilder's Brigade Mounted Infantry. Union 15 killed, 60 wounded. Confed. 10 killed, 60 wounded, 240 missing.
10.—Rapidan, Va. Buford's Cav. Union 20 wounded.
—James City, also called Robertson's Run, Va. Pleasonton's Cav. Union 10 killed, 40 wounded.
—Blue Springs, Tenn. Ninth Corps Army of the Ohio and Shackleford's Cav Union 100 killed, wounded and missing. Confed. 66 killed and wounded, 150 missing.
11.—Henderson's Mill, Tenn. 5th Ind. Cav. Union 11 wounded. Confed. 30 killed and wounded.
—Colliersville, Tenn. 66th Ind., 13th U. S. Regulars. Union 15 killed, 50 wounded.
12.—Jeffersonton, Va. 2d Cav. Div. Army of the Potomac. Union 12 killed, 80 wounded, 400 missing.
12 and 13.—Ingham's Mills and Wyatts, Miss. 2d Ia. Cav. Union 45 killed and wounded. Confed. 50 killed and wounded.
—Culpeper and White Sulphur Springs, Va. Cav. Corps Army of the Potomac. Union 8 killed, 46 wounded.
—Merrill's Crossing to Lamine Crossing, Mo. Mo. Enrolled Militia, 1st Mo. Militia Battery, 1st, 4th and 7th Mo. Militia. Cav. Union 16 killed. Confed. 53 killed, 70 wounded.
—Blountville, Tenn. 3d Brigade of Shackleford's Cav. Union 6 wounded. Confed. 8 killed, 20 wounded.
—Bulltown, Va. Detachments of 6th and 11th W. Va. Confed. 9 killed, 60 wounded.
14.—Auburn, Va. Portion of 1st Div. Second Corps. Union 11 killed, 42 wounded. Confed. 8 killed, 24 wounded.
—Bristoe Station, Va. Second Corps, portion of 5th Corps, 2d Cav. Div. Army of the Potomac. Union 51 killed, 329 wounded. Confed. 750 killed and wounded, 450 missing. Union Brigadier-General Malone killed. Confed. Brigadier-Generals Cooke, Posey and Kirkland wounded.
15.—McLean's Ford, or Liberty Mills, Va. New Jersey Brigade of Third Corps. Union 2 killed, 25 wounded. Confed. 60 killed and wounded.
15 to 18.—Canton, Brownsville and Clinton, Miss. Portion of 15th and 17th Corps. Union 200 killed and wounded.
16.—Cross Timbers, Mo. 18th Ia. Confed. 2 killed, 8 wounded.
17.—Tampa Bay, Fla. Destruction of two blockade runners by U. S. gunboats Tahoma and Adele. Union 3 killed, 10 wounded.

OCT 18.—Charlestown, W. Va. 9th Md. Union 12 killed, 13 wounded, 379 missing.
—Berrysville, Va. 34th Mass., 17th Ind. Battery. Union 2 killed, 4 wounded. Confed. 5 killed, 20 wounded.
19.—Buckland Mills, Va. 3d Div. of Kilpatrick's Cav. Union 20 killed, 60 wounded, 100 missing. Confed. 10 killed, 40 wounded.
20 and 22.—Philadelphia, Tenn. 45th Ohio Mounted Infantry, 1st, 11th and 12th Ky. Cav., 24th Ind. Battery. Union 20 killed, 80 wounded, 354 missing. Confed. 15 killed, 82 wounded, 111 missing.
21.—Cherokee Station, Ala. 1st Div. Fifteenth Corps. Union 7 killed, 37 wounded. Confed. 40 killed and wounded.
22.—Beverly Ford, Va. 2d Pa. and 1st Maine Cav. Union 6 killed.
25.—Pine Bluff, Ark. 5th Kan. and 1st Ind. Cav. Union 11 killed, 27 wounded. Confed 53 killed, 164 wounded.
26.—Cane Creek, Ala. 1st Div. Fifteenth Corps. Union 2 killed, 6 wounded. Confed. 10 killed, 30 wounded.
—Vincent's Cross Roads, or Bay Springs, Miss. 1st Ala. (Union) Cav. Union 14 killed, 25 wounded.
27.—Brown's Ferry, Tenn. Detachment of 2d Brigade 3d Div. of Fourth Corps. Union 5 killed, 21 wounded.
—Waubatchie, Tenn. Eleventh Corps and 2d Div. of Twelfth Corps. Union 76 killed, 329 wounded. Confed. 300 killed, 1,200 wounded.
28.—Leiper's Ferry, Tenn. . 11th and 37th Ky., 112th Ill. Union 2 killed, 5 wounded.
29.—Cherokee Station, Ala. 1st Division of Fifteenth Corps. Casualties not recorded.

NOV 3.—Centreville and Piney Factory, Tenn. Detachments from various regiments, under Lieutenant-Colonel Scully. Confed. 15 killed.
—Grand Coteau, La. 3d and 4th Divisions of Thirteenth Corps. Union 26 killed, 124 wounded, 567 missing. Confed. 60 killed, 320 wounded, 65 missing.
3 and 4.—Colliersville and Moscow, Tenn. Cav. Brigade of Sixteenth Corps. Union 7 killed, 57 wounded. Confed. 100 wounded.
6.—Rogersville, Tenn. 7th Ohio Cav., 2d Tenn. Mounted Infantry. 2d Ill. Battery. Union 5 killed, 12 wounded, 650 missing. Confed. 10 killed, 20 wounded.
6.—Droop Mountain, Va. 10th W. Va., 28th Ohio, 14th Pa. Cav., 2d and 5th W. Va. Cav., Battery B W. Va. Artil.
7.—Rappahannock Station. Va. 5th Wis., 5th and 6th Maine, 49th and 119th Pa., 121st N. Y., supported by balance of Sixth and portion of Fifth Corps. Union 370 killed and wounded. Confed. 11 killed, 98 wounded, 1,629 missing.
—Kelly's Ford, Va. 1st U. S. Sharpshooters, 40th N. Y., 1st and 20th Ind., 3d and 5th Mich., 110th Pa., supported by remainder of Third Corps. Union 70 killed and wounded. Confed. 5 killed, 59 wounded, 295 missing.
8.—Clarksville, Ark. 3d Wis. Cav. Union 2 killed.
—Muddy Run, near Culpeper, Va. 1st Div. Cav. Div. Army of the Potomac. Union 4 killed, 25 wounded.
11.—Natchez, Miss. 58th U. S. Colored. Union 4 killed, 6 wounded. Confed. 4 killed, 8 wounded.
13.—Trinity River, Cal. Two Co's 1st Battalion California Infantry. Union 2 wounded.
14.—Huff's Ferry, Tenn. 11th Ohio, 107th Ill., 11th and 13th Ky., 23d and 24th Mich. Union 100 killed and wounded.
—Rockford, Tenn. 1st Ky. Cav., 45th Ohio Mounted Infantry. Union 25 wounded.
—Marysville, Tenn. 11th Ky. Cav. Union 100 killed and wounded.
15.—Loudon Creek, Tenn. 111th Ohio. Union 4 killed, 12 wounded. Confed. 6 killed, 10 wounded.
16.—Campbell's Station, Tenn. Ninth Corps, 2d Div. of Twenty-third Corps, Sander's Cav. Union 60 killed, 340 wounded. Confed. 570 killed and wounded.
17.—Mount Jackson, Va. 1st N. Y. Cav. Union 2 killed, 3 wounded. Confed. 27 missing.
17 to Dec. 4.—Siege of Knoxville, Tenn. Army of the Ohio, commanded by Major-General Burnside, complete casualties not recorded, at Fort Sanders. Nov. 29 the losses were, Union 20 killed, 80 wounded. Confed. 80 killed, 400 wounded, 300 captured.
19.—Union City. Tenn. 2d Ill. Cav. Union 1 killed. Confed. 11 killed, 53 captured.
23 to 25.—Chattanooga, Lookout Mountain, Orchard Knob and Missionary Ridge, Tenn. Fourth and Fourteenth Corps, Army of the Cumberland, Major-General George H. Thomas ; Eleventh, Geary's Div. of the Twelfth and the Fifteenth Corps Army of the Tennessee, Major-General W. T. Sherman. Union 757 killed, 4,529 wounded, 330 missing. Confed. 361 killed, 2,181 wounded, 6,142 missing.
24.—Sparta, Tenn. 1st Tenn. and 9th Pa. Cav. Confed. 1 killed, 2 wounded.

NOV. 26 to 28.—Operations at Mine Run, Va., including Raccoon Ford, New Hope, Robertson's Tavern, Bartlett's Mills and Locust Grove. First Corps, Second Corps, Third Corps, Fifth Corps, Sixth Corps and 1st and 2d Cav. Divisions Army of the Potomac. Union 100 killed, 400 wounded. Confed. 100 killed, 400 wounded.
  27.—Cleveland, Tenn. 2d Brigade 2d Cav. Div. Confed. 200 captured.
    —Ringgold and Taylor's Bridge, Ga. Portions of Twelfth, Fourteenth and Fifteenth Corps. Union 68 killed, 351 wounded. Confed. 50 killed, 200 wounded, 230 missing.
  27 to 29.—Fort Esperanza, Tex. Portions of 1st and 2d Div. Thirteenth Corps. Union 1 killed, 2 wounded. Confed. 1 killed.
DEC. 2.—Walker's Ford, W. Va. 65th, 116th and 118th Ind., 21st Ohio Battery, 5th Ind. Cav., 14th Ill. Cav. Union 9 killed, 39 wounded. Confed. 25 killed, 50 wounded.
  1 to 4.—Ripley and Moscow Station, Miss., and Salisbury, Tenn. 2d Brigade Cav. Div. of Sixteenth Corps. Union 175 killed and wounded. Confed. 15 killed, 40 wounded. Union Colonel Hatch, commanding, wounded.
  7.—Creelsboro, Ky., and Celina, Tenn. 13th Ky. Cav. Confed. 15 killed.
  8 to 21.—Averill's Raid in Southwestern Va. Union 6 killed, 5 wounded. Confed. 200 prisoners.
  10 to 14.—Bean's Station and Morristown, Tenn. Shackleford's Cav. Union 700 killed and wounded. Confed. 922 killed and wounded, 150 prisoners.
  17 to 26.—Rodney and Port Gibson, Miss. Miss. Marine Brigade. Union 2 killed.
  19.—Barren Fork, Ind. Ter. 1st and 3d Kan., Indian Home Guards. Confed. 50 killed.
  24 and 25.—Bolivar and Summerville, Tenn. 7th Ill. Cav. Union 3 killed, 8 wounded.
  28.—Charleston, Tenn. Detachments of 2d Mo. and 4th Ohio Cav. guarding wagon train. Union 2 killed, 15 wounded. Confed. 8 killed, 39 wounded, 111 captured.
  29.—Talbot's Station and Mossy Creek, Tenn. 1st Brigade 2d Div. Twenty-third Corps, 1st Tenn. Cav., 1st Wis. Cav., 2d and 4th Ind. Cav., 24th Ind. Battery.
  30.—St. Augustine, Fla. 10th Ct., 24th Mass. Union 4 killed.
    —Greenville, N. C. Detachments of 12th N. Y., 1st N. C. and 23d N. Y. Battery. Union 1 killed, 6 wounded. Confed. 6 killed.
    —Waldron, Ark. 2d Kan. Cav. Union 2 killed, 6 wounded.

1864.

JAN. 1 to 10.—Rectortown and Loudon Heights, Va. 1st Md. Cav., Potomac Home Brigade. Union 29 killed and wounded, 41 missing. Confed. 4 killed, 10 wounded.
  3.—Jonesville, Va. Detachment 16th Ill. Cav., 22d Ohio Battery Union 12 killed, 48 wounded, 300 missing. Confed. 4 killed, 18 wounded.
  7.—Martin's Creek, Ark. 11th Mo. Cav. Union 1 killed, 1 wounded.
  12.—Mayfield, Ky. 58th Ill. Union 1 killed, 1 wounded. Confed. 2 killed.
  13.—Mossy Creek, Tenn. McCook's Cav. Confed. 14 killed.
  14.—Bealton, Va. One Co. 9th Mass. Union 2 wounded. Confed. 3 killed, 12 wounded.
  16 and 17.—Dandridge, Tenn. Fourth Corps and Cav. Div. of Army of the Ohio. Union 150 wounded.
  20.—Tracy City, Tenn. Detachment 20th Ct. Union 2 killed.
  23.—Rolling Prairie, Ark. 11th Mo. Cav. Union 11 killed.
  24.—Baker Springs, Ark. 2d and 6th Kan. Cav. Union 1 killed, 2 wounded. Confed. 6 killed, 2 wounded.
    —Tazewell, Tenn. 34th Ky., 116th and 118th Ind., 11th Tenn. Cav., 11th Mich. Battery Confed. 31 killed.
  27.—Fair Gardens or Kelly's Ford, Tenn. Sturgis' Cavalry. Union 100 killed and wounded. Confed. 65 killed, 100 captured.
  28.—Tunnel Hill, Ga. Part of Fourteenth Corps. Union 2 wounded. Confed. 32 wounded.
  29.—Medley, W. Va. 1st and 14th W. Va., 23d Ill., 2d Md., Potomac Home Brigade, 4th W. Va. Cav., Ringgold (Pa.) Cav. Union 10 killed, 70 wounded. Confed. 100 wounded.
FEB. 1.—Smithfield, Va. Detachments 99th N. Y., 21st Ct., 20th N. Y. Cav., 3d Pa. Artil. and marines from U. S. Gunboats Minnesota and Smith Briggs. Union 90 missing.
  1 to 3.—Bachelor Creek, Newport Barracks and New Berne, N. C. 132d N. Y., 9th Vt., 17th Mass., 2d N. C., 12th N. Y. Cav., 3d N. Y. Artil. Union 16 killed, 50 wounded, 280 missing. Conted. 5 killed, 30 wounded.
  1 to March 8.—Expedition up the Yazoo River, Miss. 11th Ill., 47th U. S. Colored, 3d U. S. Colored Cav. and a portion of Porter's Fleet of Gunboats. Union 35 killed, 121 wounded. Confed. 35 killed, 90 wounded.

FEB. 3 to March 5.—Expedition from Vicksburg to Meridan, Miss., including Champion Hills, Raymond, Clinton, Jackson, Decatur, Chunky Station, occupation of Meridan, Lauderdale Springs and Marion, Miss. Two Divisions of the Sixteenth and three of the Seventeenth Corps, with the 5th Ill., 4th Ia., 10th Mo. and Foster's (Ohio) Cav. Union 50 killed, 158 wounded, 105 missing. Confed. 503 killed and wounded, 212 missing.
    5.—Quailtown, N. C. Detachment of 14th Ill. Cav. Union 3 killed, 6 wounded. Confed. 50 captured, including Major-General Vance.
    6.—Bolivar, Tenn. Detachment of 7th Ind. Cav. Union 1 killed, 3 wounded. Confed 30 wounded.
    —Morton's Ford, Va. Portion of Second Corps. Union 10 killed, 201 wounded. Confed. 100 missing.
    7.—Barnett's Ford, Va. Brigadier-General Merritt's Cav. Union 20 killed and wounded.
    —Vidalia, La. 30th Mo., 64th U. S. Colored, 6th U. S. Artil. Colored. Confed. 6 killed, 10 wounded.
    9.—Morgan's Mills, Ark. Detachments of 4th Ark., 11th Mo. Cav., 1st Neb. Cav. Union 1 killed, 4 wounded. Confed. 65 killed and wounded.
    9 to 14.—Barber's Place, St. Mary's River, Lake City and Gainesville, Fla. 40th Mass. Mounted Infantry and Independent (Mass.) Cav. Union 4 killed, 16 wounded. Confed. 4 killed, 48 wounded.
    10 to 25.—Smith's Raid from Germantown, Tenn., into Mississippi, Smith's and Grierson's Cav. Divisions. Union 43 killed, 267 wounded. Confed. 50 wounded, 300 captured.
    12.—Rock House, W. Va. 14th Ky. Confed. 12 killed, 4 wounded.
    14.—Ross Landing, Ark. 51st U. S. Colored. Union 13 killed, 7 wounded.
    —Brentsville, Va. 13th Pa. Cav. Union 4 killed, 1 wounded.
    14 and 15.—Waterproof, La. 49th U. S. Colored and U. S. Gunboat Forest Rose. Union 8 killed, 14 wounded. Confed. 15 killed.
    19.—Grosse Tete Bayou, La. 4th Wis. Cav. Union 2 wounded. Confed. 4 killed, 6 wounded.
    —Waugh's Farm, near Batesville, Ark. 4th Ark., 11th Mo. Cav. Union 3 killed, 4 wounded. Confed. 6 killed, 10 wounded.
    20.—Holston River, Tenn. 4th Tenn. Union 2 killed, 3 wounded. Confed. 5 killed, 10 wounded.
    20.—Olustee, or Silver Lake, Fla. 47th, 48th and 115th N. Y., 7th Ct., 7th N. H., 40th Mass , 8th and 54th U. S. Colored, 1st N. C. Colored, 1st Mass Cav., 1st and 3d U. S. Artil., 3d R. I. Artil. Union 193 killed, 1,175 wounded, 460 missing. Confed. 100 killed, 400 wounded.
    22.—Mulberry Gap, Tenn. 9th Tenn. Cav. Union 13 killed and wounded, 250 captured.
    —Drainesville, Va. Detachment 2d Mass. Cav. Union 10 killed, 7 wounded, 57 captured. Confed. 2 killed, 4 wounded.
    —Johnson's Mills, Tenn. Detachment of 24 men 5th Tenn. Cav., captured and massacred by Ferguson's guerrillas.
    23 and March 18.—Calf Killer Creek, Tenn. 5th Tenn. Cav. Union 8 killed, 3 wounded. Confed. 3 killed.
    25 to 27.—Buzzard Roost, Tunnel Hill and Rocky Face, Ga. Fourth and Fourteenth Corps and Cav. Corps Army of Cumberland. Union 17 killed, 272 wounded. Confed. 20 killed, 120 wounded.
    27 and 28.—Near Canton, Miss. Foraging Detachments of 3d and 32d Ia. Union 2 killed, 6 wounded. Confed. 3 killed, 15 wounded.
    28 to March 4.—Kilpatrick's Raid, Stevensburg to Richmond, Va. Kilpatrick's Cav. Union 350 killed, wounded and captured. Confed. 308 killed, wounded and captured.
MAR. 1.—Stanardsville and Button's Ford, Rapidan, Va. Custer's Cav. Union 10 wounded. Confed. 30 captured.
    2.—Harrisburg, La. Porter's Miss. Squadron. Union 2 killed, 14 wounded.
    5.—Panther Springs, Tenn. One Co. 3d Tenn. Union 2 killed, 8 wounded, 22 captured. Confed. 30 wounded.
    7.—Decatur, Ala. Army of the Tennessee, commanded by Brigadier-General Dodge.
    9.—Suffolk, Va. 2d U. S. Colored Cav. Union 8 killed, 1 wounded. Confed. 25 wounded.
    14.—Fort De Russy, La. Detachments of Sixteenth and Seventeenth Corps and Porter's Miss. Squadron. Union 7 killed, 41 wounded. Confed. 5 killed, 4 wounded, 260 prisoners.
    15.—Clarendon, Ark. 8th Mo. Cav. Union 1 killed, 3 wounded.
    17.—Manchester, Tenn. 5th Tenn. Cav. Confed. 21 killed.
    21.—Henderson Hills, La. Detachments of Sixteenth Corps and Cav. Div. Nineteenth Corps. Union 1 wounded. Confed. 8 killed, 250 captured.

MAR. 24.—Union City, Ky. 7th Tenn. Cav. 450 men captured by Forrest.
25.—Fort Anderson, Paducah, Ky. 122d Ill., 16th Ky. Cav., 8th U. S. Colored Artil. Union 14 killed, 46 wounded. Confed. 10 killed, 40 wounded. Confed. Brigadier-General Thompson killed.
26 to 30.—Longview and Mt. Elba, Ark. 28th Wis., 5th Kan. Cav., 7th Mo. Cav. Union 4 killed, 18 wounded. Confed. 12 killed, 35 wounded, 300 captured.
28.—Charleston, Ill. Attack on 54th Ill. by mob of Copperheads while returning to the front from veteran furlough. Union 2 killed, 8 wounded. Confed. 3 killed, 4 wounded, 12 prisoners.
29.—Bolivar, Tenn. 6th Tenn. Cav. Union 8 killed, 35 wounded.
31.—Near Snydersville, Miss. 3d U. S. Colored Cav. Union 16 killed, 3 wounded. Confed. 3 killed, 7 wounded.

APRIL 1.—Near Augusta, Ark. 3d Minn., 8th Mo. Cav. Union 8 killed, 16 wounded. Confed. 15 killed, 45 wounded.
2.—Spoonville, Ark. 29th Ia., 9th Wis., 50th Ind., with 1st Mo. Cav. Union 10 killed, 35 wounded. Confed. 100 killed and wounded.
—Crumps Hill, or Piney Woods, La. 14th N. Y. Cav., 2d La., 2d Ill. and 16th Mo. Cav., 5th U. S. Colored Artil. Union 20 wounded. Confed. 10 killed, 25 wounded.
3.—Okalona, Ark. 27th Wis., 40th Ia., 77th Ohio, 43d Ill., 1st Mo. Cav., 13th Ill. Cav. Union 16 killed, 74 wounded. Confed. 75 killed and wounded.
4.—Campti, La. 35th Ia., 5th Minn., 2d and 18th N. Y. Cav., 3d R. I. Cav. Union 10 killed, 18 wounded. Confed. 3 killed, 12 wounded
4 to 6.—Elkin's Ford, Ark. 43d Ind., 29th and 36th Ia., 1st Ia. Cav., Battery E 2d Mo. Light Artil. Union 5 killed, 33 wounded. Confed. 18 killed, 30 wounded.
5.—Roseville, Ark. Seventy-five men of 2d and 6th Kan. Cav., in engagement with guerrillas. Union 19 killed, 11 wounded. Confed. 15 killed, 25 wounded, 11 captured.
—Stone's Farm. Twenty-six men of 6th Kan. Cav., in engagement with guerrillas, 11, including Assistant-Surgeon Fairchilds, captured and massacred.
6.—Quicksand Creek, Ky. Co. I. 14th Ky. Confed. 10 killed, 7 wounded.
7.—Wilson's Farm, La. Advance Cav. of Nineteenth Corps. Union 14 killed, 39 wounded. Confed. 15 killed, 40 wounded, 100 captured.
7.—Near Port Hudson, La. Detachment 118th Ill. Cav., 3d Ill. Cav., 21st N. Y. Battery. Union 1 killed, 4 wounded.
8 and 9.—Sabine Cross Roads and Pleasant Hills, La. Portions of Thirteenth, Sixteenth and Nineteenth Corps and Cav. Div. Army of Dept. of the Gulf. Union 300 killed, 1,600 wounded, 2,100 missing. Confed. 600 killed, 2,400 wounded, 500 missing. Union Major-General Franklin and Brigadier-General Ransom wounded. Confed. Major-General Mouton and Brigadier-General Parsons killed.
10 to 13.—Prairie D'Ann, Ark. 3d Div. Seventh Corps. Union 100 killed and wounded. Confed. 50 killed and wounded.
12.—Pleasant Hill Landing, La. Seventeenth Corps and U. S. Gunboats Osage and Lexington. Union 7 wounded. Confed. 200 killed and wounded.
13.—Moscow, Ark. 18th Ia., 6th Kan. Cav., 2d Ind. Battery. Union 5 killed, 17 wounded. Confed. 30 killed and wounded.
13 and 14.—Paintsville and Half-Mount, Ky. Ky. Vols. Union 4 wounded. Confed. 25 killed, 25 wounded.
14.—Smithfield, or Cherry Grove, Va. 9th N. J., 23d and 25th Mass., 118th N. Y. Union 5 wounded. Confed. 6 wounded.
15.—Bristoe Station, Va. 13th Pa. Cav. Union 1 killed, 2 wounded.
15 and 16.—Liberty P. O., and occupation of Camden, Ark. 29th Ia., 50th Ind., 9th Wis. Union 255 killed and wounded.
17.—Decatur, Ala. 25th Wis. Union 2 wounded.
17 to 20.—Plymouth, N. C. 85th N. Y., 103d Pa., 16th Ct. and the Navy. Union 20 killed, 80 wounded, 1,500 missing. Confed. 500 killed, wounded and missing. Lieut.-Com. Flusser, U. S. N., killed.
18.—Poison Springs, eight miles from Camden, Ark. Forage train guarded by 18th Ia., 79th U. S. Colored, 6th Kan. Cav. Union 113 killed, 88 wounded, 68 missing.
—Boyken's Mills, S. C. 54th Mass., U. S. Colored. Union 2 killed, 18 wounded.
21.—Cotton Plant, Cache River, Ark. 8th Mo. Cav. Union 3 killed, 2 wounded.
21.—Red Bone, Miss. 2d Wis. Cav. Union 1 killed, 6 wounded.
22.—Near Tunica Bend, Red River, La. Three Co's 3d R. I. Cav. Union 2 killed, 17 wounded.
23.—Nickajack Trace, Ga. Detachments of 92d Ill. Union 5 killed, 9 wounded, 22 taken prisoners, 12 were shot down and 6 died from wounds.
23 and 24.—Moneti's Bluff, Crano River and Cloutersville, La. Portion of Thirteenth, Seventeenth and Nineteenth Corps. Union 350 killed and wounded. Confed. 400 killed and wounded.

APRIL 25.—Mark's Mills, Ark. 36th Ia., 77 Ohio, 43d Ill., 1st Ind. Cav., 7th Mo. Cav., Battery E 2d Mo. Light Artil. Union 100 killed, 250 wounded, 100 missing. Confed. 110 killed, 22 wounded, 40 missing.

25 and 26.—Wautauga Bridge, Tenn. 10th Mich. Cav. Union 3 killed, 9 wounded.

26.—Moro Creek, Ark. 33d and 40th Ia., 5th Kan., 2d and 4th Mo., 1st Ia. Cav. Union 5 killed, 14 wounded.

28.—Princeton, Ark. 40th Ia., 43d Ill., 6th Kan. Cav., 3d Ill. Battery. Casualties not recorded.

30.—Jenkin's Ferry, Saline River, Ark. 3d Div. of Seventh Corps. Union 200 killed, 955 wounded. Confed. 300 killed, 800 wounded.

MAY 1.—Jacksonville, Fla. 7th U. S. Colored. Union 1 killed.

1 to 8.—Hudnot's Plantation, and near Alexandria, La. Cavalry of Thirteenth and Nineteenth Corps. Union 33 killed, 87 wounded. Confed. 25 killed, 300 wounded.

2.—Gov. Moore's Plantation, La. Foraging Detachment of 83d Ohio and 3d R. I. Cav. Union 2 killed, 10 wounded.

3.—Red Clay, Ga. 1st Div. of McCook's Cav. Union 10 killed and wounded.
—Richland, Ark. 2d Ark. Cav. Union 20 killed.

4.—Doubtful Canon, Ariz. Detachment of 5th Cav. and 1st Cal. Cav. Union 1 killed, 6 wounded. Confed. 10 killed, 20 wounded.

4 to 12.—Kautz's Cav. Raid from Suffolk, Wall's Bridge, Stoney Creek Station, Jarrett's Station, White's Bridge to City Point, Va. 5th and 11th Pa. Cav., 3d N. Y. Cav., 1st D. C. Cav., 8th N. Y. Battery. Union 10 killed, wounded and missing. Confed. 20 wounded, 50 prisoners.

4 to 13.—Yazoo City Expedition, including Benton and Vaughn, Miss. 11th, 72d and 76th Ill., 5th Ill. Cav., 3d U. S. Colored Cav., 7th Ohio Battery. Union 5 killed, 20 wounded.

5.—Ram Albemarle. Roanoke River, N. C. U. S. Gunboats Ceres, Commodore Hull, Mattabesett, Sassacus, Seymour, Wyalusing, Miami and Whitehead. Union 5 killed, 26 wounded. Confed. 57 captured.

—Dunn's Bayou, Red River, La. 56th Ohio, on board U. S. Gunboat Signal, steamer Covington, and transport Warner. Union 35 killed, 65 wounded, 150 missing.

5 to 7.—Wilderness, Va. Army of the Potomac, Major-General George G. Meade, Second Corps, Major-General Hancock ; Fifth Corps, Major General Warren ; Sixth Corps, Major-General Sedgwick ; Ninth Corps, Major-General Burnside and Sheridan's Cav. Union 5,597 killed, 21,463 wounded, 10,677 missing. Confed. 2,000 killed, 6,000 wounded, 3,400 missing. Union Brigadier Generals Wadsworth, Hays and Webb killed. Confed. Generals Jones and Pickett killed and Longstreet, Pegram, Stafford, Hunter and Jennings wounded.

5 to 9.—Rocky Face Ridge, Ga., including Tunnel Hill, Mill Creek Gap and Buzzard's Roost, Army of the Cumberland, Major-General Thomas; Army of the Tennessee, Major-General McPherson; Army of the Mississippi, Major-General Sherman. Union 200 killed, 637 wounded. Confed. 600 killed and wounded.

6.—James River, near City Point, Va. U. S. Gunboat, Commodore Jones. Union 23 killed, 48 wounded.

6 and 7.—Richmond and Petersburg Railroad, near Chester Station, Va. Portion of Tenth and Eighteenth Corps. Union 48 killed, 256 wounded. Confed. 50 killed, 200 wounded.

7.—Bayou La Mourie, La. Portion of Sixteenth Corps. Union 10 killed, 31 wounded.

8.—Todd's Tavern, Va. 2d Div. Cav. Corps Army of the Potomac. Union 40 killed, 150 wounded. Confed. 30 killed, 150 wounded.

8 to 18.—Spottsylvania, Fredericksburg Road, Laurel Hill and Ny River, Va. Army of the Potomac, Major-General Meade ; Second Corps, Major-General Hancock ; Fifth Corps, Major-General Warren ; Sixth Corps, Major-General Wright ; Ninth Corps, Major-General Burnside and Sheridan's Cavalry. Union 4,177 killed, 19,687 wounded, 2,577 missing. Confed. 1,000 killed, 5,000 wounded, 3,000 missing. Union Major-General Sedgwick and Brigadier-Generals Rice, Owens and Stevenson killed, Brigadier-Generals Robertson, Bartlett, Morris and Baxter wounded. Confed. Generals Daniels and Perrin killed, Hayes and Walker, wounded, and Major-General Edward Johnson and Brigadier-General Stewart captured.

9.—Varnell's Station, Ga. 1st Div. McCook's. Cav. Union 4 killed, 25 wounded.

9 and 10.—Swift Creek or Arrowfield Church, Va. Tenth and Eighteenth Corps. Union 90 killed, 400 wounded. Confed. 500 missing.

—Cloyd's Mountain and New River Bridge, Va. 12th, 23d, 34th and 36th Ohio, 9th 11th, 14th and 15th W. Va., 3d and 4th Pa. Reserves. Union 126 killed, 585 wounded. Confed. 600 killed and wounded, 300 missing.

MAY 9 to 13.—Sheridan's Cav. Raid in Virginia, engagements Beaver Dam Station, South Anna Bridge, Ashland and Yellow Tavern. Union 50 killed, 174 wounded, 200 missing. Confed. killed and wounded not recorded, 100 prisoners. Confed. Major-Generals J. E. B. Stuart and J. B. Gordon wounded.

12 to 16.—Fort Darling, Drury's Bluff, Va. Tenth and Eighteenth Corps. Union 422 killed, 2,380 wounded, 210 missing. Confed. 400 killed, 2,000 wounded, 100 missing.

12 to 17.—Kautz's Raid on Petersburg and Lynchburg Railroad, Va. Union 6 killed, 28 wounded.

13 to 16.—Resaca, Ga. Fourth, Fourteenth, Twentieth and Cavalry Corps, Army of the Cumberland, Major-General Thomas; Fifteenth and Sixteenth Corps Army of the Tennessee, Major-General McPherson, and Twenty-third Corps Army of the Ohio, Major-General Schofield. Union 600 killed, 2,147 wounded. Confed. 300 killed, 1,500 wounded 1,000 missing.. Confed. Brigadier-General Watkins killed.

15.—Mount Pleasant Landing, La. 67th U. S. Colored. Union 3 killed, 5 wounded.
—New Market, Va. Major-General Sigel's command. Union 120 killed, 560 wounded, 240 missing. Confed. 85 killed, 320 wounded.
—Tanner's Bridge, Ga. 2d Division Cavalry Army of the Camberland. Union 2 killed, 16 wounded.

16 to 30.—Bermuda Hundred, Va. Tenth and Eighteenth Corps Army of the James. Union 200 killed, 1,000 wounded. Confed. 3,000 killed, wounded and missing.

17 and 18.—Adairsville and Calhoun, Ga. Fourth Corps. Major-General Howard. Casualties not recorded.

18.—Rome and Kingston. Ga. 2d Div. of Fourteenth Corps and Cav. Army of the Cumberland. Union 16 killed, 59 wounded.
—Bayou De Glaize, or Calhoun Station, La. Portions of Sixteenth, Seventeenth and Cav. of Nineteenth Corps. Union 60 killed, 300 wounded. Confed. 500 killed and wounded.

19 to 22.—Cassville, Ga. Twentieth Corps, Major-General Hooker. Union 10 killed, 46 wounded.

21.—Mount Pleasant, Miss. 4th Mo. Cav. Union 2 killed, 1 wounded.

23 to 27.—North Anna River, Jericho Ford or Taylor's Bridge, and Talopotomy Creek, Va. Second, Fifth and Ninth Corps, Army of the Potomac, Major-General Meade. Union 223 killed, 1,460 wounded, 290 missing. Confed. 2,000 killed and wounded.

24.—Holly Springs, Miss. 4th Mo. Cav. Union 1 killed, 2 wounded.
—Wilson's Wharf, Va. 10th U. S. Colored, 1st D. C. Cavalry, Battery B U. S. Colored Artil. Union 2 killed, 24 wounded. Confed. 20 killed, 100 wounded.
—Nashville, Tenn. 15th U. S. Colored. Union 4 killed, 8 wounded.

25 to June 4.—Dallas, Ga., also called New Hope Church and Allatoona Hills. Fourth, Fourteenth, Twentieth and Cav. Corps Army of the Cumberland, Major-General Thomas; Twenty-third Corps, Major-General Schofield; Fifteenth, Sixteenth and Seventeenth Corps Army of the Tennessee, Major-General McPherson; Army of the Mississippi, Major-General Sherman. Union 2,400 killed, wounded and missing. Confed. 3,000 killed, wounded and missing. Confed. Major-General Walker killed.

25.—Cassville Station, Ga. 1st and 11th Ky. Cav. Union 8 killed, 16 wounded. Confed. 2 killed, 6 wounded.

26.—Torpedo explosion on Bechelor's Creek, N. C. 132d and 158th N. Y., 58th Pa. Union 35 killed, 19 wounded.

26 to 29.—Decatur and Moulton, Ala. 1st, 3d and 4th Ohio Cav., 2d Cav. Div. Union 48 killed and wounded. Confed. 60 killed and wounded.

27 and 28.—Hanoverton, Hawe's Shop and Salem Church, Va. 1st and 2d Divisions Cav. Corps, Major-General Sheridan. Union 25 killed, 119 wounded, 200 missing. Confed. 475 killed, wounded and missing.

30.—Hanover and Ashland, Va. Wilson's Cav. Union 26 killed, 130 wounded.
—Old Church, Va. Torbett's Cav. Union 16 killed, 74 wounded.

JUNE 1 to 12.—Cold Harbor, Va., including Gaines' Mills, Salem Church and Hawe's Shop. Second, Fifth, Sixth, Ninth and Eighteenth Corps and Sheridan's Cav. Union 1,905 killed, 10,570 wounded, 2,456 missing. Confed. 1,200 killed and wounded, 500 missing. Union Brigadier-Generals Brookes and Byrnes killed, and Tyler, Stannard and Johnson wounded. Confed. Brigadier-Generals Doles and Keitt killed, and Kirkland, Finnegan, Law and Lane wounded.

2.—Bermuda Hundred, Va. Tenth Corps. Union 25 killed, 100 wounded. Confed. 100 killed and wounded.

3 to 6 —Panther Gap and Buffalo Gap, W. Va. Hayes' Brigade of 2d Div. Army of W. Va. Union 25 killed and wounded. Confed. 25 killed and wounded,

5.—Piedmont, W. Va. Portion of Army of West Virginia, commanded by Major-General Hunter. Union 130 killed, 650 wounded. Confed. 460 killed, 1,450 wounded, 1,000 missing. Confed. General W. E. Jones killed,

JUNE 6.—Lake Chicot, Ark. Sixteenth Corps. Union 40 killed, 70 wounded. Confed. 100 killed and wounded.

9.—Point of Rocks, Md. 2d U. S. Colored Cav. Union 2 killed.

—Mount. Sterling. Ky. Burbridge's Cav. Union 35 killed, 150 wounded. Confed. 50 killed, 200 wounded, 250 captured.

9 to 30.—Kenesaw Mountain, Marietta or Big Shanty, Ga., including general assault on the 27th Pine M't, Golgotha, Culp's House and Powder Springs. Fourth, Fourteenth and Twentieth Corps, Army of the Cumberland, Major-General Thomas ; Fifteenth, Sixteenth and Seventeenth Corps, Army of the Tennessee, Major-General McPherson ; Twenty-third Corps, Major-General Schofield—Army of the Mississippi, Major-General W. T. Sherman. Union 1,370 killed, 6,500 wounded, 800 missing. Confed. 1,100 killed and wounded, 3,500 missing. Union Brigadier-Generals Harker and McCook killed. Confed. Lieutenant-General Leonidas Polk killed.

10.—Petersburg, Va. Portions of Tenth Corps and Kautz's Cav. Union 20 killed, 67 wounded.

—Brice's Cross Roads, near Guntown, Miss. 81st, 95th, 108th, 113th, 114th, and 120th Ill., 72d and 95th Ohio, 9th Minn., 93d Ind., 55th and 59th U. S. Colored. Brigadier-General Grierson's Cav., the 4th Mo., 2d N. J., 19th Pa., 7th and 9th Ill., 7th Ind., 3d and 4th Ia., and 10th Kan. Cav., 1st Ill. and 6th Ind. Batteries, Battery F 2d U. S. Colored Artil. Union 223 killed, 394 wounded, 1,623 missing. Confed. 131 killed, 475 wounded.

—Cynthiana and Kellar's Bridge. Ky. 168th and 171st Ohio. Union 21 killed, 71 wounded, 980 captured by Morgan's Raiders.

10 and 11.—Lexington, Va. 2d Div. Army of W. Va. Union 6 killed, 18 wounded.

11.—Cynthiana, Ky. Burbridge's Cav. Attack on Morgan's Raiders. Union 150 killed and wounded. Confed. 300 killed and wounded, 460 captured.

11 and 12.—Trevillian Station, Va. Sheridan's Cav. Union 85 killed, 490 wounded, 160 missing. Confed. 370 missing.

13.—White Oak Swamp Bridge, Va. Wilson's and Crawford's Cav. Union 50 killed, 250 wounded.

14.—Lexington. Mo. Detachment 1st Mo. Cav. Union 8 killed, 1 wounded.

15.—Samaria Church, Malvern Hill, Va. Wilson's Cav. Union 25 killed, 3 wounded. Confed. 100 killed and wounded.

15 to 19.—Petersburg, Va. (commencement of the siege that continued to its fall, April 2, 1865). Tenth and Eighteenth Corps, Army of the James, Major-General B. F. Butler ; Second, Fifth, Sixth and Ninth Corps Army of the Potomac, Major-General George G. Meade. Union 1,298 killed, 7,474 wounded, 1,814 missing.

16.—Otter Creek, near Liberty Creek, Va. Hunter's Command in advance of the Army of W. Va. Union 3 killed, 15 wounded.

17 and 18.—Lynchburg, Va. Sullivan's and Crook's Divisions and Averill's and Duffie's Cav., Army of the West Virginia. Union 100 killed, 500 wounded, 100 missing. Confed. 200 killed and wounded.

19.—Capture of the Alabama, off Cherbourg, France, by U. S. Steamer Kearsage. Union 3 wounded. Confed. 9 killed, 21 wounded, 70 captured.

20 to 30.—In front of Petersburg, Va. Fifth, Ninth, Tenth and Eighteenth Corps. Union 112 killed, 506 wounded, 800 missing. Union Generals Chamberlain and Egan wounded.

21.—Salem, Va. Averill's Cav. Union 6 killed, 10 wounded. Confed. 10 killed and wounded.

—Naval engagement on the James River, near Dutch Gap. Casualties not recorded.

—Buford's Gap, Va. 23d Ohio. Union 15 killed.

22.—White River, Ark. Three Co.'s 12th Iowa, and U. S. Gunboat Lexington. Union 2 killed, 4 wounded. Confed. 2 killed, 3 wounded.

22 and 23.—Weldon Railroad, Williams' Farm or Jerusalem Plank Road, Va. Second, Sixth and 1st Division of Fifth Corps, Army of the Potomac. Union 604 killed, 2,494 wounded, 2,217 missing. Confed. 300 wounded, 200 missing.

22 to 30 —Wilson's Raid on the Weldon Railroad, Va. Kautz's and Wilson's Cav. Union 92 killed, 317 wounded, 734 missing. Confed. 365 killed and wounded.

23 and 24.—Jones' Bridge and Samaria Church, Va. Torbett's and Gregg's Cavalry Divisions. Union 54 killed, 235 wounded, 300 missing. Confed. 250 killed and wounded.

25 to 29.—Clarendon, St. Charles River, Ark. 126th Ill. and 11th Mo., 9th Iowa and 3d Mich. Cav., Battery D 2d Mo. Artil. Union 200 wounded. Confed. 200 wounded, 200 missing.

JULY 1 to 31.—In front of Petersburg, including Deep Bottom, New Market and Malvern Hill, on the 27th, and mine explosion on the 30th. Second, Fifth, Ninth, Tenth and Eighteenth Corps. Union 898 killed, 4,060 wounded, 3,110 missing. Confed loss at Deep Bottom 400 killed, 600 wounded, 200 missing.

JULY 2.—Pine Bluff, Ark. 64th U. S. Colored. Union 6 killed.
—Fort Johnson, James Island, S. C. Troops of Department of the South. Union 19 killed, 97 wounded, 135 missing.
2 to 5.—Nickajack Creek of Smyrna, Ga. Troops under command of Major-General Sherman. Union 60 killed, 310 wounded. Confed. 100 killed and wounded.
3.—Leetown, Va. 10th W. Va., 1st N. Y. Cav. Union 3 killed, 12 wounded.
Hammack's Mills, W. Va. 153d Ohio Nat'l Guard. Union 3 killed, 7 wounded.
3 to 9.—Expedition from Vicksburg to Jackson, Miss. 1st Div. Seventeenth Corps. Union 150 wounded. Confed. 200 wounded.
4.—Vicksburg, Miss. 48th U. S. Colored. Union 1 killed, 7 wounded.
4 to 5.—Coleman's Plantation, near Port Gibson, Miss. 52d U. S. Colored. Union 6 killed, 18 wounded.
4 to 7.—Bolivar and Maryland Heights. Major-General Sigel's Reserve Division. Union 20 killed, 80 wounded.
5.—Hagerstown, Md. 1st Md. Cav., Potomac Home Brigade. Union 2 killed, 6 wounded.
5 to 7.—John's Island, S. C. Major-General Foster's troop. Union 16 killed, 82 wounded. Confed. 20 killed, 80 wounded.
5 to 18.—Smith's Expedition, La Grange, Tenn., to Tupelo, Miss. 1st and 3d Divisions Sixteen Corps, one Brigade U. S. Colored Troops and Grierson's Cavalry. Union 85 killed, 567 wounded. Confed. 110 killed, 600 wounded.
6.—Little Blue, Mo. 2d Col. Cav. Union 8 killed, 1 wounded.
6 to 10.—Chattahoochee River, Ga. Army of the Ohio, Major-General Schofield ; Army of the Tennessee, Major-General McPherson ; Army of the Cumberland, Major-General Thomas—Army of the Mississippi, Major-General W. T. Sherman. Union 80 killed, 450 wounded, 200 missing.
7.—Solomon's Gap and Middleton, Md. 8th Ill. Cav., Potomac Home Brigade and Alexander's Baltimore Battery. Union 5 killed, 20 wounded.
9.—Monocacy, Md. 1st and 2d Brigades of 3d Division Sixth Corps and Detachment of Eighth Corps. Union 90 killed, 579 wounded, 1,200 missing. Confed. 400 wounded.
11 to 22.—Rosseau's Raid in Alabama and Georgia, including Ten Islands and Stone's Ferry, Ala., and Auburn and Chewa Station, Ga. 8th Ind., 5th Iowa, 9th Ohio, 2d Ky. and 4th Tenn. Cav., Battery E 1st Mich. Artil. Union 3 killed, 30 wounded. Confed. 95 killed and wounded.
12.—Fort Stevens, Washington, D. C. Twenty-second Corps, 1st and 2d Division, Sixth Corps, Marines, Home Guards, citizens and convalescents. Union 54 killed, 319 wounded. Confed. 500 killed and wounded.
Lee's Mills, near Roan's Station, Va. 2d Division Gregg's Cav. Union 3 killed, 13 wounded. Confed. 25 killed and wounded.
14.—Farr's Mills, Ark. One Co. 4th Ark. Cav. Union 1 killed, 7 wounded. Confed. 4 killed, 6 wounded.
14 and 15.—Ozark, Mo. 14th Kan. Cav. Union 2 killed, 1 wounded.
16 and 17.—Grand Gulf, Port Gibson, Miss. 72d and 76th Ill., 53d U. S. Colored, 2d Wis. Cav. Casualties not recorded.
17 and 18.—Snicker's Gap, and Island Ford, Va. Army of West Virginia, Major-General Crook and portion of Sixth Corps. Union 30 killed, 181 wounded, 100 missing.
18.—Ashby's Gap, Va. Duffie's Cav. Union 200 killed and wounded.
19 and 20.—Darksville, Stevenson's Depot and Winchester, Va. Averill's Cav. Union 37 killed, 175 wounded. Confed. 300 wounded, 200 captured.
20.—Peach Tree Creek, Ga. Fourth, Fourteenth and Twentieth Corps, Major-General Geo. H. Thomas. Union 300 killed, 1,410 wounded. Confed. 1,113 killed, 2,500 wounded, 1,183 missing. Confed. Brigadier-Generals Featherstone, Long, Pettis, and Stevens killed.
22.—Atlanta, Ga. (Hood's first sortie). Fifteenth, Sixteenth and Seventeenth Corps, Major-General McPherson. Union 500 killed, 2,141 wounded, 1,000 missing. Confed. 2,482 killed, 4,000 wounded, 2,017 missing. Union Major-General McPherson and Brigadier-General Greathouse killed.
22.—Decatur, Ga. 2d Brigade of 4th Division of Sixteenth Corps. Confed. Major-General Walker killed.
23 and 24.—Kernstown and Winchester, Va. Portion of Army of West Virginia. Union 1,200 killed and wounded. Confed. 600 killed and wounded.
26.—Wallace's Ferry, Ark. 15th Ill. Cav., 60th and 56th U. S. Colored Troops, Co. E 2d U. S. Colored Artil. Union 16 killed, 32 wounded. Confed. 150 wounded.
26 to 31.—Stoneman's Raid to Macon, Ga. Stoneman's and Garrard's Cav. Union 100 killed and wounded, 900 missing.
26 to 31.—McCook's Raid to Lovejoy Station, Ga. 1st Wis., 5th and 8th Iowa, 2d and 8th Ind., 1st and 4th Tenn., and 4th Ky. Cavalry. Union 100 killed and wounded, 500 missing.

JULY 27.—Mazzard Prairie, Fort Smith, Ark. Two hundred men of 6th Kan. Cav. Union 12 killed, 17 wounded, 152 captured. Confed. 12 killed, 20 wounded.
  28.—Atlanta, Ga. (second sortie, at Ezra Chapel). Fifteenth, Sixteenth and Seventeenth Corps, Major-General Howard. Union 100 killed, 600 wounded. Confed. 642 killed, 3,000 wounded, 1,000 missing.
  28 to Sept. 22.—Siege of Atlanta, Ga. Army of the Military Division of the Mississippi, Major-General W. T. Sherman. Casualties not recorded.
  29.—Clear Springs, Md. 12th and 14th Penna. Cav. Confed. 17 killed and wounded.
  30.—Lee's Mills, Va. Davis' Cav. Union 2 killed, 11 wounded.
  —Lebanon, Ky. One Co. 12th Ohio Cav. Confed. 6 killed.

AUG. 1 to 31.—In front of Petersburg, Va. Second, Fifth, Ninth and Eighteenth Corps Union 87 killed, 484 wounded.
  2.—Green Springs, W. Va. 153 Ohio. Union 1 killed, 5 wounded, 90 missing. Confed. 5 killed, 22 wounded.
  5.—Donaldsonville, La. 11th N. Y. Cav. Union 60 missing.
  5 to 23.—Forts Gaines and Morgan, Mobile Harbor, Ala. Thirteenth Corps and Admiral Farragut's Fleet of War Vessels. Union 75 killed, 100 drowned by sinking of the Tecumseh, 170 wounded. Confed. 2,344 captured.
  6.—Plaquemine, La. 4th Wis. Cav., 14th R. I. Heavy Artil. Union 2 killed.
  7.—Moorefield, Va. 14th Penna., 8th Ohio, 1st and 3d W. Va., and 1st N. Y. Cav. Union 9 killed, 22 wounded. Confed. 100 killed and wounded, 400 missing.
  7 to 14—Tallahatchie River, Abbeville, Oxford and Hurricane Creek, Miss. Hatch's Cav. and Mower's Command of Sixteenth Corps. Casualties not recorded.
  9.—Explosion of ammunition at City Point, Va. Union 70 killed, 130 wounded.
  10 and 11.—Berryville Pike, Sulphur Springs Bridge and White Post, Va. Torbett's Cav. Union 34 killed, 90 wounded, 200 missing.
  13.—Near Snicker's Gap, Va. 144th and 149th Ohio. Union 4 killed, 10 wounded, 200 missing. Confed. 2 killed, 3 wounded.
  14.—Gravel Hill, Va. Gregg's Cav. Union 3 killed, 18 wounded.
  14 to 16.—Dalton, Ga. 2d Mo. and 14th U. S. Colored.
  14 to 18.—Strawberry Plains, Va. Second and Tenth Corps and Gregg's Cav. Union 400 killed, 1,755 wounded, 1,400 missing. Confed. 1,000 wounded.
  15.—Fisher's Hill, near Strasburg, Va. Sixth and Eighth Corps and 1st Cav. Division Army of the Potomac. Union 30 wounded.
  16.—Crooked Run, Front Royal, Va. Merritt's Cav. Union 13 killed, 58 wounded. Confed. 30 killed, 150 wounded, 300 captured.
  17.—Gainesville, Fla. 75th Ohio Mounted Infantry. Union 16 killed, 30 wounded 102 missing.
  —Winchester, Va. New Jersey Brigade of Sixth Corps and Wilson's Cav. Union 50 wounded, 250 missing.
  18, 19 and 21.—Six-mile House, Weldon Railroad, Va. Fifth and Ninth Corps and Kautz's and Gregg's Cav. Union 212 killed, 1,155 wounded, 3,176 missing. Confed. 2,000 wounded, 2,000 missing. Confed. Brigadier-Generals Saunders and Lamar killed, and Claigman, Barton, Finnegan and Anderson wounded.
  18 to 22.—Kilpatrick's Raid on the Atlanta Railroad. Union 400 wounded.
  19.—Snicker's Gap, Pike, Va. Detachment of 5th Mich. Cav. Union 30 killed, 3 wounded (all prisoners taken and the wounded were put to death by Mosby).
  —Martinsburg, Va. Averill's Cav. Union 25 killed and wounded.
  19.—Pine Bluff, Tenn. River, Tenn. Detachment of Co. B 83d Ill. Mounted Infantry. Union 8 killed and mutilated by guerrillas.
  21.—Summit Point, Berryville and Flowing Springs, Va. Sixth Corps, and Merritt's and Wilson's Cav. Union 600 killed and wounded. Confed. 400 killed and wounded.
  —Memphis, Tenn. Detachment of 8th Iowa, 108th and 113th Ill., 39th, 40th and 41st Wis., 61st U. S. Colored, 3d and 4th Iowa Cav., Battery G 1st Mo. Lt. Artil. Union 30 killed, 100 wounded. Confed. 100 killed and wounded.
  21 and 22.—College or Oxford Hill, Miss. 4th Iowa, 11th and 21st Mo., 3d Iowa Cav., 12th Mo. Cav. Confed. 15 killed.
  23.—Abbeville, Miss. 10th Mo., 14th Iowa, 5th and 7th Minn., 8th Wis. Union 20 wounded. Confed. 15 killed.
  24.—Forth Smith, Ark. 11th U. S. Colored. Union 1 killed, 13 wounded.
  —Jones' Hay Station and Ashley Station, Ark. 9th Iowa and 8th and 11th Mo. Cav. Union 5 killed, 41 wounded. Confed. 60 wounded.
  24 and 25.—Bermuda Hundred, Va. Tenth Corps. Union 31 wounded. Confed. 61 missing.
  24 to 27.—Halltown, Va. Portion of Eighth Corps. Union 39 killed, 175 wounded, Confed. 130 killed and wounded.

AUG. 25.—Smithfield and Shepherdstown or Kearneysville, Va. Merritt's and Wilson's Cav. Union 20 killed, 61 wounded, 100 missing. Confed. 300 killed and wounded.
—Ream's Station, Va. Second Corps and Gregg's Cav. Union 127 killed, 546 wounded, 1,769 missing. Confed. 1,500 killed and wounded.

27 and 28.—Holly Springs, Miss. 14th Iowa, 11th U. S. Colored Artil., 10th Mo. Cav. Union 1 killed, 2 wounded.

29.—Smithfield, Va. 3d Div. Sixth Corps and Torbett's Cav. Union 10 killed, 90 wounded. Confed. 200 killed and wounded.

31.—Block House, No. 5, Nashville and Chattanooga Railroad, Tenn. 115th Ohio. Union 3 killed. Confed. 25 wounded.

31 and Sept. 1.—Jonesboro', Ga. Fifteenth, Sixteenth, Seventeenth and Davis' Cavalry Divisions of Fourteenth Corps. Union 1,149 killed and wounded. Confed. 2,000 killed, wounded and missing. Confed. Brigadier-Generals Anderson, Cummings and Patten killed.

SEPT. 1 to 8.—Rosseau's pursuit of Wheeler in Tenn. Rosseau's Cav., 1st and 4th Tenn., 2d Mich., 1st Wis., 8th Iowa, 2d and 8th Ind., and 6th Ky. Union 10 killed, 30 wounded. Confed. 300 killed, wounded and captured.

1 to Oct. 30.—In front of Petersburg. Army of the Potomac. Union 170 killed, 822 wounded, 812 missing. Confed. 1,000 missing.

2.—Fall of Atlanta, Ga. Twentieth Corps. Confed. 200 captured.

2 to 6.—Lovejoy Station, Ga. Fourth and Twenty-third Corps. Casualties not recorded.

3 and 4.—Berryville, Va. Eighth and Nineteenth Corps and Torbett's Cav. Union 30 killed, 182 wounded, 100 missing. Confed. 25 killed, 100 wounded, 70 missing.

4.—Greenville, Tenn. 9th and 13th Tenn., and 10th Mich. Cav. Union 6 wounded. Confed. 10 killed, 60 wounded, 75 missing. Confed. General John Morgan killed.

6.—Searcy, Ark. Detachment 9th Ia. Cav. Union 2 killed, 6 wounded.

10.—Capture of Fort Hell, Va. 99th Pa., 20th Ind., 2d U. S. Sharpshooters. Union 20 wounded. Confed. 90 prisoners.

13.—Lock's Ford, Va. Torbett's Cav. Union 2 killed, 18 wounded. Confed 181 captured.

16.—Sycamore Church, Va. 1st D. C. and 13th Pa. Cav. Union 400 killed, wounded and captured. Confed. 50 killed and wounded.

16 and 18.—Fort Gibson, Ind. Ter. 79th U. S. Colored and 2d Kan. Cav. Union 38 killed, 48 missing.

17.—Belcher's Mills, Va. Kautz's and Gregg's Cav. Union 25 wounded.

19 to 22.—Winchester and Fisher's Hill, Va. Sixth, Eighth and 1st and 2d Divisions of the Nineteenth Corps. Averill's and Torbett's Cav., Major-General Phil Sheridan. Union 693 killed, 4,033 wounded, 623 missing. Confed. 3,250 killed and wounded, 3,600 captured. Union Brigadier-Generals Russell and Mulligan killed, and McIntosh, Upton and Chapman wounded. Confed. Major-General Rhodes and Brigadier-Generals Gordon and Goodwin killed, and Fitz Hugh Lee, Terry, Johnson and Wharton wounded.

23.—Athens, Ala. 106th, 110th and 114th U. S. Colored, 3d Tenn. Cav., reinforced by 18th Mich. and 102d Ohio. Union 950 missing. Confed. 5 killed, 25 wounded.
—Rockport, Mo. 3d Mo. Militia Cav. Union 10 killed.

24.—Fayette, Mo. 9th Mo. Militia Cav. Union 3 killed, 5 wounded. Confed. 6 killed, 30 wounded,

26 and 27.—Pilot Knob or Ironton, Mo. 47th and 50th Mo., 14th Ia., 2d and 3d Mo. Cav., Battery H 2d Mo. Light Artil. Union 28 killed, 56 wounded, 100 missing. Confed. 1,500 killed and wounded.

27.—Centralia, Mo. Three Co's 39th Mo. massacred by Price. Union 122 killed, 2 wounded.
—Marianna, Fla. 7th Vt., 82d U. S. Colored and 2d Maine Cav. Union 32 wounded. Confed. 81 missing.

28 to 30.—New Market Heights or Laurel Hill, Va. Tenth and Eighteenth Corps and Kautz's Cav. Union 400 killed, 2,029 wounded. Confed. 2,000 killed and wounded.

29.—Centreville, Tenn. 2d Tenn. Mounted Infantry. Union 10 killed, 25 wounded.

29 and 30.—Leesburg and Harrison, Mo. 14th Ia., 2d Mo. Militia Cav., Battery H 2d Mo. Light Artil.

30 and Oct. 1.—Poplar Springs Church, Prebles Farm, Va. 1st Div. Fifth Corps and 2d Div. Ninth Corps. Union 141 killed, 788 wounded, 1,756 missing. Confed. 800 wounded, 100 missing.
—Arthur's Swamp, Va. Gregg's Cav. Union 60 wounded, 100 missing.

OCT. 2.—Waynesboro', Va. Portion of Custer's and Merritt's Cav. Union 50 killed and wounded.

OCT. 2.—Saltville, Va. 11th and 13th Ky. Cav., 12th Ohio, 11th Mich., 5th and 6th U. S. Colored Cav., 26th 30th, 35th, 37th, 39th, 40th and 45th Ky. Mounted Infantry. Union 54 killed, 190 wounded, 104 missing. Confed. 18 killed, 71 wounded, 21 missing.

5.—Jackson, La. 23d Wis., 1st Tex. and 1st La. Cav., 2d and 4th Mass. Battery. Union 4 killed, 10 wounded.

—Allatoona, Ga. 7th, 12th, 50th, 57th and 93d Ill., 39th Ia., 4th Minn., 18th Wis. and 12th Wis. Battery. Union 142 killed, 352 wounded, 212 missing. Confed. 231 killed, 500 wounded, 411 missing.

7.—New Market, Va. 3d Div. Custer's Cav. Union 56 missing.

7 to 11.—Jefferson City, California and Boonsville, Mo. (Price's Invasion), 1st, 4th 5th, 6th and 7th Mo. Militia Cav., 15th Mo. Cav., 17th Ill. Cav., Battery H 2d Mo. Light Artil.

7 and 13.—Darbytown Road, Va. Tenth Corps and Kautz's Cav. Union 105 killed, 502 wounded, 206 missing. Confed. 1,100 killed and wounded, 350 missing. Confed. General Gregg killed.

9.—Tom's Brook, Fisher's Hill, or Strasburg, Va. Merritt's, Custer's and Torbett's Cav. Union 9 killed, 67 wounded. Confed. 100 killed and wounded, 180 missing.

10.—East Point, Miss. 7th U. S. Colored. Union 10 killed, 20 wounded.

11.—Fort Donnelson, Tenn. Detachment 4th U. S. Colored Heavy Artil. Union 4 killed, 9 wounded. Confed. 3 killed, 25 wounded.

13.—Reconnoissance to Strasburg, Va. Major-General Emory's and Crook's troops. Union 30 killed, 144 wounded, 40 missing.

13.—Dalton, Ga. Troops under Colonel Johnson, 44th U. S. Colored. Union 400 missing.

—Buzzard Roost, Ga. One Co. 115th Ill. Union 5 killed, 36 wounded, 60 missing.

15.—Glasgow, Mo. 43d Mo., and detachments of 17th Ill., 9th Mo. Militia, 13th Mo. Cav., 62d U. S. Colored. Union 400 wounded and missing. Confed. 50 killed and wounded.

19.—Lexington, Mo. 5th, 11th, 15th and 16th Kan. Cav., 3d Wis. Cav. Casualties not recorded.

—Cedar Creek, Va. (Sheridan's Ride.) Sixth Corps, Eighth Corps and 1st and 2d Divisions Nineteenth Corps, Merritt's, Custer's and Torbett's Cav. Union 588 killed, 3,516 wounded, 1,891 missing. Confed. 3,000 killed and wounded, 1,200 missing. Union Brigadier-Generals Bidwell and Thorburn killed, Major-Generals Wright, Ricketts and Grover, and Brigadier-Generals Ketchem, McKenzie, Penrose, Hamlin, Devins, Duval and Lowell wounded. Confed. Major-General Ramseur killed and Battle and Conner wounded.

21 and 22.—Little Blue and Independence, Mo. Kansas Militia, 2d and 5th Mo. Militia, 2d Col. Cav., 5th. 7th. 11th, 15th and 16th Kan. Cav., 1st, 2d, 4th, 6th, 7th, 8th and 9th Mo. Militia Cav. Casualties not recorded.

23.—Hurricane Creek, Miss. 1st Ia. and 9th Kan. Cav. Union 1 killed, 2 wounded.

26 to 29.—Decatur, Ala. 18th Mich., 102d Ohio, 68th Ind. and 14th U. S. Colored. Union 10 killed, 45 wounded, 100 missing. Confed. 100 killed, 300 wounded.

27.—Hatchers's Run, Va. Gregg's Cav., 2d and 3d Divisions, Second Corps, Fifth and Ninth Corps. Union 156 killed, 1,047 wounded, 699 missing. Confed. 200 killed, 600 wounded, 200 missing.

27 and 28.—Fair Oaks, Va. Tenth and Eighteenth Corps and Kautz's Cav. Union 120 killed, 783 wounded, 400 missing. Confed. 60 killed, 311 wounded, 80 missing.

28.—Destruction of the Rebel ram Albemarle, by Lieutenant Cushing and 13 marines. Union 3 wounded, 11 captured.

—Morristown, Tenn. General Gillem's Cav. Union 8 killed, 42 wounded. Confed. 240 missing.

28 and 30.—Newtonia, Mo. Colonel Blunt's Cav. in pursuit of Price. Confed. 250 wounded.

29.—Beverly, W. Va. 8th Ohio Cav. Union 8 killed, 25 wounded, 13 missing. Confed. 17 killed, 27 wounded, 92 missing.

30.—Near Brownsville, Ark. 7th Ia. and 11th Mo. Cav. Union 2 killed.

NOV. 1 to 4.—Union Station, Tenn. 10th Mo. Cav. Union 2 killed, 2 wounded, 26 missing.

5.—Fort Sedgwick, or Fort Hill, Va. Second Corps. Union 5 killed, 10 wounded. Confed. 15 killed, 35 wounded.

9.—Atlanta, Ga. 2d Div. Twentieth Corps. Confed. 20 killed and wounded.

12.—Newtown, Nineveh and Cedar Springs, Va. Merritt's, Custer's and Powell's Cav. Union 84 killed, 100 missing. Confed. 150 missing.

13.—Bull's Gap, Tenn. 8th, 9th and 13th Tenn. Cav. Union 5 killed, 36 wounded, 200 missing.

16.—Lovejoy Station and Bear Creek Station, Ga. Kilpatrick's Cav. Confed. 50 captured.

17.—Bermuda Hundred, Va. 209th Pa. Union 10 wounded, 120 missing. Confed. 10 wounded.

NOV. 18.—Myerstown, Va. Detachment 91st Ohio. Union 60 killed and wounded. Confed. 10 killed and wounded.
20.—Macon, Ga. 10th Ohio Cav., 9th Pa. Cav., 92d Ill. Mounted Infantry, 10th Wis. Battery.
22.—Griswoldville, Ga. Walcott's Brigade, 1st Div. Fifteenth Corps and 1st Brigade 3d Div. Cav. Union 10 killed, 52 wounded. Confed. 50 killed, 200 wounded, 400 missing.
—Rood's Hill, Va. Torbett's Cav. Union 18 killed, 52 wounded.
—Lawrenceburg, Campbellville and Lynnville, Tenn. Hatch's Cav. Union 75 killed and wounded. Confed. 50 killed and wounded.
26.—Saundersville, Ga. 3d Brigade 1st Div. Twentieth Corps. Union 100 missing. Confed. 100 missing.
26 to 29.—Sylvan Grove, Waynesboro', Browne's Cross Roads. Kilpatrick's Cav. Union 46 wounded. Confed. 600 killed and wounded.
29 and 30.—Spring Hill and Franklin, Tenn. Fourth and Twenty-third Corps and Cav. Union 189 killed, 1,033 wounded, 1,104 missing. Confed. 1,750 killed, 3,800 wounded, 702 missing. Union Major-Generals Stanley and Bradley wounded. Confed. Major-General Cleborne, Brigadier-Generals Adams, Williams, Strahl, Geist and Cranberry killed, Major-General Brown and Brigadier-Generals Carter, Manigault, Quarles, Cockerell and Scott wounded.
30.—Honey Hill or Grahamsville, S. C. 25th Ohio, 56th and 155th N. Y., 26th, 32d, 35th and 102d U. S. Colored, 54th and 55th Mass. Colored. Union 66 killed, 645 wounded.

DEC. 1.—Stoney Creek Station, Weldon Railroad, Va. Gregg's Cav. Union 40 wounded. Confed. 175 captured.
—Twelve miles from Yazoo City, Miss. Detachment of 2d Wis. Cav. Union 5 killed, 9 wounded, 25 missing.
1 to 14.—In front of Nashville, Tenn. Fourth, Twenty-third and 1st and 2d Divisions of Sixteenth Corps and Wilson's Cav. Union 16 killed, 100 wounded.
1 to 31.—In front of Petersburg. Army of the Potomac. Union 40 killed, 320 wounded.
2 and 3.—Block House No. 2, Mill Creek, Chattanooga, Tenn. Detachment 115th Ohio, 44th and two Co's 14th U. S. Colored. Union 12 killed, 46 wounded, 57 missing.
3.—Thomas' Station, Ga. 92d Ill., Mounted Infantry. Union 2 killed, 1 wounded.
4.—Block House No. 7, Tenn. General Milroy's troops. Union 100 wounded. Confed. 100 killed and wounded.
5 to 8.—Murfreesboro', Tenn. General Rosseau's troops. Union 30 killed, 175 wounded. Confed. 197 missing.
6.—White Post, Va. Fifty men of 21st N. Y. Cav. Union 30 wounded.
6 to 9.—Deveaux's Neck, S. C. 56th and 155th N. Y., 35th and 107th Ohio, 26th, 32d, 34th and 102d U. S. Col., 54th and 55th Mass. Colored, 3d R. I. Artil. and U. S. Gunboats. Union 39 killed, 390 wounded, 200 missing. Confed. 400 killed and wounded.
7 to 9.—Eden Station, Ogeechee River, Ga. Fifteenth and 17th Corps right wing of Sherman's Army.
7 to 11.—Weldon's Railroad Expedition. Fifth Corps 3d Div. of 2d Corps and 2d Div. Cav. Corps, Army of the Potomac. Union 100 wounded.
8 and 9.—Hatcher's Run, Va. 1st Div. Second Corps, 3d and 13th Pa. Cav., 6th Ohio Cav. Union 125 killed and wounded.
8 to 28.—Raid to Gordonsville, Va. Merritt's and Custer's Cav. Union 48 wounded.
10 to 21.—Siege of Savannah, Ga. Fourteenth, Fifteenth, Seventeenth and Twentieth Corps of Sherman's Army. Union 200 wounded. Confed. 800 missing.
12 to 21.—Stoneman's Raid from Bean's Station, Tenn., to Saltville, Va., including Abingdon, Glade Springs and Marion. Union 20 killed, 123 wounded. Confed. 8 killed, 126 wounded, 500 missing.
13.—Fort McAllister, Ga. 2d Div. of Fifteenth Corps. Union 24 killed, 110 wounded. Confed. 250 missing.
14.—Memphis, Tenn. 4th Ia. Cav. Union 3 killed, 6 wounded.
15 and 16.—Nashville, Tenn. Fourth Corps, 1st and 3d Divisions Thirteenth Corps, Twenty-third Corps Wilson's Cav. and detachments colored troops, convalescents. Union 400 killed, 1,740 wounded. Confed. 4,462 missing.
17.—Franklin, Tenn. Wilson's Cav. Confed. 1,800 wounded and sick captured.
17 to 19.—Mitchell's Creek, Fla., and Pine Barren Creek, Ala. 82d and 97th U. S. Colored. Union 9 killed, 53 wounded, 11 missing.
20.—Lacey's Springs. Custer's Cav. Union 2 killed, 22 wounded, 40 missing.
25.—Fort Fisher, N. C. Tenth Corps and North Atlantic Squadron. Union 8 killed, 38 wounded. Confed. 3 killed, 55 wounded, 280 prisoners.
28.—Egypt Station, Miss. 4th and 11th Ill., 7th Ind., 4th and 10th Mo., 2d Wis., 2d N. J., 1st Miss. and 3d U. S. Colored Cav. Union 26 killed, 88 wounded. Confed. 500 captured. Confed. Brigadier-General Gholson killed.

1865.

JAN. 2.—Franklin, Miss. 4th and 11th Ill. Cav., 3d U. S. Colored Cav. Union 4 killed, 9 wounded. Confed. 20 killed, 30 wounded.

2d and 3d.—Nauvoo and Thornhill, Ala. 15th Pa. Cav., Detachments of 10th, 12th and 13th Ind. Cav. and 2d Tenn. Cav. Union 1 killed, 2 wounded. Confed 3 killed, 2 wounded, 95 captured, and Hill's supply and pontoon train destroyed.

11.—Beverly, W. Va. 34th Ohio and 8th Ohio Cav. Union 5 killed, 20 wounded, 583 missing.

13 to 15.—Fort Fisher, N. C. Portions of Twenty-fourth and Twenty-Fifth Corps and Twenty-fifth Corps and Porter's Gunboats. Union 184 killed 749 wounded. Confed. 400 killed and wounded, 2,083 captured.

14 to 16.—Pocataligo, S. C. Seventeenth Corps. Union 25 wounded.

16.—Explosion of the magazine at Fort Fisher, N. C. Union 25 killed, 66 wounded.

25 to Feb. 9.—Combahee River and River's Bridge, Salkahatchie, S. C. Fifteenth and Seventeenth Corps. Union 138 killed and wounded.

FEB. 5 to 7.—Dabney's Mills, Hatcher's Run, Va. Fifth Corps and 1st Division Sixth Corps and Gregg's Cav. Union 232 killed, 1,062 wounded, 186 missing. Confed. 1,200 killed and wounded. Union Brigadier-Generals Morrow, Smythe, Davis, Gregg, Ayres, Sickles and Gwyn wounded. Confed. General Pegram killed and Sorrell wounded.

8 to 14.—Williston, Blackville and Aiken, S. C. Kilpatrick's Cav. Confed. 240 killed and wounded, 100 missing.

10.—James Island, S. C. Major-General Gilmore's Command. Union 20 killed, 76 wounded. Confed. 20 killed, 70 wounded.

11.—Sugar Loaf Battery, Federal Point, N. C. Portions of Twenty-fourth and Twenty-fifth Corps. Union 14 killed, 114 wounded.

15 to 17.—Congaree Creek and Columbia, S. C. Fifteenth Corps. Union 20 killed and wounded.

18.—Ashby Gap, Va. Detachment 14th Penn. Cav. Union 6 killed, 19 wounded, 64 missing.

18 to 22.—Fort Anderson, Town Creek, and Wilmington, N. C. Twenty-third and Twenty fourth Corps, and Porter's Gunboats. Union 40 killed, 204 wounded. Confed. 70 killed, 400 wounded, 375 missing.

22.—Douglas Landing, Pine Bluff, Ark. 13th Ill. Cav. Union 40 wounded. Confed. 26 wounded.

27 to March 25.—Sheridan's Raid in Virginia. 1st and 3d Divisions Cavalry Corps. Union 35 killed and wounded. Confed. 1,667 prisoners.

MAR. 6.—Olive Branch, La. 4th Wis. Cav. Union 3 killed, 2 wounded.

—Natural Bridge, Fla. 2d and 99th U. S. Colored. Union 22 killed, 46 wounded.

8 to 10.—Wilcox's Bridge, N. C. Palmer's, Carter's and Ruger's Divisions. Union 80 killed, 421 wounded, 600 missing. Confed. 1,500 killed and missing.

16.—Averysboro', N. C. Twentieth Corps and Kilpatrick's Cav. Union 77 killed, 477 wounded. Confed. 108 killed, 540 wounded, 217 missing.

19 to 21.—Bentonville, N. C. Fourteenth, Fifteenth, Seventeenth and Twentieth Corps, and Kilpatrick's Cav. Union 191 killed, 1,168 wounded, 287 missing. Confed. 267 killed, 1,200 wounded, 1,625 missing.

20 to April 6.—Stoneman's Raid into Southwestern Va. and North Carolina. Palmer's, Brown's and Miller's Cavalry Brigades.

22 to April 24.—Wilson's Raid, Chickasaw, Ala., to Macon, Ga. Union 63 killed, 345 wounded, 63 missing. Confed 22 killed, 38 wounded, 6,766 prisoners.

25.—Fort Steadman, in front of Petersburg, Va. 1st and 3d Divisions Ninth Corps. Union 68 killed 337 wounded, 506 missing. Confed. 800 killed and wounded, 1,881 missing, assault of the Second and Sixth Corps. Union 103 killed, 864 wounded, 209 missing. Confed. 834 captured.

26 to April 9.—Siege of Mobile, Ala., including Spanish Fort and Port Blakely. Thirteenth and Sixteenth Corps and U. S. Navy. Union 213 killed, 1,211 wounded. Confed. 500 killed and wounded, 2,952 missing and captured.

29.—Quaker Road, Va. Warren's Fifth Corps and Griffin's 1st Division, Army of the Potomac. Union 55 killed, 306 wounded. Confed. 135 killed, 400 wounded, 100 missing.

31.—Boydton and White Oak Roads, Va. Second and Fifth Corps. Union 177 killed, 1,134 wounded, 556 missing. Confed. 1,000 wounded, 235 missing.

—Dinwiddie C. H., Va. 1st, 2d and 3d Cavalry Divisions Army of the Potomac. Union 67 killed, 354 wounded. Confed. 400 killed and wounded.

APRIL 1.—Five Forks, Va. 1st, 2d and 3d Cavalry Divisions and Fifth Corps. Union 124 killed, 706 wounded. Confed. 3,000 killed and wounded, 5,500 captured.
    2.—Fall of Petersburg, Va. Second, Sixth, Ninth and Twenty-fourth Corps. Union 296 killed, 2,565 wounded, 500 missing. Confed. 3,000 prisoners.
    3.—Namozin Church and Willicomack, Va. Custer's Cavalry. Union 10 killed, 85 wounded.
    3.—Fall of Richmond, Va. Confed. 6,000 prisoners, of whom 5,000 were sick and wounded.
    5.—Amelia Springs, Va. Crook,s Cav. Union 20 killed, 96 wounded.
    6.—Sailor's Creek, Va. Second and Sixth Corps and Sheridan's Cav. Union 166 killed, 1,014 wounded. Confed. 1,000 killed and wounded, 6,000 prisoners.
    —High Bridge, Appomattox River, Va. Portion of Twenty-fourth Corps. Union 10 killed, 31 wounded, 1,000 missing and captured.
    7.—Farmville, Va. Second Corps. Union 655 killed and wounded.
    8 and 9.—Appomattox C. H., Va. Twenty-fourth Corps, one Division of the Twenty-fifth Corps and Sheridan's Cav. Union 200 killed and wounded. Confed. 500 killed.
    9.—Lee surrendered to the Armies of the Potomac and James. Major-General U. S. Grant. Confed. 26,000 prisoners.
    17.—Surrender of Mosby to Major General Hancock. Confed. 700 prisoners.
    26.—Johnson surrendered to the Armies of the Tennessee, Georgia and Ohio ; Major-General W. T. Sherman. Confed. 29,924 prisoners.
MAY 10.—Capture of Jefferson Davis at Irwinsville, Ga. 1st Wis. and 4th Mich. Cav. Union 2 killed, 4 wounded, caused by the pursuing parties firing into each other.
    Tallahassee, Fla. Surrender of Sam Jones' Command to Detachment of Wilson's Cav. ; Major-General McCook. Confed. 8,000 prisoners.
    11.—Chalk Bluff, Ark. Surrender of Jeff Thompson's Command to forces under General Dodge. Confed. 7,454 prisoners.
    13.—Palmetto Ranche, Tex. 34th Ind. 62d U. S. Colored and 2d Tex. Cav. Union 118 killed and wounded.
    26.—Surrender of Kirby Smith to Major-General Canby's Command. Confed. 20,000 prisoners.

NOTE.—This list does not include all, or nearly all, of the encounters between forces of combatants during the war, and many omissions will doubtless be noted ; but it was all we could succeed in verifying up to the time of going to press, as far as the organizations engaged are concerned and the result of the engagement.

XXX.

CORPS, BRIGADE, REGIMENTAL AND BATTERY VETERAN ASSOCIATIONS, WITH NAMES OF SECRETARIES.

Society of the Army of the Potomac, Horatio C. King, Potter Building, New York City.
Society of the Third Army Corps, Colonel Edward D. Welling. Pennington, N. J.
Society of the Fifth Army Corps, General Frederick T. Locke, 1341 Broadway, New York City.
Society of the Sixth Army Corps, Captain George B. Fielder, Jersey City, N. J.
Society of the Burnside Expedition and Ninth Army Corps, General C. H. Barney, 32 Nassau street, New York City.
Society of the Twelfth Corps, John J. H. Love, Montclair, N. J.
Society of the Nineteenth Army Corps, Major Thomas B. O'Dell, 67 Wall street, New York City.
The Cavalry Society of the Armies of the United States, Major L. L. Barney, Elmira, N. Y.
Society of the Army of Northern Virginia (Virginia Division), Carlton McCarthy, Richmond, Va.
Pickett's Division Association, Charles T. Loehr, Richmond, Va.
Philadelphia Brigade Association, John W. Frazier, Registry Bureau, Dept. Survey, Philadelphia, Pa.
76th New York Veteran Volunteers, A. P. Smith, Cortland, N. Y,
9th New York Cavalry, Veteran Association, A. C. Robertson, Harmony, N. Y.
107th New York Regimental Association, A. S. Fitch, Elmira, N. Y.
108th New York Veteran Association, J. George Cramer, Rochester, N. Y.
1st New York Light Battery L (Reynolds), ——, Rochester, N. Y.
123d New York Veteran Association, Lieutenant Donald Reid, Lakeville, N. Y.
100th Pennsylvania Veteran Volunteers (Roundhead's Society), J. C. Stevenson, New Castle, Pa.
4th New York Independent Battery Association, James R. Hill, 237 Broadway, New York City.
4th New York Cavalry Veteran Association, Joseph A. Moore, Mount Vernon, N. Y.
Company H, 1st Mass. Volunteer Infantry, James R. Gerrish. Chelsea, Mass.
54th New York Veteran Association, William C. Smith, New York City.
Battery B, New York Artillery Association, John M. Scoville, Baldwinsville, N. Y.
Social Union 97th New York Volunteers, Arch. B. Snow, Boonville, N. Y.
134th New York Volunteers, Henry Y. Bradt, Schenectady, N. Y.
42d New York (Tammany Regiment), Thomas H. Mallon, 303 Fulton street, Brooklyn, N. Y.

2d New Hampshire Association, Thomas B. Little, Concord, N. H.
3d New Hampshire Association, D. Archer Brown, Penacook, N. H.
5th New Hampshire Association, J. M. Davis, Haverhill, Mass.
6th New Hampshire Association, J. B. Sanders, Dover, N. H.
7th New Hampshire Association, H. F. W. Little, Manchester, N. H.
8th New Hampshire Association, Jacob T. Chandler, Concord, N. H.
9th New Hampshire, John E. Mason, Washington, D. C.
11th New Hampshire Association, J. B. Sanborn, Tremont, N. H.
12th New Hampshire Association, R. W. Musgrove, Bristol, N. H.
13th New Hampshire Association, C. W. Hobbs, Pelham, N. H.
14th New Hampshire Association, Lieutenant E. D. Hadley, ——.
15th New Hamshire Association, E. B. Huse, Enfield, N. H.
1st New Hampshire Cavalry Association, J. H. French, Penacook, N. H.
Sharpshooters' Association, H. A. Redfield, Dover, N. H.
Veteran Band Association, D. Archer Brown, Penacook, N. H.
Prisoners of War Association, J. Lane Fitts, Candia, N. H.
Lowell Veteran Association, P. F. Gammell, Lowell, Mass.
National Veteran Association, T. M. Fletcher, Littleton, N. H.
31st Massachusetts Volunteers, H. M. Coney, Boston, Mass.
Lamoile Valley Veterans' Association, D. J. Safford, Morrisville, Vt.
49th Massachusetts Volunteer, Captain A. V. Shannon, Lee, Mass.
121st New York Volunteers, J. M. Lovejoy, Smith Valley, N. Y.
152d New York Volunteers, Harris Greenwold, Cooperstown, N. Y.
61st Illinois Survivors' Association, P. D. Whitzell, McPherson, Kan.
30th Indiana Volunteers, J. N. Ohlwine, Cromwell, Ind.
54th Indiana Volunteers, J. H. Van Valkenburg, Tipton, Ind.
54th Ohio Volunteers, L. P. McCollum, 297 Hunter street, Columbus, O.
11th Pennsylvania Infantry, H. Byers Kuhns, Greensburg, Pa.
23d Pennsylvania Infantry, W. J. Wray, 2923 Reno street, Philadelphia, Pa.
26th Pennsylvania Infantry (Washington Guards), W. B. Wright, 258 North 22d street, Philadelphia, Pa.
27th Pennsylvania Infantry, Henry Mauk, 332 Brown street, Philadelphia, Pa.
28th Pennsylvania Infantry, John P. Nicholson, Philadelphia, Pa.
29th Pennsylvania Infantry, David Gillen, Burlington, N. J.
31st Pennsylvania Infantry (2d Reserves), Charles Devine, 509 E. North street, Phila., Pa.
38th Pennsylvania Infantry (9th Reserves), Henry W. Strickler, Pittsburg, Pa.
39th Pennsylvania Infantry (10th Reserves), W. W. Scott, 95 Fifth avenue, Pittsburg, Pa.
40th Pennsylvania Infantry (11th Reserves), R. S. Davis, Blairsville, Pa.
41st Pennsylvania Infantry (12th Reserves), Chill W. Hazzard, Monongahela City, Pa.
42d Pennsylvania Infantry (Bucktails), W. H. Rauch, 713 Girard avenue, Philadelphia Pa.
46th Pennsylvania Infantry, James A. Shipp, Shamokin, Pa.
49th Pennsylvania Infantry, Rev. I. Newton Ritter, 2026 North 21st street, Philadelphia, Pa.
53d Pennsylvania Infantry, A. B. Mann, Condersport, Pa.
56th Pennsylvania Infantry, J. M. Stoever, Chester, Pa.
57th Pennsylvania Infantry, D. W. Gore, Cheshequin, Pa.
61st Pennsylvania Infantry, David Ginther, 506 Walnut street, Philadelphia, Pa.
63d Pennsylvania Infantry, R. Howard Miller, Pittsburg, Pa.
68th Pennsylvania Infantry (Scott Legion), Alfred Craighead, 1736 North 16th street, Philadelphia, Pa.
69th Pennsylvania Infantry (Paddy Owen's Regulars), A. W. McDermott, 4905 Girard avenue, Philadelphia, Pa.
71st Pennsylvania Infantry, W. H. Landell, U. S. Mint, Philadelphia, Pa.
72d Pennsylvania Infantry (Baxter's Fire Zouaves), William Prior, 1110 Dickinson street, Philadelphia, Pa.
74th Pennsylvania Infantry, Henry Hesserich, Pittsburg, Pa.

75th Pennsylvania Infantry, Herman Nachtigal, southeast corner 23d and Arch streets, Philadelphia, Pa.

82d Pennsylvania Infantry, W. H. Ridhoffer, 920 Walnut street, Philadelphia, Pa.

84th Pennsylvania Infantry, Mose E. Miechant, 625 Walnut street, Philadelphia, Pa.

88th Pennsylvania Infantry, John D. Vautier, Federal street, Philadelphia, Pa.

90th Pennsylvania Infantry, W. W. Mayberry, 37 North 10th street, Philadelphia, Pa.

91st Pennsylvania Infantry, A. D. Caldwell, 3601 Spruce street, Philadelphia, Pa.

93d Pennsylvania Infantry (Lebanon Infantry), E. C. Euston, George H. Ahler, Lebanon, Pa.

95th Pennsylvania Infantry (Goslin Zouaves), David Ayres, Wildreer street, Phila., Pa.

98th Pennsylvania Infantry, A. B. Baemish, 855 North 8th street, Philadelphia, Pa.

99th Pennsylvania Infantry, Washington M. Worrall, 1856 North 21st street, Phila., Pa.

102d Pennsylvania Infantry, James A. McLaughlin, County Treasurer's Office, Pittsburg, Pa.

105th Pennsylvania Infantry, Miss Kate M. Scott, Brookville, Pa.

107th Pennsylvania Infantry, Captain Samuel Lyon, Blairsville, Pa.

109th Pennsylvania Infantry (Curtin Light Guards), Thomas E. Lewis, 2005 Norris street, Philadelphia, Pa.

110th Pennsylvania Infantry, J. C. M. Hamilton, Tyrone, Pa.

111th Pennsylvania Infantry, Noah W. Lowell, Erie, Pa.

114th Pennsylvania Infantry (Collis Zouaves), B. L. Myers Frankford, Philadelphia, Pa.

115th Pennsylvania Infantry, Jeremiah J. Sullivan, 226 Madison street. Philadelphia, Pa.

116th Pennsylvania Infantry (Irish Brigade), Joseph W. Yocum, Columbia, Pa.

118th Pennsylvania Infantry (Corn Exchange), George W. R. Carteret, 1640 South 16th street, Philadelphia, Pa.

121st Pennsylvania Infantry, John Gallraith, 211 South 6th street, Philadelphia, Pa.

139th Pennsylvania Infantry, Charles W. Green, 142 Ohio street, Allegheny City., Pa.

147th Pennsylvania Infantry, Lieutenant J. P. Nicholson, Philadelphia, Pa.

148th Pennsylvania Infantry, D. S. Keeler, Bellefonte, Pa.

149th Pennsylvania Infantry (2nd Bucktails), W. R. Johnston, Bellevue, Pa.

150th Pennsylvania Infantry (3d Bucktails), Charles P. Haupt, Main street, Germantown, Pa.

151st Pennsylvania Infantry, W. L. Owens, Granville, Pa.

153d Pennsylvania Infantry, Thomas D. King, Northampton Co., Pa.

155th Pennsylvania Infantry, Henry A. Breed, Pittsburg, Pa.

3d Pennsylvania Cavalry ("Young's Light"—60th Vols.), Andrew J. Speese, 227 South 4th street, Philadelphia. Pa.

4th Pennsylvania Cavalry (64th Vols.), D. C. Phillips, 428 Duquesne street, Pittsburg, Pa.

6th Pennsylvania Cavalry (Rushe's Lancers—70th Vols.), Alfred S. Pallon, Philadelphia, Pa.

8th Pennsylvania Cavalry (89th Vols.), J. M. Vanderslice, 16 N. 7th street, Philadelphia, Pa.

16th Pennsylvania Cavalry (161st Vols.), F. D. Sarmin, Mifflintown, Pa.

17th Pennsylvania Cavalry (162d Vols.), H. P. Meyer, Lebanon, Pa.

18th Pennsylvania Cavalry (Continental—163d Vols.), J. A. Wilt, Towanda, Pa.

Battery H, Pennsylvania Artillery (3d Heavy), John H. Uhler, Lebanon, Pa.

Battery B, Pennsylvania Artillery, J. A. Gardner, Newcastle, Pa.

30th Pennsylvania Infantry (1st Reserves), B. F. W. Urban, Lancaster, Pa.

34th Pennsylvania Infantry (5th Reserves), W. Hayes Grier, Columbia Pa.

35th Pennsylvania Infantry (6th Reserves), Milton McFarland, Scranton, Pa.

62d Pennsylvania Infantry, Bernard Coll, Pittsburg, Pa.

73d Pennsylvania Infantry, John P. Titus, 2035 Turner street, Philadelphia, Pa.

106th Pennsylvania Infantry, William B. Rose, 717 Sansom street, Philadelphia, Pa.

119th Pennsylvania Infantry, John A. Weidersheim, Philadelphia, Pa.

140th Pennsylvania Infantry, Rev. John Lyman Milligan, Allegheny, Pa.

143d Pennsylvania Infantry, J. D. Campbell, Beach Haven, Pa.

145th Pennsylvania Infantry, John C. Tilton, Erie, Pa.

1st Pennsylvania Cavalry, Colonel William Penn Lloyd, Mechanicsburg, Pa.

Battery F, 1st Pennsylvania Artillery, Joel H. Schmehl, Reading, Pa.

Battery G, 1st Pennsylvania Artillery, Luther Seiders, Reading, Pa.
Battery C, Independent Pennsylvania Artillery, James Stephenson, Pittsburg, Pa.
Battery E, Independent Pennsylvania Artillery, John P. Nicholson, 1308 7th street, Philadelphia, Pa.
Battery F, Independent Pennsylvania Artillery, John C. Shaler, Pittsburg, Pa.
10th New York Cavalry, Mark Bronell, Cortland, N. Y.
5th New York Independent Battery, Lieutenant John V. Grant, 16 New Church street, New York City.
5th New York Duryee's Zouaves' Veteran Association.
39th New York Veterans, A. V. Bergen, Brooklyn, N. Y.
41st New York Infantry, C. Borneman, 214-224 E. 22d street, New York City.
45th New York Infantry, Francis Irsch, 113 Old Slip, New York City.
57th New York Infantry, John J. McConnell, 513 W. Forty-fifth street, New York City.
62d New York Infantry, Hon. Edward Brown, City Court, New York City.
68th New York Infantry, C. Wehr, New York City.
Excelsior Brigade, John M. Coyne, New York City.
70th New York Infantry, John M. Coyne, Custom House, New York City.
73d New York Infantry, John Ross, New York City.
Shaler's Brigade Association, William J. Wray, 3923 Reno street, Philadelphia, Pa.
65th New York Infantry, Colonel Samuel Truesdell, 18 Broadway, New York City.
122d New York Infantry, Colonel O. V. Tracy, Syracuse, N. Y.
67th New York Infantry, Captain A. H. Doty, 16 Court street, Brooklyn, N. Y.
80th New York Vols. (20th New York State Militia), R. Loughran, Kingston, N. Y.
83d New York Vols. (9th N. Y. State Militia), W. W. Marks, 442 E. 26th street, N. Y. City.
64th New York, Rodney R. Crowley, Randolph, N. Y.
8th New Jersey, William H. Howard, Newark, N. J.
3d New York Independent Battery, James Warren, 309 Grand street, New York City.
86th New York, A. M. Dunham, Knoxville, Pa.
73d New York, Micheal Feeny, Eighth street near Broadway, New York City.
Batteries Irish Brigades (McMahon's & Hogan's) ―――― Sullivan, New York City.
Maryland Union Survivors of Gettysburg, W. F. Matthews, Baltimore, Md.
Florida Bivouac No. 1, United Veterans of the Blue and the Gray, M. R. Burns, Brookville, Fla.
Florida Camp No. 1, Confederate Veterans, W. W. Tucker, Jacksonville, Fla.
Company E, 20th Illinois Infantry, J. A. Edmiston, Clinton, Ill.
137th New York Infantry, Major M. W. Corbett, Public Stores, New York City.
125th New York Infantry, W. D. Taylor, 2230 Sixth avenue, New York City.
123d New York Infantry, Lieutenant Donald Reid, Lakeville, N. Y.
157th New York Infantry, Captain George L. Warren, Cortland, N. Y.
97th New York Infantry, B. B. Mayfield, Utica, N. Y.
44th New York Infantry, Edward Low, Box 692, P. O., Albany, N. Y.
Battery D, New York Artillery, S. M. Thayer, Gouverneur, N. Y.
Battery I, New York Artillery, Jacob Hehr, 306 Cortland street, Buffalo.
Battery M, New York Artillery, Captain Charles E. Winegar, 1103 Pacific street, Brooklyn.
Society of the First Army Corps, James M. Andrews, Jr., Saratoga, N. Y.
140th New York Infantry, Patrick C. Flemming, Rochester, N. Y.
146th New York Infantry, F. M. Flandreau, Rome, N. Y.
Irish Brigade Association, General Denis F. Burke, New York City.
63d New York Infantry, William Moran, Coroner's Office, New York City.
69th New York Infantry, Colonel John Nuttal, Coroner's Office, New York City.
88th New York Infantry, Captain W. L. D. O'Grady, 98 Maiden Lane, New York City.
Clark's Battery, B, 1st New Jersey Light Artillery.
90th Pennsylvania Infantry, John A. Schweer.
5th New York Cavalry, Lieutenant Charles M. Pease, Crown Point, N. Y.

14th Brooklyn War Veteran Association (84th New York Infantry), John Layton, Brooklyn P. O.
1st United States Sharpshooters, Captain Charles J. Buchanan, Albany, N. Y.
1st New York Battery, W. E. Webster, Auburn, N. Y.
11th New York Battery, Captain George W. Davy, 59 Park avenue, Albany, N. Y.
13th New York Battery, Diederich Funk, 99 Gold street, Brooklyn, N. Y.
149th New York Infantry, John Gebhard, Syracuse, N. Y.

UNITED VETERANS OF THE BLUE AND THE GRAY.

FLORIDA BIVOUAC NO. 1.

The headquarters of the United Veterans of the Blue and the Gray will be established on the field at Gettysburg during the Re-Union, and designated by its banner, its position to be assigned by the Committee of the Society of the Army of the Potomac.

The organization was suggested to Mr. L. Y. Jenness, the present Commander, by the Re-Union on the Battlefield of Gettysburg, and at Evansville, Ind., during the summer of 1887. After consultation with two or three other gentlemen, Mr. Jenness issued a call, which was responded to on the evening of August 16, 1887, by L. Y. Jenness, 32d Mass.; W. C. Zimmerman, 4th Alabama; Thomas P. Lloyd, 4th Georgia; C. C. Peck, 40th Wisconsin; J. W. Fleming, 4th Alabama; John P. Cobb, 2d North Carolina; M. R. Burns, 5th Mississippi Cavalry; H. Van Petten, 23d Michigan; C. C. Wickersham, 1st Indiana Light Battery; G. W. Thomas, 3d Florida; S. Weeks, 1st Florida Cavalry; A. H. Ravisies, 8th Alabama; J. A. Armistead, 39th Battalion Virginia Cavalry; Turner Landrum, 3d Florida; J. C. Preist, Dickerson Cavalry; H. J. McCoy, 65th Ind.; J. R. Temple, 59th Ohio Volunteers; S. Stringer, Surgeon P. A. C. S.; John M. Reddick, Florida Infantry; Fred. L. Robertson, 2d South Carolina. Florida Bivouac No. 1, U. V. B. G., was then formed, a simple set of by-laws adopted, and the following officers were elected for the succeeding year:

J. W. Jenness, Commander; J. W. Flemming, First Lieutenant Commander; C. C. Peck, Second Lieutenant-Commander; S. Stringer, Surgeon; M. R. Burns, Adjutant; H. Van Petten, Chaplain; C. C. Wickersham, Quartermaster; A. H. Ravisies, Commissary; T. P. Lloyd, Lieutenant of Guard; S. Weeks, Color Bearer; J. M. Reddick, Chief Musician; Fred. L. Robertson, Assistant Adjutant.

The idea has been cordially taken hold of in twelve States in the Union. The uniform is a handsome combination of blue and gray, and the badge a bronze canteen with a Federal and Confederate soldier in relief, swapping coffee and tobacco between the lines, as in days of old.

XXXI.

A PRISONER IN GETTYSBURG.

I do not know who the Confederate Provost Mashal was during the occupancy of Gettysburg by General Lee. I wish I did, for a more gallant-appearing officer I never met, and of the social and agreeable kind, too. Without doubt the Confederate officers, if not the men, as a rule, entertained a much more bitter feeling towards the enemy than did the Unionists. It was quite the custom for the haughty Southron, clad in shabby gray—oftentimes unkempt and unclean—when taken prisoner, to draw himself up with a cold and repellant air, and refuse all but "official" intercourse with his captors. This was particularly the case in the early stages of the war, but somehow it has a softening, humanizing effect upon men to die together, though by each other's hands, and so by the close of the war both sides had grown quiet amiable, glad, I suppose, to be humanized by having somebody else killed.

The Provost Marshal of Gettysburg was, however, not of the repellant kind. He was a Lieutenant-Colonel, a very handsome man and with a uniform quite fresh and bright. We had been wounded on the first day—myself and many others I mean. Most of us had been knocked over in the early afternoon, and had been carried back to the town and to a church which had been made an hospital. We had not been there long when such of us as could hobble to the door saw what was left of the First Corps—which had been, while acting as the advance guard of the army, broken and defeated but not dismayed—marching by the flank through the town. I was one of the hobblers, and I shall never forget the firm, set, determined features of the men. We couldn't go with them, but we afterwards learned that they met that "Confederate ally," Hancock, outside and on another day there was another tale to tell.

We hobbled back to our cots again, not much the better for what we had seen, and soon an attendant came and told us the Rebels had relieved our guards and they were collecting all the non-wounded men except the stewards, nurses, &c., and sending them to the rear. As most, if not all of the non-wounded men were skulkers and coffee-coolers that didn't matter much. I managed to save my man, who had carried me from the field, by tying a white handkerchief aroud his arm.

It was about eight o'clock in the evening when the Lieutenant-Colonel came in—the Provost Marshal I mean. He approached the group of cots occupied by officers, and greeted us quite cheerily. "Good evening gentlemen," he said. "I trust none of you is seriously hurt. You have your own surgeons and men here, and they will not be disturbed."

We saw that he was not of the repellant sort and so soon began to ply him with questions. He was quite communicative. Lee's Army was practically all up and flushed with victory. The Union army was very much demoralized. "We shall walk over it to-morrow," he said. And then he added something about the time they expected to arrive in Philadelphia.

Now, the truth is I had always been rather an optimist in this matter of preserving the Union, and although things certainly did look rather black, I somehow had no confidence in that trip to Philadelphia, and so I replied to the Colonel.

"I say, Colonel, if there should happen to be any 'just cause or impediment' which prevents that walk-over would you mind dropping in and telling us about it?"

He laughed a little and said he would.

We listened to the horrible din all the next day; the roar of artillery and the rattle of musketry, (which seemed to us to come from every direction), often with bated breath. Some of us had sad duties, too. There were those who were seriously hurt, and as their wounds took on that condition which indicates death's firmest grasp, those of us again who could hobble about were called to their bedside to receive their dying messages. "I would like to have seen it over," said one, and another who had lain in a stupor, suddenly opened his eyes, and to the ear bent to his lips, muttered, "Tell my mother—" but the tale was never told.

It was late in the evening of the second day when the Lieutenant-Colonel appeared again. He smiled as usual when he approached us, though I fancied not as cheerily as before. "It has been a terrible day," he said. The Army of the Potomac was all in front of Lee now, and the fight had been raging with varied success all day and had closed with the advantage all in favor of the South. He spoke of the position on Cemetery Hill as a very strong one, and said its capture was a necessity. They had been waiting for Pickett, and to-morrow afternoon at four a charge would be made upon it and it would be taken.

We were in much improved spirits. We had all some experience, and knew that when very hard fighting was the order that if the Army of the Potomac was not whipped very soon it was not apt to be whipped at all.

"If the Army of the Potomac is planted," said one, "you won't be able to dig it up."

And as the Colonel was about retiring I called after him, thus:

"I say, Colonel—that strong position of which you speak—that is a matter in which we have much interest, as you will concede. Would you mind calling or sending us word about the time you take it."

He laughed pleasantly again. "You will see," he said.

We knew when the charge took place well enough. It was to us, in the noise which was made, as though all hell had broken loose. We knew from the sounds and the signs, too, when it had failed.

It grew still, as night crept on. The Colonel was late in making his appearance, and there was no smile in response to our eager greetings.

"Yes, the charge has failed. There has been a dreadful loss." He lingered but a little while, and was reticent. He said, however, that another charge was to be made at four o'clock in the morning, and the position would be taken.

"Do not fail to notify us, Colonel," I said.

"No, I will not. Good night."

"That is good-bye," I said to an officer on a stretcher beside me.

Our sleep was rather of the desultory character, and we were all wide enough awake at four o'clock, but there were no sounds indicating a charge.

A little later an attendant rushed in. "Our men are skirmishing through the town," he said. We hobbled to the street, and there sure enough were the boys in blue, moving after the manner of skirmishers, quick, eager, alert, watchful, gradually moving through the town. We gave a rather feeble cheer of welcome, and then were driven to cover by two or three shots in rapid succession from sharpshooters over towards the Seminary. Lee and his defeated battalions, brave among the bravest, had struck a rock they could not break, and were marching back to the "sacred soil." With the rear-guard was the handsome, dark-eyed Lieutenant-Colonel, who did not come to tell us of the second charge.

WILLIAM J. STARKS,
104th New York Vols.

XXXII.

THE FORCES ENGAGED AT GETTYSBURG.

The number of men who took part in the battle will ever be a subject of controversy, owing to the long marches previous to the battle and the impossibility of estimating the number of stragglers counted as present but who did not participate in the fighting.

The nearest approximation and possibly the fairest is that of the Comte de Paris, which we use here as a fair statement.

The Army of the Potomac bore on its return, on July 1, 1863, 2,750 men who took no part in the battle, 7,000 Artillery, 10,500 Cavalry, and 85,500 Infantry, a total of 105,750 men and 352 pieces of Artillery, but deducting the Heavy Artillery in reserve at Westminster, the guards on supply trains, the stragglers, &c., the effective force of Meade was from 82,000 to 84,000 men, with 327 guns.

The Army of Northern Virginia, on May 31, 1863, contained an effective force of 88,754 officers and men, of whom the following were under arms: General Staff and Infantry, 59,420 men; Cavalry, 10,292; Artillery, 4,756; a total of 74,468 men, with 206 pieces of Artillery. Deducting all the losses by various means, the Brigades and Regiments absent, stragglers, &c., and adding the conscripts and Brigades, the Army of Northern Virginia arrived on the Battlefield of Gettysburg with 5,000 men more than it had on May 31, 1863—or in the neighborhood of 80,000 men. Deducting the mounted men from this, Lee brought into actual combat during the three days of July, from 68,000 to 69,000 men and 250 guns, against Meade's 82,000 or 84,000 men and 300 guns collected on the field.

Meade had, therefore, from 18,000 to 19,000 men more than his adversary, a superiority of nearly one-fourth, which, unfortunately for him, he was unable to turn to advantage.

The following is a table of organizations in both armies:

MEADE'S TROOPS

	Infantry.	Cavalry.	Artillery.	Total.		Infantry.	Cavalry.	Artillery.	Total.
Maine	10	1	3	14	Delaware	2	..	..	2
New Hampshire	3	..	1	4	West Virginia	1	2	1	4
Vermont	10	1	..	11	Ohio	13	1	4	18
Massachusetts	19	2	4	25	Indiana	5	1	..	6
Connecticut	5	..	3	8	Illinois	1	2	..	3
Rhode Island	1	..	5	6	Michigan	7	4	1	12
New York	69	8	15	92	Minnesota	1	..	..	1
New Jersey	12	1	2	15	Wisconsin	6	..	..	6
Pennsylvania	68	10	7	85	U. S. Regulars	13	4	25	42
Maryland	3	2	1	6					
Total						249	39	72	360

LEE'S TROOPS.

	Infantry.	Cavalry.	Artillery.	Total.		Infantry.	Cavalry.	Artillery.	Total.
Virginia	49	20	37	106	Louisiana	10	..	7	17
North Carolina	36	4	4	44	Mississippi	11	..	1	12
South Carolina	14	2	5	21	Arkansas	1	..	..	1
Georgia	38	3	7	48	Tennessee	3	..	..	3
Florida	4	..	..	4	Texas	3	..	..	3
Alabama	13	..	2	15	Maryland	1	1	4	6
Total						183	30	67	281

The Confederates always kept their regiments filled up by conscripts or recruits, while the Union Army maintained a number of skeleton organizations by sending out new men in new regiments, hence the noticeable discrepancy in the number of organizations.

XXXIII.

ABSOLUTION UNDER FIRE.

AN INCIDENT IN THE IRISH BRIGADE AT GETTYSBURG.

(WITH ILLUSTRATION.)

The troops that arrived upon the field or changed their positions did so leisurely and unmolested. Sickles came up and went into position on our left, and Geary took his division over to Culp's hill. About 10 o'clock picket firing was heard out towards Little Round Top, continuing at intervals until long after noon, at times becoming quite sharp. But three o'clock came, and still no signs of the general engagement. The boys had partly recovered from their fatigue, and were actually beginning to enjoy life; some of them indulged in a quiet game of euchre, while others toasted their hard tack or fried a little bacon at the small fires in the rear of the lines. Shortly after three o'clock, a movement was apparent on our left. From where we (Caldwell's Division) lay, the whole country in our front, and far to our left, away to the peach orchard and to Little Round Top, was in full view. Our division stood in brigade columns, and when it became evident that something was going to take place, the boys dropped their cards regardless of what was trump—even the man who held both bowers and the ace—and all gathered on the most favorable position to witness the opening of the ball. Soon the long lines of the Third Corps are seen advancing, and how splendidly they march. It looks like a dress parade, a review. On, on they go, out towards the peach orchard, but not a shot is fired. A little while longer, and some one calls out, "There!" and points to where a puff of smoke is seen arising against the dark green of the woods. Another and another cloud until the whole face of the forest is enveloped, and the dread sound of the artillery comes loud and quick; shells are seen bursting in all directions along the lines. The bright colors of the regiment are conspicuous marks, and the shells burst around them in great numbers. The musketry begins, the infantry became engaged, and the battle extends along the whole front of Sickles' Corps. Now the sounds come from Little Round Top, and the smoke rises among the trees, and all the high and wooded ground to the left of the peach orchard seems to be the scene of strife. An hour passes and our troops give way and are falling back; but slowly, very slowly, every inch of ground fought for. The Third Corps is not in the habit of giving it up, and they hold their own well; but the odds are against them and they are forced to retire.

Now help is called for, and Hancock tells Caldwell to have his division ready. "Fall in!" and the men run to their places. "Take arms!" and the four brigades of Zook, Cross, Brook and Kelly are ready for the fray. There is yet a few minutes to spare before starting, and the time is occupied in one of the most impressive religious ceremonies I have ever witnessed. The Irish Brigade, which had been commanded formerly by General Thomas Francis Meagher, and whose green flag has been unfurled in every battle in which the Army of the Potomac had been engaged, from the first Bull Run to Appomattox, and was now commanded by Colonel Patrick Kelly of the Eighty-eighth New York, formed a part of this division. The brigade stood in columns of regiments, closed in mass. As a large majority of its members were Catholics, the Chaplain of the brigade, Rev. William Corby, proposed to give a general absolution to all the men before going into the fight. While this is customary in the armies of the Catholic countries in Europe, it was, perhaps, the first time it was ever witnessed on this continent, unless, indeed, the grim old warrior, Ponce de Leon, as he tramped through the everglades of Florida, in search of the Fountain of Youth, or De Soto on his march to the Mississippi, indulged in this act of devotion. Father Corby stood on a large rock in front of the brigade. Addressing the men, he explained what he was about to do, saying that each one could receive the benefit of the absolution by making a sincere act of contrition and firmly resolving to embrace the first opportunity of confessing their sins, urging them to do their duty well, and reminding them of the high and sacred nature of their trust as soldiers, and the noble object for which they fought, ending by saying that the Catholic Church refuses Christian burial to the soldier who turns his back upon the foe or deserts his flag. The brigade was standing at "Order Arms." As he closed his address every man fell on his knees, with head bowed down. Then stretching his right hand towards the brigade, Father Corby pronounced the words of the absolution: "Dominus noster Jesus Christus vos absolvat et ego, auctoritate ipsius, vos absolvo ab omni vinculo excommunicationis et interdicti in quantum possum et vos indigetis, deinde ego vos absolvo a peccatis vestris, in nomini Patris, et Filii, et Spiritus Sancti. Amen." The scene was more than impressive,

THE IRISH BRIGADE AT GETTYSBURG.
BY KIND PERMISSION OF MAJOR P. M. HAVERTY.

it was awe-inspiring. Nearby stood Hancock, surrounded by a brilliant throng of officers, who had gathered to witness this very unusual occurrence, and while there was profound silence in the ranks of the Second Corps, yet over to the left, out by the peach orchard and Little Round Top, where Weed and Vincent and Haslett were dying, the roar of the battle rose and swelled and re-echoed through the woods, making music more sublime than ever sounded through cathedral aisle. The act seemed to be in harmony with all the surroundings. I do not think there was a man in the brigade who did not offer up a heartfelt prayer. For some it was their last; they knelt there in their grave-clothes—in less than half an hour many of them were numbered with the dead of July 2. Who can doubt that their prayers were good? What was wanting in the eloquence of the priest to move them to repentance was supplied in the incidents of the fight. That heart would be incorrigible indeed that the scream of a Whitworth bolt, added to Father Corby's touching appeal, would not move to contrition.—*Major Haverty's Illustrated Catholic Almanac.*

BABY'S SHOE.

The following incident is told by Adjutant Thomas J. Courter of John M. Wheeler, Post No. 94, Department of New Jersey:

John M. Wheeler fell during the battle of Banks' Ford, a part of the Chancellorsville campaign, May 3, 1863, and died in the hands of the enemy. His wife and only baby boy were ever in his thoughts. Once when one of those "boxes from home" came to the front, and to our tent—and we always shared our boxes of good things together—and the knick-knacks and the little articles for comfort that loving hands had made were being unpacked, he found a little baby shoe. The wife wrote that as they were packing the box the little fellow toddled across the floor and threw it in, and they would not take it out, but let it go down to papa in the army.

The shoe was found near the heart of the wounded man, when cared for by the surgeon.

Pennsylvania Railroad

The Shortest and Best Route
To The
Battlefield of Gettysburg.

The route traverses the fairest section of the Commonwealth of Pennsylvania. It passes through the celebrated Agricultural Districts of Chester and Lancaster Counties, as well as the picturesque scenery of the famous Cumberland Valley.

Connecting at Harrisburg with the Cumberland Valley Railroad and then at Gettysburg Junction (near Carlisle) with the Gettysburg and Harrisburg Railroad, trains run direct to the

MOST CELEBRATED BATTLEFIELD OF MODERN TIMES.

The field itself furnishes a sketch of the battle. Monuments or Tablets mark the spot where every important event occurred, and one unfamiliar with the history of the fight may trace each line of attack or retreat, the exact location of the contending forces, and note the spot where each hero fell, or each heroic struggle occurred.

NINE HOURS FROM NEW YORK,
Via Philadelphia and Harrisburg

Excursion Tickets at Very Low Rates.

CHAS. E. PUGH,	J. R. WOOD,	SAM'L CARPENTER
Gen. Manager.	*General Pass. Agent.*	*Eastern Pass. Agent.*

849 Broadway, New York.

The New York Graphic

PUBLISHED DAILY AND WEEKLY,

At The Graphic Building, 39-41 Park Place, New York.

THE DAILY GRAPHIC

is the Only Illustrated Daily Newspaper published in the world.

Its aim and purpose is to give quick, accurate and interesting illustrations of the current events of the day, with descriptive and news matter relating thereto.

It contains the LATEST and most INTERESTING Local and General News for THE FAMILY CIRCLE.

Its motto is and always will be,

"The Best ... the Best People."

It does ... blish scandals or sensation... unfit for Family Reading.

It is ... in Principle, Accurate i... ient, Clean in Tone, and is ... und and Entertaining for ... ers.

It ... a special field of its own ... which is not filled by any ... er published.

THE DAILY GRAPHIC,

under its NEW MANAGEMENT, has become the Best Family Newspaper published in the United States.

Its circulation is rapidly increasing. During the last three months its Subscriptions, Local Sales and Advertising Patronage have more than

DOUBLED,

which is good evidence of its increased popularity and usefulness.

Ask your Newsdealer for

THE DAILY GRAPHIC.

Price 3 Cents, or $9 Per Annum, Payable in Advance.

Address communications to

THE AMERICAN GRAPHIC CO.

39-41 Park Place, New York City.

GETTYSBURG
AND
HARRISBURG
RAILROAD.

SHORT AND DIRECT LINE
TO THE
Great Battlefield of Gettysburg,
Via HARRISBURG AND THE CUMBERLAND VALLEY RAILROAD.

EXCURSION TICKETS
On Sale from All Points on Pennsylvania Railroad and its Connections
ALL THE YEAR ROUND.

Through Coaches from Harrisburg connecting in Union Depot with all Through Trains East and West on Main Line of Pennsylvania Railroad.

This Line closely follows the route of Lee's Army to Gettysburg, passing through the South Mountain at Mount Holly Gap, and enters the Battlefield on Seminary Ridge, the scene of the first day's engagement.

For any information apply to your Station Agent, or to

WM. H. WOODWARD,
Superintendent,
Carlisle, Pa.

For Time Table during the Re-Union of 1888, see Article III. of this Book.